Dwelling in Language

Margrét Gunnarsdóttir Champion

Dwelling in Language

Character, Psychoanalysis and Literary Consolations

PETER LANG
EDITION

Bibliographic Information published by the Deutsche Nationalbibliothek
The Deutsche Nationalbibliothek lists this publication in the Deutsche Nationalbibliografie; detailed bibliographic data is available in the internet at http://dnb.d-nb.de.

Cover image:
©"ÖNB Vienna: Cod. 2759, fol. 2v".
Illuminated Initial Letter, *Wenceslas Bible.*

Library of Congress Cataloging-in-Publication Data

Champion, Margrét Gunnarsdóttir, 1953-
Dwelling in language : character, psychoanalysis and literary consolations / Margrét Gunnarsdóttir Champion. — Peter Lang Edition.
pages cm.
ISBN 978-3-631-64437-9
1. Discourse analysis, Literary. 2. Narration (Rhetoric) 3. Psychoanalysis. 4. Psycholinguistics. I. Title.
P302.5.C43 2013
808.001'4—dc23

2013024499

ISBN 978-3-631-64437-9

Peter Lang Edition is an Imprint of Peter Lang GmbH.

Peter Lang – Frankfurt am Main · Bern · Bruxelles · New York · Oxford · Warszawa · Wien

www.peterlang.de

In memorian
Hilmar Stefán Karlsson, 1957–1987
Margrét Jónsdóttir, 1904–1996

Preface and Acknowledgements

Teaching a course in the Victorian novel this semester, I have been reminded again and again of the uncanny sway realistic character has over the reading mind. Dorothea Brooke, Jane Eyre, Tess, Pipp, Joe and Miss Haversham beckon to teacher and students to follow them along fabulous terrains, mazes of language, both familiar and strange, never fully known, yet for a short while, our world, our *Dasein*. From what source issues the vital principle of character, its "absent presence," its call on our engagements, sympathies, fierce liking or loathing, our willing suspension of disbelief? Reading through Jacques Lacan's ideas about self, language and ethics, this book theorizes literary characters as a disinterested, aesthetic authority, indeed a guide into the fiction, but an impersonal guide, equipped with the desire for the other's good. By submitting one's will to mastery to the transvaluative language embodied in characters, a potential psychic reformation takes place, an alienation of self, which fosters perception of difference.

During the writing of this book, many flesh-and-blood characters have been my guides and benefactors. First, I would like to mention members of the staff at the Department of English, Uppsala University, who, while I worked there as a research fellow, encouraged me and inspired me in the early stages of thinking through the ideas at the back of this book. Particularly enriching encounters were those with Professor Gunnar Sorelius and the late Docent Michael Srigley, true scholars and Renaissance men, who opened up vistas of learning. During the 1990s, the literary seminars in the department were often voyages of discovery, and they still motivate me in my work as teacher and critic. For their generous and enlightening discussions, I want in particular to thank Dr Anna Forsberg Morris Uddén, Dr Christer Larsson, Foreign Lecturer Daniel Ogden, Dr Irina Rasmussen Goloubeva, Professor Irene Gilsenan Nordin, Professor Monica Fryckstedt, Dr Anna Swärd, Dr Åke Strandberg, Docent Helga Drougge, Dr Kristina Hildebrand, Dr Christina Cullhed, Docent Alan Shima and Dr Barbro Almqvist Norbelie. The fertile and collegiate environment provided at the Uppsala department has fuelled my work through the years.

Several research grants have funded the work on this book. Stipends from the Humanities Faculty, University of Iceland, the Icelandic Centre for Research, the Swedish Research Council and the Humanities Faculty, Gothenburg University, supported early drafts of the work. The publication of the book was facilitated by a subsidy from a Swedish Humanities and Social Sciences Foundation, Stiftelsen Lars Hiertas Minne. The incipient ideas appeared in article form in "From Plaint to Praise: Language as Cure in 'The Wanderer,'" *Studia Neophilologica* 69 (1998), reissued in chapter form in Roy Liuzza's (ed.), *Old English Literature: Critical Essays* (New Haven: Yale University Press, 2002). I thank The Taylor & Francis Group for the permission to reprint an abridged version of the article here. Finally, my sincere gratitude goes to the editorial staff at Peter Lang Publishing House. Supportive beyond the call of duty, Ute Winkelkötter deserves special mention.

I would like to dedicate this book to the memory of my grandmother, Margrét Jónsdóttir (1904–1996), and my brother, Hilmar Stefán Karlsson (1957–1987). They are my personal "present absences," always my touchstones.

M.G.C.

Gothenburg
March 2013

Table of Contents

Introduction: The Ideality of Difference

In literature, character is a multivalent site, drawing to itself, like a magnet, the various concerns of the fictional world as well as the interest of readers. As Roland Barthes suggested so convincingly, proper names (or their equivalents, personal pronouns or typical names) imbue textual signifiers with the aura of *person* (1974: 67–6): Sarrasine, Anna Karenina, David Copperfield seem to exist both in fiction as dispersed language and in reality as living individuals.[1] No other element of literary fictions traverses the bound between nondiscursive and discursive realms as insistently as does literary character.

Because of this fuzzy realism, the concept of character has resisted an encompassing theoretical description and remained on the margins of a poetics, moving uneasily between critical paradigms. With the advent of structuralism in the early 1970s, the humanist conception of character as a full, unified *being* was reduced to its a-psychological role in a series of narrative actions.[2] Interesting attempts were made by reader-response oriented critics to harmonize the poles of mimesis and structure, but the outcomes were rather disappointing: Anglo-American critics, in particular, tended to confirm a traditional, hegemonic view of the self, assuming that readers identify naturally with such a construct.[3] As literary study has become more and more interdisciplinary in recent years, diverse models for character have been proposed, emerging from fields such as ethics, psychoanal-

1 Roland Barthes. *S/Z: An Essay*. Trans. Richard Miller (New York: Hill and Wang, 1974).

2 Vladimir Propp's *Morphology of the Folktale*. Trans. L. Scott (Austin: University of Texas Press, 1928; 1968) was a major influence. See also the early Roland Barthes in "Introduction to the Structural Analysis of Narrative," in *Image/Music/Text*. Trans. Stephen Heath (New York: Hill and Wang, 1977), 79–124, and Tzvetan Todorov's "Narrative Men," in *The Poetics of Prose*. Trans. Richard Howard (Ithaca: Cornell University Press, 1977), 66–79.

3 See here John Frow's critique, in "Spectacle Binding: On Character." *Poetics Today* 7 (1986): 227–250, of Seymour Chatman's misreading of Barthes' semic code from *S/Z*. Chatman equates the Barthesean seme with A. C. Bradley's analysis of traits in Shakespearian tragedy, conceptions that derive from totally different ideologies, radical modernist versus traditionalist humanist. Seymour Chatman. *Story and Discourse: Narrative Structure in Fiction and Film* (Ithaca: Cornell University Press, 1978).

ysis, sociology, semiotics and the cognitive sciences.[4] Despite the dissimilarity of these approaches, they all, at some point, grapple with the problem of the *split* or division inherent within the character concept: How does a theory account for character as Janus, a double-faced entity, looking inside and outside, in the same instant?

My book examines this conceptual ambivalence within a psychoanalytic framework and argues that the mental and libidinal processes explored, in particular, by Freud and Lacan – identification, transference, the drives, desire and *jouissance* – establish character's identity, constitute and define its very mode of being in imaginative discourse. In contrast to the impasses experienced by the critical approaches outlined above, the sense of a deadlock between mimesis and structure, my study postulates that an eclipsed ontological speculation affects the paucity of theoretical models and, in fact, obstructs the task of building "a systematic, non-reductive but also non-impressionistic theory of character" (Rimmon-Kenan 1983: 29).[5] An alternative poetics, anchored in the Lacanian subject,

4 John Frow's "Spectacle Binding: On Character" (1986) contains interesting suggestions for a psychoanalytic, Freudian and Lacanian theory of character. Also, along psychological lines, making use of Karen Horney's theories about the self, is Bernard Jay Paris' *Imagined Human Beings: A Psychological Approach to Character and Conflict* (New York: New York University Press, 1997). The critical voice within semiotics of character is Uri Margolin, especially in "Individuals in Narrative Worlds: An Ontological Perspective." *Poetics Today* 11(Winter, 1990), 843–871. In general, for the pluralizing of approaches in the late 1980s, see the special issue of *Poetics Today* (1986) on "Theory of Character."
Focusing upon the philosophy of narrative, a recent issue of *The Journal of Aesthetics and Art Criticism* 67 (2009) presents two articles on character, both with an ethical inflection: George Currie. "Narrative and the Psychology of Character" (61–71) and Alessandro Giovannelli. "In Sympathy with Narrative Characters" (83–95).
Departing from previous studies in her concentration upon early modern texts, Elizabeth Fowler theorizes character as a *social person*, an adaptable transhistorical category, embodying both discursive features and their institutional base. *Literary Character: The Human Figure in Early English Writing* (Ithaca: Cornell University Press, 2003).
In recent years, a resurgent interest in the problematics of character is manifest in a spate of books grounded in the cognitive sciences, the most noteworthy being Murray Smith's *Engaging Characters: Fiction, Emotion and the Cinema* (Oxford: Oxford University Press, 1995) and Blakey Vermeule's *Why Do We Care about Fictional Characters?* (Baltimore: The John Hopkins University Press, 2010). Celebrating this resurgence, the 42nd volume of *New Literary History* (Spring 2011) is dedicated to character, publishing several essays with a sociological and cognitive focus. Although, in a broad sense, psychology is at issue in many recent publications on character, no work theorizes from a Lacanian perspective.

5 Shlomith Rimmon-Kenan. *Narrative Fiction: Contemporary Poetics* (Colombus: Ohio State University Press, 1983.

defamiliarizes the realist/ego-centered premise of previous investigations, both highlighting and undercutting the narcissistic drive for character as self-reflection. In the following chapters, my analyses will show character to be a phenomenon of viscerality, in its representative personhood binding readers to the fiction, but at the same time, subverting that bond by evoking the insentience of the signifier. Conceiving the character construct as vitalist metaphor, as an incremental *letter* – material sign, *prosopopeia* and *ethos* – instead of as a mimetic person, the psychoanalytic approach avoids the aporias of hegemonic essentialism, preserving an ethical, transvaluative bond between reader and text. In this introduction, the main concerns of my book crystallize in sections, which discuss the rhetoricity of character, its ethical nature as an uncanny accommodation in language and its transhistorical function as a modality of the Lacanian analyst.

What's in a Letter?

No less than poetry, Jacques Lacan contends, psychoanalytic experience encapsulates the profundity and power of words. Despite a negativistic philosophy, a tragic view of human lack, of the "want-to-be" (*manque-à-être*), Lacan's conception of language is creationist, as Gilbert D. Chaitin argues, a secularized theology, conferring on the logic of the signifier the absolute creativity of an immutable deity.[6] Influenced by Alexandre Koyré's theorization of "theological voluntarism," the Newtonians' paradoxical legitimation of their empirical investigations as both aligned with and absolutely separate from the realm of the divine, Lacan appropriates the "emancipation of the signifier" as the primary law of discourse, inflitrating and codifying both formalist science such as mathematics and communication in social worlds; the *Name-of-the-Father* in Lacanian psychoanalysis constitutes a signifying operation, manifest, on one hand, "through the combination of the little letters of science, " on the other hand, "through the creative use of the letters of language" (Chaitin 64–5).

6 Gilbert D. Chaitin. *Rhetoric and Culture in Lacan* (Cambridge: Cambridge University Press, 1996). Chaitin links creationism to Augustinian theology and traces the historical process of its secularization through the scientific revolutions of the sixteenth and seventeenth centuries, a process theorized by philosophers of science as "voluntarism," the separation of divine absolutism from human logic. "Freeing God from the constraints imposed by Leibniz's 'sufficient reason,'" Newtonians maintained a theological idealism, paradoxically legitimating their independent queries into natural law. The signifier thus becomes disentangled from the divine word, is released into discourse, as if *ex nihilo* (64).

From the early linguistically inflected work such as "The function and field of speech and language in psychoanalysis" (1953) and "The agency of the letter in the unconscious or reason since Freud" (1957) to the later considerations of "the feminine exception" in *Encore* (1972–3) and of Joycean creativity in *Le sinthome* (1975–6), the propellor of a liberating agency within signifying systems is the metaphoric function, which interacts with metonymic negativity to endow the speaking subject with both uniqueness and imaginative intervention despite the entrapment of the libido in structure.[7] Because of its mobile substitutive propensity, metaphor produces the "poetic spark," channelling unconscious energies into the rigours of the symbolic register. Reading *Beyond the Pleasure Principle* (1920) in "The function and field of speech and language in psychoanalyis," Lacan traces the metaphorics of the subject in the guise of Freud's grandson as he playfully constructs alienating tropes which compensate for primary loss, for the mother's absences and the otherness of her desire. In his language game of "fort-da," uttering differential sounds in tune with casting back and forth a toy reel, to coincide with his mother's departures and arrivals, the child strangely inscribes his desire into symbolic law, of necessity submitting to it but at the same time singularly intervening. Against the tendency toward univocality facilitated by metonymic linearity, an assoicative process, which "permits the elision in which the signifier installs the lack-of-being in the object relation" (*Écrits* 164), thereby instituting the tragedy of desire as never fulfilled, metaphoric structure, "substitut[ing] signifier for a signifier," releases unconscious signifying material into meaningful contexts, so that "an effect of signification is produced that is creative or poetic" (*Écrits* 164). If, as Lacan indicates, science displays the discourse of metonymic displacement *par excellence*, then analytic discourse is both conditioned by the scientific/master signifier and subversive of it in its privileging of metaphoric condensation as the ground for subjectivation and mental freedom.[8]

Psychoanalysis and literature share a faith in the regenerative workings of language, in a type of elegaic process which effects a binding of subjective libido to systems of official or symbolic utterance. Anchored in the materiality of signification, the Lacanian subject inhabits a positionality rather than essence, fated

7 The essays from the 1950s are in *Écrits*. Trans. Alan Sheridan (New York: W. W. Norton, 1977), 30–113; 146–178. *Encore* is seminar XX: *Le Séminaire. Livre XX. Encore*, 1972–73, ed. Jacques-Alain Miller (Paris: Seuil, 1975); and *Le sinthome* is seminar XXIII: *Le Séminaire. Livre XXIII. Le sinthome*, 1975/76, in *Ornicar?* 6–11 (1976–7).

8 See an interview conducted with Lacan during his seminar series *The Other Side of Psychoanalysis* (1969–1970), printed in *The Seminar of Jacques Lacan, Book XVII: The Other Side of Psychoanalysis*. Trans. Russell Grigg (New York: W. W. Norton, 2007), 143–149.

to self-division and alienation from an irreducibly lost primal object it perpetually desires. Elaborating upon the death drive in *The Ethics of Psychoanalysis* (1959–1960), Lacan uses the word *captivity* (*la prise*) to emphasize the primordial nature of the human constitution as an unconscious field, an inaccessibility, which traps the pscyhe in an insentient logic, the cause of *Spaltung*, the split or gap, in relation to which "the functioning of desire as such is to be articulated" (258).[9] It is precisely the intractability of articulation, the substitutions and displacements involved in expression and communication, and the ensuing painful sense of lack, which pathologizes psychology, producing libidinal "sticking point[s]" and destructive *jouissance* (258–9). The understanding of the Freudian unconscious as a discursive field, as operated by "the agency of the letter," should, Lacan insists, be taken *à la lettre*, "quite simply literally"; the letter, in fact, substantiates the human voice in communication: it is "the material support that concrete discourse borrows from language" ("The agency of the letter" 147). In Lacanian psychoanalysis, being and the letter are inextricably linked; thus, the declarations at the end of "The agency of the letter" that "the symptom *is* a metaphor" and that "desire *is* a metonymy" are not figurative expressions but elucidations of the unconscious real, the literality of being (175; Lacan's emphasis).

Primarily, *Dwelling in Language: Character, Psychoanalysis and Literary Consolations* argues that character in literature evokes the materiality of being, the very insentience at the heart of vitality, and that in that capacity it operates as a modality of the Lacanian analyst, triggering a transferential activity, which accommodates subjects to irreducible *Spaltung*. Exhibiting in its etymological development the ambivalences narratological critics, in particular, have struggled against, on one hand, translating as a chirographic mark – an engraving, a printed symbol, an inscription –, and, on the other hand, suggesting a personality – moral features, psychological traits, distinctive reputation – literary character emerges as the effect of metaphoric substitution, where the human name replaces and conceals the artificiality, which grounds it.[10] What I'm interested in tracing in this book is how this Janus-like condition, this ruptured viscerality, consolidates both the narcissistic desire for self-identity and the innate sense of resistance to such unity. Character's ontological identity, as established in the following chapters, is the Lacanian mirror of alienation: the zone of character magnetically binds readers and audiences to the fiction in their processes of ego-driven identification, simultaneously subverting such a bond through a reflection of radical otherness. In the encounter with sublimity, the audience's psychic organization is (poten-

9 *The Ethics of Psychoanalysis: The Seminar of Jacques Lacan: Book VII*. Trans. Dennis Potter (New York: Routledge, 2008), esp. 258

10 See the nineteen entries for *character* in the *Oxford Dictionary Online* (www.dictionary.oed.com).

tially) transformed and ego-centered hegemony turned into a condition of ethical responsibility.

To a great extent, the "case studies" in the second half of *Dwelling in Language* ontologize character as a consolatory trope, as the *jouissance* of the Other in language. The activity of the figures in the various texts, poetry from Anglo-Saxon England, the fourteenth-century romance, *Sir Gawain and the Green Knight*, Graham Swift's novel, *Last Orders* (1996), and Virgina Woolf's *To the Lighthouse* (1927), inscribe, to a more or less intense degree, elegaic restitution, traumatic intimations of the real of desire transmuted into poetic denial and pure desirousness. What is iterated globally and transhistorically in the character construct is the (Lacanian) *letter* as a fragment of the real, of that which resists symbolization, "the obscurity and opacity" beyond language and communication (*The Ethics of Psychoanalysis* 258). Literature, as Jean-Claude Milner suggests, surpasses scientific discourse in its rehearsal of Kantian "sophistication," the negative capability of maintaining a balance in the mind between painful truth and fantasies of surpassal; *belles lettres*, in Milner's phrase, use letters to "spell out what exceeds the letter," appropriating and sublimating the very artifice which constitutes this realm (38).[11]

My readings telescope the zone of character as the carrier of the excess of the letter, which by instigating the audience's hermeneutic pleasure, guides it into mental sophistication, an accommodation to the impossibility of the real and to irreducible difference. In Virginia Woolf's *To the Lighthouse*, Lily Briscoe's, the artist's, struggle with representation, her helpless crying out for the departed, loved friend, "Mrs Rasmay! Mrs Ramsay!" (196; 219), and her "sudden intensity" (226) of closure, the line she draws in the middle of the canvas, the cohesive center, emblematize character's mode of being as poetic denial of inaccessiblity, a mark of negativity, which in "its attempt at something" (225) captures the vitality of desire.[12] As Karen Smythe notes in an essay on Woolf's "fiction-elegies," the rhetoric of person in art operates catachretically, a transfer of names from the life-sphere unto absence (esp. 65). Not unlike Roland Barthes' paradigm of semes, which gather beneath the proper name, fleshing out the protagonist in Balzac's novella, an incarnation in language takes place, a type of *prosopopeia*, "giving face" to the inanimate. According to Smythe, who relies on Paul Ricoeur, in mod-

11 Jean-Claude Milner. "Lacan and the Ideal of Science," in Alexandre Leupin, ed. *Lacan and the Human Sciences* (Lincoln: University of Nebraska Press, 1991), 27–42.

12 Virginia Woolf. *To the Lighthouse* (Penguin Boooks, 1992). Note Woolf's comment in a letter to Rogoer Fry that she "meant nothing by The Lighthouse"; yet it marks the vital spark of her art. Quoted in Hermione Lee's introduction to the Penguin edition (xxi).

ernist elegy, this rhetorical process of personification, "induc[ing] the reader [...] to possess magically the absent thing, body or person," shapes a "trope of mourning," enabling restitution after loss (66).[13]

The psychoanalytic poetics of character I propose in this book builds on just such an activity of incorporation, the initially narcissistic assimilation of prosopopeia, which, through the complex intersubjective dynamics of transference, is transformed into an *other-regarding* constitution. Because of character's almost magical incarnation, the word turned into flesh, the situation staked out is an aesthetic modality of the analytic relation, generating unconscious energies and through the transference channelling the ineffable into modes of new subjective knowledge. In both aesthetic communication and the specialized terrain of psychoanalysis, the analysand-analyst relation, entrenched misrecognitions and repressions of fundamental fantasies corroborate the captivity to unconscious opacity, resisted, at first, in repetitions, but during the transferential process, worked through and brought to the surface of the *talking cure*. Significantly, transference denotes both linguistic and psychological registers, a "carrying over" of meaning from one context to another, from, for instance, imaginary constructions to symbolic figurations. In fact, Lacan stresses the symbolic dimension of transference, the intersubjective structure, which facilitates the subject's truth to emerge.[14] In *Rhetoric and Culture in Lacan*, by profitably linking Lacan's work to philosophers of language such as I. A. Richards and Susanne K. Langer, Gilbert D. Chaitin examines the psychoanalytic situation as staging the metaphorics of subjectivity, how latent configurations condition a symptom, which appears to participants as a text, amenable to reading, interpretation and attachments to rejuvenating signifiers (esp. 114–121).

Here, the catalyzing agent is the analyst as both "the subject supposed to know" (who, in reality, Lacan states, "knows nothing" (1977: 267)) and enigmatic desire, a presence to whom the analysand attributes emotions and thoughts, at first, a troubling gaze, but potentially a liberating nexus of meaning. By embodying indeterminacy, the analyst precipitates the irruption of the signifier into the transference: driven by narcissistic identifications, which condition and conflate all

13 Karen Smythe. "Virginia Woolf's Elegaic Enterprise." *NOVEL: A Forum on Fiction* 1 (1992), 64–79. Smythe cites Ricoeur here from "The Metaphorical Process as Cognition, Imagination, and Feeling," in Sheldon Sacks, ed. *On Metaphor* (Chicago: University of Chicago Press, 1979), 148.
Barthes' argument in *S/Z: An Essay* is summarized in chapter one of this book.

14 Lacan's faith in the transference can be gauged in this early statement from the seminar, *Freud's Papers on Technique* (1953–54): "Each time a man speaks to another in an authentic and full manner, there is, in the true sense, transference, symbolic transference – something which takes place which changes the nature of the two beings present" (109). *The Seminar. Book I. Freud's Papers on Technique*, 1953–54. Trans. John Forrester (New York: Norton, 1998).

relationships, the analysand initially expects a transparent communication, where his self-identity is confirmed and his specular unity supported; however, a revelatory moment of being in the transferential situation is the articulation of *demand* toward the enigma of the analyst, "*Che vuoi?*" – "what do you want from me?" – a self-divided address, which enables "the crossing of the plane of identification," disrupting deception and bringing back "the experience of the subject to the plane at which, from the reality of the unconscious, the drive may be made present" (1977: 274). Thus, the analyst's desire directs subjects into confrontations with their own libidinal otherness, (potentially) transforming the narcissistic ego into an other-regarding constitution.[15]

The transformational dynamic I have synoptically presented here endows literary character with an ontological identity as aesthetic analyst. As the zone which binds audiences to the fiction, character prompts ego-driven identification, both affirming and subverting such a process in its status as sublime *prosopopeia.* As in the case of the Lacanian analyst, character's libido is an enigmatic, generative force in the aesthetic experience, most succinctly understood as an ethical directive that in a state of pure desirousness wills the reader's good. Significantly, again, interlacing with the psychoanalytic situation, the good desired does not entail moral reform or curing a deluded ego, but the reader's singular subjectivation, his or her confrontation with the unique truth of absolute difference.

Zones of Hospitality

Because of its zeal for, evocation and support of fragile singularities, literary character prepares a ground for transvalued socio-cultural orders. My study seeks to demonstrate how character inhabits unfinalizable zones in discourse, within which ideological conflict takes place, usually effecting the inscription of the private libido into official signification.[16] From a psychoanalytic perspective, the works under inspection contain valuable material for a theory of character because they inaugurate events of *suture*, the barred, or divided, subject's

15 In the last section of *The Four Fundamental Concepts of Psycho-Analysis* (1964), "In you more than you," Lacan is quite explicit about "the liquidation" of transference being the rupturing of narcissistic deception (esp. 267–274). *The Four Fundamental Concepts of Psycho-Analysis*. Trans. Alan Sheridan (Penguin Books, 1977).

16 I'm referring to *character zones* in M. M. Bakhtin's sense of narrative loci "densely saturated" with hybrid utterance. Bakhtin understands a character's voice as a "field of action," "a sphere of influence," which extends "beyond the boundaries of the direct discourse allotted to him" (316;320). *The Dialogic Imagination*. Trans. Caryl Emerson and Michael Holquist (Austin: University of Texas Press, 1981).

active stitching into master signifiers, which operate in the social register and within habitual reality by eliding the "unknown knowledge" of the unconscious.[17] Belonging to both medical and mathematical registers, suture as an activity is associated with artificial closure, on one hand, with surgical interference, on the other hand, with finalizing a potentially infinite set of numbers by including within it an exception to the rule, a limit, an impossibility. In an influential article on the implications of Frege's set theory for the psychoanalytic subject, Jacques-Alain Miller reveals the mathematician's paradoxical "truth," the necessity to dilute self-identical propositions with "the name, or signifier, of something that is excluded from the set of objects on which it operates" (Chatain 1996: 220); the logic of the signifier, of the relations instituted in the symbolic by the assumption of the Name-of-the-Father, can be broadly designated as just such a paradox of identity: *suture*, an operation of excess within the ideal, consolidates the realm of master signifiers, both enabling them to function as markers of univocity and uncovering the gaps, the cuts, over which they incompletely slide.[18] As a positionality within the fissured symbolic, the Lacanian subject emblematizes the impossible real of desire, which both grounds and exceeds the closed set of socio-cultural knowledge. It is precisely as such a "non-universalizable 'I'" (Chatain 1996: 219) that the subject of the unconscious escapes the restrictions of history and culture, potentially regenerating thought and replacing essentialist images with new signifiers of difference.

In its mode of being as an other-regarding agent, literary character exposes and subverts the totalizing strategies of official signification, in its fragile interventions disclosing the logic of suture, the very lack which grounds the field of the Other itself. *Dwelling in Language* attempts to mark within the character zone the communication channels between subjective desire and interpellating ideologies, which in the shape of master signifiers restrict freedom, eclipse mutual responsibility and prevent the full reign of justice. In *Deor*, one of the more accomplished Old English poems, the metaphorics of subjectivity generates the speaker-character's "word-power," ultimately fracturing the stoic *Weltanschauung*, which compels subjects to resign themselves to the Christian corroboration of sacrifical economies. Graham Swift's *Last Orders* depicts four characters journeying through the English landscape, telescoping moments of subjectivation, as filial adherence to paternal signifiers and to conventional vision is transformed into tragi-comic suturing onto the historical narrative of the nation. On one level, a fable of the transition from narcissistic identifications to the self-divided subject, the medieval

17 Dylan Evans uses this Lacanian expression in *An Introductory Dictionary of Lacanian Psychoanalysis* (London: Routledge, 1996), 219.

18 Jacques-Alain Miller. "Suture." *Screen* 18.4 (1977/78), 24–34. I rely on Chatain's helpful synopsis in *Rhetoric and Culture in Lacan*, esp. 219–222.

romance *Sir Gawain and the Green Knight* enacts a transvaluation of values in the figure of the *errant* knight whose singular *jouissance* erupts into the colonizing discourse which relentlessly seeks to suppress it. The feminine exception underpins character construction in Virgina Woolf's *To the Lighthouse*, where Henri Bergson's radicalization of the image of thought and Lacan's understanding of Woman's non-universality can be profitably linked to elucidate the novel's production of new knowledge, flowing from the maternal *eros*, the disinterested desire for the other's good, lying at the very heart of the object of art.

The ethical transformations enacted in these works are sustained by the character zones, within which the discourse of the (Lacanian) analyst accrues, condensing, in the words of Bakhtin, a "sphere of influence," which encroaches upon other textual spaces, in fact, hybridizing the whole artifact, causing "characters [to] overlap and infect each other" (1981). Sharing with Bakhtin a sense of the incompleteness of the field of *logos*, Lacan, in *The Other Side of Psychoanalysis* (1969–70), maps the four discourses of master, university, hysteric and analyst, significantly noting their historical shiftings in terms of knowledge: logical articulations of subjective positions in the discursive realm, the schemas interact in a "relationship of weaving, of text – of fabric" (*The Other Side of Psychoanalysis* 54), exhibiting perforated borders.[19] The advantage the analytic communication has over the other discursive positions lies in its interrogation of master signifiers which ground symbolic knowledge, in, as Lacan emphasizes, manufacturing *doubt*, and in that very activity negotiating psychic space within social orders.[20] In order to "cross the plane of identification," to rupture the analysand's immersion in the reified images of dominant discourses, the analyst hystericizes the situation, eliciting the divided, traumatized subject, who lashes out against the social restrictions which elide the *real* of desire. What the controlled hysterical discourse aims at achieving is the analysand's alienation, a psychological disentanglement from repressive positions in the field of the Other, positions which deceptively represent the subject. The confrontation with lack causes a crisis of meaning, often accompanied by "anxiety and a sense of emptiness" (Bracher 1993: 71), entailing demands for narcissistic gratification, for assuaging identification with master signifiers.[21] However, the ethical imperative of analytic discourse is to activate singular psychic space, to stage the metaphorics of subjectivity, which enables

19 A more systematic presentation of the four discourses is provided in chapter eight of this book.

20 In *The Other Side of Psychoanalysis*, Lacan links analytic questioning to the ancient sceptics, who formed a school dedicated to doubting the totality of knowledge (30–31).

21 Mark Bracher. *Lacan, Discourse and Social Change: A Psychoanalytic Cultural Criticism* (Ithaca: Cornell University Press, 1993).

the working-through of alienation to a position of self-empowerment in *separation*. As is Freud's intent with his female patient in "Observations on Transference Love" (1915), the analyst wills the other's "mental freedom," mediating between the unconscious, and often destructive, drive and sublimations in meaningful signifiers.[22] The analyst, in fact, opens up a channel between the psyche and the social, precipitating accommodating communities and ethical rejuvenation.

Dwelling in Language proposes an ontological identity for literary character as an aesthetic analyst, who orchestrates zones of changing values and of the metaphorics of differential subjectivity. Through a Freudian/Lacanian lens, the first part of this book maps character's activity as an *uncanny* dwelling, within which the foundational narcissistic psyche is put on trial, simultaneously exposed and ethically challenged. The current resurgent interest within the humanities and social sciences in the interfaces of psychic space and socio-political realms, an interest attested to, for instance, by Kelly Oliver's and Steve Edwin's recent collection of interdisciplinary essays, *Between the Psyche and the Social: Psychoanalytic Social Theory* (2002), does not to any significant extent include aesthetic figures as potential mediators and catalysts of transvalued observances.[23] My book gestures toward such a role for imaginative discourse, ontologizing character as, in a sense, the tain in the mirror of art, the self-divisive constitution at its origin, the latent cause of desire, which makes specularity possible. As an uncanny agent, then, instead of conforming to dominant master signifiers, character enables a metaphoric transfer, a sublimation, from the ineffable psychic drives to new social configurations; in the words of Freud, from his work on narcissism, character revises *self-regard*, instituting nurturing ego-ideals and thereby precipitating inclusive communitites and compassionate leadership. "Necessary Fictions," the first part of my study, anchored in Freud's "Copernican revolution" and Lacanian poetics, makes a claim for character as the transforming conscience of art.

---

22 "Observations on Transference Love" (1915).*The Standard Edition of the Complete Psychological Works of Sigmund Freud* (hereafter referred to as SE). Vol. XII. Ed. and trans. James Strachey (London: The Hogarth Press, 1958). (This essay is discussed in chapter five of this book).

23 Kelly Oliver and Steve Edwin, eds. *Between the Psyche and the Social: Psychoanalytic Social Theory* (Lanham: Rowman&Littlefield Publishers, 2002). Other recent work which promotes relational poetics includes Kelly Oliver. *Witnessing: Beyond Recognition* (Minneapolis: University of Minnesota Press, 2001) and Morgan Brigg. *The New Politics of Conflict Resolution: Responding to Difference* (New York: Palgrave, 2008).

History of the Signifier

A near contemporary with Freud's civilization critique in *Civilization and its Discontent* (1930), D.H. Lawrence's *St Mawr* (1925), discussed in chapter six of this book, can, in my opinion, be conceived as a parable of how certain historical events turn dominant discourses into symptomatic structures, amenable to aesthetic-analytic diagnosis, destabilization and subsequent emergence of redemptive ego-ideals. Similar to Freud's perceptions, Lawrence's novella depicts the paralysis of European communities suffering beneath an oppressive super-ego, which manufactures states of war, trapping subjects in "new maladies of the soul," in sado-masochistic bonds, eclipsing the sexualized body and the natural good.[24] Although *St Mawr* does not fall within the perimeters of the genre of consolation or of elegy, it stages the mode of being of character as a vitalist structure, which instigates a form of *death-work* in transference. Broadly characterizing the psychoanalytic session as the "labor of the unconscious," as the coming to terms with negativity, with the "poor plenty" of Narcissus, Kristeva draws attention to the eschatological role of the analyst, how he both orients subjects toward mortality and accommodates them to life through their singular truth.[25] Interfacing with the existential matrix of the analytic session, literary characters, transhistorically and globally, exemplify consolation and provide a shelter from death. It is important to note, though, and underpins the argument of this book, that the character zone does not offer narcissistic gratification, but binds audiences to an *unheimliche* dwelling, facilitating their separation from reified images and ascension to a condition of ethical repsponsibility.

A tain in the mirror of imaginative discourse, character is, in my study, a transhistorical signifier, explored in its mode of being as eschatological directive, not as a realistic reflection, nor as a literary device. Significantly, the ontological intent of this study does not preclude historical specificity, character's dependence on paradigms of knowledge or on what Roland Barthes refers to as "ideologies of person;" on the contrary, *Dwelling in Language* strives to saturate

24 *New Maladies of The Soul* (New York: Columbia University Press, 1995) is the title of Julia Kristeva's study of contemporary psyhological illness, which she aligns with dominant socio-political discourses and especially with the repression and devaluation of the maternal body.

25 Relying on Kristeva's essay, "Within the Microcosm of the Talking Cure" (1983), Martha J. Reineke prefers *death-work* to death-drive, because it implies subjectivation and agency. Kristeva's essay is published in Joseph H. Smith and William Kerrigan, eds. *Psychiatry and the Humanities*. Trans. T. Gora and M. Waller (New Haven: Yale University Press, 1983), 33–48. See Reineke's *Sacrificed Lives: Kristeva on Women and Violence* (Bloomington: Indiana University Press, 1997).

the historical moment with the divisiveness of the psychoanalytic subject, in that effort endowing identity to an undertheorized construct. As chapter one, "Situating Character," will show, despite the turn from structuralist codifications to interdisciplinary persepective, which often are, as Stanley Bates asserts in a recent essay, "broadly naturalistic" (2009: 395), within literary criticism, character has remained shackled to either reductive deconstructions or to impressionistic reflections, which appear to operate from hidden assumptions about the essentialist content of human identity.[26] In fact, the often cited *problem* of character, especially within narrative theory, stems principally from a universalizing tendency, which tends to flatten out historical meaning, ironically periodizing aesthetic objects as transparent reflectors of contemporary conceptions. Even if the aim of *Dwelling in Language* is not historicizing *per se*, by defamiliarizing identification, by anchoring it in *Spaltung*, in self-division, not in conscious plenitude, this book hopes to open up the field of literary character to "the history of the signifier," which in syncopated form can be understood as the work of sublimations throughout historical time within regimes of pleasure and of the death drive.[27] In her remarkable book, *Read My Desire: Lacan against the Historicists* (1994), Joan Copjec, argues convincingly for the superiority of psychoanalytic cultural studies over Foucauldian historicism, underscoring Lacan's insight into the complexity of generative processes which underlie socio-cultural conditions within history.[28] As opposed to the visible subject in the new historicism, illuminated by techniques of surveillance and manipulated through the conflation of knowledge and power, Copjec proposes "the orthopsychic subject," the subject who grounds itself in the lack in the Other, in a "fundamental dependence on the faults it finds in representation and in itself" (38). This *manque-à-être*, this lack as well as thirst for being, engenders the metonymic libido, the desire that "*transfixes* the subject [...] in a conflictual place" and that generates the fantasies and sublimations "circumnavigat[ing] the absence that anchors the subject and impedes its progress" (38; Copjec's emphasis). Because Lacanian psychoanalysis separates the *enunciation* of the orthopsychic subject from historical knowledge, from the *statement*, it prob-

---

26 Stanley Bates. "Character." *The Oxford Handbook of Philosophy and Literature* (Oxford: Oxford University Press, 2009), 393–419.

27 "History of the signifier" is L. O. Aranye Fradenburg's coinage. Her explanation is a variant of mine: the expression indicates "Lacan's idea of a history of how the function of marking has been realized in relation to enjoyment" (255, n25). *Sacrifice Your Love: Psychoanalysis, Histroicism, Chaucer* (Minneapolis: University of Minnesota Press, 2005).

28 Joan Copjec. *Read My Desire: Lacan against the Historicists* (Cambridge: The MIT Press, 1994).

lematizes discourse to an extent precluded by positivism, conjoining the truth of the singular psyche to the totalizing systems of epochal knowledge.[29]

Similarly engaging with antagonistic scholarship, which charges the psychoanalytic enterprise with antihistoricism, medievalists interested in the theory of desire promote the inclusiveness of the Lacanian perspective, its transhistoricity as well as its attentiveness to the singular subject. A recent spate of seminal books within medieval studies attests to the relevance and insistence of premodern desire within the history of the signifier, an inclusion facilitated by a grounding in psychoanalytic social theory.[30] In both her survey in *New Medieval Literatures* (1998) and her book, *Sacrifice Your Love* (2002), L.O. Aranye Fradenburg invokes "psychoanalytic medievalism" as a methodological alternative to prevailing academic historicism, which, on the one hand, operates on positivistic principles, valorizing grand narratives as opposed to hybrid genres such as dramatic chronicles or local legends, and, on the other hand, advocates *alteritism*, the view of the "uniqueness of historical phenomena" and a concomitant pledge to mediate this responsibly and objectively.[31] Rigorously orchestrating borderlines, in terms of periodization, archival purity and "containment of the dead" (Fradenburg 2002: 48), these dominant historiographic brands share a form of professional asceticism, which according to Fradenburg, participates in a paradoxical economy of sacrifice: purporting to "give ourselves up, become other to ourselves" in order to decipher the alien past, historians, almost perversely, deny "the power of medieval texts too speak unless spoken to, by *us*" (49). The paradox of this academic rescue operation pri-

29 See especially Copjec's *tour-de-force* cultural reading of modernist France, conjoining the fetishistic subject, utilitarianism and moral law, "The Sartorial Superego" (65–116).

30 Besides L. O. Aranye Fradenburg's *Sacrifice Your Love: Psychoanalysis, Historicicsm, Chaucer*, which I discuss below as well as throughout this study, Erin Felicia Labbie's *Lacan's Medievalism* (Minneapolis: University of Minnesota Press, 2006) contributes extensively to a revaluation of the place of the premodern within histories of subjectivation. Not exclusively psychoanalytic, Paul Strohm's *Theory and the Premodern Text* (Minneapolis: University of Minnesota Press, 2002), with regard to medieval texts, undertakes "practical theory," often from a Freudian perspective, productively engaging with the textual unconscious.

31 Fradenburg's survey of recent psychoanalytic scholarship within medieval studies is "We are Not Alone: Psychoanalytic Medievalism," in *New Medieval Literatures*, Vol II, eds. Rita Copeland, David Lawton and Wendy Scase (Oxford: Clarendon Press, 1998), 249–276. In *Sacrifice Your Love*, the chapter on psychoanalysis and historicism is titled "Becoming Medieval" (43–78). The phrase "uniqueness of historical phenomena" is culled from Lionel Gossman's study of the emergence of alteritism in the nineteenth century: "History as Decipherment: Romantic Historiography and the Discovery of the Other." *Studies in Historical Change* 18 (1986): 23–57. See *Sacrifice Your Love*, 262, n10.

marily lies in its being "put into the hands of a rather dubious Red Cross: the post-Freudian, post-Einsteinian, post-Betty Friedanian subjects of the twenty-first century" (49).

As a counter historicist maneuver, psychoanalytic medievalism, informed by Lacan's return to Freud, practised by scholars such as Fradenburg, Erin Felicia Labbie and Paul Strohm, embraces *transhistoricism* as a recognition of the "signifier's ability to return" (Fradenburg 2002: 49), of the complex and subtle dialectic between alterity and sameness throughout historical time. In the introduction to the innovative collection of essays, *Premodern Sexualites* (1996), Louise Fradenburg and Carla Freccero expose the ideological premise of the opposition between the transhistorical as a universalizing gesture and the (Foucauldian) *episteme* as radical historical contingency, aptly observing that Foucault's own writing engaged with the moment or event in history as "fractured, layered," as suffused with "multiple time lines" (xix; xx).[32] Signifying continuity between the premodern and the contemporary does not of necessity imply an ahistorical conflation or a teleological development, but can, on the contrary, be perceived on the lines of the Freudian/Lacanian subject as temporalized space, as an entity crisscrossed by heterogenous pasts, as an unstable identity, marked by narcissistic desires and their infinite vicissitudes and detours. As the following chapters in this book will show, *identification* is a force field, libidinally motivated to validate self-identity, but at the same time, fissured by the logic of the signifier, by an Other, whose lack consititues the identifying subject's very cause. My book on literary character seeks to foreground sublimation as an aesthetic engagement with the negativity inherent in identification. If as Fradenburg contends, "history is a matter of knowledge production, and the knowledge it produces is a matter of life and death" (2002: 59), then in the arts and poetic creation, character's transhistoricity is generated by the continuity of the work of mourning, of the work of producing revisionary, accommodating ego-ideals despite the tragedy of desire.

32 Louise Fradenburg and Carla Freccero. "Introduction: Caxton, Foucault, and the Pleasures of History." *Premodern Sexualities*, eds. Louise Fradenburg and Carla Freccero (New York: Routledge, 1996), xiii–xxiv.

Part 1: Necessary Fictions

Chapter 1: Situating Character

As the early narratologists noted, literary character is peculiarly resistant to a theoretical description. Whereas other elements of narrative – story, plot, temporal order, narration – lend themselves easily to precise classifications, character remains elusive, hovering uneasily between mimetic wholeness and semiotic dissection. There seems to rest a kind of semantic paradox at the heart of the concept itself. On one hand, "character" refers to the self, to persons, to existence in the world; on the other, it denotes text, networks of signifiers, the technology of writing.[1]

As narrative theory has become more and more interdisciplinary in recent years so has speculation about the nature and function of literary character. The structuralist tendency to conceptual reduction has given way to eclectic approaches which take into account reading, gender, ethics, ideology and culture. Character is thus often perceived as a privileged textual space, as a point of entrance for readers into the fictional world and as hermeneutic testing ground (e. g. Frow 1986: 248; Milowicki and Wilson 1995: 217–223).[2] There is no reason, many theorists claim, to stop short at the concept's inherent aporia, its continuous shifts between absence and presence; rather the challenge of interpretation is to both account for the dissolution of constructs and to refill them with meaning (esp. Docherty 1983).[3] The paradox of character is a sign of its vitality, not of its death.

One of the more interesting outcomes of these attitudes of pluralism is an emphasis on readers' activity and on reading itself as components in the construction of characters. As a text's formal condition, character *binds* the reader to the fiction (Frow 1986: 248), and this relation has been described in a variety of ways,

1 In the heyday of narratology, many critics commented on the "problem of character." In "Structural Analysis of Narrative" (1977), Roland Barthes says, "Since Propp, the characters set the structural analysis of narrative the same problem" (105). The starting point for both Shlomith Rimmon-Kenan's (1983) and Seymour Chatman's (1978) analysis is that character is a resilient problem.
The etymology of the word seems to confirm the conceptual fuzziness. See the entries for *character* in the *Oxford English Dictionary Online*, referred to in my introduction.

2 Edward. J. Milowicki and R. Rawdon Wilson. "Ovid through Shakespeare: The Divided Self." *Poetics Today* 16 (Summer, 1995), 217–252.

3 Thomas Docherty. *Reading (Absent) Character: Towards a Theory of Characterization in Fiction* (Oxford: Clarendon Press, 1983).

depending often on the theorist's ideological orientation. An early contribution to this aspect is Roland Barthes' *S/Z* (1974), a remarkable account of the critic as creative reader. In his provocative reading of Balzac's *Sarrasine*, Barthes' central aim is to unsettle the realist work ("the readerly"; "le lisible"), to inject it with the difficult rhetoic of *the writerly* text ("le scriptible"), the text that reflects upon itself as artifice. Consequently, as regards the character/reader couple, Barthes stresses, in the first place, the *writtenness* of character, how, following certain textual indices, readers attach language to proper names. Signifiers that refer to characters are specialized *semes* or connotations that suggest the human personality, the inner life and cultural being of individuals (17). For instance, throughout Balzac's novella, various behavioral and psychological terms point to the central character, Sarrasine, which readers assemble into a paradigm of verisimilitude. Sarrasine is the sum of these semantic fragments: *turbulence, artistic gift, independence, excess, femininity, ugliness, composite nature, impiety, love of whittling, will*, etc. (191). The illusory stamp of *individuality* is the Proper Name:

> The proper name enables the person to exist outside the semes, whose sum nonetheless constitutes it entirely. As soon as a Name exists (even a pronoun) to flow toward and fasten onto, the semes become predicates, inductors of truth, and the Name becomes a subject [...] the semic raw material [...] *completes* what is proper to being, *fills* the name with adjectives. (191; Barthes' italics)

Barthes also emphasizes how these inventories are by no means stable categories. The realistic illusion is punctured when semes move between groupings as often occurs between narrators and the narrated; character is then demystified, revealed as a symbolic function or a figure (67–68). Furthermore, like thematics, classical interpretation *par excellence*, character construction is a product of "an ideology of the person," a semiotic product of cognitive, as well as cultural, conditioning (92–3; 191).

In *S/Z*, the "binding in" of reader to character, the process of identification itself, is stripped of its traditional humanist dimension and unmasked as an ideologically coded activity. As Anglo-American narratology developed Barthes' propositions, however, their radical edge became blunted, and they were subtly re-directed to an older position. Both Shlomith Rimmon-Kenan and Seymour Chatman equate Barthes' account of semes with a common-sensical naming of traits, with a kind of *folk empirics* which readers bring to texts and then harmonize with strategies of discourse such as characterizing action, speech and setting (Rimmon- Kenan 1983: 59–70; Chatman 1978: 96–145).[4] Chatman, in particular, seems to misunderstand Barthes' methods as he compares them to A.C. Bradley's analysis of Shake-

4 In *Story and Discourse* (1978), Chatman comments on the relationhip between literary character and "folk physics":

spearean characters, a prototypical empirical approach (*Shakespearean Tragedy* 1904; 1955).[5] Through a paradigm of traits, Bradley hopes to sum a character up, to "find … the genuine mainspring" of his personality, the key to Iago, Lear and Hamlet (Chatman 134). For instance, after examining the clash between Iago's public image and his private speech, Bradley concludes that the villain is motivated by *coldness*, not by envy or hate, and that this capacity for cool detachment makes of him "a twisted artist" (Chatman 1978: 136; Bradley 1955: 185–7). Quite contrary to Bradley's essentialism, Barthes' reading in *S/Z* is a demystification of the signified. The "metonymic skid," the slide of signifiers, readers experience in their relation to characters is not at all, as Chatman maintains, the path to "the key to the character," but the route itself of textual division, of the arbitrary sign (Barthes 92; Chatman 134).

Both Rimmon-Kenan and Chatman acknowledge that theoretically literary character is "a problem" (Rimmon-Kenan 1983: 29) but seem to consider the *reading* for character to be a natural procedure, emerging in a straightforward way from "the general vocabulary of psychology, morality, and any other relevant area of human experience" (Chatman 1978: 138). Similarly, James Phelan's discussion in *Reading People, Reading Plots* (1989) advocates a realistic model of character despite his interest in the rhetorical conditions of narrative.[6] According to Phelan, the audience's relationship to characters can best be understood by distinguishing between three parts – the mimetic (character as person), the thematic (character as an idea), the synthetic (character as artificial construct) – and by focusing on how different texts produce variable hierarchies. A social realist novel, like Jane Austen's *Pride and Prejudice*, for instance, privileges the mimetic dimension and induces readers to assemble the information about the heroine, Elizabeth Bennet, into a sympathetic "portrait." On the other hand experimental texts such as Virginia Woolf's *The Waves* demand a more comprehensive response from the audience as the mimetic, thematic and synthetic components blend within characters in complex and challenging ways; here, character is experienced as a fluid phenomenon, as a movement between individual essence and textual construct (*Narrative as Rhetoric* 40–42).

The event-existent distinction is a purely folk ("commonsense") attitude taught us by the codes of our culture. The culture can"naturalize" events intoo existents: "fist" in English is a noun, hence we think of it as an object; in other languages it is a verb, hence an event. Narrative analysis is based on folk, not scientific, physicis.(96, n1)

5 A. C. Bradley. *Shakespearean Tragedy* (London: McMillan, 1905; 1955).

6 James Phelan. *Reading People, Reading Plots: Character, Progression and the Interpretation of Narrative* (Chicago: University of Chicago Press, 1989). See also Phelan's *Narrative as Rhetoric: Technique, Audiences, Ethics, Ideology* (Columbus: Ohio State University Press, 1996).

In order to explain the operation of the three components of character in narrative, Phelan imbues each with what he calls *dimensions* and *functions*, "the potential to signify in a certain way and the realization of that potential" (*Narrative as Rhetroic* 29). Thus, character in satire, in *Gulliver's Travels*, for instance, has, on the mimetic level, only dimensions, a signifying potential, applied variously to different aims of the satiric critique, but does not develop into full individuality (29). *Pride and Prejudice*, of course, manages a complete mimetic function, an emotional and moral investment in the portraiture of Elizabeth, whereas the self-aware narration in *The Waves* problematizes both dimensions and functions, calling for a sophisticated, reflective audience response (30–31; 38–40).

Phelan's model of character is valuable in a variety of ways for narrative analysis, and my brief sketch does it scant justice. What is disconcerting about it, however, is the unexamined assumption that the mimetic experience is a natural one, that the end result of the novelistic *portrait* is a state of transparency where readers glance at the *essence* of individuals.[7] Even the deconstructive strategies in *The Waves*, in Phelan's opinion, are harnessed so as to engage readers directly in the mimetic dimension and to confront them with characters as whole individuals, as paradigms of ordinary traits, of selfishness, resentment, love, hate, fear, jealousy, insecurity and greed (35–42; 201). Like Chatman, Phelan does not examine the contexts of such paradigm constructions but merely assumes that they are the products of normal literary response. It is indeed surprising that a critic so attentive to writers' intention should ignore the interest of Woolf herself in unconventional psychology, in the elusive emotional life of the solitary person, and in inventing new forms to represent such a life.[8] It is also surprising that within contemporary narratology investigations into the nature and function of character tend to trivial-

7 *Portrait* is a prevalent term in Phelan's book, implying always the realistic portrait, as if art history knows no other.
In an article in *The Times Literary Supplement* (August 2003) – "Not on his picture but his book," an edited speech delivered at the National Portrait Gallery – Stephen Orgel draws attention to the unreliability of author portraits, mostly of Renaissance figures such as Sidney, Donne and Ben Jonson. Here, likeness and authenticity are shown to be complex conceptions; for instance, rather than depicting the essense of an author, these portraits constitute an iconography: they are appendages to the author's persona not reflections of him or her. In this context, it is worth noting that Virginia Woolf herself has written critically about the veneration of the portrait. See "The Fleeting Portrait," in *Granite and Rainbow* (London: Hogarth Press, 1958), 216–224.

8 Woolf's "Mr Bennett and Mrs Brown" (1923) and "Character in Fiction" (1924) are major modernist manifestos about new character. The essays are critical of Arnold Bennett's realistic, fixed notion of character, his exquisitely detailed, but static portrayals; instead, Woolf proposes her own evocation of "Mrs Brown" (the epilogue to this book examines these essays more thoroughly).

ize the psychological conditions of the concept, to turn the difficult and complex relation between readers' desire and textual structure into an *ordinary* experience, facilely mappable in the language of commonplaces.

One of the reasons for this reductive psychological view may be that the term itself – *character* – is not applicable within avant-garde, experimental texts which actually aim at subverting the conventional category of a structured self. Within critical history, there have been several attempts to eliminate the concept as it appears to represent an outmoded view of not only literary creation but of subjectivity as well. Thus, Hélène Cixous claims that "character" remains a stumbling-block to investigations into the nature of *fiction* because it presupposes a Cartesian perspective on the Ego as a masterable unity ("The Character of 'Character'" 383–5).[9] In Cixous' account, the textual *imaginary*, that subjective space which "has always been disturbed, changeable, literally populated with a mass of "Egos" (383), is overpowered by the concept of character which is of the order of the *symbolic*, a repressive socializing position. Because of its unified, closed structure, character is no less than a *censor* of subjectivity, suppressing polyvocality within its enlightened knowledge of itself as "the guarantor of the transmission of sense and of the 'the true'" (385). Readers are cajoled into full identification with this thin signifier, (mis)recognizing themselves in its illusory realistic reflection.

On the whole, Cixous' essay contains a provocative analysis of the ideological condition of what she calls the "fetishization" of character, of the "'I' who is a *whole* subject [...] conscious, knowable" (385). Without a doubt, literary history has encouraged a narcissistic link between the rise of the middle class in the early eighteenth century, the novel and realistic character and has, for better or worse, universalized this relation, projecting the enlightened self backwards and forwards in history, onto quite different texts, audiences and cultural contexts. However, if realism is an ideology, constructing its own version of the person in the language of literature, then it is a critique of that ideological distortion that is valuable, not the dismantling of the distorted concept. As Barthes contends, character functions as a kind of *figure* of reading and writing, activities which are invariably ideologically coded (see above: *S/Z* e.g. 92–3). A novelistic character such as Sarrasine is a conjunction of the naming that takes place in the interaction between readers and signifiers. Readers construct wholes out of a narcissistic desire which is filtered through culture and through the language of the specific text. This activity is neither the ordinary experience Phelan maintains it is, nor is it fully explained by Cixous' view of character as symbolic suppression. Rather it is a network of relations – ideological, psychological, cognitive, ethical and semiotic. Theorists tend

9 Hélène Cixous. "The Character of 'Character'." *New Literary History* 5 (1974): 383–402.

to unravel only one thread in that complex web, missing the *surplus* of the term, character, the way in which it exeeds its own status as structure, portrait or fetish.

There have, of course, been several attempts to account for the elusive surplus of character. Three critical approaches to the problem are particularly worthy of attention, Joel Weinsheimer's semiotic reading of Jane Austen's *Emma*, Edward Milowicki's and Rawdon Wilson's (literary) historical method and John Frow's prolegomenon for a psychoanalytic poetics.[10]

In "Theory of Character: *Emma*" (1979), Weinsheimer is interested in the *fictiveness* of literary character, in its quality as segment of text, dissociated from the real world. Unlike Cixous, who considers the concept of character to be an impediment to investigations into fictionality or, as she says, "the theater of writing" (385), Weinsheimer explores character's *polysemy*, the way in which it relates to writing, to the materiality of signs. In this reading of *Emma*, the superfluity of character manifests itself within the textual world which the critic deliberately closes in order to foreground mimetic dissolution. Here, character has no individual identity but merges indiscriminately with other characters; it has no specific characteristics, no unique voice, no style of its own, no social background, no historical continuity (194–195). In Weinsheimer's words, "character is deindividualized and contextualized or, better, is itself a context," an "indeterminate" phenomenon, belonging to the "psychology of the whole text," not to subjective experience (194).

In spite of his irreverence toward literary mimesis, Weinsheimer is well aware of the duality of the character concept, of the fact that the referential dimension can only be elided at the cost of both critical anxiety and theoretical impoverishment. Indeed, the end result of this ingenious deconstructive analysis is as "inadequate" and "partial" as would be the conception that "Emma" is a person, participating in an extratextual world (208).[11] In order to encompass character fully, the critic must be "Janus-faced," capable of "[doing] justice to both texts and persons," of harmonizing semiotic and mimetic criticism (208). Separated from a world, semiotic criticism manages only to expose arbitrariness; separated from textuality, mimetic criticism ignores the literary experience itself. A combination of approaches enables both "production" and "recovery," a focus upon character as indeterminate fiction as well as an interest in its human *meaning*, in the relation between persons and fictional representation (209).

---

10 Joel Weinsheimer. "Theory of Character: *Emma*." *Poetics Today* 1 (Autumn, 1979): 185–211. Edward Milowicki and Rawdon Wilson. "Ovid through Shakespeare: The Divided Self" (1995). I single out these three approaches because they are particularly relevant to the psychoanlytic theory of character developed in this book. Especially, Frow's suggestions are pertinent for an ontological exploration.

11 Weinsheimer contends that his method differs from Derridean deconstruction, even if the results are similar.

As I remarked above, the duality of the character concept, its elusive slippage from wholeness to dissolution, has, among contemporary theorists, come to define the critical problematic. In recent years, this problem has not been exclusively formulated within narratology but has been appropriated by fictional poetics in general, linked to pre-novelistic texts, such as classical poetry and Shakespearean drama, and to literary modes, such as the lyric, the dramatic monologue and autobiography.[12] A revealing light is cast on the historical dimension of character as a dual structure in Edward Milowski's and Rawdon Wilson's "Ovid through Shakespeare: The Divided Self" (1995). Here, the conflict at the heart of the character concept is considered as a literary convention, originating with Ovid, then re-embedded in Shakespeare's works and finally absorbed into the genre of the novel. In a way, Milowski's and Wilson's method suggests how it may be possible to mediate between a life-world model and a textual model in discussions of character, especially in their reliance on Mikhail Bakhtin's concern with *voice* in *Problems of Dostoevski's Poetics* (1984).[13] What Bakhtin emphasizes is the anteriority of a character's voice in an imagined world which readers must enter in order to grasp nuances and conflicts within a text (Milowicki and Wilson 223; Bakhtin 32). In Dostoevsky's novels, character always carries the language of value, emerging from a tangible world, imbued with existential and social struggle. Thus, almost every utterance is *dialogic*, contending with itself as another: "in every expression [there is] a crack, and the readiness to go over immediately to another contradictory expression"; in every gesture "[there is] confidence and lack of confidence simultaneously" (30). Because the polyphonic novel is a web of voices, each registering "a conviction" or a world-view as well as an openness to conflict, character becomes a kind of structure of multifariousness, anchored in textuality *and* embroiled in life.[14] In general, Bakhtin's investigations of polyphony contain rich material for a theory of literary character. I will have occasion to

---

12 The 1980s proved fertile for character study. See, for instance, the special issue of *Poetics Today* on *Theory of Character*; Joseph A. Porter. "Character and Ideology in Shakespeare," in Ivo Kamps, ed. *Shakespeare Left and Right* (New York: Routledge, 1991); Thomas Docherty. *Reading (Absent) Character: Towards a Theory of Characterization in Fiction* (1983). I will have occasion to refer more specifically to Docherty's book in the section on the Old English elegies. My introduction refers to more recent studies.

13 Mikhail Bakhtin. *Problems of Dostoevksi's Poetics*. Trans. Caryl Emerson (Minneapolis: University of Minnesota Press, 1984).

14 A related point is Bakhtin's reference to Lunacharsky's "conviction" in *Problems of Dostoevsky's Poetics*: "Lunacharsky emphasizes, and correctly, that 'all the voices playing a truly essential role in the novel are actually 'convictions' or 'points of view on the world'" (33). A. Lunacharsky's work is *On Literature and Art* (Moscow: Progress Publishers, 1973).

return to *Problems of Dostoevsky's Poetics* later in this chapter. At present, I want to briefly outline Milowicki's and Wilson's historical approach to character as a dialogic construct.

According to Milowicki and Wilson, "the split awareness" they detect first in Ovid's works culminates in novelistic consciousness, particularly in the sophisticated self-awareness of modernist narrative. Within Renaissance drama, as well as within late Renaissance romance and the first novels, this *convention* of a divided self was ubiquitous, crystallized in Shakespearean character, both in the plays and in narrative poems such as *The Rape of Lucrece* and *Venus and Adonis* (226). In the case of, for instance, Tarquin, Macbeth, Brutus and Hamlet, the cognitive dilemma assumes the form of a clash of values, which is actually debated within the mind, in an interior monologue. Shakespeare's troubled characters stage their indecision as if it was an allegorical tug-of-war between conscience and passion. In *The Rape of Lucrece*, Tarquin reasons the inevitability of rape by matching the unequal terms of "frozen conscience" and "burning will." Even before the mind engages in moral debate, it is overpowered by the latter term, by lustful anticipation which taints the ensuing argument. Thus, the character's interior monologue is mere rhetorical show; desire itself has predetermined the outcome (223–24). Nevertheless, the sense of imbalance or dissonance is acute enough to turn such situations into crucial moments of ethical and existential choice.

Milowicki and Wilson claim that Shakespearean drama hones a literary convention of character derived from Ovidian narrative. In particular, the *Metamorphoses* depicts anguished female characters torn between vice and virtue and marshalling arguments in support of illicit desire. The narrative voice is usually explicitly dialogic, a *cracked* utterance in a Bakhtinian sense, at first wavering between law and passion, then justifying transgression with ingenious rhetorical flair. These "dialogized monologues" are even cast in regular persuasive patterns: caught in a debate between duty and love, Medea structures her thought in a question-and-answer scheme, a *ratiocinatio*, which enables her to scrutinize her own feelings through conventional morality; in the process, she manages a relativization of values, convincing herself that place determines views, that Colchis, her own land, is "barbarous" and that her lover's, Jason's, homeland, which she longs for, is "civilized and cultured" (232–33). Similarly, the stories of Myrrha and Byblis tell of attempts to rationalize transgression; both female characters justify their incestuous longing by an appeal to the relativity of the law, conditioned by different cultures and the fallibility of its human makers (232–33).

To a large extent, Ovid's formalized arguments, saturated with strained passion, provide an intertextual milieu for the medieval courtly love tradition and for characterization in Chaucer's works. Milowicki and Wilson note Chaucer's sophisticated use of Ovid's rhetorical model in *Troilus and Criseyde* where the clash beween the code of courtly love and the strictures of Catholic theology exemplifies characters' relativizing ploys. Since the medieval "art of love" comprised a confused mixture of objective convention and subjective value, of authority and subversion, it empowers an individual such as Troilus to rationalize his erotic obsession. Like Ovid, Chaucer makes love itself the disturbing psychological force which pluralizes voice, splintering the illusory unity of consciousness. On the other hand, even to greater lengths than in classical narrative, Chaucerian characters are *ironic* compositions, or, as Milowicki and Wilson would say, *reductive* structures, acutely self-conscious about their inner dissonance. In *The Canterbury Tales*, the Wife of Bath anticipates the psychology of novelistic character in the reverberating divisions between self and society, the past and the present, desire and reason. The Wife's modernity lies in ironic rationalizations of her own character. Unlike Ovid's Medea and Myrrha who are convinced by their own passionate rhetoric, the Wife of Bath justifies her difference, her deviance from social norms, her sensuality and promiscuity, with the sceptic's eloquence, *tounge-in-cheek* (236–40).

Split awareness, first elaborated upon in Ovid's *Metamorphosis*, casts a long shadow over Western literature – narrative, drama, as well as the modern novel – not exclusively because it is a usable artifice but because it is a necessary ingredient in the construct of character. A self-divided character bridges world and text and engages audiences in a clash of values which is intellectually and psychologically authentic. Following Bakhtin, Milowicki and Wilson claim that because of its argumentative openness literary voice connects with person and that such a connection creates a *zone* of character, the major force in fiction, binding reader to text (245–47).

Milowicki''s and Wilson's literary historical review of a conceptual scheme, their tracing of cognitive dissonance from classical narrative to the dawn of the modern novel in late medieval times, provides a valuable contribution toward a theory of character. As the writers note themselves, their aim is to uncover *one* of the building blocks of, what Bakhtin calls, characterhood, to define an important substratum of a character's world, not to offer a whole-scale solution to the problems of the concept (245). Of necessity, such a partial approach brackets off major conceptual difficulties, especially those that have to do with the links between character and ideology, between discourse and ideology (the character's zone in history), between the cultural situation of audience and the world of persons in texts. In the following discussion, I will have occasion to expand on all of these aspects; at this juncture, I merely want to indicate the complex implications within each relation.

In the first place, although the question of *ideology* is broached by Milowicki and Wilson, it is dismissed all too offhandedly as generating only "a restrictive paradigm" (242). The writers seem to assume that there exists a direct relationship between textual structure and ideology so that Shakespeare's characters, for instance, function as "reflections of the author's own ideolgical investment" (242). Viewed in such a light a theory of character becomes exclusionary, flattening out differences: Renaissance characters turn into mouthpieces or themes, registering the political, religious and moral concerns of the period; they are deprived of their individuality, their inner complexity, the sense of which a topos such as split awareness can offer (243).

Of course, if the anchoring point for character as an ideological structure is primarily the author's world-view then the paradigm is bound to be a limited one. On the other hand, if the path followed is, as Barthes contends, that of an *ideology of the person*, an epistemological model, conditioned by a particular cultural situation, then the representational products will be as nuanced and diversified as the realms of knowledge they emerge from. Literary character may extend and propagate a certain cognitive assemblage, as in the stereotyping of gender, race or class, but it is more likely, especially in the case of individualized figures, that some static cultural knowledge is undercut, inverted and transformed. In fact, the very device of split consciousness, that Milowicki and Wilson investigate, illustrates the powers of literary convention to resist ideological structures and to revise in radical ways the representation of subjectivity. In a way, double-voicedness, the character's "sideways glance" at the otherness of the utterance (Bakhtin 1984: 32), performs ideology, the conflict between self and society. The character's dilemma, for instance, the experience of love as opposed to taboos or to social knowledge in general, does not simply negate ideology but stages its multi-faceted aspects in confrontation with individual desire. It is a dialogic *display*, neither prescriptive nor damaging, but profoundly ethical; it is a unique feature of that artisitic structure we call character.

The role of ideology in the construction of character becomes clearer if linked more concisely to zones of *discourse*. Milowicki and Wilson make the strong point that Bakhtin's dialogism manages to mediate between characters' position in the world and in text, between "existential realities" and literary voice (223). Although the writers mention the force of value in that convergence, they do not consider at any length the means by which norms in the non-discursive realm are translated into discourse. What kind of transformation takes place when social action is represented by a character's axiological sphere, his or her conflicted world of value? Is it enough to maintain, as Milowicki and Wilson do, that it is the very *authenticity* of a device such as cognitive dissonance that brings the "experience of characters closer to human experience" (229)? Is this a normative authenticity, transhistorical and authoritative? Or is it a private knowledge of the genuine, opposed to cultural standards, provocative and potentially subversive? In my opinion, such questions can only be answered from a view of the operations of ideology as it traverses non-discursive/discursive bounds in historical time.[15]

As I discussed above, the poststructural critique of literary character (e.g. Cixous; Weinsheimer) presumes that the concept itself functions as an ideological stricture, a *fetish*, produced and valorized by the Cartesian premise of bourgeois consciousness. According to such views, "character" in itself embodies an ideology of the person, with the realistic novel as the main culprit, exhibiting its portrait gallery of unified, coherent selves. In avant-garde, experimental fiction, on the other hand, the category of character is outmoded, a stumbling-block for investigations into pluralized subjectivity. By the same token, this category would be considered an anachronism within pre-novelistic genres such as the epic or medieval narrative and inapplicable to dramatic or poetic texts. In my opinion, even if this type of criticism makes use of a theory of ideology, it assumes, no less than Milowicki's and Wilson's bracketing off the ideological, an unproblematic relation between form and reality, between artistic practice and non-discursive modes of production. Character does not simply reflect a person, an authentic individual or a mystified self; rather it stakes out its own discursive realm, registering within that the multifarious *relations* that can exist between representation and the world. It is in this sense of a relational zone that character can be considered a polyphonic structure; as such, it is indeed an apt artistic register for subjectivity.

In order to show the polyphonic relation between the discourse of character and ideology, I will briefly focus on the construction of identity in a contemporary novel, Graham Swift's *Ever After* (1992).[16] The major character in Swift's text is also the narrator, and, as is so often the case in autodiegetic narratives, the voice attempts a reconstruction of the past after crisis. The narration takes place after repeated experiences of loss and the protagonist's own suicide attempt. In less than two years before the moment of writing, the closest members of the narrator's family have died, his wife, his mother and his stepfather, leaving him with a "shattered, overturned" life (3), driven to self-destruction. Most shockingly, the brush with death dislocates the narrator's sense of self so that he doesn't recognize his own face in the mirror and feels permanently divorced from his former being. In the beginning, his writing is prompted by a desire to overcome alienation, to capture the essence of self; in the process, however, it turns into an extended discovery of difference and an accompanying meditation on the consequences of self-division for human meaning.

15 The latter part of this book develops to some extent the role ideology has in determining subjective utterance.

16 Graham Swift. *Ever After* (New York: Picador, 1992).

Although the narration in *Ever After* is personally motivated, it is also permeated by the effects of major historical events. The narrator, Bill Unwin, is born on the eve of the Second World War, in December, 1936, during the very week, as he says, of the Abdication Crisis in Britain. Unwin's life, in fact, appears to be characterized by constant collisions between the violence of reality and the sublimities of romance: the father, a military man, commits suicide in "fairy-tale" Paris where the young narrator visits the Opera with his charming mother and contemplates ballerinas from afar; the new plastics industry, in the shape of his stepfather's company, Ellison Plastics, competes with Unwin's aspirations for another world, the love of literature and the theater; the perfect marriage to a famous actress is disrupted by her illness and premature death. These different worlds of hard facts and private pleasure are, however, not presented in the novel as separate realms but interact with each other in intricate ways. As the story proceeds, the narrator becomes more and more conscious of this interaction, often noting in bewilderment how a fact is nothing but artifice or how fiction comprises the real itself. Thus, in 1945, he wonders how the painted set of the city rooftops in *La Bohème* is just like the actual Paris so that he will always see it as "the incarnation of something already imagined [...] as a palpable network of 'scenes' " (13). After the war, in England, the young boy assembles a scale-model of a fighter plane, a gift from his stepfather, and as he does so experiences viscerally how it is to participate in war; he realizes the pilot's impotence, how he is, no less than the plastic figure, a puppet in the grip of the tactics and technologies of warfare: "The man didn't belong to himself. The man was plucked up from his real place and set down in the plane no less ruthlessly than I took his counterpart and glued him down by his backside" (66). At the same time, this contact with the model version of a violent reality emboldens the boy to partially act his revenge, Hamlet-like, against the mother and stepfather, in defiance of their neglect of the father's memory. He sets fire to the plastic kit and throws it like a hand-grenade into the garden where Sam and the mother sit in undeserved conjugal harmony. It is a case of defiant power literary fictions offer the embattled individual.

The divisionary force of fictional models of identity within historical reality is the narrator's major concern in *Ever After* and constitutes his zone as polyvocal character. In the novel, *characterhood*, the sense the character gives of himself as a substantial *person*, is constructed as a result of the philosophical meditation on the congruence between reality and appearance as well as of the narrator's autobiographical strategies. The narrator both *shows* and *is* (or *becomes*); that kind of self-reflective construction is uniquely the property of literary character.[17]

17 Note Bakhtin's discussion of characterhood in *Problems of Dsotoevsky's Poetics*: "Self-consciousness, as the *artistic dominance* governing construction of charac-

An additional example will further illustrate the complex building process of self in the novel. The narrator's explorations of identity, at first cursory and tinged with wonder, gather force as the conviction that "reality" is no less an ideological construct, a fiction – a falseness, perhaps – than the theatrical world he so much admires. For instance, the academic milieu he inhabits, once "the true, real permanent thing," is now considered from the *real*, active world outside it as a pretension, a "contrived film set"; still, the semantics of this *real* are so confused as to be meaningless: "the world is falling apart; its social fabric is in tatters, its eco-system is near collapse. Real: that is, flimsy, perishing, stricken, doomed" (2). Also, the stepfather's plastics industry provides the narrator with an apt semantic contradiction to figure modern reality: isn't plastics *the* post-war metaphor of phony consciousness, or, as the novel states, "the epitome of the false" (7)? Still, the narrator must contend with the strange congruence between the real and the apparent and the ensuing paradoxes and ironic effects. The stepfather's advocacy of his product as the new actuality of *substitution*, necessary in a world where " 'the real stuff is running out,' " collapses as his own wealth enables him to seek an authentic origin in Old England, an academic lineage, a *real* Tudor mansion, "fine tailoring and choice antiques" (8). Even more ironically, Bill Unwin's brave rejection of a lucrative carrer in Ellison Plastics turns against him in middle-age as, distraught after his wife's death, he accepts the Ellison Fellowship, the stepfather's endowment to the college of his forefather (another irony!).

As he writes his memories, the narrator seems often disturbed by these strange complicities between the real, the false, the individual subject and ideological construction, and his style reflects his insecurity, punctuated by question marks and unfinished sentences. If he must give up his quest for an essential self and instead survey a many-layered, complex *construction*, what is there to prevent dissolution, a dispersal of the subject within that terrible absence at the heart of things? At several points, however, the narrator hints at the difference between fictional models in literature, which do "not hide that [their] premise is illusion" (69), and the deceptive epistemological models of "the real," which present themselves as *the truth*, as in the writing of history and in the violent and tragic action such writing entails. Unwin's insight into the ethical implications of this difference crystallize when he decides to give up the *scholarly* enterprise of editing his Victorian ancestor's (great-great grandfather) Notebooks and instead to incorporate them into his own autobiographical account, the narrative we read, *Ever After*. By

ter, cannot lie alongside other features of this image; it absorbs these other features into itself as its own material and deprives them of any power to define or finalize the hero" (50; Bakhtin's emphasis). Chapter two, "The Hero, and the Position of the Author with Regard to the Hero, in Dostoevsky's Art" (47–77), is particularly revealing about the connection between character and ideology.

creatively reconstructing Matthew Pearce, instead of offering deceitful historiography, the narrator is empowered to confront relativity and to write himself as a fiction. It is a *necessary* and a good fiction, revealing to its audience how meaning is made in a senseless world.

Significantly, Bill Unwin's character is the result of his reading of Pearce's Notebooks as a *consolation* and, in turn, of his writing of his own restoration from grief. As a narrative genre, *Ever After* is a kind of post-modern elegy, a *working-through* of loss, offered to an audience as a new model of cure, as an instance of literary value, in a world blind to the ideological work of Historical Truth.[18] As Matthew Pearce discovered the amoral fictiveness of religion and found goodness only in his own conviction, even if it involved a total break with the past, so his great-great grandson confronts the masks of relativity and weaves them into an ethical texture, a fictional character, more true to experience and to history than dry, empty fact.

Ever After illustrates particularly well how literary character is embedded in historical time, how it emerges from ideological work in the real and, at the same time, contests that work through self-reflexive discourse. As Linda Hutcheon has observed about postmodern parody and historiographic metafiction, Swift's novel carries a political force, not as social realism nor as a defamiliarizing experiment but as narrative that both incorporates and disrupts the premises of Late Capitalist culture.[19] Within such a narrative, character functions as a necessary structure, concentrating within its zone a specific *epistemological* critique, a questioning of the dominant models of the person and suggestions for the building of alternative subjects. Thus, even if character is an ideological structure, complicit with dominant cultural discourses, it is also a *radical* symbol, a transhistorical, open paradigm of the person. So far, in my reading of *Ever After*, I have concentrated on the former dimension in order to promblematize the relation between aesthetic form and reality, an activity overlooked by many scholars who are especially interested in the concept of character. Still, an exposure of the ideological facet merely indicates the concept's radical openness but does not in itself manage to theorize

18 Similar concerns about the status of traditional history are raised in Swift's *Waterland* (1983; rev.ed. New York: Picador, 1992), although here there is more of an ambivalent attitude toward it. By offering alternative models – local history, family annals, stories of place and nature – the narrator, a history teacher, attempts to counter the force of Grand Narratives; *Waterland*, however, does not dismiss history, but engages with it dialogically. See my article"Cracked Voices: Identification and Ideology in Graham Swift's *Waterland*." *Critique: Studies in Contemporary Fiction* 45 (2003), 34–42.

19 See both Hutcheon's *A Poetics of Postmodernism: History, Theory, Fiction* (New York: Routledge, 1988), especially, chapter seven (106–123), and *The Politics of Postmodernism* (London: Routeldge, 1989), esp. 54–6; 72–3.

it. A comprehensive theory of character must account for the inherent *dynamics* of the concept, for its unique operation as both a temporal and transhistorical phenomenon. In other words, the concept requires a theory of *how* it exists, of its *being* – an ontology.

As I suggested at the beginning of this chapter, the "reader-response" group (e.g. Chatman, Rimmon-Kenan, Phelan) within the literature on character has not accomplished an ontology of the concept mainly due to its insistence on the naturalness of response, on text as a confirmation of ordinary experience. Although Milowicki and Wilson indicate the complex relation between convention and cultural audience they do not elucidate that relation but focus almost exclusively on the development of technique in literary history.[20] In fact, there are surprisingly few investigations of character's ontological dynamics; the most penetrating one is John Frow's essay, "Spectacle Binding: On Character" (1986), a prolegomenon for a psychoanalytic poetics of character.[21] Before I proceed to examine the psychoanalytic framework, I will outline Frow's major propositions.

As most theoretical approaches to character, Frow emphasizes the *duality* of the concept, its conjunction of textuality and realism, of rhetoric and subjectivity (245–247). Neither mimetic criticism nor structuralist poetics have managed to account for this ambivalence, the former neglecting the opacity of texts, the latter disregarding "any continuity between character and person" (230). On the other hand, psychoanalysis, as a theory of *identification*, suggests how "the person or subject [can] [...] be thought in textual terms," providing that *Janus-faced* perspective, Joel Weinsheimer called for in his essay on Jane Austen's *Emma* . Psychoanalysis offers an explanation of text or of the "writtenness of character" in terms of a psychological logic because it examines duality itself, or divisiveness, as a major constituent in ego formation (229; 238–9). Readers mobilize characters, make them exist as substantial agents, within the self-divisive drive of identification: character exists as an effect of the reader's desire for self in the place of the

20 Note the beginning of Milowicki's and Wilson's article: "The basic Ovidian contention, split awareness, is also seen as a paradigm case of how a structural form can be embedded, and subsequently reembedded in culture" (217); in fact, the critics do not consider that cultural end of the equation.

21 Thomas Docherty's *Reading (Absent) Character* (1983) is influenced by neo-Freudian thought, but does not pursue a wholescale psychoanalytic theory of character. More firmly grounded in psychoanalysis, Leo Bersani's *A Future for Astyanax: Character and Desire in Literature* (Boston: Little Brown, 1976) lacks, in my opinion, a consistent Lacanian perspective on the libidinal apparatus. Both Docherty and Bersani see character in modern and contemporary fiction as a culmination of its paradoxical status, both present and absent, a body and a word. Although Frow does not examine older texts specifically, his view of literary character as a *structure of desire* does not exclude transgeneric, transhistorical versions.

other. It is especially Freud's observations on narcissism which clarify this complex libidinal dynamic.

According to Frow, the explanatory force of narcissistic identification lies in "its ability to mediate between character as a formal structure and the reader's structured investment in it" (243). Freud's work on narcissism suggests that the work of pleasure in reading may not be fundamentally different from object choice everywhere since in all cases there is a tendency to *fantasize* the objective position (Frow 243).[22] In a love relation, for instance, the actual libidinal space may be less important than the ego's internal fantasy, its narcissistic scenario. This kind of situation is particularly well demonstrated in Freud's essay, "Mourning and Melancholia" (1917), where the melancholiac betrays his or her neurosis through misplaced reproaches of self: the apparently shameless self-accusations are actually attacks on the lost object, the resented other, who has been internalized, metamorphosed into an aspect of the ego (Frow 244; Freud 157).[23] The experience of loss thus reveals how narcissistic identification elides the boundary between subject and object so that, in Freud's words, "the loss of the object [becomes] transformed into a loss in the ego, and the conflict between the ego and the loved person transformed into a cleavage between the criticizing faculty of the ego and the ego as altered by the identification" (*Mourning and Melancholia* 159).

The *mechanisms* of this psychic movement, not its pathological circumstances, are analogous to the work of reading for fictional character. The drive to identify with characters in text is prompted by the ego-libido, by narcissistic desire which disperses itself and produces the effect of self in the sites of others. To a greater extent than any other theoretical formulation, this process enables a conceptualization of character as an ambivalent texture, as both presence and absence. Frow says that from the perspective of narcissism, a theory of character takes "account of the dialectical mirroring of subject and object positions in discourse," in other words, of the dynamics of the reader's *binding-in* to the signifying chain and the concomitant "'self'-construction in an imaginary construction of 'other,' quasi-unified selves" (243; 244).

In Frow's account, character is thus a powerful binding element in the "spectacle" of the text (as the title of his essay indicates), suggesting both the arbitrariness of signs and the necessary logic of subjective reconstruction. Besides positing narcissism as the ground of identification, Frow examines readers' activity in terms of psychoanalytic *semiotics*, especially within film theory. Lacanian scholars such as Jacques-Alain Miller and Jean-Pierre Oudart have developed psychoanalytic

22 See Freud's Essay "On Narcissism: An Introduction" (1914). *Collected Papers* Vol 4. Trans. Joan Riviere (New York: Basic Books, 1959), 30–59.

23 "Mourning and Melancholia" (1917). *Collected Papers* Vol 4. Trans. Joan Riviere (New York: Basic Books, 1959), 152–170.

concepts in order to investigate the production of subjectivity in popular discourse such as film. An important concept relating to the character construct is *suture*, used as a metaphor by Miller to theorize positionality in discourse, the way the subject links to the syntagm, the microlevel of the utterance. Entering the Symbolic Order, speakers are stitched into chains of signifiers so that there is a constant sense of the shiftiness of being. Lacan emphasizes the materiality of this experience, its *writtenness*, that subjectivity is a representational shift between signifiers: "the signifier is what represents the subject for another signifier" (Lacan 1977: 316; Frow 241).[24]

According to Miller, "suture" helps to name the oscillation between lack and presence in subjective experience (Miller 1977–1978:25–26; Frow 241).[25] In film, this operation translates into visual terms, as viewers identify with characters within chains of images and a mobile point of view. Cinematic cutting, in particular, exemplifies the paradox of character, how identity is constituted by both representation and discourse, signifying structure and the collapse of signification. For instance, in a viewing technique called "shot/reverse shot," the first shot can be conceived as neutral, discursive, enunciated by an invisible narrator, the "Absent One" (Frow 241). On the other hand, the second shot quickly overtakes the first one and subsumes it beneath its own second-order discourse, that of a particular agent within the story, representation as character. This recuperative act of the camera is explained thus by Daniel Dayan: "when shot two replaces shot one, the absent one is transferred from the level of enunciation to the level of the fiction (Dayan 1976:448; Frow 241).[26]

On the whole, Frow is rather critical of what he calls "the atomistic" level on which these theories of identification rest. His contention seems to be that Lacan's explanations of the speaking subject are narrowly bound to the sentence, to the function of "shifters" such as the personal pronoun, and that they are incapable of accounting for larger discursive categories, aesthetic experience or the psychological life in culture (242).[27] In my opinion, at this point, Frow's argument

---

24 Jacques Lacan. *Écrits: A Selection*. Trans. Alan Sheridan (New York: Norton, 1977). Lacanian concepts will be scrutinized more closely throughout the book; this sketch merely outlines the main tenets in Frow's prolegomenon.

25 Jacques-Alain Miller. "Suture." *Screen* 18.4 (1977–1978), 24–34.

26 Daniel Dayan. "The Tudor-Code of Classical Cinema," in Bill Nichols, ed. *Movies and Methods* (Berkely: University of California Press, 1976): 438–45. For a brief, helpful review of recent developments within Lacanian film theory, see Sean Homer. *Jacques Lacan* (London: Routledge, 2003), 124–8.

27 In his early linguistically oriented woork, Lacan often relies on Roman Jakobson's paper on "shifters": "Shifters, Verbal Categories, and the Russian Verb" (1957). *Selected Writings* Vol 2 (The Hague: Mouton, 1971), 130–147. Basically, "shifter" refers to the unstable position of pronouns in messages.

itself is "atomistic," paying scant attention to Lacan's rich and complex theory of subjectivity. It will be the task of the following chapters to demonstrate the explanatory power of that theory as an ontology of character.

Chapter 2: Narcissus: From Ovid to Freud

As the great tragedy of Oedipus, the myth of Narcissus conditions the psychoanalytic investigation of the mental life. The most complete version of the myth exists in Ovid's rendering in the *Metamorphoses* where it forms a long episode among many tales about transformation caused by love. Commentators rarely note the uncanny congruities between Ovid's story of a youth's incurable self-love and Freud's scientific re-telling, how the artist not only provides the psychoanalyst with a major concept, but creates as well an intricate intertextual milieu for the writings on narcissism, especially for the crucial essay, "On Narcissism: An Introduction" (1914).[1] To begin with, it will be useful to trace some of the intertextual links, in order to throw a stronger light on Freud's thoughts about this controlling psychological force.

In the *Metamorphoses*, the story of Narcissus occurs at a pivotal point within a series of accounts about the vicissitudes of love and desire, frequently involving a couple, where the pursuer is a powerful god – Pan, Apollo or Jupiter himself – and the pursued an innocent maid, an Arcadian nymph or a devotee of Diana, the virgin huntress. The otherwise imperturbable gods are always overwhelmed by their passion, and even though they know the tragic outcome, they plunge eagerly into their erotic pursuits, which invariably culminate in rape and in intolerable suffering for the young maids. One such story in Book 1 tells of Apollo and Daphne who both have been wounded by Cupid's arrows, the god by the golden arrow of love's lust, the nymph by the leaden arrow of frigid aversion. Apollo is determined to possess the girl and chases her in the forest, like a Gallic hound tracking a swift hare, hoping "at every moment that he has her, and [grazing] her hind quarters with outstreched muzzle" (43).[2] The only safe haven for the distraught girl is metamorphosis, and having uttered a prayer to be delivered from her own sexual attractiveness, she changes into a laurel tree. Later in Book 1, Mercury tells about Pan and Syrinx, a similar tale about an infatuated god, a virginal maid, a chase in a forest and vegetal transformation on the banks of a river, this time, a transformation into marsh reeds. The latent violence in both tales is exploited fully in the episode of Jupiter and Callisto, which involves the father of the gods himself in the

1 An exception to the critical neglect is Juliet Mitchell, who investigates the role of Echo in Ovid's work, in *Psychoanalysis and Feminism* (Penguin Books, 1974).

2 References to Ovid's *Metamorphoses* are to Penguin Classics (1955). Trans. Mary M. Innes.

ardent pursuit of a chaste warrior of Diana. Ready to face even the jealous wrath of Juno, his wife, for the sake of his passion, Jupiter rapes the maiden, who, as a consequence, suffers not only the shame of a despoiled huntress, but the agony of being transformed into a bear. Jupiter, however, manages to save Callisto from the relentless hate of his wife, effecting another transformation, turning the bear into a constellation in his heaven.

These three love stories convey a dynamic of desire, repeated again and again in various guises throughout the *Metamorphoses*. It is a dynamic that can best be described as a force of *negativity*, not in the sense that the outcome is always lamentable or that the whole quest, the libidinal effort, is negated, but in the sense that from the very beginning, the impossibility of fulfillment is inscribed within the drive to possess another. In all its manifestations, desire is fraught with its own *constitutional* lack so that its objects always elude its grasp, slip, slide, flee like Ovid's persecuted maidens, arrested only in states of metamorphoses, in substitution.[3] Thus, no matter how *imperialistic* the desire, how magnificiently backed up by power, glory and subjective mastery, the desired other escapes acquisition, even after such violent acts as sexual aggression and rape. In their hyperbolic transfigurations, Ovid's stories self-consciously highlight these libidinal gaps: the unattainability of the human is figured in the inhuman, in the radical difference of natural phenomenon and the animal body.

Perhaps no other story in the *Metamorphoses* is as preoccupied with the problematics of desire as is the story of Narcissus, the youth who falls in love with his own image. First, it is important to note the position of the tale in Book III, preceeded by the dramatic accounts of the birth of Bacchus and of the rise to fame of the prophet Tireisias and followed by a variety of events associated with the Bacchic festivities and "the new rites" (88). The introduction of Tireisias involves a significant episode staged among the gods, a "playful" argument between Jupiter and Juno about the stakes of sexual pleasure, whether the man or the woman gets more enjoyment out of love. To Juno's great chagrin, her husband claims women to be the winners, and Tireisias is brought in to arbiter the quarrel since "he had experienced love both as a man and as a woman," born a man, but lived seven years in the body of a woman (82). The greater pleasure of women is confirmed

3 In *Revolution in Poetic Language* (1974). Trans. Margaret Waller (New York: Columbia University Press, 1984), Julia Kristeva examines in detail Hegelian negativity, which "should not be confused with *negation* in judgment or with the "negative quantities" that Kant introduced in philosophy as a "polarity" or "opposition" (117; Kristeva's emphasis). Rather *negativity* as a semiotic/psychological/epistemological force should be understood as traversing meaning and subjectivity, ceaselessly productive because of its divided constitution. See especially chapter three in *Revolution in Poetic Language* ("Negativity as Transversal to Thetic Judgment" 117–126).

again, and Juno's disproportionate revenge is to blind the judge. As a compensation, Jupiter grants him the great honour of a prophetic gift. Subsequently, Tireisias' first major prophecy is to foretell Narcissus' fate, that he will "live to a ripe old age [...] *if he does not come to know himself* (83; my emphasis). The fulfillment of the prediction guarantees the seer's glorious reputation.

The Narcissus episode is thus locked within highly self-reflective narrative surroundings where *pleasure*, the tale's central concern (and, it is safe to say, one of the central concerns of the *Metamorphoses*, in general), is actually debated and linked to sexuality, to gender and to cultural change, in the form of the new religion of Bacchus, whose ascendency Tireisias also predicts. In fact, the prophet's comment on the fate of Narcissus, implying that man will perish in his *self*-knowledge, can be understood as a retrospective meditation upon the frivolous gods who ceaselessly cultivate their pleasure, despite the ensuing disasters and the long periods of grief. Even if, early on in the *Metamorphoses*, the Golden Age gives way to ages of strife, the gods remain children of paradise, immersed in the sensual life, with an omniscient view of the events of the world, but with no knowlegde of themselves. The story of Narcissus introduces the travails of subjectivity into the *Metamorphoses*, the fall of desire into knowledge: hence, its centrality in psychoanalysis as an explanatory model for the psychic constitution.

If pleasure in the first two and a half books of the *Metamorphoses* is the amorphous sensual life, encompassing pain and grief in the boundless libido, then in the story of Narcissus, as well as in the Bacchic rites, described in its aftermath, it turns back upon itself to expose the very negativity that drives it. Because the tale focuses on the love of self, it exemplifies what the other love stories merely suggest, that it is in the nature of pleasure to be transmuted into its own destruction, to go "beyond," as Freud says, its own principles into death.[4]

Besides the youth's lust for his own reflection, various other elements in the tale suggest this paradoxical quality of libido, this strange state of empty fullness. As the *Penguin Classics* edition indicates, the Narcissus legend is divided into three parts, the first one telling of Echo's love of the youth, the second one of Narcissus' seduction by his own reflection in a pool, the third one again of Echo's love and of her grief after Narcissus's death. Perhaps no other figure in the *Metamorphoses* captures the divisiveness of desire as powerfully as Echo, the epitome of the hollow cravings of the human voice. At the beginning of the tale, the nymph is already cursed with her handicap, the inability to speak, except in the ceaseless

4 Freud's major work on the collision of drives – Eros and Thanatos – is *Beyond the Pleasure Principle* (1923). *The Standard Edition*. Trans. James Strachey (New York: Norton, 1961). In the section on the Old English elegies below, I will examine the death drive from a Freudian perspective, especially its manifestatioon in *The Seafarer*.

repetition of others' words. It is noteworthy here, as indeed it is elsewhere in the *Metamorphoses*, that the emphasis is not so much on the mythological explanation of echo, but on the dilemma of individuals, caught in situations beyond their control: Echo's burning desire to confess her love to Narcissus is conveyed only in the mockery of meaningless words:

> [S] he wished to make flattering overtures to him, to approach him with tender pleas! But her handicap prevented this, and would not allow her to speak first; she was ready to do what it would allow, to wait for sounds which she might re-echo with her own voice. (84)

What is described here is a libidinal impasse on a par with Lacan's account of the vicissitudes of desire in language. In one of his virtuoso metaphors in "The agency of the letter in the unconscious," Lacan compares the scenario of libido to a railway system where the enunciating subject is "caught in the rails – eternally stretching forth towards the *desire for something else*" (1977: 167; Lacan's emphasis). Human desire is thus trapped in the perpetual motion of the signifying system like the wheel of a train in the ruthless technology that controls it. In linguistic terms, this is a *metonymic* process where the wish is hurled along in a series of displaced utterances. As Lacan emphasized again and again, this is not a scenario of physical appetite, of needs which are slaked as easily as hunger or thirst, but a landscape of *alienated* passions, divided from the human subject which initiated them. Only an intersubjective context – such as transference in psychoanalysis – rescues subjectivity from victimization because it submits the tyranny of the signifier to dialogue and empowers the participants to infuse the utterance with new meaning.[5]

There exists no such therapeutic situation for Echo in the *Metamorphoses*, and as a consequence, her dilemma can be understood as the pathological rock-bottom of the human voice, trapped in endless repetition of the alienated word. In fact, many of the preceeding stories of transformation foreground the tragedy of the living voice imprisoned in metaphor, desiring speech, but only able to howl like animals.[6] Echo stretches this tragedy to its limits as she withers away into a mere symbol of voice, resounding in nature as the insistent reminder of human loss:

5 See Malcolm Bowie's excellent account of the difference between need and desire in Lacanian analysis. *Lacan* (Cambridge: Harvard University Press, 1991), 131–141; see also Lacan's "The significance of the phallus" (1977: 281–291). In the section below, "The Mirror of Alienation," I will discuss Lacanian desire in greater detail.

6 See, for instance, the story of the transformation of Callisto: "a harsh growling issued from her throat, angry and quarrellsome, frightening to hear; she had become a bear, but even so her mind remained unchanged, and she declared her grief with continual lamentations" (63); the episode about Phaeton's sisters (59) and "The Prophecies of Ochyrhoe" (67–68) tell similar stories of the imprisoned human voice.

when Narcissus is dying and "sighed 'Alas,' she took up his sigh, and repeated 'Alas!'"; when he beats his breast in mourning, Echo gives back the same sounds; the youth's last words are repeated verbatim by the echoing surrounding: "'Woe is me for the boy I loved in vain!'"; his last farewell is Echo's "Farewell!" also (87). This last scene presents a fitting image of the interconnections between love and loss, of the empty fullness of human desire.

Clearly, the self-perpetuating drive this strange love story traces operates somewhat like a whirlwind on an isolated territory, destroying its own ground and rushing into death. As Juliet Mitchell notes in her discussion of narcissism in *Psychoanalysis and Feminism*, self-love is a vicious circle, leading only to its own disintegration, to madness or suicide (1974: 30–41). Both Echo's voice and Narcissus' gaze are caught in compulsive repetitions, paralyzing their will to move away from imaginary pleasures. Although the legend makes plain that the youth becomes aware of his dilemma, that the image he loves in a pool is but a shadow of himself, this knowledge does not amount to psychological insight. On the contrary, it is the occasion for mourning. Narcissus cannot bear the loss of the Golden Age of amorphous pleasure nor the self-division an awareness of such loss entails. Hence, the language of lamentation at the moment of self-discovery:

> Alas! I am myself the boy I see. I know it: my own reflection does not deceive me. I am on fire with love for my own self. It is I who kindle the flames which I must endure. What should I do? [...] My very plenty makes me poor. How I wish I could separate myself from my body! [...] Now grief is sapping my strength; [...] I have no quarrel with death, for in death I shall forget my pain. (86)

This passage illustrates particularly well the psychoanalytic concept of *lack* as constitutive of subjective being, of, what Lacan has called, *manque-à-être*, the peculiar gap at the core of plenitude.[7] Lacan's own apt English translation, the neologism "want-to-be," captures the contradiction of subjectivity and matches precisely Narcissus' mournful exclamation that "my very plenty makes me poor." *Being* is asserted and renounced in the same instance. It is a state of existential aporia, the superlative contradiction, perhaps most accurately imaged in the sixteenth-century sexual pun "to die," that is, to experience orgasm as if it were the moment of death.[8]

It is surely no coincidence in the *Metamorphoses* that the orgiastic rites of Bacchus follow in the aftermath of Narcissus' death. After this irruption of negative

7 See especially Lacan's seminar "Of the Subject of Certainty," in *Four Fundamental Concepts of Psycho-Analysis*. Trans. Alan Sheridan (Penguin Books: 1977), 29–41.

8 Lacan's *jouissance* is the psychoanalytic equivalent to this experience. In French, "jouir" is a slang expression for "to come."

desire into the Golden Age of innocent pleasures, it is only logical that worship of a different divinity should ensue. In fact, the birth of Bacchus is prompted by a kind of erotic death as Semele, his mother-to-be, is burnt to ashes by Jupiter's, her lover's, thunderbolt, which he had brought as a wedding-gift. The child, Bacchus, "not fully formed, was snatched from his mother's womb," and then "sewn into his father's thigh till the months for which his mother should have carried him were fulfilled" (82). The violence of the god's birth and his androgynous nurture characterize his cult and can be understood as a translation into cultural terms of the private aporia experienced by the love-sick Narcissus.

The best description of the Bacchic rites, which is at the same time a fierce critique, is provided by Pentheus, who is a representative of the vanishing Theban warrior culture, allied to Mars, masculinist and ascetic. In particular, Pentheus makes a distinction between kinds of violence, the purposeful, rational violence of the Theban warrior and the mad, gratuitous violence of the worshipper of Bacchus. In angry dismay, Pentheus tries to rally his companions, asking them how it is possible that men who were "undaunted by the ranks of war with weapons drawn, should quail before wailing women and tinkling tambourines, drunken madmen and disgusting fanatics?" (88). Also, the sexual ambiguity of the revellers is incomprehensible to a warrior, the fact, for instance, that the young men, his own age, wear garlands instead of helmets, and carry Bacchic wands instead of weapons (88). The whole hedonistic enterprise is offensive to Theban rationalism, and Pentheus wonders if

> Thebes will be taken by an unarmed boy, one who takes no pleasure in war, its weapons and its cavalry, but delights in tresses dripping with myrrh, in fresh garlands and garments embroidered with purple and gold. (89)

At the end of Book III, Pentheus suffers the cruel punishment for his criticism and his disbelief. In possibly the most horrid scene in the *Metamorphoses*, the doubting king confronts the mysteries on mount Cithaeron and is murdered by the mad revellers, his own mother and his relatives ripping his body to pieces.

The contrasts presented in these descriptions of the Bacchic rites between asceticism and hedonism have, of course, been elaborated upon variously by philosophers, scholars and artists, especially since Nietzsche's formulation of the principles of the Appolonian and the Dionysean.[9] It is not my intention here to elucidate further such dualities but rather to indicate the interesting connection

9 In *The Birth of Tragedy* (1872), Nietzsche considers ancient Greek culture and especially tragedy in terms of the tension between the Appolonian and Dionysean principles, between fundamentally two forms of aesthetic perception, intellectual versus sensuous. The dualistic tension must be maintained in genuine tragedy. Thus, Euripides and Socrates undermined the Dionysean aspect in their undue empahsis "on

between cultural and individual aporia in Ovid's fiction and how this connection can be profitably viewed as an intertext for Freud's discussion of narcissism. I will now turn to the psychoanalytic version of Narcissus.

As Judith Mitchell notes, relying to a large extent on Lacan's revisions, Freud's discovery of narcissism was a landmark event, moving the investigation of mind away from nineteenth-century biologism into the direction of modernity (1974: 30–32). Much of Freud's work between the *Interpretation of Dreams* (1900) and the essay on narcissism (1914) is concerned with mapping the human *drive* and with dividing sexual history into instinctual stages. The text most characteristic of this period is *Three Essays on the Theory of Sexuality* (1905) which, in spite of its revolutionary insights into the sexuality of children, is rooted in what can be termed a *physiology of the psyche*, the view that human psychology is only qualitatively, not quantitatively, different from the biological life of animals.[10] Within such a framework, a good example is Freud's discussion of the sexual instincts as a source for the neurotic symptom, where *instinct* functions as a kind of catch-all expression for repression, for emotional process, wishes and desires, not permitted to enter consciousness (1977: 77–78).[11] Even if Freud was to refine his conception of the instincts through two editions of *Three Essays* (1910; 1915), his basic definition emphasized their somatic source; it is the excitation occurring in a specific organ that mobilizes the instinct to seek discharge or gratification (83). The sexually stimulated organs Freud referred to as "erotogentic zones," and he explained the function of these in psychoneurosis, in hysteria, obsessional neurosis or paranoia, as substitute symptoms for some illegitimate erotic wish (83–84). Thus, generally in *Three Essays*, the physiological explanation tends to override the psychological one.

However, it would be a mistake to propose that in laying the foundations of psychoanalytic theory, Freud had a reductive view of human sexuality. As Jacques Lacan contends, in his revisionary critique of a "theory of instincts," Freud was uncomfortable with the biological tradition his work participated in, and in his case histories, in particular, disregarded it and even showed "disdain" for it (*Four Fundamental Concepts of Psycho-Analysis* 1977: 54–55). This scientific unease is quite obvious in the elaboration of the concept of human *drive* in the *Three Essays* as Freud attempts to make it work as a psychological force rather than as a mere somatic principle. Especially, in the discussion of what he calls "the sexual aber-

---

reason as a means to man's salvation" (262). D. W. Hamlyn. *The Penguin History of Western Philosophy* (Penguin Books, 1987).

10 Note that much of the material on the sexual theories of children was not added to the second essay until 1915.

11 Sigmund Freud. *On Sexuality: Three Essays on the Theory of Sexuality*. Trans. James Strachey (Penguin Books, 1977).

rations," Freud repeatedly notes that the instinct does not appear to be a simple source of sexual longing nor of the striving toward an object, but a psycho-somatic aggregate, complex, diffuse and only tenuously tied to the libidinal aim. For instance, the investigation of homosexuality, or of "inversion," as it was called at the time, convinces Freud that previous sexologists have had too narrow a view of the relation between sexual instinct and sexual object, that they have regarded it "as more intimate than it in fact is" (59).[12] The subject's drive toward an object is actually *deviant*, not straightforward: the confirmed homosexual man is usually not at all of the stereotypical feminine kind nor is he necessarily attracted to the masculinity of the other; homosexual object-choice is most often ambiguous, combining the characters of both sexes, "a compromise between an impulse that seeks for a man and one that seeks for a woman" (56); neither is heterosexual desire self-evident, but tends to follow devious paths, susceptible to fetishism and various types of "perverse" behaviour (e.g. 61–76). Generally, in the *Three Essays*, Freud vacillates between a biological and a psychological explanation, moving away from a purely naturalist explanation of the human libido toward a more modern conception of it as primarily a mental phenomenon.[13]

In the essay "On Narcissism" (1914), Freud, for the first time, as Juliet Mitchell observes, *irrevocably* submits the notion of drive to the structure of desire (1974: 31). The essay can be seen as a point of crisis in Freud's thinking as he confronts and subverts his previous dualistic scheme of the sexual instincts and the ego instincts, shifting the emphasis onto the sexualization of the whole human psyche (Richard Wollheim 1971: esp. 177–218; Mitchell 31).[14] Along with that shift, there is a collapse of the entire developmental theory of instincts, the supposition that sexuality matures chronologically from an "oral stage" through an "anal stage" to the pubertal "phallic stage" (*Three Essays,* especially Books 2 and 3). Observing the behavior of both children and of his neurotic patients, Freud concludes that love first emerges as *self-love*, as "an original libidinal cathexis of the ego" (33), and that this internal bond motivates all further permutations of the libido:

> Thus we form the idea of there being an original libidinal cathexis of the ego, from which some is later given off to objects, but which fundamentally persists and is related to the object-cathexes much as the body of an amoeba is related to the pseudopodia which it puts out. (33)

12 The nineteenth-century sexologists Freud refers to are among others Havelock Ellis, R. von Kraft-Ebing, I. Bloch and Magnus Hirschfield.

13 At one point, Freud states the instinct lies on "the frontier between the mental and the physical" (83).

14 Richard Wollheim. *Freud* (Fontana Press, 1971).

The implication here is that mature love, or intersubjective love, is for the self as well as for the other. Narcissism does not fade in a chronological sequence but persists in the structure of mind.

It was especially the megalomania of schizophrenic patients which convinced Freud of a *primary* state of narcissism which determines a *secondary* pathological expression. The social isolation of schizophrenics is characterized by a complete withdrawal of libido from objects and a reattachment to the ego itself. Subsequently, there occurs an illusory aggrandizement of the self, which Freud compares to the thoughts of children, to their "over-estimation of the power of wishes" and to their "belief in the magical virtue of words" (32). In his grandiose detachment, the megalomaniac is the psychoanalytic equivalent to Ovid's Narcissus: the knowlegde of self destroys them, one in madness, the other in death.

There are, however, in Freud's account, less extreme forms of pathological narcissism. For instance, neurotic patients, hysterics or obsessional neurotics, do not manifest their illness by an absolute substitution of ego for intersubjectivity, but acutally recreate the object through fantasy. In such a case, a broken erotic relation becomes internalized and is experienced just as intensely in the imagination as it was in actuality. A later study on melancholia reemphasizes this psychic capacity for narcissistic identification, how a lost object, for instance, is transferred onto the ego, causing a conflict between "the criticizing faculty of the ego," the agency that mourns, and "the ego as altered by the identification" ("Mourning and Melancholia" 1914; 1953: 157). Because he identifies with loss narcissistically, repeating it, instead of actively working through it, the melancholiac, even if it is to a lesser degree than the megalomaniac, is trapped within the vicious circle of *intra*subjective libido. In fact, the lamentations of melancholiacs resemble the hollow voice of Echo, compulsively resounding the drama of existential loss.

As I indicated above, literary character exists primarily as an effect of narcissistic identification, and its ontology can be profitably described analogous to Freud's model of imaginary reconstructions in the essays "On Narcissism" and "Mourning and Melancholia." Of course, it is possible to assert that *reading* as a mental activity is made possible by the structures of Narcissus, by primary narcissism as a persistent psychological phenomenon. Nevertheless, since character specifically binds readers to the *person* in the text, to the experience of confronting another, it functions most precisely as *the* site of the narcissistic experience. The question that arises is whether there is a substantial difference between this imaginary experience and the fantasies of neurotics and, if so, how should this difference be explained.

From a Freudian (and Ovidian/mythic) point of view there is no *fundamental* difference because the libidinal drive – desire itself – is born in the aporia of self-love and is therefore propelled by its own negative force. Just as Ovid's Narcissus was destroyed at the moment of self-discovery, the moment of glimpsing his "poor plenty," so Freud's patients evade the full force of recognition of loss, imagining instead an inner landscape of full presence. In the aesthetic experience, especially in the experience of facing the constructed *person*, the psychoanalytic process of recognition is ritualized or dramatized (depending on the form of art) so that the receiver is challenged to look, first within the context of primary narcissism, as a child desiring self-identity, secondly within an ethical texture, as a subject in a state of dissociation, seeing character in the space of its radical otherness. In the following chapters, I will coninue to show how character as a factor in cultural productions, in the aesthetic and the psychological dimensions, operates as a kind of consolatory device, a figural script which combines both Narcissus and the way to go beyond his aporia, to avoid the deadly link between personal *jouissance* and cultural terror depictied in Ovid's fiction. At this point, I want to examine how Freud described in psychoanalytic terms the healing process beyond Narcissus.

"On Narcissism" is first and foremost about love and its various manifestations as permutations of narcissistic desire. In the analytic situation, the patient's pathological self-love can be redirected outwards, toward the world of objects, the only path of the cure. It is important to reiterate that the healthy intersubjective love Freud discusses here is not to be equated with some "normal," prescriptive category, but is in all instances, no less than the megalomaniac's delusion, a structural component of narcissistic mental acitvity. Healthy erotic love co-exists with primary narcissism within the *space* of mind Freud is concerned with delineating in this essay and which is radically different from the chronological story of the instinctual phases outlined in the earlier *Three Essays on the Theory of Sexuality*.[15]

Freud's analogy, quoted above, between the libidinal ego and the body of an amoeba expresses well this spatial coexistence between primary narcissism and intersubjective love. As the libido turns outward to the world of objects, it can be differentiated into various kinds of love, grouped broadly by Freud into either "the anaclitic type" or "the narcissistic type" (47). The first kind is predominantly pre-oedipal, exemplified by the infant's attachment to the mother (or her substitute). The second type designates adult love: sexual attraction between men and women as well as homosexual attraction; the development of conjugal relations; parental love. Freud divides this second type into four categories, asserting that "a person may love [...] a) what he is himself; b) what he once was; c) what he would like to be; d) someone who was once part of himself" (47). It is important to realize, notes Freud, that these groupings are not pure, but combine in com-

15 Juliet Mitchell notes that Freud, in his later work, is concerned with a "complex 'time' of space, not a simple 'time' of place, an awareness verbally expressed, that every moment is a historical one – a summation of a person's life " (1974: 22).

plex ways to influence subjective choice. Male choice, for instance, often proceeds from the anaclitic relation to the mother as well as from on over-estimation of the ego (category a); as a consequence the loved woman tends to be idealized, a figure for mother-love and a confirmation of the man's imagined identity. On the other hand, women compensate themselves for this unsatifactory role as ideals by, in turn, idealizing their children. This kind of parent love would fall under category four above, an interesting formulation of the narcissistic dilemma (45–49). On the whole, Freud's observations on gendered object-choice are surprisingly nuanced and show how well aware he was of the role of the imaginary, of identity *construction*, in all facets of human culture.

The type of love most relevant to an investigation of literary character is described in group c: "a person may love [...] what he would like to be." The process of construction of characters in the aesthetic experience is analogous to the way in which *idealization* of self influences object choice. In his discussion of the *ego-ideal*, Freud notes how its formation is a substitute vestige from infant megalomania, a *displaced* narcissism, purified of libidinal tendencies that may be culturally offensive or unacceptable to the social environment (50–51). Essentially, the ego set up as an ideal standard is a product of *repression* alternating with narcissism; the standard is entangled with cultural demands which favor repression; in turn, internalization of strictures enhances the ideal (52). As is so often in psychoanalytic investigations, neurosis – in this case, paranoia – lays bare this normative process as idealization (or *conscience*, as Freud tentatively calls it at this time) is protested against for being like an authoritative, alien gaze, controlling from within, censoring and oppressive (52–3). Paranoiacs frequently suffer "delusions of observation," the sense of continuously "*being watched* "; they "complain that all their thoughts are known and their actions watched and overlooked" (52). In an experience of psychic regression, these patients revolt against their displaced narcissism, their enforced, alienated maturity.

Apparently, what Freud wants to re-emphasize here is the co-existence within the space of mind of narcissism in a primal state and its secondary form, the ego as ideal standard, as well as the fact that all object relations are permeated by this co-existence. Also, it is worth noting, that in this account, as always within psychoanalysis, from Freud's time, categories of normalcy are disrupted as it is questionable whether so-called "healthy" *conscience* is of a higher order of sanity than the paranoiac's protest which is truer to the divisiveness of human nature. In many respects, the ordinary sense of subjectiviy as self-identical is a pathological illusion since, as the whole essay "On Narcissism" shows, the psychic constitution is a fragmented construct, a series of displacements, of necessity deviating from the destructiveness of Narcissus' primal desire. The neurotic knows intuitively that he is being controlled from a position he has not chosen to be situated within.

It is certainly not this knowledge in itself that is pathological, or, as Lacan would say, a form of *méconnaisance*, of *misconstruction*; rather, it is its imprisonment in an imaginary register where no distinction is made between authentic knowledge and misdirected knowledge and where all articulation stagnates, cut off from intersubjective dynamic exchange.[16]

I have made these observations about the "normalcy" of knowledge here because they are pertinent to the experience of reading for literary character. If, in the first instance, the confrontation with person in text is influenced by a desire for self-identity, then, in a second, revised instance, the meeting is a complex mixture of paranoid rebellion and the emergence of a *new* knowledge of self. It is the peculiar property of character as an aesthetic object to enable the receiver to transform the restrictions of internalized idealizations, of conscience, into an *ethical* force, a property that is, in fact, lodged in the semantics of the term – character as *ethos*, character as a blueprint for how to be good.[17] At this juncture, it is important to trace the contours of an apparently paradoxical psychological condition, that of a Narcissus displaced, purified of destructive desire and exalted to a position of culturally acceptable self-love, who actually nurtures a radical agency of mind, a potential revisionary epistemology. Here, Freud's sustained exploration of the role of the "ego-ideal" in object-choice, identification and character formation offers valuable information.

In "On Narcissism," the rather condensed observations on idealization and on mental censorship are developed further in the postulation of a *super-ego* in *Group Psychology and the Analysis of the Ego* (1921), *The Ego and the Id* (1923) and in chapters seven and eight of *Civilization and its Discontents* (1930).[18] As Freud's preoccupation with paranoia suggests, the early writings on the ego-ideal propose that it is much more of a *libidinal* agency than the ego, which has a closer affiliation with consciousness and with selective repression.[19] Even if the ideal is set up

16 For an extensive commentary on "méconnaisance," see Lacan's *Le Seminaire II: Le Moi dans la théorie de Freud et dans la technique psychoanalytique* (Paris: Seuil, 1978); see also Shoshana Felman's illuminating discussion of this seminar in "Beyond Oedipus: The Specimen Story of Psychoanalysis," in *Psychoanalytic Criticism*, ed. Maud Ellman (London: Longman, 1994), 76–102.

17 In Greek, "ethics" means "matters concerned with character." See, for instance, Stephen Watts' introduction to the Wordsworth Classics edition of Aristotle's *Nicomachean Ethics* (1996), xii-xiv.

18 Sigmund Freud. *Group Psychology and the Analysis of the Ego*. Trans. James Strachey (New York: W. W. Norton, 1955); *The Ego and the Id*. Trans. Joan Riviere (New York: W. W. Norton, 1960); *Civilization and its Discontents*. Trans. James Strachey (W. W. Norton, 1961).

19 In *The Ego and the Id*, Freud uses ego-ideal and super-ego synonymously, and I will follow him in not making a distinction between the two.

as purged of sexual drives, especially as it is set up for inspection by consciousness and by others, it is grounded in primary narcissism and in an identification which is immediate and, as Freud remarks several times, directly *homosexual*.[20] For instance, in his study of Leonardo da Vinci (1910),[21] Freud maintains hat in one type of homosexual love, the young boy's narcissistic attachment to his mother – his identification with her, as a result of his love for her – is not abandoned in adult object choice, so that every partner reflects the mother, as imagined through love of self. Such relations do not at all suggest that the super-ego is weak, and, in fact, they are not qualitatively different from heterosexual love, which also emerges from a narcissistic ground, even if repression here has been under more social control. In whatever form, adult love highlights the co-existence within mind between primary narcissism and a revised narcissim; what makes this condition special and different from the blindly libidinal nature of primal choice, is the detachment – or, as Freud say, the *self-regard* – encouraged through the establishment of the super-ego (see especially 1914: 55–59). It is especially the experience of the Oedipal conflict which influences the role of the super-ego in mature love.

As he makes his suggestive remarks on love in the concluding pages of "On Narcissism," Freud characteristically reveals his sensitivity to language. A feature of idealization, *self-regard* ("Selbstachtung") refers to the mental agency that watches in a way that enhances respect for self. If internalization of another's gaze – of the parent or the lover, for instance – does not harmonize with the subject's well-being, in other words, if the libidinal object is not felicitously placed within the narcissistic reservoir, then the psychological outcome may become either the paranoiac's painful sense of being controlled from without or an almost masochistic lowering of self-esteem, common to the experience of Freud's hysterical women, who were often oppressed by idealized males.[22] Happiness, Freud indicates, is a state of balanced self-regard, where primary narcissism has been transformed through love of another into a satisfactory ego-ideal (1914: 57–58). On the other hand, the outcome of the Oedipal experience, the central event in subjective life, is usually a truncated gaze, a flawed view of self, modified by excessive repression and the building of a disciplinary, rigid, even prudish, super-ego.

---

20 See other comments on homosexual love in "On Narcissism" (53) and in *The Ego and the Id* (21).

21 Sigmund Freud. *Leonardo Da Vinci and a Memory of his Childhood*. *SE* Vol XI. Trans James Strachey (London: Hogarth, 1957).

22 The case history of *Dora* exemplifies a young female patient's strained idealization of an older man. Of course, women in general suffer from a discrepancy beteen a need for narcissistic harmony in love and the "patriarchal gaze," social demands they have internalized about the duty to serve a man rather than experience pleasure as his equal.

As presented in the later work, *Civilization and its Discontents* (1930), Freud's views of the super-ego as a moral product of Western culture are, despite the inherent ideological critique, pessimistic and almost dejectedly resigned. Because the super-ego originates within the dissolution of the Oedipus complex, as the prime agent of its repression, it is essentially a structure of identification with the *father* and with the father's prohibition against incestuous desire. Freud emphasizes that the processes of identification here are more complex than previous libidinal attachments since they are patterned as negative reactions: the ego identifies with the father as a repressive authority, turning against narcissistic choice in general as well as the specific rivalry of the Oedipal situation. As a consequence, the relation of the super-ego to the ego is first and foremost that of a moral censor; it does not merely demand obedience to the father, as might be formulated in the "precept: 'You *ought to be* like this (like your father)'"; rather, the super-ego "also comprises the prohibition: 'You *may not be* like this (like your father) – that is, you may not do all that he does; some things are his prerogative'" (1923: 24). Caught within the Oedipal triangle, the child perceives the threat of the powerful father and responds by incorporating this threat, not so much in the image of the father's person, but in its *position as obstacle* to desire. The super-ego thus exists both as moral burden and illicit desire. It is, Freud contends, the prime mover of psychic conflict (1923: 24–25).

As cultural demands take over the father's role, the ego-ideal is infiltrated by "the influence of authority, religious teaching, schooling and reading," and the more intense the repression was at the Oedipal stage, the more dominating is the ideal, now "in the form of conscience or perhaps of an unconscious sense of guilt" (1923: 24–5). In his ventures into broader anthropological views, Freud often reveals a pessimistic attitude to morality as an oppressive force, the instigator of psychological dilemmas, expressed in neurotic illness or alleviated in a discontented social conformism. Especially, during the elaborations of the role of the super-ego in individual and cultural life, in the last two chapters of *Civilization and its Discontents*, Freud's language, despite the scientific sheen, betrays his dislike of observations he seems compelled to make. In Western culture, the relations between individual and community appear to be trapped within a vicious circle of aggressive energies, where the ego, the most conscious, realistic factor in Freudian mental topography, is dominated by a vengeful super-ego, which ceaselessly crushes "dangerous desire," ruling the mind like a sadistic dictator. Civilization manages the wild narcissism of its subjects by obtaining "mastery over [...] aggression by weakening and disarming it and by setting up an agency within him to watch over it like a garrison in a conquered city" (79). It is as if ethical relations exist in a state of war; only through slavish subjection to a law of moral emergency do individuals build a successful community.

Nevertheless, as psychoanalytic expertise can testify, repressed desire does not vanish but persists in the structure of mind, often in unconscious form, the cause of psychic misery, which can range from neurotic illness to the general state of unhappiness, Freud so dejectedly describes in *Civilization and its Discontents*. Because of the stern supervision of the super-ego, the sense of a persistent, illicit wish produces *guilt*, the most powerful factor in determining moral relations. At the same time as the child identifies with the father's prohibitive function in the Oedipal situation, he becomes aware of himself as guilty, as a trespasser against an authority that loves him. As this realization deepens within the child, he becomes more and more fearful of, at first, losing the love of the father and, later, with the incorporation of the super-ego, of losing the love of his own self-regard (esp. 83). Thus, in Freud's account here, all subjective relations, the displaced narcissism of the individual subject as well as object-choices in the world, the life of Eros, are determined by fear, anxiety and a sense of guilt. Further, in this connection, *virtue* seems an arbitrary category, fabricated in fearful submission to a guilt-invoking super-ego. Clearly, in the view of *Civilization and its Discontents*, "something is rotten" in the economy of psychic life.

As I discuss above, the legend of Narcissus, as told by Ovid in the *Metamorphoses*, illustrates the link between individual destructive desire and cultural aporia, as expressed in the terror of the Bacchic rites. Freud's underlying worry in *Civilization and its Discontents* relates to the question of how to manage negativity, the constitutional lack of the psyche, within culture, or, in other words, how to *moralize* it, transform it into responsible displacement. Is it possible for Narcissus to depart from himself and to become sifted outward through the stern apparatus of the super-ego and still return to a balanced economy, to happiness?[23] Since Freud's text is conceived primarily as descriptive, as a reflection of the state of contemporary culture, his answers to this central question are only implied in a subdued ideological critique and a skeptical view of dominant moral categories. On the other hand, the whole psychoanalytic ouevre, Freud's investigations as well as post-Freudian re-readings, suggest revised ethical models for Narcissus, new

23 Freud's final paragraph is ambivalently hopeful, the note of doubt perhaps due to the last sentence, which was added in 1931, when the threat of Hitler was emerging. I quote the last half of the parapraph, an expression of Freud's belief in Eros as a constitutive cultural force:

Men have gained control over the forces of nature to such an extent that with their help they would have no difficulty in exterminating one another to the last man. They know this, and hence comes a large part of their current unrest, their unhappiness and their mode of anxiety. And now it is to be expected that the other of two 'Heavenly Powers,' eternal Eros, will make an effort to assert himself in the struggle with this equally immortal adversary. But who can foresee with what success and with what result? (104)

cultural spaces, within which he will know his own difference without sorrow. In my opinion, the role of fictional models in such new constructions has not been considered in full detail and the following analyses of literary texts, medieval as well as modern, will hopefully illuminate the dialogue between the narcissistic subject, cultural community and cultural production. In order to highlight the transvaluative potential in Freud's writing, it will, to begin with, be necessary to examine major Lacanian concepts and post-Freudian psychoanalytic developments; the focus will be on the relation between the Lacanian subject and the questions I have raised about displaced Narcissus and the role of desire in culture.

Chapter 3: The Mirror of Alienation: Jacques Lacan's Theory of the Subject

"Man speaks ... but it is because the symbol has made him man" (1953: 65)

Jacques Lacan has remarked that Narcissus is Freud's greatest discovery, and his own investigations into subjectivity are to a large extent devoted to mapping the faces of differentiation, etched in psychic experience upon the narcissistic constitution.[1] Where Lacan goes beyond Freud's conceptions in "On Narcissism" is primarily in the theorization of the *moment* of the birth of negativity, that is, of that psychic event depicted as a tragic paradox in Ovid's fiction – Narcissus' gaze upon his *poor plenty.* In his essay, Freud concentrates upon some internalizing strategies the ego has at its disposal to replace the loss of the primary self, especially idealization and how love of self may be transformed into care for the objective world; on the other hand, Lacan focues on the situation of the *lack* itself and postulates it as the constitution of human being. If Freud's momentous insight is Narcissus as a libidinal agency of mind, then Lacan's is Narcissus' as a specular reflection, an image cast off the surface of a mirror.

Both Freud and Lacan consider the function of the ego as an envelope of the narcissistic constitution; even if their emphasis differs somewhat – Freud underlining the active powers of ego, Lacan its entrapment – both thinkers pose the "I" as a container of identifications, a patched mask, a guise, a *construct.* Contrary to classical psychology, based on the philosophical premise of the Cartesian ego, the *Cogito*, being as fully conscious in thought, Lacan, in his early and path-breaking essay on the "mirror stage," shows how the first intimations of a sense of self in a child occur in a state of *division* and how the ego is fabricated as a cloak to hide an existential gap.[2] Basically, what happens within the psychological context of this

1 See, for instance, Lacan's promotion of Freud's "truly Promethean discovery" in the introduction to "The function and field of speech and language in psychoanalysis," 32–39.

2 "The mirror stage as formative of the function of the I as revealed in psychoanalytic experience" (1949). In *Écrits*, 1–7.
Note misunderstandings regarding Freud's view of the ego as fully conscious in *The Ego and the Id.* To some extent, Freud was constrained by biologism in his postulation of the ego as a system of perceptions and therefore conscious. On the other hand, he states in no uncertain terms that a large part of the ego is hidden; despite the importance of the ego-id antithesis in this work, Freud states: "the ego is not sharply separated from the id; its lower portion merges into it" (24).

event of the mirror is that the infant (between the ages of six to eighteen months), physically and mentally weaker than a chimpanzee, suddenly encounters an image of itself, a coherent representation, and is, as a result, seduced into an almost megalomaniac sense of its own vital centrality and centredness. The "trotte-bébé [...] sunk in his motor incapacity and nursling dependence" gazes in startled glee at a harmonic body in apparent control of itself and of its relation to things and persons around it (1–2). At first, Lacan seems to describe this event as a moment of recognition, the first insight into self-identity; it is, however, in his further elaborations, like Narcissus' mistaken gaze, an epistemological mirage, a fatal moment of a constitutional *méconnaissance* (the failure to recognize; misconstruction).[3]

It is thus in a sense of the mirror-image as a kind of seductive trap or *lure* that the ego emerges in a primary identification.[4] In narcissistic blindness, the child assumes his reflected body as if it were an *imago*, a primordial form that can be assimilated directly, in an ideal collocation. Lacan refers to this form of identification as "Ideal-I" and contends that it determines all the subject's secondary identifications, all later permutations in the symbolic order of culture (2).[5] The ego as an imaginary unit, a *fictional* whole, directs the emergence of subjectivity, and will, to a large extent, construe the position the subject takes in relation to himself and to others. As prepared by primary identification, the very ground of self-knowledge is misconceived, promising nurture to an autonomous subject, when, in fact, human origin is self-divided, a contradiction, a split.

Lacan's commentary on the spectacle of the child and the mirror bears an uncanny resemblance to Tireisias' observations on Narcissus, in Ovid's account. Both utterances, one psychologically prophetic, the other cosmically so, are preoccupied with the tragedy of origins, with *alienation*, not self-identity, as the ground of human subjectivity. Tireisias predicts Narcissus' fate – the boy will "live to a ripe old age [...] *if he does not come to know himself*" (83) – and thus articulates the paradox of identity, that it is lack itself which constitutes being. Unlike Ovid's frivolous gods, who pursue pleasure without pain, Narcissus faces the knowledge of his own lack – his *poor plenty* – and perishes in its melancholy avowal. Similarly, in the mirror-stage essay, the Lacanian child's initial "flutter of jubliant activity"

3 It is somewhat ironic that within popularized psychology, in particular, the theory of the mirror has itself been misconstrued as a drama of the discovery of self-identity. With Malcolm Bowie, one wonders at the thrirteen year delay between the introduction of the concept of the mirror at the Marenbad Congress in 1936 and the publication of the essay in 1949. Was it deliberate on Lacan's part to let error circulate? (Bowie 1991: 22–23).

4 In French, *leurre* refers to both illusion and decoy.

5 The "Ideal-I" is from Freud's *Ideal-Ich*, not too be confused with the *ego-ideal*, the later construction of the super-ego.

(1) is soon combined with surges of anxiety arising from a deepened awareness of the gap between subjective discord and the symmetrical *imago*. This anxiety often surfaces in the aggressive play of children but registers most intensely in dreams, in what Lacan calls "imagos of the fragmented body" (11).[6] Like the precocious surrealism of Hieronymus Bosch's paintings, "aggressive dreams" portray a demonic phantasmagoria: "images of castration, mutilation, dismemberment, dislocation, evisceration, devouring, bursting open of the body" (1948: 11). The ego as envelope around these contradictory *imagos*, the wholeness of Narcissus contending with his disintegration, is first and foremost a defense mechanism, a mask hiding the very conflict from which it emerges. Lacan emphasizes that ego-structure enables the human subject to "[symbolize] the mental permanence of the *I* "; it is, however, powerless to erase its own divided ground, at the same time, figuring loss, the subject's "alienating destination" (1949: 2).

It is important to note that in the early writings, Lacan begins to elaborate a difference between the "I" at the site of the ego, within the *imaginary* context of the mirror, and the "I" at the site of subject, within culture, within *symbolic* space. The mapping of the emergence of symbolic being can be seen as roughly parallel to Freud's investigation into secondary identifications, especially into the construction of the ego-ideal after the Oedipal phase, which I surveyed in the preceding pages. However, early in his career, Lacan returned to Freud with a structuralist hindsight, highlighting his linguistic interests and revising the major psychoanalytic concepts of the unconscious, repression, Oedipal complex and super-ego. At the risk of simplifying, it can be claimed, at this point, that Freud's concern with secondary agencies of mind, with displacement and substitution, both in the work of the unconscious and within object relations (as in, for instance, the structure of super-ego) was worked over again and again by Lacan to produce a systematic theory of the subject ("systematic" here not be taken to mean "schematic"). Structuralist linguistics and structuralist anthropology provided him with the methods by which to trace the processes of the subject on his or her way to an "alienating destination" in culture. The role of language in that process is of paramount significance, not least in revealing the dynamics of *aesthetic identification*, the impact of fictional models upon subjective knowledge.

As I protested above, John Frow, in his essay on psychoanalysis and literary character, gives a reductive account of Lacan's Symbolic Order, viewing the subject's place in that order merely at the level of the sentence, as if Lacanian categories do not manage larger discursive units. Lacan does indeed show a great deal of interest in the structure of the sentence, and in his first major piece on

6 "Agressivity in psychoanalysis" (1948), in *Écrits*, 8–29; see also "The mirror stage," 4–5.

linguistics and psychoanalysis – "The function and field of speech and language in psychoanalysis"[7] – as well as in general in his papers during the 1950s and 1960s reveal his indebtedness to structural linguistics, especially to the work of Ferdinand de Saussure, Roman Jakobson and Otto Jespersen. For instance, in the "Rome Discourse," the outlining of interactions between the imaginary and the symbolic registers and of the different sites of the ego and the symbolic "I" is, to a large extent, informed by Jakobson's definition of *code*, *message* and *shifter* (in "Shifters, Verbal Categories and the Russian Verb" (1957)). The structuralist concept of code corresponds roughly to Lacan's realm of signifiers, the realm of the *Symbolic*, as an impersonal, formal system of rules; the *message* links up to code in a way similar to the relations of individual speech (*parole*) to language, to the rule of signifiers (*langue*): in order to mean, speech must plug into the formally logical operations of discourse. According to Jakobson, as a grammatical category, *shifter* always refers to an element of code that binds in specific ways to the *sender* of the message such as, most obviously, the personal pronouns, as well as adverbs that localize the person (e.g. "here," "there," and "yonder"), and any word that indicates mood or subjective orientation. In fact, Jakobson departed from other linguistic definitions of shifters, such as C. S. Peirce's and Jespersen's, by emphasizing the subjective elements. Thus, he provides Lacan with a minimal signifying structure from which to oversee the appearance of the psychoanalytic subject in language.[8]

However, Lacan's often miniscule attention to the subject of the sentence, to the appearance and disappearance of the signifying subject, is only a necessary moment of investigation in a much larger and more intricate theoretical project. Even if the Symbolic Order is in most respects a structuralist conception, a linguistic universe existing prior to, and independent of, subjectivity, Lacan is not primarily concerned with marking the formal relationships between speaker and utterance; rather his aim is to account for, in as precise terms as possible, the psychological *effects* of structure on the human constitution. As the crucial texts on language and psychoanalysis show, this investigation encompasses in complex ways all levels of human communication, from the minimal level of the *letter* itself, the very materiality of utterance, through the units of a sentence, to the sub-

7 "The function and field of speech and language in psychoanalysis" (1953), in *Écrits*, 30–113. This essay is often referred to as the "Rome Discourse." It was originally a report too the Rome Congress held at the Istituto di Psicologia della Università di Roma, 26 and 27 Spetember, 1953; first published in *La Psychanalyse*, vol. I, 1956: 81–166.

8 See Anthony Wilden's section on *shifters* in his commentary on the "Rome Discourse," in *Speech and Language in Psychoanalysis* (Baltimore: The Johns Hopkins University Press, 1968), 183–5.

ject's position in the discourses of ideology and of culture. An essay from 1957, "The agency of the letter in the unconscious or reason since Freud," originally delivered as a lecture to the Philosophy Group at the Sorbonne, illustrates particularly well Lacan's synthetic powers as he harmonizes within a uniquely radical vision the insights of Freud into language and the psyche, Saussure's discovery of the arbitrary sign, a philosophical critique of the Cartesian ego as well as a venture, often from a Heideggarian perspective, into a new epistemology, into the terrain of the Other. The following discussion will rely on this essay since it introduces the major premises of the Lacanian subject, all of which have a bearing on my consideration of character as both a structure in language and a complex epistemological node in the discourses of culture.[9]

If the essay on the "mirror stage" focused on the ego as a structure of imaginary unity and permanence, then "The agency of the letter ..." follows the path from fantasy to the "alienating destination" in the symbolic order. What enables Lacan to ground his concept of alienation in a concrete context, and thereby, of course, distinguish it from more elusive existential notions, is Ferdinand de Saussure's formulation of the linguistic sign as a *divided* structure. Contrary to the ruling positivist opinion of his day, which tended to view the sign as an unproblematic word, with natural ties to the objective world, Saussure, in *Cours de linguistique générale* (1915), proposed it as a dual entity, with, on one hand, a *signifier*, the mark of an articulation, and, on the other, a *signified*, the concept, with reference to real objects and ideas.[10] The relationship between signifier and signified is *arbitrary*, Saussure claimed, fixed in history by convention alone. Diagrams from the *Cours* show how reality is conceived in signification as continuous flux, a constant movement of waves, whereas below this depiction, separated by a barrier, are orderly rows of signs or marks, which appear momentarily to arrest the flow, to capture a slice of it, like a snapshot, the camera snatching a static image from the rush of everyday life.

As he appropriates the Saussurean sign, Lacan makes some important adjustments to emphasize its impact upon the advent of the subject in language. In the first place, he turns the structuralist algorithm around so that signified/signifier becomes S/*s*, with the reminder that it should be "read as: the signifier over the signified, 'over' corresponding to the bar separating the two stages" (149). As Malcolm Bowie so succinctly remarks, the disproportionate connection here, the "capital letter and the Roman type" in the upper position, "[suggest] that a moral rather than a simple topographical inferiority is at issue: the signified retreats to

9 This essay was originally delivered as a speech to the Philosophy Group of the Fédération de étudiants ès lettres, at the Sorbonnes, 9 May, 1957; first published in *La Psychanalyse*, vol. 3 (1957: 47–81); in *Écrits*, 146–178.

10 Ferdinand de Saussure. *Cours de linguistique générale* (1915; Paris: Payot, 1965).

the lower position, shrinks into the lower case and withers into italic type" (1991: 64). Within psychoanalysis, Lacan indicates, throughout "The agency of the letter ...," there will be a new science of the signifier, with a reshuffled emphasis on the *effects* of symbolic articulation on the signifed as well as on the *relationships* between signifiers, on the vicissitudes of subjectivity as it slides within the horizontal flow of the utterance. Because the signifed is *barred* from the symbol, it can never bloom into full meaning, into the presence of a self-identical moment, but remains in constant motion, anticipating fulfillment, but fatally "caught in the rails – eternally stretching forth towards the *desire for something else*" (167).

Thus, Lacan stresses these two major properties of the signifier: first, that it operates like language itself, "that it should be articulated," that it is, in fact, like a *letter*, localizable in the symbolic order, a specific place the subject must contend with; secondly, signifiers relate to one another within the syntactic logic of language like links in a *chain*: the most vivid image of such a structure is that of interlocked rings in a necklace, which in turn is linked to another necklace made of locked rings (152). Within the signifying chain, meaning skips along, carrying along with it a seemingly powerless subject. This linearity, contends Lacan, is artificial, rigorous and restrictive; "all our experience runs counter to [it]," but, all the same, in order to become a subject, a speaker within culture, it is impossible not to submit to its law (154). The other side of language, Lacanian psychoanalysis emphasizes again and again, is madness, the hallucinatory world of psychosis.[11]

What kind of subject is it then that is stitched into the interlace of signifiers, moving along in series of appearances and gaps, finding itself a provisional place in shifting pronouns and transient adverbs? In his lucid expositions, in *The Lacanian Subject* (1995), Bruce Fink notes how Lacan, during his "structuralist phase" in the late 50s and early 60s, was preoccupied with demarcating signifiers that would articulate the negativity of desire, *split being* as authentic experience.[12] As a matter of fact, the French language contains a word that approximates such a strange articulation, the word *ne* (usually a part of the negation *ne pas*), which grammarians call an expletive, but, when linked to subjective utterance, has a more complex semantic function. Most often, *ne*, when cropping up without *pas*, is an element in standard expressions such as *avant qui'il n'arrive, pourvu qui'l ne soit arrivé* or *craindre qu'il ne vienne*, and in this capacitiy "seems to introduce a certain hesitation, ambiguity, or uncertainty into the utterance in which it appears, as if to suggest that the speaker is denying the very thing he is asserting" (1995: 39). In a passage from "The subversion of the subject and dialectic of desire in

11 See, for instance, comments in "The agency of the letter ...," 154; also, see "On a question prliminary to any possible treatment of psychosis, " in *Écrits*, 179–225.

12 Bruce Fink. *The Lacanian Subject: Between Language and Jouissance* (Princeton: Princeton University Press, 1995).

the Freudian unconscious," critical of grammarians' narrow definitions of this "expletive," Lacan himself makes a point about the strangeness of *ne* by using it in a sentence: "... *avant qu'il ne soit avéré qu'ils n'y comprennent rien*" (298).[13] Here, he derides the same grammarians for being obtuse about the significance of this word; Alan Sheridan translates the whole sentence thus: "May the weight that I give it persuade them to think again, *before it becomes obvious that they have missed the point*." Although the English does not quite capture the ambiguous force of the statement, it is clear that, as Lacan contends, an omission of *ne* would diminish that force, turning the attack into petty personal resentment (298). *Ne* is not a harmless filler in a sentence nor is it negation; rather it indicates a moment of *irruption* into orderly discourse, a reminder of ambivalent desire, the speaker's way to say that he "*both wants and does not want*." It is best defined, as Lacan does, as "no-saying" (*dit-que-non*), a particle of negativity.[14]

Such ambiguous flickers within the rigour of the signifying chain indicate the work of subjectivity, which struggles to express its own sense of alienated being. Still, it is not only the signifier *ne* that registers the otherness of desire; as Lacan shows in "The agency of the letter ...," the larger operations of discourse – what Roman Jakobson referred to as the metonymic and the metaphoric processes – prepare crooked paths and narrow byways for desire, within which it insistently moves, often in an ambiguous or a contrary relation to statements themselves.[15] Even if the linearity of the statement, of the *enoncé*, seems, in Lacan's writings, to overtake all articulation, it is only one dimension in discourse, a "necessary" one, but, at the same time, "not sufficient" (154). Beneath the articulated statement (linguists call it "the enunciated"), infiltrating it, is *speaking* itself, proceeding from a second vertical dimension of language, from the polyphony of words and from the their dialectical rhythm. Because language exists in culture, as an intersubjective medium, a texture of others and of others' desire, it enables speakers to use words creatively, to make them "signify *something quite other* than what [they say]"

13 "The subversion of the subject and dialectic of desire in the Freudian unconscious" was originally delivered as a lecture at a conference entitled "La Dialectique," held at Royaumont, in September 1960; in *Écrits*, 292–324.

14 The standard examples of *ne* are taken from Fink (1995: 39). See also Fink's discussion of "but" as the English equivalent to *ne*, for instance, in the expressions "I will not deny but that it is a difficult thing" or "I do fear but that my grandfather will recover" (39). Lacan's explanations of this signifier, as, in general, his discussions of the unconscious dimension within words, bears a great resemblance to Mikhail Bakhtin's "dialogic word." I will have occasion to elaborate on ambiguity in my examination of elegiac discourse below.

15 For Jakobson's discussion of metaphor and metonymy, see "Two Aspects of Language and Two Types of Aphasic Disturbances, " in *Fundamentals of Language* (The Hague: Mouton, 1956), 55–82.

(155; Lacan's emphasis). Poetic discourse, in particular, illustrates these complex interactions between statement and speaking, because it highlights the creative potential of figurative expression.

With references to poetry, it can be shown, that if language, the domain of signifiers, is an impersonal social law, then its displaced status, its figurative nature, also suggests its profundity, its richness and fecundity, that can be manipulated, not only by the artist, but by any subject in culture. Metonymy and metaphor are the largest functional categories which epitomize the two faces of language, the former as a line of association between elements, the second as a pure substitution of one element for another. In order to show the preponderance of these figures in all types of discourse, poetic speech, the language of analysis, the most sophisticated writing as well as the most humdrum conversation, Lacan's definitions are clear and concise: metonymy is based on a "*word-to-word*" connection whereas the formula for metaphor is "*one word for another*;" in the grammar from childhood, "thirty sails" stood for the imposing fleet of ships, without referring directly to this signified, managing to both suggest it and obscure it; the line from Victor Hugo, "*His sheaf was neither miserly nor spiteful*," establishes a similar ambiguous relation between signifer and meaning as the figure – "his sheaf" – replaces the owner, in fact "usurp[ing] his place," through its superiour munificence (157–158). Both examples crystallize a rhetoric of difference: speaking subjects always articulate a foreign language, divorced from the fullness of meaning. Neverthelss, the relational matrix within which speaking occurs, the connection between signifiers and the fleeting presence of the signified, is also a space of subjective *invention* or, at least, it suggests the possibiltiy of such as space. As Lacan observes about Hugo's line: "So, it is between the signifier in the form of the proper name of a man and the signifier that metaphorically abolishes him that the poetic spark is produced" (158).

Throughout Lacan's writings metaphor occupies a privileged position as an indicator of both the complex ambivalences of language and of the travails of subjectivity in signification. Because it is so purely a *substitution*, re-*placing* one element with another, metaphor is superior to metonymy in figuring the divisiveness that lies at the heart of all human articulation. The very structure of metaphor offers a glimpse of the subject's relation to meaning, how s/he is either barred from it or in an imaginary relation to it and then sometimes surprisingly in strange control of it. In chapter five on "Transference," I will examine the role of metaphor in the analytic situation and how this role is performed in similar ways in art, and very specifically so in figures of character. Here, since the focus is upon the construction of the subject in language, I will try to demonstrate how metaphor participates in that construction.

In Lacan's delineations of the Symbolic Order, it is always implied that the entrance into it, if difficult, even traumatic, is *necessary* (e.g. *Écrits*: 154). If the individual is not literally carried away by the movement toward alienation, in other words, if there is not a passage from fantasy to a position in culture, then there will be no subjectivity, only a hallucinatory existence in psychosis. Already in "The function and field of speech and language in psychoanalysis" (1953), there are demonstrations of the power of metaphor to figure loss as the subject is separated from his imaginary fulfillments and inducted into the universe of split symbols. The example Lacan uses is drawn from an episode in Freud's *Beyond the Pleasure Principle* (1920) which depicts a child's reaction to his mother's abrupt disappearances. Freud notes that his one and a half year old grandson, normally well behaved and obedient, is in the habit of angrily tossing away toys, especially when his mother suddenly vanishes. These small temper tantrums are subsequently refined in a game the boy invents to coincide with the mother's comings and goings: he plays with a wooden reel, casting it away with the syllable "fort" ("there") and pulling it back with the sound "da" ("here"). Both psychoanalysts link this game to a child's entry into culture, Freud describing it as a moment of "instinctual renunciation," Lacan as "the moment in which desire becomes human [...] [and] the child is born into language" (SE: 1961: 14; *Écrits*: 103). In its simple compactness, "*fort-da*" exemplifies succinctly the properties of metaphor as formative in subjectivity: it is a three-dimensional figure of alienation, pleasure and mastery. Primarily, it empowers the child to negotiate his desire within discourse, to both submit it to a law and to infuse it into the processes of this law. As Lacan observes, "fort" and "da" are "vocables [...] in the system of the concrete discourse of the environment," signifiers that inevitably affect the subjective constitution; at the same time, through these sounds, the little boy manages to "[raise] his desire to a second power," to transform his fantasy of a narcissistic unity with the mother into a kind of aesthetic pleasure, detached and in control of the object (103).

Lacan's own metaphor – *desire raised to the second power* – captures beautifully the dynamic of linguistic deplacement. Desire is neither totally repressed nor resolved, but *raised* from an inferior level to a great height where it persists, not in subjugation, but in power. As a consequence of the entry into the Symbolic Order, the subject is barred from the signified, from meaning; this does not mean, however, that s/he cannot participate in the production of meaning, even in the construction of him/herself as a significant agent. Indeed, the way in which Lacan's expression merges a mathematical idiom with the language of the passions exemplifies the creative control metaphor delegates to speakers. As is stated in "The agency of the letter ... ," even if metaphor "abolishes [...] the proper name of man," setting up the bar, the divisveness within his identity, it also, in the process, produces "the poetic spark," the startling beauty of subjective intervention (158).

The role of metaphor in the construction of subjectivity becomes more fully realized during the Oedipal phase, with the full assumption of what Lacan refers to as the "paternal metaphor" or the "Name-of-the-Father."[16] Both the "fort/da" game of Freud's grandson and the Oedipal drama constitute facets of – what psychoanalysis calls – *primal repression*: in the first instance, narcissistic loss is overcome in its own metaphor, which strangely retains desire through the act of repressing it; to an even greater extent, the second instance of Oedipus facilitates repression as the father intervenes in the child-mother scenario, enforcing libidinal substitution against the threat of castration. Overwhelmed by awe for paternal authority, the child opts for a kind of symbolic castration, where the imaginary relation to the mother, and to exteriority in general, is subjected to the realm of socialized signifiers. As with "fort/da," the Symbolic register the father legislates does not abolish desire, but paradoxically inscribes it at the moment of superceding it.

In his reading of Freud's account of the Oedipus phase, Lacan notes that, despite the primarily localized emphasis on it as a family dilemma, the older psychoanalyst frequently underlines the father's *symbolic* function, the *structural* role he fills, rather than exclusively his biological impact. For instance, Freud's fable of the inaugural primal murder of the father suggests the symbolic acquisition of the child as he simultaneously overtakes castration and an authoritative position in culture.[17] Also, as my overview of the Freudian super-ego indicated, the child's incorporation of the paternal threat does not involve the father's person as much as it does his structural function as obstacle to desire. In general, Lacan gathers Freud's structuralist hints to propose a revised theory of Oedipus as primarily a conflict between the semiotic registers of the imaginary and the symbolic. It is within such a context that the identification with the father's demand can be understood as an accession to *metaphor*, to the *Name*-of-the-Father.

A closer look at the processes of *castration* as the symbolic motor within the Oedipal conflict will clarify the dynamics of subjective construction here. In her lucid exposition of Lacan's seminars on *The Formations of the Unconscious* (*Les formations de l'inconscient*, 1957–8), Anika Lemaire observes that the dissolution of the Oedipus complex coincides with the child's identification with the father "as he who *has* the phallus" and that, in essence, the scene of this complex can be viewed as a transition from *being* to *having* (1977: 82–83).[18] In the early stage of

16 See especially "Function and field of speech and language in psychoanalysis" and "On a question preliminary to any possible treatment of psychosis."

17 See *Totem and Taboo* (1913). *SE* Vol XIII (London: Hogarth Press) (143), and *Civilization and its Disconents* (87–90). Note Lacan's comment in "On a possible treatment of psychosis …": through killing the Father, "the subject binds himself for life to the Law" (199).

18 Anika Lemaire. *Jacques Lacan*. Trans. David Macey (London: Routledge, 1977). The seminar *Le formations de l'inconscient* is unpublished. Besides Lemaire's explication, a partial summary is provided by Jean-Bertrand Pontalis in *Bulletin de Pscyhologe*, XII 2–3, November 1958, 182–92, and XII 4, December 1958, 250–6.

primary narcissism, the maternal relation is that of undifferentiated desire, within which the infant, male or female, strives to *be* the object of the mother's want, the phallus itself. Because of this imaginary fusion with the mother, the young child appears as if without subjective contours, a mere appendix to the mother's body, with no existentially concrete position marked for him. During the second phase of Oedipus, the father's intervention occurs as a ban on narcissistic intimacy, an autonomous *injunction* against incestuous desire: "[the father] deprives the child of the object of its desire and he deprives the mother of the phallic object" (82). Thus, through paternal authority, the threat of castration works across the mother-child couple, compelling them to submit an imaginary unity to the detached rule of the Symbolic. Lemaire notes that this second Oedipal phase is of paramount importance as a transition to the final identification with the father as castrating authority and possessor of the phallus. As Freud also intimated, the conflict of Oedipus is resolved when the child internalizes the paternal position as a *Law*, as metaphoric control in a detached discourse. The drama, then, culminates in a place of *having* the phallus.

The child's arrival in the Symbolic order, however, is a tormented victory, an assumption of an identity, which is conditioned by absence or loss. Just as Freud's grandson's figurative mastery worked through loss, but did not abandon it, so the *naming* of desire at the Oedipal stage retains its lack in every act of speaking it. The establishment of the *phallus* as the central symbolic site must be viewed in this light as the paradox of being in language: the subject *becomes* as substitue of itself; it *has* only at the price of loss and it *is* only at the price of division. Thus, the prevalent critiques of this symbolism as only phallocentric are misdirected, since, as Jacqueline Rose points out, Lacan does not posit the phallus as the source of alienated identity but rather as its "ghost," the absent presence that haunts it in discourse as a cultural fact (1982: 40).[19]

The Phallus as emblem of paradoxical mastery within discourse has inscribed within it the effects of primal repression. In his ground-breaking article on psychosis – "On a question preliminary to any possible treatment of psychosis" (1959) – Lacan shows how the emergence of the phallic signfier in the imaginary coincides with the subject's accession to symbolic orders and how the process can, in fact, be mapped in a formula analogous to the formal operation of metaphor (200–201). In its substitutive function, metaphor replaces one signifier with another, thereby crossing the bar of signification to alter the substance of the signified. This is Lacan's formula:

19 Jacqueline Rose. "Introduction – II," in *Feminine Sexuality: Jacques Lacan and the école freudienne*, eds. Juliet Mitchell and Jacqueline Rose (New York: W. W. Norton, 1982).

$$\frac{S}{\$} \cdot \frac{\$'}{x} \rightarrow S\left(\frac{I}{s}\right)$$

The elision of the first signifier ($\$'$), represented by the line across it, is necessary for a successful outcome of metaphor. Similarly, in the paternal metaphor, *the Name-of-the-Father*, as master signfier, replaces the desire for the mother so that the process can be formalized as:

$$\frac{\text{Name-of-the-Father}}{\text{Desire of the Mother}} \cdot \frac{\text{Desire of the Mother}}{\text{Signified to the subject}} \rightarrow \text{Name-of-the-Father}\left(\frac{\text{O}}{\text{Phallus}}\right)$$

Here, the subject's transition from *being* to *having* is mapped as successful metaphor: the narcissistic desire to be a phallic extension of the mother is repressed and transformed into a differently situated symbol, a name in socialized discourse. Of course, the fact that this name is forged in a state of repression makes it an ambiguous representation of subjectivity, retaining within itself residues of traumatic losses, an otherness to itself, full and empty at the same time. In the next section, I will consider further the status of the split subject, with particular reference to its appearance in aesthetic discourse as *character*.

Chapter 4: The Other's Desire

The paternal metaphor illustrates particularly well the outlines of the divided subject within the Symbolic order: the assimilation of the primal signifier – the phallus – serves as a blueprint of signification in general, the logic of substitution, where the name both cancels out and retains subjectivity. Above, I concentrated on the processes of alienation at the level of the speaking, or enunciating, subject, as these could be marked in particular words and figures. In this section, I will, for the most part, stay within the Oedipal resolution, but focus more exclusively on the *libidinal* dynamic, on the subject's emergence as a *desiring* being. It will then become clearer how fictional models participate in the formation of self-knowledge.

In the seminars from 1964 – published in English as *The Four Fundamental Concepts of Psycho-Analysis* (1977) – Lacan frequently makes a useful distinction between alienation and separation, where the former process refers to the confrontation with the otherness of language and the latter with the Other's desire, designated sometimes as mOther's desire, the fundamental libidinal experience. Arriving at his *alienating destination* in language, the subject plugs into a place already prepared for him, for instance, a shifter, a personal pronoun or a deictic, which humanizes him, but provides him with little more than a fleeting foothold. Making use of J.-A. Miller's formulation, Bruce Fink notes that alienation resembles an occupation within the empty set – {0} – of set theory, "a symbol which transforms nothingness into something by *marking* or *representing* it" (1995: 52; Fink's italics). In other words, the signifer initiates subjectivity by *positioning* it in discourse, leaving it room for a *trace*, but in no way filling it or embodying it. What the signifier ensures for the subject is the circumstance of existence, not the possibility of going beyond its concrete place.

On the other hand, separation, occurring in the last stages of the Oedipal drama, forges a more substantial subject, a *desiring being*, who overrides the level of pure signifiers in its specific relations to others. In essence, the experience of separation is on a par with the assimilation of the phallus in the paternal metaphor, I descibed above: the desire to *be* the mother's wish, to exist with her in dyadic bliss, is castrated, cut off from its illusory nexus, and transformed into a detached position of *having*; still, it is important to realize that primary narcissism is a formative stage for subjectivity, grounding all subsequent libidinal experience, because in this state the child's desire is born as the mOther's desire. Since the context of the mother-child couple is not a realm of pure pleasure, but already socialized, inundated by the full/empty register of signifiers, the narcissistic relation is characterized by the *mobility* of desire, its very condition in a *lack*, which can never be ideally filled. The child perceives this supplementarity in the mother, the way in which want continuously exceeds its objects, and strives to arrest it, by becoming the want itself. During this subjugation, the operation of desire is revealed in its complexitiy as always *of the Other*: "man's desire finds its form as the desire of the Other" ("Le désir de l'homme, c'est le désir de l´Autre"). Only in an imaginary register, can the illusion be sustained that the state of desiring itself is pure, whole and self-present.[1]

The narcissistic union is disrupted by the third term of the father as prohibition. The paramount significance of the accession to the father's name is elucidated by Lacan in the essay on psychosis (1961), especially in the distinction drawn there between repression in neurosis and foreclosure in pscyhosis. Even though the price of adopting the "phallus" entails a state of permanent division, – the tragedy of desire, as Lacan states it on several occasions – the failure to do this exacts a more terrible doom of mad exile from the human experience. If the father's name is not adopted, the alienating bar between signifier and signified not founded, then the subject's potential place in the signifying order vanishes, leaving only a *hole*, an irreparable absence, in the universe of symbols. In psychosis, the foreclosure, the unconditional expulsion, of the Law of an Other in discourse, results in the *delusional metaphor*, the imagined collapse of division between signifier and signifed. Hence, the figurative nature of the signifier is mistaken as a literal embodiment, confronting experience from the outside; as Malcolm Bowie observes:

> The signifier is 'unleashed' and gives birth not to an abundance of sense but to a vociferous tribe of imaginary beings. The imaginary becomes real, we might say, by passing through the symbolic dimension without being submitted to its exactions and obliquities. (1991: 109)

The accession to the paternal signifier, and the attendant process of repression, provide the subject with – what Lacan often refers to as – *anchoring points* (*points de caption*) in the interlinked, mobile chains of human discourse. Of necessity, the illusory mother-child utopia is interrupted by phallic prohibition so that the primary desire ruling it can both be named and repressed. This inaugural event of

---

1 Besides the seminar on the Other in *The Four Fundamental Concepts of Pscyho-Analysis* (esp. 203–230), see Lacan's paper in *Écrits*, "The subversion of the subject and the dialectic of desire in the Freudian unconscious" (292–324); the above quote is from that essay (311).

separation dissolves the Oedipus complex: now the shifting, meager place in the Symbolic is fleshed out by a *specific* being, the desiring subject.

As Freud so memorably outlined in his essay "On Narcissism," primary narcissistic desire does not evaporate at the end of Oedipus, but persists in psychic structure, partly repressed, and partly cathected to objects in intersubjective space. Lacan's retrospective view of the narcissistic constitution and especially of the object relations it establishes is particulary relevant for an examination of the role literary characters play in identification and subjective knowledge. In fact, Freud's image of the *amoeba* with its tentacles of love, ruled by "an original libidinal cathexis of the ego," by Narcissus himself, crystallizes in Lacan's account of desire in language, of the object *a* as the new guise of the mOther's desire.[2]

The libidinal force which creates a space for the split subject beyond alienation, at the mere level of signifiers, is the psychic remainder, and reminder, of narcissistic desire, of the hypothetical pre-oedipal union. If phallic separation opened up a gap between subject and Other, naming undifferentiated desire and thereby positioning it in another register, then this separation, at the same time, enacted a transformation of the mOther's desire into – what Lacan came to call – object *a*, the italicized *a*, standing for a heterogeneous other, partly repressed, partly fantasized, and partly real. Perhaps, the most outstanding feature of this objective relation is the capture of *excess* in the mOther's desire, of the child's confrontation with its sheer foreignness, the inscrutable way in which it by-passed him in the want for something else. Whereas the pre-oedipal child only intimates this engima and imagines, even experiences, its solution, the alienated subject comes to *know* its permanent opacity. The libidinal feat here consists of the surpassal of alienation in *fantasy*: the subject fantasizes a relation to otherness, based on the rem(a)inder of narcissistic bliss.

The dynamics of transition here from pure narcissism to object *a* are formulated by Lacan as a positioning of the subject toward the *cause* of the Other's desire (esp. Fink, 59–60). What becomes important for the subject is to establish a relation with object *a* which reveals that he constitutes himself the cause of the Other's desire, giving another twist to Lacan's dictum, "Le désir de l'homme, c'est le désir de l'Autre": "Man's desire is for the Other to desire him." However, since there is no way to arrest the supplementarity of desire, to wrest from it its conditioning in lack, the ideal object relation would be, as Brian Fink suggests, a scenario of pure *desirousness*, a kind of libidinal spectacle, where the subject momentarily experiences psychic balance, an irruption into the Symbolic of sub-

---

2 My presentation of object *a* owes a great deal too Bruce Fink's exposition in *The Lacanian Subject* (esp. 59–68; 83–97). See also Lacan's "The subversion of the subject and the dialectic of desire in the Freudian unconscious" (*Écrits*: 292–324).

lime joy (e. g. 60). In his evocative discussion of object *a*, Brian Fink suggests that such a scenario is outlined by Lacan, in Seminar VIII (*Le transfert* 1960–61), in Alcibiades encounter with "a certain something" in Socrates, with "a precious, shiny, gleaming something," the emanation itself of desirousness. Plato calls this "agalma": it is an experience of otherness, which arouses desire in a pure state; it is born of the signifier and escapes it, in happiness.[3]

In his seminar papers on fantasy and the analytic situation, Lacan continues to fine-tune his concept of the object *a*, especially the form it takes as the binding force of the relation between analyst and analysand.[4] In many ways analogous to aesthetic discourse, the analytic setting constitutes a field of fantasy where the analysand's various and complex attachments to object *a* are performed, their more or less successful manifestations serving as major elements in the cure. What is primarily at stake in analytic interactions is the particular pleasure produced as a result of the game played with the object *a*, or, in other words, the kinds of *jouissance* reigning in the analysand's fantasy. As I pointed out in the section on Ovid's Narcissus, psychoanalytic *jouissance* connotes a range of pleasures arising out of the primary experience of negativity, the lack in being (*manque-à-être*), and therefore belongs to a different semantic register from ordinary enjoyment. The most extreme understanding of the state of *jouissance* is as a kind of orgiastic death, the final, even apocalyptic, pleasure, hinted at in the renaissance sexual pun "to die." From that point, down the ladder of meaning, there are varieties of pathological "pleasures," often unequally mixed with pain and suffering, such as neurotic obsession, sadism, hysteria and more or less serious forms of perversions. Most often, pathological *jouissance* is the point of entry into the analytic situation. The cure, then, depends to a large extent on the staging of the fantasy in such a way that a repositioning toward the object *a* ensues and a different order of pleasure is orchestrated; the highest, even the most noble, order of pleasure is the encounter with otherness as *agalma*, a meeting with the sense of primal bliss, together with a glimpse of a realm beyond alienation. In this state of *jouissance*, the desiring subject is in full control of his own destiny.

My claim concerning literary characters is that as personified nodes in aesthetic discourse, they function as instigators of this kind of second-order, *noble jouissance*, prompted by the reader's or viewer's staging of a new relation to otherness in fantasy. Perhaps, no literary character has functioned so prominently

---

3 My account is slightly different from Fink's, but builds on his observations (esp. 59–60). Lacan's text is Seminar VIII, *Le transfert*, 1960–61, ed. Jacques-Alain Miller (Paris: Seuil, 1991).

4 Seminar XIV, *La logique du fantasme*, 1966–7 and Seminar XV, *L'acte psychanalytique*, 1967-; these are unpublished, but Fink discusses them at some length (esp. 61–68).

throughout history as a node of identification as has Shakespeare's *Hamlet*, written about tirelessly from innumerable ideological perspectives and treated by both Freud and Lacan as prototypical material for the case study of the modern individual. Before I examine transference in analysis as technique for understanding character, I will focus on a few examples from Lacan's seminar text, "Desire and the Interpretation of Desire in *Hamlet*" (1958–9), in order to determine to what extent a psychoanalytic reading can serve as a standard for reading character in literature in general.[5]

The three-part text on *Hamlet* was initially given as a series of seminars in April 1959, and it continues Lacan's elaboration upon the Oedipal situation, with particular attention to the consititution and vicissitudes of desire. The first part, "The Object Ophelia," concentrates upon the role the character of Ophelia plays as shifting object in Hamlet's Oedipal dilemma; the second part, "Desire and Mourning," elucidates the connection between loss, mourning and signification; the last section, "Phallophany," considers the effects of castration in terms of the work of mourning, linking Hamlet's final act to his authentic vision of the paternal signifier. Throughout the essay, psychoanalytic knowledge and the particulars of literary exploration ineract to shed a light on character in text as site of desire.

In the first place, Lacan's reading of Shakespeare's play is instructive in its view of character as a textual *construct*, a network of signifiers, rather than a mimetic representation. All psychoanalytic experience indicates, according to Lacan, that subjectivity emerges "in a certain position of dependence upon the signifier," not as a transparent "reflection [...] of what are called interhuman relationships" (11). What is at stake in *Hamlet*, the very substance of its tragic power, is the subject's complex and pathetic (and pathological) relation to the pure signifier of self-division, the *Name of the Father* itself. Because he fails to adequately name his primary desire, to both repress and figure it in the site of the split subject ($), Hamlet remains in a state of narcissistic attachment to the mother, rehearsing her desire throughout the play, not subjectifying his own. Thus, identifying with his mother's lust, with her "instinctive voracity," as she pays no heed to the difference between the noble King and his despicable brother, Hamlet resists the act of revenge, even though he discerns this difference, and then is fully convinced of Claudius' criminality. Subjugated to the mOther's desire, Hamlet remains in a state of procrastination during most of the play, his occasional spurts of energy no more than symptoms of that pathetic dependency. In Lacan's reading, the play's

5 Seminar VI, *Le désir et son interprétation* , 1958–9. I'm using the final three sessions of this seminar translated by James Hulbert in "Desire and the Interpretation of Desire in *Hamlet*." *Yale French Studies* 55/56 (1977), 11–52.

libidinal dynamic, its *topolgy* of desire, is generated in the Oedipal relationship, in the moment Hamlet fails to assume his lack (11–13).

Another important dimension of Lacan's reading, arising out of the concern with Hamlet's Oedipal dilemma, is the analogy drawn between the contours of *fantasy* in the analytic situation and in literary text. Above, in the discussion of object *a*, I noted that the analysand's process of separation involves a movement beyond speech to a transformed object relation, ideally produced in a space of blissful psychic reorganization. As Lacan points out in the first part of the *Hamlet* seminar, the fantasized object *a* belongs "in the normal state of affairs [...] [to] the circuit of the unconscious," unless an extraordinary situation or event brings it "to the level of the message," to a more or less explicit formulation within the register of the Symbolic. Perhaps the most significant point of contact between knowledge in psychoanalysis and in literature is the privilege each accords the "crossover" from unconscious fantasy to symbolic performance (14). The analytic situation creates a platform for subjective fantasy, staging various, and varying, relations to the object in desire; similarly, literature foregrounds the interaction between the imaginary and the symbolic, often most devoted to enigmatic irruptions into the logic of the signifier. In this way, the analogies drawn between character in literary text and the subject in psychoanalysis are substantial ones, not merely rhetorical comparisons. The matrix of analysis and of literature is of the same order of subjective existence.

The specific nature of Hamlet's fantasy is that he is trapped "in the hour of the Other" (*l'heure de l'Autre*; *leurre*: lure, trap, delusion) (18), ceaselessly repeating the trauma of his division, unable to arrest it, to control it in a state of separation. If fantasy in general can be formalized as $\$\lozenge a$ (the split subject's imaginary relation to the object), then Hamlet's pressure rests on \$, the moment of the split itself, asking of it questions, Lacan observes, similar to clinical cases of obsessional neurosis. Unlike perverse behavior, which accents the object *a*, often concretizing it as a fetish, neurosis seeks to recover a lost relationship in *time*, fantasizing the object as permutations of primary narcissistic crisis. Shakespeare's tragedy dramatizes its hero compulsive fantasy on two interrelated levels, in the communication with Ophelia and in the communcation with language itself.

For Lacan, the episodes involving Hamlet and Ophelia illustrate particularly well the circuit of the object *a* from unconscious fantasy to the level of the message. The play indicates that during the happy time before the King's murder, the young prince cherished Ophelia, writing her sincere, if stilted and clumsy, letters of love. However, during a scene occuring shortly after Hamlet's first encounter with his father's ghost, a strange reversal seems to have taken place, affection turned to disgust, gentleness to cruelty, love to hate.[6] Ophelia herself reports the incident to her father, in the detailed language, Lacan notes, of "a clinical observation" (21): in both appearance and manner the young man is transformed, his clothes dishevelled and the look on his face "so piteous in purport/As if he had been loosèd out of hell" (II i, 93–95); also, his agression is uncharacteristic, in the way he grabs her arm and glowers at her in rude intimacy. As usually, Polonious misinterprets the situation, concluding that here is to be found the root of Hamlet's madness, "the very ecstasy of love" (101). On the other hand, Lacan detects in the character's change an interplay of identifications, bonds of *love*, in fact, but more profound and complex than the superficial stateman could ever guess at.

Because Hamlet's Oedipal dilemma is unresolved, trapping him at the narcissistic hour, Ophelia has, up to the scene in question, occupied for him the place of the mOther's desire, the fantasized mother-child unity. The mother's remarriage to Claudius, the King's brother, works for Hamlet as a second Oedipal challenge to repress primary desire and ascend to the father's *name*, to a position of symbolic identification with the *phallus*. However, the ghost's shocking revelation about fratricide and about the mother's lascivious nature upsets the circuit of identifications in Hamlet's fantasy: instead of undergoing symbolic castration himself, he elaborates its *substitution* in the figure of Ophelia, his former love. As if playing some ingenious psychic game, Hamlet moves object *a* from its privileged union with subjectivity to a depersonalized place outside the self, where he can pretend both to master it and to reject it. Lacan contends that it is as the outcome of a *substitue* self-division that Ophelia occupies the role of the phallus itself. Hence, the play's focus is upon the transformation of love into cruelty:

> The subject is no longer the object: he rejects it with all the force of his being and will not find it again until he sacrifices himself. It is in this sense that the object is here the equivalent of, assumes the place of, indeed is – the phallus. (23)

As Bruce Fink suggests, an awareness of how crucial a concept *substitution* is in psychoanalytic theory is needed for a full appreciation of Lacan's reading of *Hamlet*, especially of this surprising view of Ophelia's role (182).[7] In this regard, Freud's work on fetishism is significant, since, in the later essays in particular, he developed the connection between the fetish, the threat of castration and renunciation. A late, unfinished essay, published posthumously, "Splitting of the Ego in the Process of Defence" (1938; 1940), suggests, through clinical observation,

6 Lacan discusses scene one in Act II as if it follows immediately upon the meeting with the ghost, whereas it is almost certain that a considerable time has passed, possibly two months.

7 Bruce Fink, "Reading Hamlet with Lacan," in *Lacan, Politics, Aesthetics*, eds. Richard Feldstein and Willy Apollon (Albany: SUNY Press, 1996), 181–198.

that neurotic fetishism exemplifes a special configuration of the event of castration in subjective history.[8] Here, Freud starts to outline a case of the subject who *splits* in the very act of a botched renunciation: in order to both retain infantile sexual pleasure and confront the loss of that pleasure, entailed by the father's threat, the subject fantasizes a substitute object, often with erotic connotations and endowed with a phallic shape – for instance, the nose, the foot, or even the little toe (!). In the displaced organ, castration can be both controlled and denied. For Lacan, *Hamlet* dramatizes this complex psychic ambivalence in the interaction between the hero and Ophelia, which erupts into the play as phallic fantasy. Whereas Freud's analysand typifies substitutive strategies as erotic *perversion*, Shakespeare's character telescopes those as an existential/narcissistic dilemma: Hamlet knows, yet does not know, the pain of his own self-division.

Trapped within an imaginary register, within, as Lacan says, "the hour of the Other," fantasizing substitutions for the loss he never assumed fully, Hamlet does not only construe a strange relation to Ophelia, but elaborates as well a pathological linguistic (and semiotic) universe. As I indicated in the discussion above, the event of castration is represented by the paternal metaphor which ushers the subject into its appointed place within the structures of the Symbolic. Although Hamlet clearly has been partly initiated into discourse, the complex Oedipal dynamic in the play eclipses the process of separation from the mOther's desire in signification; that is to say, since Hamlet does not face loss from a detached position, he ceaselessly searches for a stable object in language: the failure to accomplish this induces a pathetic relation with the signifier, the play's prevailing attitude of *melancholia*.

In particular, in the second part of his essay, Lacan expounds the connection between desire, mourning and signification. Just as Hamlet appears obsessed with narcissistic loss, repeatedly defending himself against its insistence, so the play as a whole struggles to restructure its world after the many deaths it suffers – the death of King Hamlet, of Polonius, of Ophelia. In fact, both the hero's psychology and the structures of the play itself are suffused with melancholy grievance, which, as Lacan states, accompanies "insufficient mourning" (39). Early in the the play, Gertrude, Hamlet's mother, surmises correctly that her son's "distemper" is caused by "his father's death and our o'erhasty marriage" (Act II, ii, 54–55). Clearly, little ceremony follows upon Polonius' death, his murder staged in a grotesque fashion, and his body last seen as Hamlet drags it by the feet off the stage. Neither is Ophelia's suicide properly mourned, her burial in Christian ground even questioned, both by the priest and the gravediggers (Act V, i; Lacan: 40–41). These

8 Sigmund Freud. "Splitting of the Ego in the Process of Defence" (1938). SE XXIII (London: Hogarth, 1966).

deaths as well as the abrupt rites of mourning contribute to the disordered – the "rotten" – state of things in the play.

What emerges from Lacan's discussion of desire and mourning is that ritual operates as a kind of substitute language for loss, a higher order of symbols than the ordinary system of signification. As psychic structure, grief (and/or melancholia) bears an inverse relation to *foreclosure* in psychoses since both experiences lead to the opening up of a gap or a *hole* in the subject's world: on one hand, the psychotic rejects symbolic castration, expunging the paternal signifier and thereby leaving a primal hole in the web of language; on the other hand, the mourner, shocked, for instance, by the death of a loved one, confronts an irreparable void in the *real*, in the uncanny existential space ouside of speech and communication.[9] Lacan also emphasizes how the substitutive processes are inversely similar for madness and grief; in the first case, hallucinations overtake the symbolic lack and in the second case, "swarms of images [...] assume the place of the phallus," sometimes resembling delusions, as in the figure of the ghost in *Hamlet* (38). Ritual participates in the movement of signifiers triggered by loss, and Lacan indicates that it is only its higher-order, encompassing function "that can fill the hole in the real." For restitution to take place, "the work of mourning is accomplished at the level of the *logos*: I say *logos* rather than group or community, although group and community, being organized culturally are its mainstays" (38).

In *Hamlet*, the work of mourning is not harnessed to run its course for the benefit of individual and community, resulting in the melancholic structure of play, with its obsessive repetitions, complaints, mockeries, and dejected games of language. Although Lacan does not specifically focus on this, the *pathos* of subjectivity in the play, its pathological dependency on the signifier, becomes evident in the contrast set up between the dramatic aesthetic Hamlet favors, and elucidates to the players in Acts II and III, and the drama itself of his tragic fate. In both "play-scenes," Hamlet posits character in drama as a kind of ritualized *mirror* which casts back to an audience intense passion, framed and formalized by the actor's temperate skill. An excellent play, the young prince maintains, should be emotionally refined, "set down with as much modesty as cunning" (Act II, ii, 416–7), avoiding cheap, "savory" tricks, aimed at catching the crude attention of the groundlings. Just before the performance of the tragedy, the *Murder of Gonzago*, before the King and Queen, Hamlet expounds his theory of an "honest method" in drama:

---

9 The *real* comprises one of the major human dimensions, together with the symbolic and imaginary registers. Although it tends to be defined variously in Lacan's writings, there is always a sense of its resistance to symbolization: "the real is the impossible"(*The Four Fundamental Concepts of Psycho-Analysis* 167). It is important to realize that the *real* has nothing to do with reality or with realism.

there should exist a judicious reciprocity between an audience and the depiction of human nature upon the stage; extravagance betrays the purpose of art, which is

> to hold [...] the mirror up to nature; to show virtue her own feature, scorn her own image, and the very age and body of the time his form and pressure. Now, this overdone, or come tardy off, though it make the unskilful laugh, cannot but make the judicious grieve; the censure of the which one must, in your allowance, o'erweigh a whole theatre of others. (Act III, ii, 21–25)

This conception of the artistic *mirror* has a classical heritage, first oulined by Aristotle in the *Poetics* as imitation of action in tragedy, a compendium of aspects of reality, not photographic reflections. Here, character operates as an agent who abstracts human behavior from contemporary contexts; thus, it occupies a site of ideality, much closer to its *ritualistic* function in ancient drama than to psychological realism.[10]

The *pathos* of the character of Hamlet crystallizes in this view of the discrepancy between idealized character in drama and the passive, hollow protagonist, unable to act as a ritualized, therapeutic, example for his audience. An instructive case, which expresses one of the central dilemmas of the play, is Hamlet's first long meditative soliloquy, occurring immediately after he listens to the main player recite a speech from the tragedy of Priam.[11] Having witnessed the actor's superb skill in conveying a scene of death and grief, Hecuba's mourning her slain husband, Hamlet is moved to reflect on his own apathy, his inability to harness passion in the proper act of revenge. The language of the speech is typical of melancholic self-accusations as Hamlet curses himself for villainy, cowardice and "pigeon-livered" inaction. In contrast to the actor's controlled identification with "a fiction [...] a dream of passion," the young prince mopes about in a dull dream, "Like John-a-dreams, unpregnant of my cause,/And can say nothing" (Act II, ii, 542–3). This comparison between two registers of grief, one ritualized, the other melancholy, throws a double light on *character* as a site of desire in literary text, as both a movement toward a sublime, idealized condition and as a ritualized node of *object a*, an instigator of noble fantasy in audiences and spectators.

The reciprocity between witness and representation, onlooker and actor, in the above scene, clarifies this double function of literary character. Clearly, the actor who rehearses Aeneas' tale and who weeps for Hecuba already occupies a ritualized space, both exercising a sublime fantasy and mirroring its dynamic to an impressed audience. It is significant that even Polonius, apparently branded by

10 Note Hamlet's well-known comment about actors: "let them be well used, for they are the abstract and brief chronicles of the time" (Act II, ii, 498–99).

11 This play is not given a title, but the speech is referred to by Hamlet as "Aeneas' tale to Dido"; the subject is from Virgil's *Aeneid* where Aeneas tells of Pyrrhus' killing of Priam, the aged king of Troy.

Hamlet as a "barren spectator" (Act III, ii, 38), is touched by the actor's performance, remarking on his change of colour and the "tears in's eyes" (Act II, ii, 495). For Hamlet, the powerful impact of this scene is a psychological turning point, prompting his own quest toward an idealized site, where passion is perfomed with exquisite beauty, touching the hearts of even the crudest groundlings. *Hamlet* is deeply interested in the processes of this "character-making," investing its creative energies in constructing a fictional model which both confirms and contemplates its own being. Hence, the magnetic pull of its protagonist, captivating audiences with its uncanny modernity across historical time.

Lacan's psychoanalytic reading of Hamlet's entrapment within the hour of the mOther, which I have here supplemented by a look at the "play within the play," helps to orient attention to the dramatic movement in the play as *ritualistic libido*, the longing for a system of symbols which both enacts loss and offers a consolation for it. In *The English Elegy*, Peter Sacks (1985) notes that despite the dominant mood of dejection in *Hamlet*, there is within the play a drive toward an Oedipal resolution, worked out most fully within the circumstances of the hero's death.[12] Sacks contends that the attitudes of the play are closer to the genre of elegy than to the melancholia of revenge tragedy, because, especially in the final scene, there emerges renewed faith in the consolatory powers of the *logos*, of communal rites (82–3). Hamlet's avowal in the first act, shortly after his father's death, that there is an unbridgeable rift between the rhetoric of grief – "all forms, moods, shows of grief" (Act I, ii, 82) – and its inner, affective reality – "that within which passes show" (85) – is substantially modified in his final plea to his friend, Horatio, "to tell my story" (Act V, ii, 331), to repair his "wounded name" and "report me and my cause aright/To the unsatisfied" (Act V, ii, 321–2). The seeds of this confidence in offical narrative are, according to Sacks, sown in the episodes involving Hamlet and the players, which I investigated above. In my view the communication here should not only be stressed as a crisis of the conscience of King Claudius (Sacks: 86), but, first and foremost, as Hamlet's psychological epiphany: what is revealed to him is the affective power of character in art, how "dream[s] of passion" can effect and transform the viewer's psychic constitution. The last words to Horatio are permeated with that epiphanic insight.

12 Peter Sacks. *The English Elegy* (Baltimore: The Johns Hopkins University Press, 1985).

Chapter 5: Transference

In the previous section, I have primarily attempted to draw attention to how Lacan's psychoanalytical interpretation of Shakespeare's *Hamlet* contains suggestions for a model of literary character as a ritual of human desire. The enactment of grief in the play within the play triggers in Hamlet a noble wish to both imitate the "dream of passion" and to instil in his own onlookers a similar wish for a second-order transformation. The last scene of the tragedy is particularly instructive in this regard: here, despite the many deaths and the sense of tragic fatality, the central interaction is marked by a renewed faith in the virtuous life – in honour, the noble deed, the "name ungored" (V, ii, 232).

As Lacan intimates in the last section of the *Hamlet* seminar, aptly called "Phallophany," the unclouded view of virtue in the play's last act emerges logically from Hamlet's symbolic castration, his disentanglement, in the face of death, from the mOther's desire. The trail of "character-making" is thus primarily a narcissistic process, a movement through psychological crises, at first inadequately assumed as a fantasy of substitution, and then, in the final stages, bravely faced as absolute lack. The honourable space created in *Hamlet*''s last scene can, in Lacan's reading, be participated in as *logos*, as proper ritual, because the *pathos*, the pathology, of the tragic hero has given way to *ethos*, to character in its authentic function as an "honest," "wholesome," and "handsome" mirror of its time (II, ii, 420–421). Hamlet's descriptions here of the "excellent play" (415) are attached to his own figure by the audience of his tragic fate. Thus, it is possible to contend that as a model for literary character, Hamlet embodies the *transferential* relationship between fiction and onlooker or reader; in a way similar to the young prince's libidinal reconstitution, as he responded to the speech of an actor, the audience transfers its own narcissistic desire unto fictional character, in the process experiencing a (potential) psychic transformation. The event of artistic transference is, as I have pointed out earlier, of the same existential substance as the relation between speaker and listener in the psychoanalytic situation. Before turning to the specifics of the analogy, I want to examine another of Lacan's literary explorations, his analysis of Sophocles' *Antigone*, in the seminar on *The Ethics of Psychoanalysis* (1959–1960).[1]

1 Seminar VII, *The Ethics of Psychoanalysis* (1959–1960). Trans. Dennis Porter (London: Routledge, 1992).

Lacan's commentary on the heroine of Sophocles' play crystallizes some of the points I have been making about the ritual force of literary character. As Jean-Michel Rabaté makes clear, the part of Lacan's ethics seminar called "The Essence of Tragedy" is to some extent built upon Hegel's commentary on *Antigone* in the *Phenomenolgy of Spirit*, with the main emphasis on the conflict between Creon, the representative of the Law, and Antigone, the embodiment of the "unwritten values of the family" (69).[2] The play starts in *medias res* just after Antigone's two brothers have been killed in war, one honorably, for the city of Thebes, the other treacherously, against his own kin, and the ensuing action revolves around Creon's decision to punish the traitor, Polynices, according to the laws of the city, by denying him last rites and burial in holy ground. The sister, Antigone, defies the cruel verdict by covering up the condemned body, thereby committing a crime against the state, punishable by death. In Hegel's view, tragedy is born through the clash of values, the realm of politics, underwritten by legal codes, versus the ethics of family, spiritualized, in proximity to the ineffable order of the divine.

In many respects, Lacan's analysis relies on Hegel's dichotomy between state and individual, but also departs from it by adding weight to Antigone's side, especially through considerations of the character's combined aesthetic and ethical powers. The essence of the tragic lies less in the play's axiological tension than in the heroine's uncanny impact on the audience, an impact that, unlike the cumulative force in *Hamlet*, remains integral and strong from the beginning of the action to its very end. How is one to define, Lacan asks, this combination of forces in Antigone's character, "this power of attraction" (247), which impinges on the spectators and draws them to it as if it were a magnet?

To an even greater extent than Hamlet, Lacan intimates, the character of Antigone carries an archetypal force, both in the sense of tapping into primary desire, the mOther's desire, and in the sense of marking Being (*l'être*) as such, the limit zone between life and death. In his seminars, Lacan repeatedly draws attention to the unorthodox status of his reading of Sophocles' tragedy, especially how he departs from the conciliatory views of the great commentators such as Hegel and Goethe. For instance, a passage close to the end of the play, Antigone's speech of self-justification, her elevation of blood-ties to her brother as being of a superior order than the kinship of husband or children (ll 995–1004, in *Penguin Edition*, 1982),[3] scandalized many nineteenth-century readers, among them Goethe, who both noted it and wished it away: "I wish that one day some scholar will reveal to us that this passage is a later addition" (quoted in Lacan 255). Similarly, Lacan

2 Jean-Michel Rabaté. *Jacques Lacan: Psychoanalysis and the Subject of Literature* (Palgrave, 2001).

3 Sophocles. *Antigone* (Penguin, 1982). All further references to *Antigone* are to the line numbers in this edition.

emphasizes how many critics have been ill at ease with the apparent contradiction between the inflexible Antigone of the first half of the play and the passionate, lamenting heroine of its later episodes. The consensus seems to be that this lack of verisimilitude in the tragic hero is a textual corruption, a later addition by writers less discerning than Sophocles (280).

In Lacan's view, however, Antigone's final complaint articulates a certain scandal which clings to the character's image from the beginning of the tragedy to its very end. After the Chorus, almost always dazzled by Antigone's radiating strength, asserts "even I would rebel against the king" (895), horrifed at Creon's tyranny, the heroine responds with her "lamentation on life"; her sorrows are mounted one on top of the other: she will be a living being in the kingdom of the dead, entombed without a tomb of her own; at this point, she is an emblem of the living dead, without friends, helpful kin, husband and children; she has never known the joys of the conjugal bed; she is, in fact, an avatar of Niobe, the half-goddess, whose grief for her dead children turned her to stone. Lacan underscores how this passage of Antigone's complaint occurs at the *limit-zone*, at the point where the heroine's petrification, so to speak, becomes visible. All along, Antigone has articulated her death-like condition: in the very first speech, she identifies herself with the alomst unbearable griefs of her father, Oedipus (1–13); in the ensuing dialogue with the sister, Ismene, expressing her determination to bury the traitor brother, she claims that punishment by death "will be a glory," because she "will lie with the one I love and loved by him" (86–7); shortly afterwards, she defies Creon, appropriating his death-sentence as her own reward, "alive in the midst of so much grief" (517). Thus, Antigone's scandal pertains to her espousal of Hades, her passionate drive for death.

What is particularly illuminating in Lacan's reading of the play is his view of the involvement of the Chorus in Antigone's tragic passion. Although the Chorus in ancient Greek drama usually consists of the community of wise elders, it performs an important stand-in role for the general audience, especially in its capacity as impressionable witness. In *Antigone*, the Chorus, initially allied with law and order, and with Creon's edict, during the course of the play and the communication with the young heroine, switches sides, or, as Lacan states, "lose[s] its head" (281) in the magnetic pull of heroic transgression. The Chorus' admiring gaze becomes especially clear in the episode, referred to above, of Antigone's visible petrification, that is, of her ultimate arrival in the liminal zone of a living death. The image which dominates at this moment is of character as desire; it irradiates a "glow of beauty" (281), a "violent illumination" (281); it draws the Chorus, and by implication the audience, with it across permissible limits, making of them accomplices in crime, so that they reverse their former opinion on justice and the rightness of civil law. By gazing upon the beauty of tragic character, the onlooker's psychic constitution is (potentially) transformed; it is an experience similar to Hamlet's viewing of the tragedy of Priam: a purely honorable space is created, where passion extends beyond its pathological roots in narcissism to sublime spectacle. As archetypal characters, both Hamlet and Antigone illustrate Lacan's interpretation of "agalma," Plato's name for Socrates' beauty: their splendor dazzles spectators so that they experience pure joy, detached from the realm of objects, oriented close to the authentic source of their own Being.

Because they retain an originary aesthetic and ethical force, tragic heroes such as Hamlet and Antigone delineate an *ontology*; in other words, they exemplify what it fundamentally means to exist as a character in literature. What is primarily at stake in this fictional concept, what, in fact, vitalizes it, so that it materializes in the audience's experience, exists for it as a point of psychic reference, is the activity of *transference*. My concluding commentary here will trace the major features of that activity.

As Lacan discusses at some length at the beginning of the seminar on *Antigone*, a common meaningful process for both aesthetics and psychoanalysis is *catharsis*. In the *Poetics*, Aristotle propounds his theory of tragedy via a list of vital ingredients – Spectacle, Character, Fable (or Plot), Diction, Melody, and Thought – as well as in terms of the dramatic effect on the audience. In essence, tragedy is "the imitation of an action that is serious and also, as having magnitude, complete in itself;" its dramatic incidents arouse "pity and fear, wherewith to accomplish its catharsis of such emotions" (Book VI: 230).[4] To modern readers, the allusion to *catharsis* is cryptic, passed over by Aristotle as if it were a commonplace in his culture, too well known for explication. Still, as Lacan points out, there is consensus among commentators that the term has both psychological and medical associations, "purgation" or "purification" capturing best its sense and function. There are problems, however, Lacan notes, in placing too much emphasis on *emotional* cleansing, since in another passage on catharsis, this time in Book VIII of the *Politics*, Aristotle links it to a state of exalted *excitement* certain disquieting music produces. Listeners to this type of music, on a par with "hot jazz *(le hot)* or rock 'n' roll," reach heights of Dionysean frenzy and then become calm (245). Much more seems to be involved than the participant's emotional revision. "What is this pleasure," Lacan asks, "to which one returns after a crisis that occurs in another dimension, a crisis that sometimes threatens pleasure, for we all know to what extremes a certain kind of ecstatic music may lead?" (246).

What Lacan is suggesting here is that the propelling force within catharsis is desire, in its psychoanalytic dimension, and it is precisely within this libidinal

---

4 *The Rhetoric and The Poetics of Aristotle*. Trans. W. Rhys Roberts and Ingram Bywater (New York: The Modern Library, 1954).

territory that the matrices of aesthetics and psychoanalysis merge. It was, in fact, in the early encounter with hysterics that Freud and Breuer formulated their theory of the cure and proposed *catharsis* as the apt description of the psychic fulfillment experienced as the outcome of the lifting of repression (*Studies on Hysteria* 1895; Lacan 244).[5] Of course, in *Studies on Hysteria*, psychology is still entangled with biology, and the medical sense of catharsis as "discharge" or "abreaction" overrides that of libidinal purification. Again, however, Lacan emphasizes Freud's awareness of contemporary aesthetic thoughts, notably his interest in Greek tragedy and also a possible connection with an Aristotelean scholar, Jakob Bernays, who wrote with discernment about the Greek understanding of rituals of desire (246–7).

Throughout his career, Freud probed and developed the cathartic field of the psychoanalytic situation. Although there is considerable difference in attitude between the early work on hysteria and the later papers on technique – primarily, between the neophyte's optimism and mature scepticism – a red thread running through the writings on analytic practice *as such* is the remarkable fact of transference, as a defining factor both in the analyst/analysand relation and in the outcome of the cure. As Lacan has pointed out, a crucial insight for Freud, in the work with Breuer, occurred during sessions with hysterics, who, by telling their dreams and secret fantasies, implicated the listening analyst in unconscious space. Despite his neutrality as a physician, Freud's communication with his patients resembled more that of a reader's with seductive texts than that of a detached authority with his clientele. Thus, the awareness of his own inevitable participation in the patients' inner lives led to Freud's discovery of the unconscious: "It was while listening to hysterics that he *read* that there was an unconscious" (quoted by Shoshana Felman 1977: 118; Lacan's emphasis).[6] The implications here are, of course, infinitely rich and complex for both psychoanalytic and literary/aesthetic projects. In both cases, *intersubjectivity*, the border-crossing between self and other, overrides the model of critical authority versus enigmatic object. Perhaps, most of all, as Lacan, again, observes, the realization that criticism itself becomes affected, even contaminated, by the field of the object, leads to fruitful self-reflections on the dynamics of the analytic situation. Everything in Freud's "resulting rules through which he established the practice of psychoanalyis is designed to counteract this consequence, to conduct things in such a way as to avoid being affected" (Felman 118).

Freud's analytic rules emerge to a large extent from, and interact with, his work on transference, both in his case histories and then, on a metpsychological level, in

5 Sigmund Freud and Joseph Breuer. *Studies on Hysteria* (1895). SE II (London: Hogarth Press, 1955).

6 Shoshana Felman. "Turning the Screw of Interpretation." *Yale French Studies* 55/56 (1977), 94–207.

the later papers on technique. As many commentators have noted, the first independent study of hysteria – *Dora: An Analysis of a Case of Hysteria* (1905) – presents a seminal account of the psychoanalytic situation, not least important for Freud's own involvement in his analysand's pathology.[7] In his postscript to the narrative of Dora, Freud attributes the failure of the cure to the unconscious conflict between analyst and analysand, in the process offering his first detailed observations on the phenomenon of transference. Because the analytic situation occupies in a sense an *other* place, – like Freud's dreams, "ein anderer Schauplatz" – various forms of repressed material surface, not least material attached to significant childhood relationships and experiences within the family. The unique therapeutic context does not only, as Lacan says, "stage the reality of the unconscious" (*The Four Fundamental Concepts of Psycho-Analysis* 89) within the analysands' autobiographical accounts, their memories, dreams and associative dialogues, but, in the most striking manner of all, within a dramatization, "an acting out," of past events, usually associated with members of the family – father, mother, siblings, or, as in Dora's case, a potential lover. In all cases, the analyst himself functions as the catalyst of psychic dramas, as a sort of stand-in figure for embodied memory.

As Freud emphasized again and again, transference is both a difficult, tricky mechanism and the most useful tool in the psychoanalytic cure.[8] As early as Dora's case, the *ambivalence* of transference is touched upon, the way, on the surface, it appears as a straightforward act, in all essentials a direct translation of past experience. Freud likens such acts with printed copies, exact reproductions of the original. On the other hand, there occur more subtle, "artful" expressions, which have "gone through a stylization [...] a *sublimation* [...] and those attain consciousness when, in an inventive manner, they become attached to concrete details in the relationship with the doctor" (116). As opposed to "reproductions," Freud calls these "revisions" (117).

Although the term, *sublimation*, is rarely used again for the analysand's activity, it is a conception with significant connections to artistic discourse and to the textual situation between character and audience.[9] As I have remarked earlier, the

---

7 Sigmund Freud. "Fragment of an Analysis of a Case of Hysteria" (1905). SE VII (London: Hogarth Press, 1953). For a discussion of the significance of this case study see Peter Gay's biography: *Freud: A Life for our Time* (London: J. M. Dent&Sons, 1988).

8 "The Dynamics of Transference" (1912). SE XII (London: Hogarth Press, 1958); "Remembering, Repeating and Working Through" (1914), SE XII (London: Hogarth Press, 1958).

9 In other contexts, of course, Freud worked toward a theory of sublimation, especially in consideration of aesthetic and intellectual activity, such as *Leonardo da Vinci and a Memory of Childhood* (1910).

divergencies between the private, pathogenic material of psychoanalysis and the public arena of literary contracts are not fundamental ones, but criss-cross within the same existential matrix: for instance, in both circumstances, repression plays a crucial role in the formation of symptoms, even if the analytic session treats those as pathological emotions and aesthetic discourse, such as Aristotle's *Poetics*, as every-day emotions, heightened to a state of "pity and fear" (Book IV). Subsequent chapters will focus more closely on aesthetic versions; at this point, I want to examine the sublimating forces in Freud's relation of transference.

The specialized framing of the psychoanalytic situation is first and foremost affected by the establishment of a pact between patient and doctor, which ideally should operate as a controlling force from beginning of treatment to the moment of cure.[10] On several occasions, Freud refers to the respective *tasks* of the participants, where, on one hand "the sick ego promises us the most complete candour [...] to put at our disposal all the material which its self-perception yields it," and, on the other hand, the analysts "assure the patient of the strictest discretion and place at his service [...] experience in interpreting material that has been influenced by the unconscious" (*An Outline of Psycho-Analysis* (1939), 173).[11] Although both partners assume active roles, it is obvious that the situation would not work without the superior knowledge of the analyst, who penetrates the ignorant *id* and attempts to give "[the patient's] ego back its mastery over lost provinces of his mental life." As Freud says, this division of labor, this pact, "constitutes the analytic situation" (1939: 173).

In reality, however, mainly due to the dynamics of transference, the patient's promise of "complete candour" is not upheld. Instead of adhering to the fundamental rule of keeping in check his or her self-criticism, patients sublimate the repressed material and produce ingenious, often deceptive, structures, which block dialogue and delay, or even destroy, the possibility of therapeutic results. Whereas other intractable analytic material, such as dreams and free associations, become, in the end, conscious procedures, parts of a person's life-history, sublimations remain resistant to scrutiny, in many ways similar to palimpsest texts, with seemingly endless layers of meaning. It is only with a convincing approach to and interpretation of sublimated transference that the patient experiences relief from symptoms and a sense of coherence in the story of her life.

The point to be emphasized here, as it touches significantly upon literary analysis and literary character, is the field of new knowledge produced through the final co-operation of patient, unconscious material and analyst. Freud often likens

10 I use "patient/doctor" interchangeably with "analysand/analyst," because the former are Freud's terms.

11 *An Outline of Psycho-Analysis* (1939). SE XXII (London: Hogarth Press, 1964). See especially chapter VI: "The Techinque of Psycho-Analysis."

the analytic scene to a battle-zone, where the "allies," the ego and the analyst, fight a war against the "enemy" of *id*, repression and especially the resistances, which keep repression in its place. In one of the most informative essays about transference, "Remembering, Repeating and Working-Through" (1914), this scene of struggle is outlined in concrete detail, showing the problems of narcissistic sublimation, and offering the allies advice on how to attack the artful enemy. The crucial idea here, the fascinating aspect of the analyst/analysand relation, is *repetition*, the fact that, instead of remembering the past, of recounting it in dialogue with the analyst, the patient *acts out* the pressing, but repressed, circumstance. In the beginning of treatment, contrary to expectation, the patient is not a voluble teller, but remains forgetful and silent about his "eventful life-history" (150). The only way in which the past becomes known is through repeated acts; the doctor becomes a kind of "objective correlative," a trigger for repressed personalities, which, for instance, instead of recounting difficult childhood situations, re-live them in the course of psychoanalysis. Thus, a patient does not recall his defiant attitude toward authoritative parents, but behaves in such a way toward the analyst; he does not give examples of sexual frustrations, but exhibits a defeatist attitude, "complains [...] he is fated never to carry through what he undertakes"; he is without awareness of his shameful and guilt-ridden past, but expresses unease over the present treatment, preferring to keep it a secret to family and friends (150).

To a large extent, analysis constitutes a process of enlightenment, whereby *memory* replaces pathological display. In line with his prevalent war metaphors, Freud notes how *acting out* serves as the patient's defense strategy, his weapons of resistance to the task of knowing himself. During treatment, the doctor must "wrest [these weapons] from him one by one" (151), must, in other words, turn from a role of passive correlation into active interpreter. The most important aspect of the cure is just this: the development of the transference into a positive instrument for "curbing the patient's compulsion to repeat and for turning it into a motive for remembering" (154). Once the process of remembering has started, psychoanalysis changes from battle-zone into *playground*, where past and present, real life and imaginary obsessions, unconscious and consciousness coalesce in an "intermediate region," where ordinary laws of reality are suspended (154). Upon this extraordinary time/space unit, a "new condition" is constructed, where the illness itself, as a visible artifice, as opposed to the previous opaque symptomology, opens itself up to scrutiny and to the healing interventions of the doctor (154). Although resistances may persist for some time to come, the harnessing of transference as the patient's own self-analytic tool initiates a *cathartic* environment, to use Freud's medical term, "abrecating" the stifled affective life, liberating the sick individual from the strangulated hold of repression.

In order to show more concretely the dynamics of transference, I want in conclusion briefly to present another of Freud's papers on technique, "Observations on Transference Love" (1915). What is at stake in this paper is the illness as *artifice*, as a kind of composition, open to positive change, created through the complex and shifting relationship between analyst and analysand. Freud's focus here is upon the frequent tendency during treatment of female patients to fall in love with their doctor. Since, in its initial stages, psychoanalysis resembles a battle-ground, involving skirmishes between forgetful acting out and powerful *imagos* of authority, it is a condition amenable to a passionate relation.[12] The resistance to "working-through" the repressed life creates, in a sense, physical intimacy, especially between female analysands and the figure of the doctor, whom they invest with unconscious erotic power. This intimacy is further complicated by the dangers besetting the doctor himself, who is almost always susceptible to the phenomenon of *counter-transference*; as I pointed out above, listening to the psychological discourse of others, the analyst is made aware of his own unconscious. Although such a relationship operates on the same emotional principles as love in the real world, it is, Freud emphasizes, *not real*, but a special product of the whole artifical composition of psychoanalysis. As with illness in general, initially, transference-love is a weapon of resistance; if managed skillfully, it too will be transformed into a tool of self-discovery.

As regards literary studies, what is particularly interesting about this transferential dynamic is that love for another is turned into self-analytic tool. In both cases, in psychoanalysis and in literature, communication is raised to the level of *art*, constructed and malleable; nevertheless, the (potential) outcome of participation in such acts entails a heightened sense of being, "mental freedom," Freud contends, on one hand, *catharsis*, Aristotelean purgation of "pity and fear," on the other. As I discussed above, in relation to both Hamlet and Antigone, both are powerful archetypal figures, drawing to themselves, like magnets, the interests of the dramas they appear in as well as the desire of audiences. Like the dazzled Chorus in Sophocles' play, the spectator of tragic character experiences rapture, which resembles love: gazing upon Priam, Hamlet or Antigone, the viewer's narcissistic disposition, entangled with infantile repressions, is transported, via identification and displacement, to a state of sublime grace. In psychoanalytic, and more specifically, Lacanian terms, this process is one of discovering a libidinal space beyond alienation: in mature love, as well as in open confrontation with object *a* in art, the

---

12 One of the uses of *imago* in psychoanaysis is for the analyst as authority figure, for instance, parental authority figure. See Jean Laplanche and Jean-Bertrand Pontalis. *The Language of Psychoanalysis*. Trans. Donald Nicholson-Smith (London: Hogarth Press and the Institute of Psychoanalysis, 1973).

subject moves, even if momentarily, beyond division, on the level of signifiers, to a new objective relation, to elevated joy in the knowledge of otherness.[13]

In "Observations on Transference Love," Freud, as if in anticipation of Lacanian *jouissance*, notes how the analytic love-relationship is a double-edged instrument, *genuine*, despite its artificiality, *essential* despite its pathological context. All the ingredients of so-called "normal" love are part and parcel of transference love: narcissistic identification, infantile repression and repetition of infantile patterns, a tendency to favor fantasy over reality, and an overvaluation of the traits of the loved one (168–169). The patient's love for her analyst is certainly not a fake one, nor is it created out of thin air as soon as analysis starts. Rather it exists as a pre-disposition in the narcissistic psyche, intensified by the dynamics of transference. Thus, Freud advices other analysts neither to reject nor to succumb to this attraction, but to harness it and to preserve it as the force of desire itself. The analyst must keep "within the limits prescribed by ethics and technique"; his aim must be to liberate the female patient from the infantile fixations, which impair her love and also make sure that she does not "dissipate it in the treatment, but keep[s] it ready for the time when, after treatment, the demands of real life make themselves felt" (169). Toward the end of this paper, Freud defends analytic technique against contemporary sexual prejudice, comparing the analyst to a chemist, who, in the process of his explorations, discovers "highly explosive forces" (170). Despite the risks and dangers of such powerful substances, scientists have not ceased their investigations; nor should psychoanalysis dilute the substances of its human laboratory. Transference-love crystallizes in analytic space: it issues from a narcissistic constitution, moving through sexual attachment to a higher form of self-love. If managed well, it is the "mental freedom" of Freud's female patient, enabling her to live a more fully conscious life. Thus, transference-love is an ethical directive and has its equivalent in *ethos,* artistic models of character, which impress us, dazzle us and teach us how to live.

13 See also my discussion above, in "The Other's Desire."

Chapter 6: *St Mawr*: Character and Ethics

As rituals of desire, characters, such as Antigone and Hamlet, create, with some reservations, effects of the *uncanny.* Ideally, spectators, who are guided into a process of self-elevation, will undergo ambivalent, even conflicting, emotions, as they face the tragic hero, so like themselves, and yet as if imbued with superhuman strength. In the *Poetics*, in prescribing the conditions for the tragic effect, Aristotle emphasizes that the hero, like mimetic action itself, must imitate the ordinary individual – "the intermediate kind of personage" – whose misfortune is neither caused by a "fear-inspiring" situation nor by inherent vice, but "by some error of judgment"; the arousal of "human feeling in us," the evocation of pity and fear, occurs only through such generalized identification (e. g. Book 13: 238). However, this flaw of character, this *hamartia*, exceeds expectations, involving overpowering, complex, strange, *uncanny* forces, which resist attempts to explain them or know them. In Sophocles' tragedies, for instance, the heroes' self-destructive persistance defies ordinary understanding, but, as Lacan points out, attracts and scandalizes at the same time. Similarly, Shakespeare's Othello, Macbeth and Hamlet arouse our everyday pity, but disturb us also, in their overweening passion – in jealousy, ambition, filial love. I want to maintain that *cathartic* ambivalence is a defining feature of literary character, crystallized in the fates of tragic heroes, but prevalent for the aesthetic experience in general. Below, my discussion of D. H. Lawrence's novella, *St Mawr*, seeks to map this ambivalence within the parameters of the Freudian *uncanny.*

It will, however, be necessary to list several reservations, pertaining mostly to Freud's seminal paper, "The 'Uncanny'" (1919).[1] The major focus of the analysis is Hoffmann's tale "The Sand-Man," from the volume *Nachtstücken*, as Freud intimates in the beginning paragraph, one of the pioneering ventures of psychoanalysis into aesthetics. The subject of the 'uncanny,' Freud claims, is a neglected, "remote region" of art, as a conception, veiled with as much mystery as it is as a sensation (368). The purpose of the paper is to penetrate the sense of the *unheimliche*, which is, in popular parlance, associated with "all that is terrible – all that arouses dread and creeping horror" (368). To a large extent, Freud's disquisition pursues a scientific explanation in psychoanalysis for the Gothic ambience of the

1 "The Uncanny" (1919). *Collected Papers*. Vol 4. Trans. Joan Riviere (New York: Basic Books, 1959), 368–407.

conception. Thus, major analogies are made between psychology in general, neurosis and the fate of the major character in Hoffman's story, the student, Nathaniel. The uncanny effect, the sense of inexplicable horror, can be investigated as a property of the title figure, "The Sand-Man," who is both a childhood fantasy and an authentic psychological force. In Nathaniel's experience, this figure is introduced by his mother as a kind of folklore devil, who punishes naughty children by ripping out their eyes; also, in early childhood and during his student years, the Sand-Man appears as a real personality: he is the lawyer Coppelius, who is involved in the father's death, and he is an Italian optician, Guiseppe Coppola, whose pocket-telescope brings upon Nathaniel suffering, madness and eventually death. Freud wants to underline the proliferation of the title figure: "for the conclusion of the story makes it quite clear that Coppola the optician really is the lawyer Coppelius and thus also the Sand-Man" (383).

According to Freud, the psychoanalytic equivalent to the fictional concern with loss of the eyes is the fear of castration. As always, sensitive to charges from the anti-psychoanalytic camp, Freud makes clear that the relation between bodily organs is a substitutive one, and that the binding element is the "peculiarly violent and obscure emotion" evoked by the *threat* of castration, that is, by the threat of fragmentation, of a self-division (384). In my claim that an uncanny relationship exists between spectator, or reader, and literary character, it is this broader sense of castration I want to take advantage of, rather than the specific masculine anxiety about sexual organs. What underlies the "Sand-Man's" uncanny effect is not so much Nathaniel's penis *angst* as it is a "castration-complex," a network of repressed fears of separation from the mother. In the psychoanalytic Oedipal drama, and especially in Lacan's elaboration, castration, or the threat of castration, is not a real act, but a *symbolic* interference in the potentially incestuous union between infant and mother. The Father's demand is cultural articulation which positions the individual in the differential chain of significations. It is the inaugural event of psychological splitting: the Name-of-the-Father, an authorial voice, is assumed at the price of alienation.

It is this "castration-complex," this latent fear of separation, which is fundamental in the character-viewer relation. As he widens his discussion of the uncanny, Freud includes another of Hoffman's tales, "The Devil's Elixir" ("Elixire des Teufels"), which extends some of the themes in "The Sand-Man," but now more focused on the idea of a *double*, series of identical figures, who, for instance, communicate through telepathy, who "[possess] knowledge, feeling and experience in common with the other [...] in other words, [undergo] doubling, dividing and interchanging of the self" (387). Although in the general survey of Doubles – Der Doppelgänger – Freud ventures perhaps too far into Victorian anthropology, the psychoanalytic insights are truly fertile and firmly linked to important conclusions from the paper "On Narcissism" (1914).[2] As fathers and anti-fathers proliferated in "The Sand-Man," expressing the young man's conflicting attitude toward his father, his love for him as well as his wish to kill him, so the figure of the double in general is an ambivalent one, registering both the *heimliche* and the *unheimliche*, a sense of integrated unity and fear of its loss. Thus, the double in literature registers the narcissistic desire, which is jolted in the child's enounter with its image during the mirror phase; like this reflection in the mirror, the double is a kind of *lure*: initially, it traps the viewer into a vision of self-identity, whereas its truth is an alienated figure, an other. Herein lies the uncanniness of doubles: they are *ghosts* of narcissism, reflecting the same in another substance.

Fundamentally, literary characters are doubles, representations of ourselves in a foreign medium. Although I do not mean to imply that Gothic horror envelops every type of character, the principle of the uncanny as ambivalent emotion, narcissistic and fearful, can be said to define characters as an aesthetic group. In particular, what makes this uncanny function theoretically fruitful is its *ethical* potential. As Freud discussed at some length in his previous paper on narcissism, self-love is a double-edged condition: Ovid's Narcissus was trapped in pathological libido, preferring death to coming to terms with the "empty fullness" of his representation; on the other hand, post-analytic Narcissus, the self-observant individual, emerging from successful transference, implies elevated libido, love of self, which has transcended morbidity. In literary art, characters, as the nodes in discourse, where the self sees itself as if in a mirror, function as such points of elevation; they anchor ethical self-observation: they come into existence out of fear of the loss of eyes, transformed into the eye – the "I" – of aesthetic conscience. For the remainder of this section I will attempt to show how D. H. Lawrence's *St Mawr*, in many respects, allegorizes this ethical function, providing a blue-print for character, in general, as a special type of conscience.

Not a Gothic tale, by any stretch of the imagination, *St Mawr* nevertheless manifests a concern with the uncanny in a terrifying dimension. If "The Sand-Man" (as well as Freud's analysis) focuses on the ambivalent father-son bond as defining factor of the castration-complex, then Lawrence's narrative broadens this factor to an intense scrutiny of both individual and cultural loss. In his early book on

2 If there is a dated component in Freud's work, it is the sometimes culturally mechanistic view he takes of the "development of the ego"; for instance, in "The Uncanny," there is an equation between primary narcissism, the mind of a child, and "primitive man" – "the ancient Egyptians, who made images of the dead in lasting material" (387). Nevertheless, as many recent commentators have noted (e. g. Lacan, Juliet Mitchell), Freud is more apt than not to forget his cultural equation and to contradict himself with regard to the developmental state of the ego. In his papers on technique, for instance, he empahsizes memory as synchronic space, not chronology.

Lawrence, Frank Kermode contends that *St Mawr* is "one of the most achieved of his works" (111), because it manages to integrate in a powerful way doctrine and narrative, metaphysics and physicality, symbolism and realism. In my reading also, *integrity* is a fundamental value the novella advocates, as an aesthetics, as well as an ethical philosophy. Lawrence's observations in his essay on Nathaniel Hawthorne, in *Studies in Classical American Literature* (1923), that artistic union emerges from a reconcilation between "conscious understanding and [...] passional understanding" (139) could serve as the ideal aim *St Mawr* works toward.[3] In the story, confronted with threats of devastating losses, integrity is retrieved as a human value through the diverse experiences of the characters, whose libidos – their more or less passionate consciousness – are ritualized in the encounter with the title figure, the magnificent horse, St Mawr.

Often read as a social satire, Lawrence's novella, on the surface, portrays an insipid, even impotent, 1920s society, fuelled by dull pleasure-seekers, *laissez-faire* sympathizers, mean-spirited "humanitarians" and cowardly, ignoble men.[4] The satirical setting is primarily bourgeois, and quasi-aristocratic, Britain, urban and rural, although it is important to keep in mind that the greatest poser in the tale, Rico Carrington, alias Sir Henry, is a displaced Australian, fortune-hunter turned sham artist. On the other hand, the more imposing, even redeemable, individuals in the story are Americans, a mother-daughter couple, Mrs Witt and Lou Witt, born in Louisiana and stationed in Texas. The privileged satiric viewpoint is Mrs Witt's as she lashes out at English pettiness, class arrogance, pompous manners, as well as the claustrophobic smallness of the Shropshire landscape. Touching the very nerve of the narrative, Mrs Witt's most vicious remarks are reserved for the decline of maleness, especially pointed in her mockery of a young Shropshire gentleman, Fred Edwards, the archetypal "fair young man," with his "little brush moustache" and blue, shallow, sentimental eyes (59). However, the critique in *St Mawr* reaches deeper than social satire: the rule of the mediocre, sham art, weak men and shallow conversations over tepid tea-cups are merely symptoms of a deeper illness lying at the core of civilization itself. The possibility for the individual of extricating herself from this illness is *St Mawr*'s major concern.

The symptom of greatest decay is modern marriage. Although "some inscrutable bond" holds Lou and Rico together, their union lacks substance, operating only on willfulness and nerves, and a kind of sado-masochistic dynamic: "As soon as one felt strong, the other felt ill. As soon as the ill one recovered strength,

3 D. H. Lawrence. *Studies in Classical American Literature* (1932). (New York: Viking Press, 1969).

4 See, for instance, Richard Aldington's comments in the "Introduction" to the Penguin Books edition. D. H. Lawrence. *St Mawr and The Virgin and the Gipsy* (Penguin Books, 1950). All references to *St Mawr* are to the Penguin edition.

down went the one who had been well" (14). Mrs Witt's contempt for Rico as a son-in-law is implied by the narrative as a whole, which shows the couple drifting apart into chaste friendship, tolerating each other without sexual love. Especially, with Lou's purchase of St Mawr and during the family's late summer holidays in Shropshire, close to the Welsh border, does the sick premise of the marriage reveal itself. What had previously seemed satisfactory – the house in Westminter, the fashionable company they kept, the air of *joie de vivre*, of "having a good time," the Platonic amiability – shows itself for what it is: a substitute formation for deep discontent.

According to Freud, psycho-neurotic symptoms are both processes of libidinal replacement and *symbols*, special types of signifiers, firmly associated with an unconscious wish.[5] As the manifest content in dreams disguises as well as obliquely satifies a (dangerous) sexual wish, and articulates the unconscious in the rhetoric of displacements and condensations, so the symptom, more or less pahtological, stands for the *return of the repressed* in waking life. In other words, the symptom has a unique significance as it imbues the symbolic register with repressed desire to a greater extent than any other semantic unit. In *St Mawr*, the linguistic, or symbolic, associations with the repressed are particulary evident; even if, in the beginning, the narrative states that both Lou and Rico are "drifters," that neither of them "would [...] go down in any society" (14), the marriage is doomed as a certain kind of modern institution, practical, passionless, built on nerves and power of will. What returns in the story is the repressed sexual body. The general task of the narrative becomes the construction of a healthy signifier of the human body, a symbol powerful enough to regenerate the system of modern culture.

In my opinion, it is something of a misconception among several commentators on the tale to maintain that the horse, St Mawr, is a commonplace, Lawrentian symbol of primitive energy and pantheistic subversion, and, in general, as Graham Hough, puts it, "a short-hand notation for what Lawrence wants" (182).[6] Although the figure of the horse is without a doubt a central semantic unit in the narrative, it functions less as a straightforward "cure-all" than a complex libidinal ritual, engaging the major characters as well as readers in acts of psychological and spiritual cleansing. In a way similar to the cases of Hamlet and Antigone, St Mawr prompts a desire for honorable space where Being (*l'être*) itself is enhanced in healthy narcissism. As I discussed in the previous section, a similar transferential dynamic defines the relationship between analysand and analyst, on one hand, and

5 Sigmund Freud. *Inhibitions, Symbol and Anxiety* (1926). SE XX (London: Hogarth Press, 1959); also, see definition of "substitute-formation" in Jean Laplanche's and Jean-Bertrand Pontalis' *The Language of Psychoanalysis* (1973; 1988).

6 Graham Hough. *The Dark Sun* (London: Duckworth, 1956).

spectator/reader and artistic object, on the other. When the "acting out," as damaging defense strategy, in psychoanalysis has given way to wholesome remembering, it is, in Freud's account, as if a battle zone has been transformed into a field of play, where the illness is put on display, as a kind of a-temporal artifact, amenable to analysis and healing. In *St Mawr*, the figure of the horse assumes the role of analyst, at first triggering outbursts of discontent from Rico, Lou and Mrs Witt, and then successively staging this discontent as confrontation between character and psychic illness. As is the case with the Freudian analyst, the role of St Mawr changes from "objective correlative" to active intervention; also, as in psychoanalysis, *cure* is a co-operative effort: the healthy integrity established at the end is the common product of psychanalysis, individual consciousness, and the powerful strife toward aesthetic and ethical grace.

The malaise the major characters – Rico, Lou and Mrs Witt – suffer from, and by implication the cultures they are a part of, is to a large extent a symptom of repressed *vision*. As correlating object, the plaintive behavior the horse triggers in the characters reveals first of all their distorted sight, their inability to perceive the separateness of phenomena. It is by no means coincidental that Rico is presented as a fake artist, a portrait painter whose motivation for work is only social status, popularity and membership in prestigious academies, – that is, a build-up of a *career*, instead of dedication to vocation. In *The Dark Sun* (1956), Graham Hough considers Lou's gift of St Mawr to her husband a weakness of plot, since it falsifies Rico's personality and tastes, his preference for cultured company over sportmanship and horses (esp. 105). However, as is the case with every significant character in the story, Rico's relationship with the horse is more of a ritual, a symbolic trial, one could say, than a literal element of plot. Thus, Rico's authenticity, his art, his psychology, ethical constitution and his very maleness are put on trial during the collisions with St Mawr. In a way, the situation is similar to a transference in psychoanalysis approaching deadlock: despite the most intense efforts the analyst does not manage to lead the analysand out of a corrosive pattern of repetitions. Rico persists in *acting out* repression, resisting the therapeutic promise of the character of St Mawr.

Significantly, initial descriptions of Rico compare him to a horse, stressing his likeness to his adversary. In his depths, the career-oriented, slick Sir Henry harbours a wild animal, a force of terrible anger, which he holds at bay, "afraid of himself, once he let himself go" (18). In confrontations with others, his wife and mother-in-law, in particular, he must be on his guard not to "bite," not to "erupt like some suddenly wicked horse," set off by the repressed fuse of "life-long anger" (18). This wildness can be said to constitute Rico's uniqueness, his potential for development into an integrated individual, because it poses a threat to his conventional *gestalt*, to his vision of the world as bourgeoise heaven:

> this pretty-pretty picture of charming young wife and a delightful little home and a facinating success as a painter of fashionable, and at the same time 'great' portraits: with colour, wonderful colour, and at the same time, form, marvellous form. (18)

The term used to designate this view – *tableau vivant* – underscores the relation with Rico's artistic eye: from this eye issues a stale portrait, pretty and colorful, perhaps, but marked by the absence of passionate consciousness which truly creates.

Only in occasional spurts, primarily within scenes of collisions with St Mawr, does Rico's anger find expression. A climactic turning-point in the novella occurs during the Shropshire episode as Lou, Rico, Mrs Witt, the groom, Lewis, and their fashionable neighbours go horseback-riding into the countryside to survey ancient rock formations on the hilly terrain, close to the Welsh border, the Devil's Chair and the Needle's Eye. Woven densely with many of the major concerns in the narrative – marriage, maleness, Englishness, spirits of place, creation and destruction, repression and aggression – the episode culminates in Rico's temper tandrum and outbreak of rage against St Mawr, whom he is riding carelessly and clumsily. As the horse rebels against the rider, shying away and rearing his powerful legs, Rico's desperate maneuvers result in an accident, bringing man and horse to the ground in a kind of perverse embrace; the eruption of repressed anger underlines an uncanny relation: as they rest helplessly on the ground, attention is drawn to the similarites in their postures, their heads "straining," St Mawr's eyes "starting from the the naked lines of his nose," and Rico's eyes "also starting from his yellow-white face, among the heather" (74). However, the close connection established remains a dead-lock: analysand and analyst never move beyond pathological *acting out*, incapable of scrutinizing repression as the individual's potential.

It is significant that the disastrous visit to the Devil's Chair is framed by Lou's reflections, in the first place, on maleness and, in the second place, on evil. In a conversation with her mother on the differences and similarities between men and animals, Lou attempts to articulate her vision of healthy malehood, contrasting the *libido* of St Mawr – "that great burning life in him" – with the diminished erotic life of men, the suppressed, or half-dead animal in them – "a deadness in them" (56). Although Lou makes it clear that she does not wish for animality in itself, not for brute cave men, her image is of "a pure animal man [...] lovely as a deer or a leopard, burning like a flame fed straight from underneath" (57–8). This new man bears some resemblance to St Mawr's groom, Lewis, who, according to Lou, has a "real mind," "a good intuitive mind [...] knowing things without thinking them," as opposed to the so-called clever men, Rico and Dean Vyner, who are like "tame dogs," with the animal in them "gone queer and wrong" (57). What is at stake here in Lou's ruminations is disagreement about the meaning of enlightenment:

for modern men, all is seen and known; they are "really old women, knitting the same pattern over and over again" (56). On the other hand, Lou's imagined "pure animal man" cultivates what the narrative later refers to as "the third eye" (e. g. 62), authentic sight, which issues from the darkness of the psyche, and brings to light an exquisite *integrity*, where knowledge is creative becoming, not sterile fact.

I will return to Lou's meditation toward the end of this section. At this point, in relation to Rico's failed transference, I want to emphasize how, in some respects, this critique of maleness can function as the psychoanalytic premise for the "castration complex" and the dimension of the uncanny in the narrative. As Freud insisted in his discussion of Hoffman's "The Sand-Man," the preoccupation with the loss of eyes is a substitutive sign – a symptom – of castration anxiety as a *complex*, a complex network of repressed fears of separation from the mother and of the psychic split experienced during the mirror stage and the Oedipal trial. Individual subjects harbour an ambivalent attitude, fear as well as attraction, toward the father figure, because the authority of its Name entails both a suppression of narcissistic pleasure as well as necessary precondition for a healthy participation in culture. In literature, characters assume the positions of such authority figures – fathers, analysts, those, in Lacan's expression, "who are supposed to know" (e. g. *The Four Fundamental Concepts of Psycho-Analysis*, seminar 18). However, the knowledge literary figures wield is of a special kind and requires that receivers are willing to participate in a situation of dynamic transference, where the product of the interchange is scrutinized in the light of conscious, yet performative, love, resulting in a revised conception of self. In Lawrence's novella, St Mawr functions as a node of analytic authority for both the characters and for readers; in fact, the test for, for instance, Rico, Lou and Mrs Witt consists, to a great extent, in whether they develop into *characters*, that is, into versions of St Mawr, as ethical observers, powerful enough to engage the audience in an act of productive transference. Rico, of course, fails: despite the uncanny effect, the horse has on him, Rico does not move beyond stale vision. In the Devil-Chair episode, the conquest of the common-place mind, of "slow, so dead, so deadly dull" men (56), over post-transferential integrity results, at this point in the narrative, in an attitude of despair, expressed powerfully through Lou's meditation upon Evil.

In an interesting paper, "Symbolic Seeing: Lawrence and Heraclitus," Mara Kalnins maintains that contrary to critical opinion about Lawrence's pessimism in his later writing, a new direction in his thought is discernible in the last poems, essays and especially in his final book, *Apocalypse* (1931), a synthetic, affirmative view of the human condition, influenced by organic pre-Socratic philosophy.[7]

7 Mara Kalnins. "Symbolic Seeing: Lawrence and Heraclitus." *D. H. Lawrence: Centenary Essays*, ed. Mara Kalnins (Bristol: Bristol Classical Press, 1986), 173–190.

Although *St Mawr* is written six years earlier than *Apocalypse*, it can be considered to contain in a preliminary and exploratory manner Lawrence's assertions in the later work about symbolic seeing, poetic intelligence and the harmony of consciousness. Whereas the concern with revealing a common source for perception and with integrating intuition and reason, emotion and intellect, religious impulse and scientific mind is articulated directly in the last essays, in *St Mawr* dual consciousness is dramatized in the encounter between the individual subject and cultural registers. In the Devil-Chair scene, after the collapse of the relation between Rico and St Mawr, the hope for a harmonic flow between man, woman, nature and culture collapses also, so that this episode seems to telescope the pessimistic attitude and dark satiric tone of the novella. Having witnessed Rico's accident in a kind of horrified stupor, and then spotting a dead adder in the grass, "its head crushed, its gold-and-yellow back still glittering dully," reminiscent of the deadlocked posture of man and animal, Lou is shocked into "a vision of evil," sensing it no longer as "a mere negation of good," but as an existential condition, as "dark-grey waves" which envelope "the whole world [...] in one great flood" (76). This vision resembles a reversed bibilical revelation: it is as if the kingdom of Hell has replaced Heaven or Milton's Satan has succeeded in his demonic sedition.

Nevertheless, instead of reading this crucial passage as a statement of *St Mawr's* disillusioned ideology, it is more fruitful for an understanding of the novella to examine it as a stage in the education, or training, of *poetic vision*, undertaken chiefly through Lou's experiences. As Kalnins stresses, throughout his work, and most straightforwardly in the later essays, Lawrence tended to discuss the purpose of human existence in terms of artistic creation, advocating *self-creation* as the highest value: "[the aim of one's life was] to create oneself [...] create that work of art, the living man, achieve that piece of supreme art, a man's life."[8] This potential in every human individual for being in full control over existence, for making and re-making the self, as artists and scientists enrich the objective world, expands along with the cultivation of, what Lawrence called, "poetic intelligence," the synthetic consciousness of imagination and reason. In order to retrieve this, to extend intelligence, individuals must engage in "the essential act of attention, the essential poetic and vital act [...] [which] "'discovers' a new world within the known world." [9] Unlike Rico and Mrs Witt, who fail to extend an integrated intelligence, Lou achieves a supreme act of self-discovery through cultivation of attention. As I will attempt to show,

8 From *The Letters of D.H. Lawrence*, ed. J.T. Boulton et al (Cambridge: Cambridge University Press, 1979–85), i-iii; ii; quoted in Kalnis 186.

9 *Phoenix*, ed. E. D. MacDonald (London: Heineman, 1936), 261;255; quoted in Kalnins 186.

after the Devil's-Chair episode, she moves beyond the evil surface of culture to new ethical space.

At this point in the narrative, Lou's negative epiphany is thus primarily prompted by her inability to retrieve, what she refers to as "quick thinking," the expanded intelligence, which sees with the inner eye. Also, it is important to emphasize that this realization is not limited to the failure of manhood but involves the moral bankruptcy of Western culture, in the England of post-war Europe, in particular. The small group of young people on the trip, Rico and the Shropshire neighbours, Flora and Elsie Manby, and the "sentimental" Frederick Edwards, exemplify a diseased civilization, where natural passion is repressed and the social apparatus is characterized by a sado-masochistic dynamic: society is like a game ("it's good sport" 77) whose rules do not articulate the nature of the people involved, but cover up a sick intercourse of aggression and humiliation. The key word Lou ascribes to this sort of behaviour is "undermine": the social principle is to keep up smooth and slick appearances, "keep the surface easy, and have a good time"; at the same time, "*let us undermine one another. There is nothing to believe in, so let us undermine everything*" (Lawrence's italics; 77). This Judas mentality, this cold immorality at work in Western culture, supports the horrors of war and the political movements built up them:

> The evil! The mysterious potency of evil. She could see it all the time, in individuals, in society, in the press. There it was in socialism and bolshevism: the same evil. But bolshevism made a mess of the outside of life, so turn it down. Try fascism.
>
> Fascism would keep the surface of life intact, and carry on the undermining business all the better. All the better sport. Never draw blood. Keep the haemorrahge internal, invisible. (78)

Here, the attitude and the arguments resemble those Freud expressed in his work on the super-ego and, in particular, in *Civilization and its Discontent* (1930), a near contemporary with Lawrence's novella. According to Freud, repression in culture can be traced back to the formation of individual identity during the Oedipal drama, and most specifically to the strengthening of the superego, as the threatening father, or father figure, is internalized in his most authoritative role of *obstacle* to desire.[10] Both Lawrence and Freud take pains to show that an unhealthy, and an unhappy, psychological constitution issues from an overly rigid identification with a prohibitive superego; as we saw was the case with Rico, suppressed aggression leads to destructive behavior; the strongest critique in *Civilization and its Discontent* is against forms of authority which obtain "mastery over [...] aggression by weakening and disarming it and by setting up an agency with [the individual] to watch over it like a garrison in a conquered city" (79).

10 See my discussion above in chapter two.

Thus, sickness is a kind of morality, slavish self-denial and fearful submission to a castrating conscience.

It turns out, though, that *St Mawr* harbours a more hopeful view of the human predicament than Freud's book, and can even be seen to extend the cautious optimism expressed in the latter's final paragraph (added in 1931): the task now lies with the individual subject to resist the oppressive gaze of culture and to explore within himself a "third eye," a new source of self-observation and, as a consequence, of transvalued morality. Aware of the threat Hilter posed to the world, of the beginning of an arms race and of the violent exploitation of nature, carried on in the name of progress, Freud ventured to glimpse the victory of Eros over death: "and now it is to be expected that the other of the two 'Heavenly Powers,' eternal Eros, will make an effort to assert himself in the struggle with his equally immortal adversary. But who can foresee with what success and with what result?" (104). After the epiphany of evil, Lou decides to "depart from the mass," to seek in solitude a clean space, away from the Western eye, which is part and parcel of this evil, censoring the "passionate principle of creative being" and ignoring "the natural good" (79). Even if this quest will be carried out in chastity, its aim is Eros, the kind of love discovered in a new sight.

Lou's activities here are extremely important because eventually she takes on, for the readers of the novella, the function that St Mawr had for her; in other words, on the highest level of development, Lou can be compared to the analysand, who has experienced successful transference and who has been enriched in a new mode of perception. In the first part of the novella, St Mawr is, in a sense, Lou's *eye*: through the encounter with the otherness of his existence, she re-discovers herself; on the other hand, in the New Mexican scenes in the latter half, the horse recedes into the background and Lou takes on his role. She becomes our eyes; through her, we may come to " 'discover' a new world within the known world."

What enlightenment thus means in *St Mawr* is primarily a retrieval of *thingness*, an education in vision, which guides the eye (and the "I") toward the separate being of phenomena in the world. After Lou's insight into evil and the beginning of her break-up with Rico, evidences gather as to the incurable corruption of Europe, and the only alternative for mother and daughter is a return to America, to "the great bare spaces of Texas" (81). As if to subtly underscore that the deadlock Lou witnessed on the individual level persists in culture, the narrative tarries in the English setting, depicting mother and daughter engaged in the dull roundabouts of tea-drinking and "undermining" chit-chats. A revealing episode occurs in Lou's Westminister house just before the trip to America: a former acquaintance, the Irish painter and socialite, Laura Riding, pays a visit, and a curious dialogue takes place between the two women about family, London, the groom, Lewis, Rico, St Mawr, beauty and wickedness. As so often in *St Mawr*, characters are introduced through remarks on the peculiarites of their *eyes*, and in this case we are told of Laura's "sharp eyes [that] would see everything" (128). Not only is the young woman's sight literally quick and all-encompassing – she had spotted her friend at Paddington station the day before – but she appears to harbour the powers of the inner eye, the expanded poetic intelligence, Lou craves and quests for. During their conversation, it appears as if Laura has also discovered the "real within," – the evil machination of society, the failure of manhood, the need to cultivate chastity, the uncanny force of St Mawr. As her light gossip turns into more serious talk, Laura notes how "monstrous" people as a rule tend to be, especially the showy riders in Hyde Park, and her hypocritical relatives in Ireland, and how an individualist must refuse to "play their game" (129). Also, her painter's gaze highlight Lewis' "peculiar eyes" and his "psychic powers" (130). During a visit to St Mawr at the Mews, Laura "eye[s] him round with those gimlet, sharp eyes of hers," overcome by his extraordinary beauty, as if he indeed suggested for her, as for Lou, the essence of uncanny separateness.

The apparent sympathy between Lou's and Laura's vision, however, clinches the evidence against Western mentality. Cleverly, the narrative brings into concentrated relief the hopelessness of the situation: in spite of the munificience of the young woman's response, of the fact that her perception is that of a talented artist, intuitive, quick, sharp and attentive, she does not truly see, not advance much beyond Rico's programmed views. As Freud discussed, in successful transference, illness is disentangled from distorted time and space, and resituated in a clean site, as an artifact, amenable to interpretation, analysis and cure. Nothing changes in Laura's encounter with St Mawr; all she sees is ego-centered, bourgeois reality, the narcissistic version of self. Unlike Lou, who only "care[s] about [...] the horse himself, his real nature," the *thing* in itself, Lou perceives only an object, "his perfect *bone*" (Lawrence's emphasis), his "show qualitites" and his breeding (131). The meeting with Laura enhances the urgency of Lou's quest for re-vision and strengthens her own role in the narrative as enlightened guide.

As the earlier Shropshire episode, the last scene of the novella's "American section," the evocation of the New Mexican landscape, of the situation of Lou's ranch and its history, is framed by, on one hand, Lou's reflections on maleness and, on the other hand, by a version of evil, now crystallized in Mrs Witt's cynical perspective. For both mother and daughter, the American excursion proves to be disillusionary, summed up in Mrs Witt's "grim silence," as she watches her self-satisfied, tipsy and silly compatriots touring Havana, for them only "this city of sunshine and alcohol" (135). Although at first their native ground, Texas, impresses them with its fabulous vistas and cheerful inhabitants, so self-reliant, despite their apparent naivity, the end result is again Lou's French phrase, "plus ça change, plus c'est la même chose": nothing has changed, in the sense that if

American culture is less decadent than English culture, then it is just as superficial, harbouring "no meaning in anything save the obvious, the blatantly obvious" (137). What is particulary disconcerting is that instead of the insidious, undermining social games of the English, Yankees operate on "film psychology." In Lou's estimation, the cowboys surrounding her at the Texas ranch are caricatures, hollow men, who define themselves through the gaze of film heroes, or of the colourful book-jackets of chain-store fiction. They exemplify what can, in Lacanian terms, be described as a purely imaginary *Gestalt*: they are trapped in misrecognition, in the mirror-stage fantasy of self-identity through an external source of reflection.[11]

In the course of this American episode of *St Mawr*, one narrative thread unravels the break-up of the mother/daughter couple, the two women's different reactions to the several dead-ends they run into – dead-ends of community, of individual psychology, of existential meaning. On one of their many escape routes, at a fiesta in Santa Fé, Mrs. Witt, again reminded of the shallow tourist, even among the native artists of New Mexico, at first, in a rather paradoxical gesture, appears to both reject the show, by locking herself up in silence in the hotel room, and to conform to it, by reading bad novels, the sort of productions the cowboys, the tourists and the general populace indulge in and imitate; however, perhaps not surprisingly, toward the end of the novella, Mrs Witt has become at one with a point of view of cynicism, which, as we shall see, harkens back to the social Evil Lou elaborated on in the Shropshire episode. Indeed, *St Mawr* ends with an extremely cynical remark: after Lou's rapturous speech about her love of the ranch and her sense of mission in the American wilderness, Mrs Witt closes the novella with a comment on the cheapness of the place, in dollars, compared with "all there is to it," in Lou's description. Cynicism is heaped on cynicism in this last sentence, as the mother mentions the trivial detail of the name of the ranch – Las Chivas – as an ingredient in the exquisite wholeness her daughter had praised: "Then I call it cheap, considering all there is to it: even the name" (165).

In contrast to her mother, despite her disillusionment, Lou moves beyond the proliferations of dead-ends to a place which promises to nurture her newfound knowledge, discovered in the transferential relationship with St Mawr, and held in fragile suspension through episodes leading to the journey to the New Mexican ranch. In order to alert the reader to the *messianic* pull of Lou's character in this last scene of the novella, its frame echoes the construction of the Shropshire episode, co-mingling feminist critique with moral renuciation. Together with this frame, what is repeated with an intensified force is the critique of Western vision and a redoubled attempt to lift the repression of the "third eye," post-transferen-

11 See especially Lacan's essay, "The mirror stage as formative of the function of the I as revealed in psychoanalytic experience" (1949).

tial intelligence, which binds together in an integral knot the "natural good" of the individual and "the passionate principle" in general of all creative being. At the risk of minimizing other significant elements of this last splendid scene of *St Mawr*, what I want primarily to emphasize is the elevation of the *authentic* work of art, brought to its fullness here and channelled to its audience through its most concentrated element – character; in the process, the act of seeing New Mexican space becomes invested with the mystic power of St Mawr, with, as Lou wants to maintain, sacredness: the object is rescued from its mechanical relation to the observer and encircled with numinosity, with the *aura* of the thing.

In one of the most insightful statements in the twentieth century about the relationship between the work of art, capitalistic (re)production and mass culture – "The Work of Art in the Age of Mechanical Reproduction" (1936) – Walter Benjamin traces the socio-historical path of what he calls "the decay of the aura" in the medium of modern perception (224).[12] For Benjamin, the film industry and the techniques of film crystallize the dissolution of aesthetic authenticity, of the unique, essential work of art, situated in a specfic place and time, "testimony to the history it has experienced" (223). Because film both constructs and caters to the desire of the masses for *proximity*, for the utilitarian closeness of objects, former modes of perception, grounded first in cult and ritual, and then in secularized traditions, bound to a sense of the art work as unapproachable, – in antiquity, divine, in romanticism, sublime – undergo a kind of democratic re-organization: " 'a sense of the universal equality of all things' " replaces uniqueness, and transitoriness, associated with the now reproducible object, replaces the "substantive duration" of the historical thing (225).

In Benjamin's estimation the concept of *aura*, both with regard to cultural artifacts and to aspects of nature, is the effect of "a distance, however close it may be." Thus, a majestic landscape on a summer afternoon may cast its spell on the observer, not because he or she feels at home in it, but because of its difference, the other-wordly dimension it seems to exist in (224–5). A similar connection is established between the beholder and the work of art, in its circumstance of unique creation: in the tragic theater, for instance, it is the existential gulf between aesthetic patterns and the mundane reality of the audience which effects the latter's recognition, identification and cathartic purification; the framing of a painting by Turner or Matisse also underlines the different realm within which art resides, in some respects approximate to the viewer's knowledge, but *distant* nontheless; authentic art is imbued with an enlightened grace ordinary life can only catch glimpses of, but can neither utilize nor consume. Benjamin emphasizes how the

12 Walter Benjamin. "The Work of Art in the Age of Mechanical Reproduction." *Illuminations* (1955). Trans. Harry Zohn (Fontanta, 1970), 219–253.

fact that the art work is embedded within a tradition enhances its uniqueness, its otherness and hence its aura. Thus, a modern producion of *Antigone*, adapted perhaps to suggest the radical youth culture of the European community, retains its artistic power, to large extent, as the uppermost layer in the palimpsest of tragic tradition; no matter how alike Antigone is to the wilful political teenager, the unique grace of her character, created in ancient Greece and a testimony to that historic circumstance, overrides any tendency to turn tragedy into filmic show. At the start of tradition, art was ritual, and although the secularization of modern culture dismisses the religious associations, "it is significant that the existence of the work of art with reference to its aura is never entirely separated from its ritual function" (225–6).[13] I want to claim that in the final scenes in *St Mawr*, D. H. Lawrence, acutely aware of the cultural issues Benjamin raises, aims at retrieving the "ritual function" of the art work amid the rule of mass consumerism, capitalistic reification and film psychology.

In the previous discussion of Hamlet and Antigone, as well as of Freud's conceptions of castration, I emphasized the function of literary character as a *ritual of desire*, as a node of identification in artistic discourse, imbued with both the authority of the analyst – "the subject supposed to know" – and the force of the uncanny – the *unheimliche*, the home that is not a home. Thus, literary character as the binding, charismatic activity in the art work is doubly effective: in the sense that it harbours the uncanny, it challenges its audience to confront self-division, both the desire for the double and the fact of castration, as separation from archaic unity; in the second place, in the role of analyst, character is a potential catalyst for the viewer's, or reader's, transformation, for the triggering of "the third eye," a superior mode of perception, which weaves together in an integral whole the human individual and the environment, life and death, beauty and decay, knowledge and mystery. In *St Mawr*, this is a mode of perception infinitely superior to the other "eyes," that have dominated the narrative – Mrs. Witt's alternating satire and cynicim, Rico's stale conventionality, Laura's reifying vision, the superficial seeing of both the English and Americans, their blocked imaginary *Gestalt*, breeding cultures of empty utilitarianism and frenzied consumption.

One of the more startling aspects of the "New Mexican" scene in *St Mawr* is how the attempt to re-create the landscape is not only rendered in narrative and in description, but also in terms of *a painting*, thus almost turning the metaphorical frame around it – Lou's reflection on the decline of manhood and Mrs. Witt's cynical remarks – into a literal border between viewer and work of art. As Lou, together with Phoenix, one of the grooms who had followed mother and daughter

13 The specific examples here are mine, but the underlying ideas are for the most part a recapitulation of Benjamin's, esp. 225–6.

from England to America, arrives at the gate of the ranch, it is as if her perception, already inspired, sharpened and composite, is superseded by a cosmic perspective, which, throughout the scene, controls and encompasses its many-layered composition. What this cosmic eye aims at highlighting in its brilliant creative strokes is precisely their *aura*, in Benjamin's definition: "we define the aura […] as the unique phenomenon of distance, however close it may be" (224). At first, the ranch appears in its mundane situation as a place where men and women have struggled to make a living, added buildings, plumbed for water, cleared land, planted alfalfa, beans and potatoes, raised goats, fought off vermin. It is a view resembling a nineteenth-century landscape painting, filled with exquisite details, attending to high and low with the same rapt attention: the running water in the bath-house, the five hundred Angora goats, the swarming pack rats, the Rocky Mountains, the "motionless desert," the previous owners – a schoolmaster, a trader, a woman from New England. Thus, at first glance, the composition underscores aspects of the *heimliche*, how this ranch and its surroundings could be the ordinary man's and woman's home; it could perhaps in miniature represent natural selection, humanity's struggle for survivial in the wilderness.

However, the drift of this portrayal is not to fine-tune elements of the known, but to effect a disorientation, an impression of the distance between the human viewer and the work of art. The apparent realistic levelling of the nineteenth-century landscape turns out to be a strange – an *uncanny* – equality, where the individual is brought to an encounter not with every-day reality, nor with Darwinian nature, but with, as Lou formulates it, the sacred spirit of a place. As was the case with St Mawr himself, place here functions as a kind of testing-ground for the characters, as the authoritative figure of analyst who challenges them to re-organize their perception and to retrieve the unknown from the known. In my previous discussion of transference, and especially of Freud's essays, "Remembering, Repeating and Working-Through" and "Observations on Transference Love," it became clear that cure consisted to a large extent of the patient's comprehension of her illness as artifact, as a pliable object, created in the extraordianty time-space unit of the psychoanalytic encounter. In particular, the female analysand, who falls in love during treatment, lays bare the force of human desire in all forms of interactions with the objective world. As Freud points out, if, in such a situation, love is managed expertly, the artifact of the woman's illness can be infused with erotic power, manipulated now in the service of her self-knowledge. Thus, love in transference, operating both on authentic pscyhological principle and as misrecognition, the narcissistic blindness in identification, develops into the creative core of a patient's conscious life: what is established is "mental freedom," a healthy integrity, as opposed to the previous pathological narcissistic whole.

In *St Mawr*, a similar dynamic is at issue in the perception of the aura of place. Although they react in different ways, both Lou herself and her predecessor, the trader's wife, the woman from New England, perceive this sanctity with the kind of passionate awareness Lawrence advocates in his comments on Nathaniel Hawthorne. In some respects, though, the case of the New England woman can be compared with that of Rico's in the first half of the novella, in that transference for both leads to dead-lock, not to emancipation. In fact, Lou's forerunner loves the place with the kind of misguided intensity Freud's patient directed at her analyst, and it is extremely significant that her eye creates the most magnificent vista of the scene: as in transference-love, there is the revelation of the subject's archaic desire for the object.

Even if, in her interactions with the spirit of place, the New England woman does not achieve Lou's state of healthy rapture, the logic of her love, its psychologically authentic component, perceives beauty in its *ne plus ultra* realm, in its absolute, distant splendor. Several times attention is drawn to how the woman's connection to the place is different from the men's, that, in fact, she loves with "a sort of sex passion, [which intensifies] her ego, making her full of violence and of blind female energy" (152). At first, in tune with the realistic depiction, she nurtures her domesticity, her sense of the ranch as her home, building a fence around the cabins, digging a kitchen garden, preparing the basin of "a pool with a tiny fountain jet" (152). A mundane, feminine role, however, does not satisfy her, and she becomes as if possessed by "blind frenzy, [...] an intoxication," thrillingly subdued by the strange beauty around her. In her perception, the landscape – the circle of pine-trees, on the downslope from the alfalfa field, the mountains, the canyon and the desert itself – is featured almost like an intangible, demonic lover: the guardian pine-tree, shadowing her cabin, attracts her through a powerful, albeit perverse libido, "a passionless, non-phallic column, rising in the shadows of the pre-sexual world" (152); the group of trees on the downslope exude the same kind of otherworldy sensuality, "hedg[ing] one in with the aroma and the power and the slight horror of the pre-sexual primeaval world" (153); the distant splendor of the desert, the infinite vistas of mountains, mesas, and valleys, the play of light and color, overwhelms the observer with inhuman desire, as if earthly paradise is "a question simply of living through the eyes, into the *distance*" (155; Lawrence's emphasis).

The reactions of the New England woman are reminiscent of Lou's earlier confrontation with St Mawr, the way he seemed both demonic and a harbinger of "another darker, more spacious, more dangerous, more splendid world than ours" (34). Like Freud's analysand, both women fall in love with this splendid world and want only to enter it and merge with it. However, the reason for their different vocations in the novella is that the older woman reaches a stalemate in transferential relation, unable to fuse the aesthetic aura with "the near things" (155), that is unable to re-organize her knowledge of herself through her experience of encounter with absolute otherness. On the other hand, Lou arrives at the ranch in a post-transferential state, searching only for the appropriate place – that extraordinary time-space unit – to match her newly created artifact, her discovery of herself as a differential, yet integral, individual. Whereas, in the beginning the New England woman experiences only rapt intoxication, and does not pay heed to the perverse destructiveness, the *inhuman* libido of the place, Lou is immediately aware that the holiness she perceives, "the latent fire of the vast landscape," is not only the pure flame of desirable beauty, not only Eros, but fed also with Thanatos, the drive for death:

> she realized that the latent fire of the vast landscape struggled under a great weight of dirt-like inertia. She had to mind the dirt, most carefully and vividly avoid it and keep it away from her, here in this place that at last seemed sacred to her. (147)

Toward the end of one of her most influential feminist essays, "Women's Time" (1979: 1981), Julia Kristeva speculates that with the demise of both religion and radical politics, *aesthetic practices* will increasingly infiltrate discourse and authorize the emergence of new identity –

> the process [that] could be summarized as an *interiorization of the founding separation of the socio-symbolic contract*, as an introduction of its cutting edge into the very interior of every identity whether subjective, sexual, ideological, or so forth. (Kristeva's emphasis; 210)[14]

Having presented a critical overview of the women's movement – the first-generation benefactors from the earliest suffragettes, accepting the political windfalls and conforming to the Symbolic, the second generation rejecting separation and the father's Law, in a spirit of destructive anarchy – Kristeva outlines contemporary signifying space where difference itself, as the authentic effect of the trauma of castration, is interiorized, and in that very process, on the level of "personal and sexual identity," disrupting the nucleus of that identity itself (209). In her estimation, aesthetic practices will replace religious discourse, in particular, in the articulation of "a new ethics," a code of the *singularity* of the human individual, who assumes accountability for both restriction – guilt and the nurture of conscience – and *jouissance* – pleasure without neurosis (210–211).

As *St Mawr* draws to a close, it becomes increasingly clear, that Lou's functions as a filter for a Kristevan type of aesthetic practice, a language permeated with the aura of distance, searching for the proper medium, within which to utter the new sense of human singularity. As if to exemplify Kristeva's discus-

14 Julia Kristeva. "Women's Time." *The Kristeva Reader*, ed Toril Moi. Trans. Alice Jardine and Harry Blake (New York: Columbia University Press, 1986), 188–211.

sion of a conflict between an older and younger generation of women, in the last pages of the novella, mother and daughter argue about and, in fact, break up over the issues of religion, malehood and marriage, and the meaning of personal identity. At this point, Mrs.Witt brings only her cynical eye to the ranch, viewing it with a combination of indifference and satire, calling its beauty "a cold egg" (162), castigating her daughter for being "conventy," like many women of her own generation, who retreated into religion, in the "imbecile" hope for *"something bigger"* (164), and finally, uttering clichés only, about the need to keep up illusions of self-identity, in other words, the need to conform to things as they are. In contradistinction to the mother's cynically dry and empty speech, Lou's last peroration is an inspired articulation of her experience of otherness, and, in many ways, concentrates in individual practice, in the language of literature, what the entire New Mexican episode attempted aesthetically to deliver: aura glimpsed as distance, through the desiring eye, is transported into language, the words of the singular human being. Thus, as Lou, and the little New England woman before her, confronting, in rapture, the absolute beauty of the land, the audience of *St Mawr* encounters Lou's strange words, retaining an ordinary sense, but also as if created by an otherworldy mentality, poetic, rhythmical, primeaval and ecstatic.

To continue the parallel with Kristeva's outline, Lou's last speech exemplifies the start, the exploratory beginning, of post-transferential mentality, of the mind and language, which confronts castration, and accepts both the restrictions of conscience and the possiblity of exquisite joy. Perhaps to a greater extent than any other segment of *St Mawr*, Lou's speech is the *uncanny* in text; in response to her mother's clichèd version of the unmarried woman, "spend[ing] your life keeping to yourself," Lou's words come pouring out of her, as if the "wild spirit" she talks of is already in control of the very substance of her thoughts:

> Do you think I mind! There's something else for me, mother. There's something else even that loves me and wants me. I can't tell you what it is. It's a spirit. And it's here, on this ranch. It's here, in this landscape. It's something more real to me than men are, and it soothes me, and it holds me up. I don't know what it is, definitely. It's something wild, that will hurt me sometimes and will wear me down sometimes. I know it. But it's something big, bigger than men, bigger than people, bigger than religion. It's something to do with wild America. And it's something to do with me. (165).

The epistemological ambiguity here, the way Lou both knows and does not know the spirt of the wilderness, is consistent with dominant features of the uncanny, as discussed by Freud, and as experienced through characters in fiction and art. At this final stage in *St Mawr*, what is brought home to readers is their own homelessness, their eternal separation from the archaic unity they once knew in narcissistic bliss. What rescues this insight from being a dead-lock, is the possibility to go beyond it, to experience a different kind of bliss, *jouissance*, without pathology or neurotic violence. In this final moment, the dynamics of identity, we have witnessed in the novella, are concentrated, so that the sanctity of the title words – *St Mawr* – beckons us and invites us to partake of their power.

Part II: Case Studies

Chapter 7: The Psychological Tradition in Old English Poetry

In literature, characters bind audiences to fictions through their *effects* rather than through their immediate presence. Even if familiar names – Antigone, David Copperfield, Emma Bovary, Dorian Gray – evoke personalities, they operate less as mimetic elements than as containers for a work's semiotic activity. As Roland Barthes contends in *S/Z*, individuality in fiction is a penumbra of the Proper Name: "[as] soon as a Name exists (even a pronoun) to flow toward and fasten onto, the semes become predicates, inductors of truth, and the Name becomes a subject" (191). Semantic fragments with special reference to the human sphere, to psychology, economics, aesthetics, morality, and so on, invite readers to participate in a kind of character-making, resulting in a coherent paradigm, consonant both with the verbal texture and with the ideological context of reading. In Balzac's novella, *Sarrasine*, the eponymous protagonist is a sum of nominations: *turbulence*, *independence*, *excess*, *femininity*, *impiety*, *ugliness*; similarly, Flaubert's Emma Bovary can be said to be a product of adjectives such as *romantic*, *vain*, *narcissistic*, *unfaithful*, *self-indulgent*, *shallow* and *stupid*.[1] The selection of traits is, of course, neither a natural nor a neutral process; the important point to be made, however, is that the semiotic view of character foregrounds not only its *writtenness*, its embeddedness in the textual fabric, but its extra-textual dimension as well, its specialized dependence on human meaning.

The human endeavor involved in character construction affects textuality as such. In my view, psychoanalytic theory, developed in the first part of this book, manages most comprehensively to account for the "character-effect," because of its focus on text as libidinal scenario. Characters are first and foremost psychoanalytic structures because their very existence depends upon desiring subjects – upon narcissistic, Oedipal and post-transferential subjects. Thus, the nomination of traits, semiotics is interested in, implies more than the realistic paradigm; what is at stake is the Lacanian understanding of "the naming of desire," the successful outcome of transferential relation. As Lacan has shown in the essay on *Hamlet*, restitution for individual and community occurs only when the protagonist regains confidence in the healing powers of ritual: at the end of the play, Hamlet offers his

1 These adjectives and nouns may or may not appear in the text; the point is that the reader is involved in the construction of identity, most oftern projecting his or hers ideologically saturated vision.

own "wounded name" as public spectacle, as, in fact, the character in the drama of his life, imbued with cathartic powers.[2] Although the processes of construction are slightly different, Antigone, in Sophocles' tragedy, also ritualizes desire, dazzling the audience with the beauty of brave and relentless transgression. In chapter six above, "*St Mawr*: Character and Ethics," I aimed to illustrate how the magnetism of characer is an aspect of its *aura*, how in the quest for a home in the work of art, the viewer, or reader, is guided into an experience of her own misrecognition; it is an experience similar to that of transference in pscyhoanalysis: cure consists of the analysand's discovery that the past is a construction, not natural history. Instead of a pathological dependence on desire, the analysand disentangles herself from it and, in the voice of individualized mastery, *names* it.

The complex effects of character construction through transference are the driving forces of all works of fiction. In distinction from previous chapters, which focus on archetypal models, this section is concerned with mapping a particular terrain, the aesthetic and cultural consequences of the "work of character" in a group of early medieval poems, often referred to as the Old English elegies. It may be claimed a disadvantage to this type of analysis that the critical consensus about these texts, and about traditional texts in general, minimizes the psychological features I have drawn attention to in the previous discussion. The prevalent estimation is that while capable of producing works of considerable sophistication, the oral-performative cultures which fostered Anglo-Saxon poetry lack introspective resources and a sense of psychological depth. Many contemporary scholars in the area of orality and oral literature draw on Walter J. Ong's seminal study – *Orality and Literacy: The Technologizing of the Word* (1982) – in order to characterize the Anglo-Saxon mind-set as dependent on mnemonics, type-cast information, formulas and repetition, as opposed to chirographic interiority (69–70).[3] Alvin A. Lee, for instance, discusses the heroic tradition in *Beowulf* in these terms, emphasizing the "mnemonic servicability" of "heavy" or "outsize" figures and the ubiquity of stark contrasts of character, so that experience may be organized "in some sort of permanently memorable form" (12).[4] In primary orality, in particular, where there exists no technology of writing to relieve the mind of the burden of tradition, the images of individuals in epics, narratives or song necessarily function as carriers of cultural memory, not as selves, equipped with unique, complex psychological lives.

2 In *The English Elegy*, Peter Sacks discusses the last scene in *Hamlet* from a Lacanian point of view (86).

3 Walter J. Ong. *Orality and Literacy: The Technologizing of the Word* (London: Methuen, 1982).

4 Alvin A. Lee. *Gold-Hall and Earth-Dragon: Beowulf as Metaphor* (Toronto: University of Toronto Press, 1998).

Contrary to critical preoccupation with the inner lives of novelistic characters, recent readers of Old English verse have to a large extent concentrated on anthropological context and especially on the transitions within orality from primary oral culture to situations of textual productions.[5] Whereas the tendency had been to work either with oral "literature," often employing tools developed by classical oral-formulaic theory, *or* with the literate text, the fully Christianized and authored text, for instance, medieval scholars such as A. N. Doane, John Foley, Carol Braun Pasternack and Katherine O'Brien O'Keeffe bring into purview the event of *transcription* itself, that is, the mental shifts and changes accompanying the "technologizing of the word."[6] In his introduction to the influential anthology, *Vox intexta: Orality and Textuality in the Middle Ages* (1991), A.N. Doane notes the paradoxical nature of the "oral text," an intricate composite, which modern readers encounter as chirographic reality, whereas a medieval audience interpreted it as a kind of sound script, as "traces of an existence that was normally vocalized" (xii). The early medieval text, as well as the ancient Greek one, incorporate "echo[s] of the voice" as well as the multiform conditions of the original performance: "the phonics, the breathings, the stalls, the timbre, the gestures, and the communal surroundings" (xiii). Agreeing with Doane's points about the *complexity* of such transitional documents, John Foley, in an article from the same volume, proposes that scholars abandon "the Great Divide model," the binary opposition between oral and literary aspects, and instead aim at "evolving a theory [...] that explains the complex, hybrid nature of the work" (37).[7] The world from which tradition emerges, whether in the form of Old English poetry or the Homeric epic, is a border-line world, infused with change on all levels of experience, mental, psychological, communal and national. Contrary to the notion that traditional societies were fixed and conservative, these critics, and many other medieval specialists, emphasize their transitional nature, their *liminality*, in fact, the spaces of renewal they stake out amid the decay of old forms.[8]

Of particular interest in relation to my investigation of character and psychoanalysis in Old English poetry is Carol Braun Pasternack's discussion of the hybrid oral text in *The Textuality of Old English Poetry* (1995). Following to a

5 See the influential studies, *Vox intexta: Orality and Textuality in the Middle Ages*, eds. A. N. Doane and Carol Braun Pasternack (Madison: The University of Wisconsin Press, 1991); Carol Braun Pasternack. *The Textuality of Old English Poetry* (Cambridge: University of Cambridge Press, 1995).

6 These scholars generally desire to loosen the stranglehold Milman Parry's and Albert Lord's "Oral Theory" has had upon traditional literature, past and present.

7 John Miles Foley. "Orality, Textuality, and Interpretation," 34–45.

8 The anthology in question, *Vox intexta*, is representatiave of the most enlightened work in this area; I will have occasion to examine *liminality* more fully in relation to Old English poetry.

large extent Katherine O'Brien O'Keeffe's *Visible Song*, a ground-breaking study of Old English manuscripts, especially of the physical appearance of verse – style, structure and techniques of copying – Pasternack's starting point is the conception of *transition*.[9] One of O'Keeffe's conclusions is that the nature of Old English verse is "collaborative," that is, that the poems modern readers confront are the end products of oral composition and the creative interferences of scribes, who transmit the heritage. What is more, although the "writtenness" of the poetry to some extent suggests a chirographic culture and mind-set, the texts' traditional format dominates their understanding; a different kind of knowledge is required from the reader of Old English verse than from the reader of a fully written text: "early readers of Old English verse read by applying oral techniques for the reception of a message to the decoding of a written text" (21; quoted by Pasternack 5). Thus, hybrid textuality undermines a hermeneutics of authorship, intentionality and the unique creative act.

Pasternack develops the critique of the authored text, which she maintains continues to dominate Anglo-Saxon literary studies. Even critics who build upon O'Keefe's theory about collaborative production find it diffucult to accept scribes as creators of poems, since they did not "remak[e] the text in any significant way" but merely interpolated more or less skillfully (Pasternack 7). Douglas Moffat, for instance, worries that the modern critic will be unable to analyze scribal intervention, as so few copies were made of Old English manuscripts, and he can only envision calling scribes "quasi-poets" if their artistry matches that of the original author (Moffat 814; quoted by Pasternack 7).[10] Similarly, Michael Lapidge is willing to accept the fluidity of the verse and the fact of scribal manipulation but cannot resist viewing such aspects as false layers which modern editors and critics must penetrate to reach the original ground of the single author's conception (8).[11] Pasternack perceptively remarks upon this critical desire for individuality and originality: the dictate is that "one person functions as author and creates a determinate text, which we call a 'poem,' and others who alter that text trample on that territory, which the critic must restore before he or she can analyse it properly" (7).

An important step in the dismantling of the author fixation is a sustained critical attention upon the hybrid text itself, upon what Pasternack calls the *inscribed* text, in order to underline its combination of vocality and writing. Unlike oral per-

9 Katherine O'Brien O'Keeffe. *Visible Song: Transitional Literacy in Old English Verse*. (Cambridge: Cambridge University Press, 1990).

10 Douglas Moffat. "Anglo-Saxon Scribes and Old English Verse." *Speculum* 67 (1992), 805–27.

11 Pasternack discusses Michael Lapidge's "Textual Criticism and the Literature of Anglo-Saxon England." *Bulletin of the John Rylands University Library of Manchester* 73 (1991), 17–45.

formance itself, with the figure of the poet orchestrating meaning to some extent, his voice and gestures connecting elements of the traditional material, guiding the audience into a perception of closure, the written composition is a fluid phenomenon, open to new interpretations and new constructions. Paradoxically, despite its traditionality, inscribed verse invites innovative responses from subsequent poets, scribes, performers and readers. In order to support this notion of openness, Pasternack relies on the work done by scholars of orality on compositional techniques, on the stylistic studies of Katherine O'Brien O'Keeffe and Malcolm Parkes (*Pause and Effect*) and on the general visual layout of Old English manuscript verse.[12] For instance, Albert B. Lord's description of "themes" as key organizational units in Serbo-Croatian song informs Pasternack's "movement," a broad structural category, embodying a patterned verse sequence, which expresses a particular sense or message.[13] In Old English verse, these movements function similarly to oral composition, "communicating [...] via the ear rather than the eye," recognizable as aural patterns or as semantic cues (Pasternack 11). Readers accustomed to oral performance would tend to voice the written words and, as Pasternack says, "hear these cues," grasp the meaning of a passage almost like listeners to music sense rhythmic varieties, dissonance and harmonies (11).

As transitional discourse, combining oral voice with the new medium of writing, inscribed verse implies both a traditional and an innovative reader. Unlike fictions in chirographic cultures, shaped by the consciousness of single authors, Old English poetry is not limited by modern ideas of authorship, but is generated and received by multiple subjects (esp. 17–9). One of Pasternack's strongest points is that because of their genesis in tradition poems such as *The Dream of the Rood*, *The Wanderer* and *The Seafarer* lack a subjective center and that, in spite of their first-person speakers, they do not fictionalize authorial experience (14). In "Hearing from Books: The Rise of Fictionality in Old English Poetry," Ursula Schaefer makes a similar claim about the early poet-figure, that instead of the sustained speech of a single mentality, the "I" here functions as transitional device, to ease the shift from oral to written communication.[14] Schaefer further defines this function as "conditional fictionality," as the incipient stage in literary history of fully embodied narrators (Schaefer 125). Formulaic language and conventional themes as well as the anonymity of the verse are, of course, further evidence of its communality and of the absence of single authority. Instead of constituting deter-

12 Malcolm Parkes. *Pause and Effect: An Introduction to the History of Punctuation in the West* (Berkely: University of California Press, 1993).13

13 See Lord's seminal account of oral composition, *The Singer of Tales* (Cambridge: Harvard University Press, 1960).

14 Ursula Schaefer. "Hearing from Books: The Rise of Fictionality in Old English Poetry," in *Vox intexta*, 117–136.

minate form, Old English poetry can be considered multiform and polyphonic, each version a "new creation" in the traditional lineage, the speech of "successive 'authors,' (singers, reciters, scribes)" (Zumthor *Toward a Medieval Poetics* 47; quoted by Pasternack 17).[15] Thus, readers of inscribed verse contend with an idea of "implied tradition," non-originary, flexible and open to improvization, not with the "implied author" of novelistic fiction (17).

The *complex* notion of tradition which Pasternack's study promotes is a welcome contribution to Anglo-Saxon scholarship. Nevertheless, it seems to me a reductive move to establish such a firm and organic connection between authorship and subjectivity, to the point of exclusion of the latter in Old English verse. Although the case against the author fixation is a necessary historicizing gesture, it does not follow that tradition is without subjective consciousness, friction-free in the encounter between oral poet or performer and formulaic speech. In fact, in her discussion of readers, Pasternack acknowledges the possibility of individualized interpretations, where text is not only decoded but creatively appropriated (21–26). Since manuscript verse implies no authors, neither in their physicality nor in autobiographical traces such as the embodied "I" or signature, the active reader assumes a role similar to that of oral poet or scribe, producing a new version, "colour[ing] the words with [his or her] own gestures and inflections, introducing [his or her] own subjectivity" (22). Because of its structural layout in manuscript, with discrete movements orchestrated without apparent narrative connection, and because of its vocality, with echoes from a diversity of oral performances, inscribed verse is more amenable to readers' participation than either written fictions or performed tradition. This type of verse exists in multiple layers of connotations, guiding different readers into different rehearsals of individual and communal experience; again, despite the oral-traditional residue, the hermeneutic situation remains open, and what is more, highly subjective, even idiosyncratic: "each reading will attempt resolution in a different way, perhaps including readings which refuse any resolution" (25).

It is interesting to note that in oulining this reading dynamic, Pasternack draws to some extent upon Lacanian psychoanalysis, especially the view that desire in language, and in interpretation, is metonymic, that is, that the human drive for resolution is constituted by a lack, bound to remain "unsatisfied, impossible, misconstrued (*méconnu*)."[16] In the encounter with the hybrid, enigmatic text, the

15 Paul Zumthor. *Toward a Medieval Poetics*. Trans. P. Bennett (Minneapolis: University of Minnesota Press, 1992).

16 Quoted by Pasternack from Lacan's *Four Fundamental Concepts of Psycho-Analysis* (154; 24). Gillian R. Overing also uses a Lacanian model of interpretation in *Language, Sign and Gender in Beowulf* (Carbondale: Southern Illinois University Press, 1990).

reading mind strives to supply syntactic connections between seemingly disconnected units, and during the quest for unity and closure is inundated in memory with cross-references and intertextual echoes. If then, as Pasternack claims, the active reader's product is on a par with the products of poets, performers and scribes, the latter, transmitted in manuscript form, and available to a modern audience, must operate on similar libidinal principles, displaying the vicissitudes of desire in the metonymic rush of language. Of particular relevance is the condition of the *transitional* text, the oral-traditional situation inscribed in the words of the emerging culture of writing. Just as the stylistic surfaces, critics such as Carol Pasternack, Malcolm Parkes and Katherine O'Brien O'Keeffe investigate, the psychology of poetic composition undergoes transitional strain, as the oral mindset, formulaic, didactic and communal, submits to the reflective, interiorizing mode, fostered by the technique of writing. As will become clearer in my analysis of the major Old English elegies – *The Wanderer, The Seafarer, The Wife's Lament* and *Deor* – the libidinal work in the poetry, the drive toward *new* subjectivity, is directly related to the intermediate cultural situation, to the interface between traditional and reflective mentality, between the language of convention and the language of the inner life. Because they display a heightened sense of psychological conflict and cultural change, these poems belong to a generic group, which privileges *character* to an extent not found in other poems from the Anglo-Saxon period. My next section is an examination of this generic space.

a. Alterior Space

Within Anglo-Saxon scholarship, there have been persistent attempts to establish a common critical principle for a group of seemingly specialized poems from *The Exeter Book*, an anthologized manuscript, compiled toward the end of the tenth century. Current parlance generally agrees that seven or eight of those poems belong to the genre of elegy, although that designation is to a large extent based on readers' intuition rather than on precise definitions of Old English elegiac form. As T. A. Shippey maintains in *Old English Verse* (1972), the selection of *The Wanderer, The Seafarer, Deor, Wulf and Eadwacer, The Wife's Lament, The Husband's Message* and *The Ruin* as "elegies" displays a certain "arbitrariness which might usefully be challenged" (54), if only for the reason that in the manuscript, they are not placed next to each other, but converge on a variety of verse – religious narrative, maxims, riddles, dialogue and allegory.[17] Although there have

17 T. A. Shippey. *Old English Verse* (London: Hutchinson, 1972). In her critical edition of the elegies, Klinck includes this group together with *The Riming Poem* and *Res-*

been several attempts to formally link adjacent poems, for instance, *Wulf and Eadwacer* to the following group of riddles (1–59), *The Wanderer* and *The Seafarer* to the gnomic lists and hortatory verse they border on, the opinion persists that the above poems share a specialized discourse, strangely elusive, perhaps, but urgent, intense, and permeated with lyrical passion.[18]

Perhaps the underlying baffling factor is the elegies' shared emotional texture rather than common themes, incidents and ideologies. Readers of the poems often note that that they evoke a "melancholy mood," that they are filled with "longing" and that they brood upon the losses and sorrows of earthly existence. Unlike the mostly doctrinaire religious verse and the traditionalist epic narrative, poems such as *The Wanderer*, *The Wife's Lament* and *Wulf and Eadwacer* appear similar to the personal utterance in romantic or modern lyric, secretive, ambiguous and psychologically exploratory. In one of the finest considerations of the elegies' consolatory function, T.A. Shippey remarks on their individualized immediacy and on the combination within them of autobiographical trial and stoic wisdom. The two seemingly disjunctive parts of *The Wanderer* and *The Seafarer*, for instance, should be understood as poetic *process*, as mental development, rather than structural unit, moving from the individual's experience to the acquisition and communication of mature insight (58–9). Similarly, in his edition of *The Wife's Lament*, *The Husband's Message* and *The Ruin* (1961), R. F. Leslie emphasizes the "immediate situation" of the poems and their expression of "a particular experience" (2).[19] Leslie further notes that the powerful appeal these poems make even to a modern audience is a result of their strange mixture of opaqueness and urgency: "any increase in the purely informative content would weaken their dramatic impact" (2). Implying an akin preference for the elegies' enigmatic ambience, S. A. J. Bradley, especially, in his commentary on *Wulf and Eadwacer*, notes the contrast between its carefully crafted form and its obscure content; nevertheless, without an adequate understanding of the poems' background or of the relationships it delineates, readers are invariably jolted by its intense articulation of "of an apparently adulterous sexual passion" (365).[20] Erotic passion and sensuous perception are often seen as features not only of *Wulf and Eadwacer*, but of *The Wife's Lament* and *The Seafarer* as well: even if enigmas persist, *The Wife's Lament* is

ignation. I agree with Klinck about the inclusion of these two. Anne L. Klinck. *The Old English Elegies: A Critical Edition and Genre Study* (Montreal: McGill-Queen's University Press, 1992).

18 Shippey sees the elegies as mixed forms, intimately related to the wisdom literature *The Exeter Book* exemplifies (53–79).

19 R. F. Leslie, ed. *Three Old English Elegies* (Manchester: Manchester University Press, 1961).

20 S. A. J. Bradley, ed. *Anglo-Saxon Poetry* (Everyman, 1995).

generally considered to be a "female" elegy, uttering the frustrated passion of a woman separated from her lover; although a love affair is not at the center of *The Seafarer*, the conflict within the mind of the speaker is often interpreted in psychological terms, as, for instance, M. R. Godden does in the claim that "two centers of consciousness" exist in the poem, "an inner, urgent, passionate personality and a more reluctant self which controls action" (306–7).[21]

Although the critical commentary here, and in many more instances, on the Old English elegies shows a high regard for their complex interiority and an awareness of their insistent emotional appeal, there have no attempts been made to move such considerations to the center of a discursive, or generic, definition. In the designation of the group of poems as elegies, the reference point seems to be the intuitive grasp of their psychological dynamic, of their interest in personal experience, and in the life of mind and emotion, but is most often left on the periphery of critical evaluation, as if such interests are merely incidental embellishments. The criterion for Old English elegy has remained vague, as Shippey states it, "inoffensive if unhelpful" (53), implying both indistinct literary and mental categories such as "mood," "tone," "melancholy," "passion," and "longing."[22] In other words, there is within the criticism an appreciation of a specialized psychological component in certain poems in the Anglo-Saxon literary corpus, without there at the same time being any kind of theoretical justification for such appreciation. Although Anne L. Klinck, in the latest, fine and comprehensive edition, writes extensively about the poems' generic environment, she resists offering a precise definition, preferring a broad paradigm to discursive specificity. Building upon historical information about origin and influences as well as upon structuralist genre theory, Klinck concludes with an operable, but as Shippey would say, "inoffensive" category, drawn in large features of common themes, mood, tone and vocabulary: "Old English elegy is a discourse arising from a powerful sense of absence, of separation from what is desired, expressed through characteristic words and themes, and shaping itself by echo and leitmotiv into a poem that moves from disquiet to some kind of acceptance" (1992: 246).

21 M. R. Godden. "Anglo-Saxons on the Mind." *Old English Literature: Critical Essays*, ed. R. M: Liuzza (New Haven: Yale University Press, 2002), 284–314. Furthermore, note this typical observation by R. F: Leslie on *The Wife's Lament*: "It is one of the few poems in Old English literature dealing with a relationship between a man and a woman, and the only comprehensive study of a woman's thought and feelings" (3); Shari Horner's recent "Enclosed Subjects: *The Wife's Lament* and the Culture of Early Medieval Monasticism" examines this situation from the perspective of gender theory, in *Old English Literature* (2002: 381–391).

22 My point is not to criticize the use of such terms but merely to underline their lack of a theoretical base.

In a comparison with the *Exeter* riddles' psychological vocabulary, Klinck does contend that the elegies explore questions of identity, and that words often express personal intention as well as states of mind, "wretchedness, sorrow, dreariness and woe, or longing and expectation, or absent brightness and joy" (227). As is the tendency in the critical commentary, however, this type of observation does not assume a central role, but operates on the surface of analysis, pointing to general poetic similarities. In my view, if the fleeting, often peripheral concern with the interiorized life of the elegiac group is moved to the center of formal and hermeneutic concerns, it will become clear that a psychological dynamic is neither one feature among many nor an incidental embellishment, but the *constituent,* the discursive life itself, of Old English elegy. Within the transitional cultural context, especially within the technological shift from oral tradition to chirographic mindset, the poems' interest in autobiographical experience – as Shippey suggests, in the process from trial to wisdom – merits a systematic investigation, not only to establish a generic criterion, but to elucidate their function for a contemporary audience. In a study of the Anglo-Saxon interest in mind and soul, M. R. Godden, following the anthropologist, Rodney Needham, draws attention to the intimate connection between a culture's psychological ideas and their linguistic expression, pointing, in particular, to the vernacular writers' rich and varied use of words for inner experience.[23] Similarly, in the following discussion, I want to uderline the centrality of the speaking subject in Old English verse, the conflations and conflicts between experience and utterance, loss and speech act, the imaginary and the symbolic. As I suggested above, poems such as *The Wanderer*, *The Seafarer* and *The Wife's Lament* share a space of alienation within Anglo-Saxon culture, because within them, there is a drive toward *new* subjectivity, propelled by the shift from oral-traditional exteriority to the inwardness of written text. What these, and other poems within the elegiac group, work toward constructing is *character*, a psychoanalytic structure composed of the libidinal interchanges between an audience and its cultural language in a time of transition. What the most successful of these poems effect is consolatory troping in the shape of the human, a mirror of alterity, reflecting loss, mourning, crisis and restitution in creative self-knowledge. Undoubtedly, their powerful impact, even on an audience of the twenty-first century, is due to this *character effect*, the language still saturated with the desire to renew it.

Because the Old English elegies share a concern with loss and separation, as well as an attitude of, and education in, resignation, there have been several speculations within the scholarship about their originary function as poems of

23 Godden focuses on words for mind and soul in *The Seafarer and the Wanderer* (esp. 298–304).

consolation. In 1919, Levin Schücking, for instance, proposed that the elegies belonged to the Germanic tradition of *Totenklagelied* or funeral lament, which, on the evidence of scenes from *Beowulf* and the Norse *Poetic Edda*, operated as both private and communal rites.[24] Although no such laments have survived, three funeral scenes in *Beowulf* depict a probable context for them: at the end of the narrative, while preparations are underway for the dead king's pyre, the mourners "sadly complain[ing] of their distress" (3171), the spotlight is upon a kind of elegist, a Geatish woman, "with hair bound up, [who] sorrowfully sang a sad lament for Beowulf, saying that she dreaded evil days of mourning, filled with great slaughter, terror of the enemy, harm and captivity" (3150–3155);[25] a similar glimpse of a grieving woman is offered in the so-called Finn episode, recounted by Hroþgar's minstrel during a feast, of Hildeburh at her brother's and son's funeral pyre, lamenting and uttering "mournful dirges" ("Ides gnornode, / geomrode giddum," 1117b-18a); again, the third setting is Beowulf's wake, the twelve warriors, riding around the fire, expressing their sorrow and eulogizing their king:

> They composed an elegy (eulogy?) about the hero, praising his nobility and extolling his deeds of valor, for it is meet that a man should praise his lord in words and love him in his heart when his spirit leaves his body. (3171–77)

Clearly, there is some differentiation of function here, as the female reciters bemoan first and foremost their personal loss, whereas the warriors articulate a more ceremonialized, communal sense of grief. Indeed, Schücking postulates a role within Anglo-Saxon culture for lamenting women such as Hildeburh and the Geatish woman, whose *sorhleoð* (song of sorrow) at funerals expressed their own bereavement of a loved one, and further contends that the Old English elegies, as well as the Lament of the Last Survivor and the Father's Lament in *Beowulf* (2247–66 and 2444–59), are its direct descendants. Such specific roles for female mourners is attested to in ancient Greek culture, where, according to Margaret Alexiou, "praise of the dead was traditionally assigned to the men, lamentation to the women" (*The Ritual Lament in Greek Tradition* 248).[26]

In *The Old English Elegies*, Anne L. Klinck conveys her scepticism about such an origin for the poems in ritual lament, since their subject matter is rarely the type of specific bereavement narrated in the Finn espisode (230–31). As is

---

24 Levin L. Shücking. "Das angelsächische Elegiendichtung." *Englische Studien* 73 (1938), 1–31.

25 The translation here is Constance B. Hieatt's, from *Beowulf and Other Old English Poems* (Bantam Books, 1967).

26 Margaret Alexiou. *The Ritual Lament in Greek Tradition* (Cambridge: Cambridge University Press, 1974).

evident from the definition of the genre, cited above, Klinck focuses on broad existential issues as hallmark of the poems, rather than individual life crisis (246). Even though the "love poems," *The Wife's Lament*, *The Husband's Message* and *Wulf and Eadwacer* mourn the absence of a loved one, their situations lack the concreteness of funeral elegy, which evokes names, families and biographical details. The object of loss the elegiac group as a whole elaborates is, according to Klinck, a heterogeneous one, comprising questions of life and death and of communal identity, often formulated in traditional themes of alienation, exile, pligrimage, transcience and the search for stability (e. g. 225–6). Klinck does, however, admit the possiblity of an oral-performative environment as the initial setting of the poems, where "narration by a real person of his own woes would have developed into a genre of lament by fictitious persons, which we see in some of the elegies" (230). As is the case with Germanic ritual lament, such songs have not survived, but a few images from chronicles and epic do support the hypothesis: for instance, in *Histories of the (Vandal) Wars*, Procopius gives an account of Gelimer, sixth-century king of the Vandals in North Africa, who, on the brink of defeat in war, composes a song on his misfortune, to the accompaniment of a harp (ca. 550; Klinck 262–3); in *Beowulf*, not only minstrels are memorializers, but Hroþgar himself, king of the Scyldings, plays a mournful tune, "told a tale both true and sad [...] would begin to mourn his youth and strength in battle: his heart was stirred as the aged man remembered many things" (2108–2117).[27] Interestingly, what is being suggested here is the vocal setting of the orality-literacy shift, investigated by contemporary medieval scholars such as A.N. Doane and John Foley; Klink's concluding comment is pertinent within that discussion:

> it seems reasonable to infer that some of the traditional language of the elegies is descended from a genre of autobiographical oral poems, originally chanted to the harp, which narrated the speaker's misfortunes, rather than from a genre of death-poems, specifically. (231)

Thus, in spite of her scepticism about Schücking's theory of a genre of *Totenklagelied*, Klinck retains an autobigraphical origin for the poetry, indicating its mixture of private grief, traditional language and existential themes. An earlier, perceptive examination of such a conjunction is T. A. Shippey's chapter on the elegies in *Old English Verse*, "Wisdom and Experience: The Old English Elegies" (1972: 53–79). Shippey's major concern is in mapping the implications of the chapter title, how personal knowledge of hardships in the world is transformed in the grind of poetic work into a moral vocabulary and a communal purpose. Poems such as *The Wanderer*, *The Seafarer* and *The Wife's Lament* are in sense "consolation poems," not because they resolve crisis in a didactic manner, but

27 The examples are Klinck's. It is interesting to note that here Beowulf himself, at his homecoming, is recounting recent history, the exploits in the land of the Danes.

because they offer as cure "poetry itself, the expression and formalisation of raw experience" (56). The journey motif so prevalent in the verse foregrounds this pattern whereby the spontanaeous outburst of calamatiy is worked through and gradually controlled within the trajectory of public speech. As so many Old English "elegiac" words, *sið* – journey – operates on various levels, encompassing literal travel, as well as "the path of life," the individual's travails and exploits across the spectrum of experience. In fact, the typical name for the Old English poet is *Widsith*, the "widely travelled" *or* "widely experienced," the one whose autobiographical trial is translated into traditional lore (55). In Anglo-Saxon culture, and by implication in oral cultures, poetry carries social and moral authority difficult to envision for a modern audience. Shippey's discussion makes clear, however, that despite the anonymity of the verse and its immersion within formula and tradition, it is born in a state of crisis, within the individual psyche. Thus, *consolation* is to some extent the effect of character, as I have formulated that concept in psychoanalytic terms: the Old English poems work through pain and loss in order to re-frame their experience in the language of community. The image of self most of them construct embodies that conjunction: the public speech of interiority.

Elaborating upon the journey motif, Shippey makes the important point that in terms of structure, the elegies should be viewed as a process, not as a predetermined unit (56). *The Wanderer*, *The Seafarer* and *Deor*, in particular, are dualistic structures, beginning with an individualized speaker, undergoing woe, and concluding with a stoic voice, uttering philosophical advice, Christian doctrine or hortatory warnings. From a modern point of view, it may be claimed that the shifts from private to public mode in *The Wanderer* and *The Seafarer* are abrupt and unconvincing, and both have had a rather long critical history of dispute about stylistic coherence and assignment of voices.[28] On the other hand, Shippey concentrates on the poems' cultural setting, especially on their "performative" milieu, which "demands a certain involvement from reader or listener, and repays him not with abstract knowledge but with the strenghtening of mind, an awareness of human limitations and of the way they are conquered" (60). This observation matches recent work in both historical orality and, in general, anthropological studies of performance in contemporary oral-traditional societies. As transitional literature, caught in the shift between an oral mode of communication to written interiority, Anglo-Saxon texts bear the mark of both ritualistic experience and subjective psychology. Below, I will begin by outlining some of the features of ritual, and then turn to a psychoanalytic / Lacanian investigation.

28 My discussion of individual poems will include some of that critical history,

With modernity, Walter Benjamin tells us in "The Storyteller," "experience has fallen in value" (1936; 1970: 84).[29] Whereas in the past, and especially within the economic and social structure of the Middle Ages, where communities were characterized by the interpenetration of classes, work and trade, oral storytelling communicated both local traditions and individual knowledge, after the catastrophe of the First World War, "men returned from the battlefield grown silent – not richer but poorer in communicable experience" (84). Tactical warfare, and the mass destruction it effected, crystallized the tendency in modern development to valorize impersonal power and minimize the value of the individual citizen. Paradoxically, in modern society, despite the expansion of democratic institutions and their underpinning of liberal ideology, the vital connection between individual agency and communal structure has dissolved, leaving only a gap between private persons, on one hand, and a faceless system of authority, on the other. Concomitantly, cultural forms which represent a collective heritage and interest lose ground, in the first place, for the novel, the representative of the solipsistic psyche, and in the second place, for the mass media, with its promotion of *information*, our "new form of communication" (88).[30] In the modern setting, readers and listeners no longer depend on the educational process of the professional storyteller, who leads them from experience into wisdom, but consume transient, and often sensational, news reports, which are "already [...] shot through with explanation," leaving no room for individual involvement in the eventfulness of the world (89).

In Benjamin's overview, the oral story operates like the individual's navel-string to the centers of community. Performance of stories resembles ritualistic rehearsals, where self-forgetful listeners, often at work themselves, weaving and spinning, in the almost sacred space of community, are assimilated into local memory, through the teller's extraordinary craft (91). The ritualistic character of oral stories becomes particularly apparent in what Benjamin calls "an orientation toward practical interests," in their usefulness to an audience (86). For instance, the storytellers, who are Benjamin's main concern, Leskov, Gotthelf and Hebel, offer concrete advice about science, agriculture and "the perils of gas light." However, instruction is not necessarily in the form of overt statements, but more often embedded in narrative as "a moral," or traditional lore, achieved, Benjamin makes clear, with the harmonizing of individual lives with the tellers' encyclopedic knowledge of history, tradition and communal identity. The storyteller is "a man who has counsel for his readers," not in the form of didacticism, but as open-ended

29 Walter Benjamin. "The Storyteller." *Iluminations*. Trans. Harry Zohn (Fontanta, 1970), 83–109.

30 Of course, literary history is presented in elliptical form in "The Storyteller," since Benjamin's concern is to draw up the broad differences between the social function of stories in modern times and in the past.

propositions about psychology, morality and social practice. Unlike explicit doctrine, "counsel [is] woven into the fabric of real life"; it is the trajectory the art of storytelling follows in attaining "the epic side of truth, wisdom" (87). According to Benjamin, no modern structures encompass this trajectory, because narrative no longer belongs to "the realm of living speech," but has become a private affair, exemplified by the silent contract between the self-enclosed world of the novel and a solitary reader (87; 100).

Benjamin's concerns in "The Storyteller" touch on those in the contemporaneous "The Work of Art in the Age of Mechanical Reproduction" (1936; 1970), although the latter is less interested in verbal art than in the difference between the authentic artistic image and modes of reproduction, in particular, photography and film. In the discussion of *St Mawr* above, I noted with regard to character construction, Benjamin's conception of *aura*, as an almost sanctified quality of a work of art, emanating from its uniqueness and from its unbridgable distance from real life (esp. 224–5). In the final scene of Lawrence's novella, the figure of Lou assumes uncanny authority because, in a post-transferential state, she transcends archaic desire to a superior epistemological level, where the aura of aesthetic practice is re-confirmed and activiated in the service of future identities. Even if, on the surface, Old English poetry appears as if descended from a different genetic heritage than the modernist novella, my investigation links the narrative desire of both forms for a language – images, metphors, symbols – to contain a sense of *new* subjectivity, instigated by transitional, even traumatic, cultural events. My point is neither to claim an anachronistic precociousness for the Anglo-Saxon subject, nor to flatten out historical differences in the construction of character, but to underline the recurrence of a mental *structure*, which transects cultural differences and historical bounds. In the early medieval period, a ritualized situation, the oral-traditional perfomance, underpins the work toward a new cognitive structure in the elegies, and the conflation between this setting and their images and tropes must be taken into account as a parameter of interpretation. Following Benjamin, it is possible to claim that this poetry, being so close to the source of art in ritual, is imbued with spontaneous aura, that it constitutes, in fact, to some extent a form of cult, producing quasi-religious symbols, venerated on a par with Christian icons (Benjamin esp. 227–8). While I do not subscribe to a view of Old English poetry as a product of cult activity, I want to highlight its links to ritual, not least for the fact, that modern aesthetic practice, such as Lawrence's *St Mawr* recreates a ritualistic condition for narrative through character; it is, of course, a condition modified by historical and cultural difference, but articulated by a an unalterable structure, transecting time and place.

The Old English poems I will primarily be concerned with – *The Wanderer*, *The Seafarer*, *Resignation*, *The Wife's Lament* and *Deor* – share a processual form, intimately related to ritual processes in pre-industrial societies, and exceptionally receptive to the communal integration of individuals, Benjamin foregrounds as the hallmark of oral storytelling. As I noted above, three of these poems are dualistic discourses, clearly marked by diachronic development from dejected lamentation to stoic acceptance: the speaker in *The Wanderer* moves from vivid memory of the past, through its hallucinatory recall, to a detached view of human destiny; *The Seafarer's* persona is a voyager, literally and metaphorically, crossing the ocean as a religious exile – *peregrinus pro amore dei* – at first expressing ambivalent desire for the heavenly home, but, in the latter half of the poem, embracing and explicating Christian doctrine; in *Deor* dualistic composition is reversed, since the speaker's identity does not emerge until with the last strophe, a Boethian figure, who has achieved consolation through the memorializing of, as well as sympathy with, the misfortunes of others. Although *Resignation* and *The Wife's Lament* are less obviously process poems, their speakers are transitional figures, the former a compunctious sinner, questing for God, the latter a forlorn woman, uttering her tale of woe, in solitary confinement, in an almost surrealistic version of no-man's-land, between the nostalgic past and a fearful future. In broad outline, all the elegies are generated by an individual's life crisis – sudden loss of kin and community, professional calamity, betrayal in love, psychological and religious conversion. In all cases, the elegiac speakers find themselves in a state of separation, which ushers them into an exploration of their cognitive, psychological and existential situation; this intermediacy in the poetry is best characterized as *liminality*, as the emergence of new forms and entities among the dissolution and decay of the old; liminal exploration "is through a limbo of statuslessness," out of which the enlightened individual is reconciled with a new modality of social order (Turner 1969: 97).[31] On the model of pre-industrial ritual, the Old English elegies are forms of *rite de passage* – rites of passage – performative poems, which guide listeners into a rehearsal and celebration of their common humanity, in the face of psychological and cultural crisis.

In Victor Turner's *The Ritual Process* (1969), a pioneering account of ritual practices and ritual symbolism among Central African cultures, the need to perform ritual is shown to coincide with conflict and crisis in the life of community (11–12). One of the performances Turner describes in detail is a rite of the Ndembu tribe, of northwestern Zambia, called *Isoma*, connected specifically with women, and also referred to as "ritual of procreation" (11). The Ndembu stage these rites as curative processes for wives, who suffer from conditions of barrenness, thought to be caused by offended ancestral spirits or "shades." In terms of social relations and

31 Victor Turner. *The Ritual Process: Structure and Anti-structure*. (Ithaca: Cornell University Press, 1977).

loyalties, the situation is quite complex, since the tribe practices matrilineal descent together with virilocal marriage, that is, it assigns children's lineage through the mother, but residence through the father. Consequently, upon marriage, a woman tends to stay on in her husband's village and raises her children there; because the matrikin, residing in another village, demand the loyality of mother and child, this arrangement turns out to be a contradictory one, frequently erupting in quarrels within the family, and even in divorce. Within the belief system of the Ndembu, infertility is the curse of the matrilineal shades, the "deceased mother or mother's mother or some other senior deceased matrilineal kinswoman," whom the victim has ignored in favor of new life in her husband's community. Ritual cure consists in bringing the barren woman back into the fold of her maternal lineage: she is guided into remembrance of past allegiances and imbued with a "sharpened awareness of where her and her children's loyalites lie" (13). The ultimate goal of this process is then not only "magical," that is, restoration of fertility through an appeasement of the dead, but also therapeutic, the harmonizing of individual identity with the demands of the group.

The semantics of the name – *Isoma* – indicate that restitution occurs on a variety of levels, physical, psychological, conjugal and social. The individual who is caught in *Isoma* has "slip[ped] out of place or fastening," a state of dislocation, referring to a woman's miscarriages, as well as to her distorted indentity, caused by an imbalance in social relations (15–16). Like elegiac structure, the curative process in ritual is diachronic and tripartite: during the first phase, *Ilembi*, the candidate is separated from the outside world and brought within the sacred space of the rites; after a variety of symbolic activities, during the second phase, *Kunkunka*, the woman, together with her spouse, is enclosed within a hut-like structure, for a period of time, barred from all communication with secular life; the third phase, *Ku-tumbuka*, is that of communal rejoicing, "a festive dance, celebrating the removal of the shade's interdiction and the candidate's return to normal life" (14). Through affliction, isolation, sacred instruction, reflection and social re-integration, individual life-crisis is brought under sympathetic control. What is particulary noteworthy is that an equally high value is placed on subjective experience and social re-entry. As is the case with the Anglo-Saxon poet, only personal trial reaches "the epic side of truth, wisdom."[32]

A particularly good example of individualism in this Ndembu ritual is offered by perfomances connected with the symbolism of trees. In his discussion of the early phase of ritual, when doctors gather medicinal herbs from the sacred site, Turner draws attention to a principle of *revelation* which underlies the names of curative objects. Not only do the various medicines treat the patient's physical

32 The quote is Benjamin's from "The Storyteller" (80).

condition, but their natural origin within specific ceremonial trees invests them with therapeutic powers, not far removed from "the talking cure" in psychoanalysis (25–6). Thus, in its symbolic dimension, the important *mulendi* tree carries a double meaning: on one hand, it has a "slippery," dangerous surface, "from which climbers are prone to slip and come to grief"; on the other hand, its glossy bark constitutes part of its effectiveness as medicine, as its use "makes the 'disease' (*musong'u*) slip away from the patient" (25). With regard to the barren woman, this double-sided symbolism brings to the fore the hiddenness of her condition, functioning, Turner contends, like so many Ndembu symbols, by "express[ing] simultaneously an auspicious and inauspicious condition" (25). One of the most significant principles in ritual action is *ku-solola*, "to make appear, to reveal," to empower the patient to *name* or to realize the embodiment of the hidden in speech or in symbols (25–6). Essentially, what Turner describes here is the curative process in the psychoanalytic situation, exemplified by Freud's discussion of the analytic session as an "intermediate region," where the previously concealed illness is turned into artifact, amenable to the healing interferences of the doctor as well as to the creative rearrangements of the analysand.[33] In both processes, the outcome of cure is the subject's detachment, the view from the other's place, in the shape of analyst or socialized symbolism. It is also the elegiac process, the construction of character as a consolatory symbol within the site of the Other's desire.[34]

Turner's description and analysis of the tripartite, processual form of the women's ritual, *Isoma*, has embedded within it the experiences of a suffering individual, who through a kind of communal psychotherapy achieves enlightenment about her own identity. On similar lines, the latter part of *The Ritual Process* is devoted to an investigation of "the developmental cycle" in the life of individuals, in terms of communal rites – *rites de passage* – with particular emphasis upon their intermediate phase, the period of liminality. Here, the focus is almost exclusively upon episodes in the lives of ritual subjects, although those experiences are shown to be, no less than in fertility rituals such as *Isoma*, intimately bound up with social operations. Rites of passage ceremonialize major changes in an individual's life, movements or transitions from one phase of life to another, for instance, from "place, state, social position and age" (94). As in the case of the barren woman in *Isoma*, events such as puberty, menstruation, migration, political ascendancy or retirement from office might have hidden psychological repercussions, where the experience of *passage*, in those situations not socially

33 See "Remembering, Repeating and Working-Through" (1914; esp. 154).

34 Indeed, Turner notes the resemblance between the effects of ritual symbol and the practice of the modern psychoanalyst: "This is not so very far removed from the practice of the modern psychoanalyst. When something is grasped by the mind, made capable of being thought about, it can be dealt with, mastered" (26).

symbolized, is made visible as collective phenomena. The most conspicuous, and most intense, ritual phase is the liminal interval, occuring between the subject's initial separation from community and the final re-integration. Again, not unlike suspended time in psychoanalysis, where past, present and future seem to co-exist in synhronized space, liminality occupies a kind of cultural free zone, where ritual subjects pass through radical revison of both individual and communal identity. The major characteristic of the liminal state is its *ambiguity*: it unsettles the certainties of the past and undermines the predictions for the future. Within it, the individuals are transformed into "threshold people," border-line persons who "elude and slip through the network of classifications that normally locate states and positions in cultural space" (95). It is as if ritual devises an anarchic social experiment where customary norms are turned upside down, social hierachies disintegrate and subjective identities flow and mix in indeterminate mixtures:

> Liminal entities are neither here nor there; they are betwixt and between the positions assigned and arrayed by law, custom, convention, and ceremonial. As such, their ambiguous and indeterminate attributes are expressed by a rich variety of symbols in the many societies that ritualize social and cultural transition. (95)

Of greatest significance for "liminal entities" is the overturn of social structure and the immersion in the experience of community, or, as Turner prefers to call it, *communitas*.[35] Ritual temporality is a "moment in and out of time," within which subjects move through dialectical processes of "high and low, communitas and structure, homogeneity and differentiation, equality and inequality" (96; 97). Because neophytes have been removed from everything known, both in terms of their social position and their sense of being, they are particularly receptive to the undifferentiated human element, which lies at the root of social endeavor. Liminal *communitas* consists of relationships without normative distinctions, such as "caste, class, or rank hierarchies or of segmentary oppositions"; it is unstructured, egalitarian and ambiguous, an organic "limbo of statuslessness" (97). For instance, in installation rites, where a former commoner is inducted into political office, such as that of a tribal chief, the pre-requisite is a "stripping off of preliminal and postliminal attributes," so that the individual enters ritual space, naked, sexless, powerless, ready to be humbled by the insults of the weak ("The Reviling of the Chief-Elect"), and to be tested in ascetic trials, at times "crouch[ing] in a posture of shame and modesty," or deprived of sleep at night and ordered to perform strenuous menial tasks (100–102). At the end of this passage, stripped of authority, reviled, shamed and humbled, the chief-elect is ready for a public installation and the wielding of responsible power, because not only has he shown

35 Turner prefers the Latin *communitas* to community, as he says, "to distinguish the modality of social relationships from an 'area of common living'" (96).

self-mastery, but, more importantly, because he has come into contact with human interrelatedness itself, the sacred origin of social structure. As Turner points out, in tribal societies, there is not a binary opposition between the secular and the sacred, but political office is sanctified by its carrier's experience in liminality: "something of the sacredness of transient humility and modelessness goes over, and tempers the pride of the incumbent of a higher position and office" (97). Like Shakespeare's King Lear, stripped of the paraphernalia of royal power, in tattered rags, mingling with the homeless, the destitute and the simple-minded, the tribal chief-elect in Ndemba culture achieves insight into the sacred bonds of *communitas*: "recognition [is given] to an essential and generic human bond, without which there could be *no* society" (Turner's emphasis; 97).

Framed within different cultural perimeters and articulated within a poetic, rather than a dramatic, idiom, the Old English elegies nevertheless rehearse a *rite de passage*, operating on the principles of liminal knowledge, ethical education and dialectical reintegration described by Victor Turner in *The Ritual Process*. The first-person speakers in the major poems – *The Wanderer*, *The Seafarer*, *The Wife's Lament*, *Resignation* and *Deor* – are liminal entities participating in a ritualistic performance, prompted by a crisis in the lives of both individuals and community. Although these speakers are not political aspirants, they passionately seek authority: the transitional/liminal zones in the poems stake out experimental voices, which move from social separation, through the interrelations of *communitas*, to more or less successful roles as cultural spokesmen. Below, I will examine in detail the poetic processes in *The Wanderer* and *Deor* which are the aesthetically most satisfying ones in culminating in redemptive symbolism. Character is constructed, in *The Wanderer*, as a multi-layered symbol, a conglamoration of the hidden and the visible, representative for both individual and community of a complex historical moment. *Deor*, whom Shippey has called "that most perfect of Old English poems" (1972: 75), also weaves a symbolic texture, emblematic for the elegies' strife for cultural authority: here, character is the poet himself, the widely experienced one, who achieves wisdom in the liminal state, re-creating the language of tradition. Although the other three poems are less successful in harmonizing subjective trial with communal concerns, they reach considerable psychological depths in their moments of liminal exploration: *The Seafarer* makes manifest the ambiguous reversals of *communitas*, and is particularly interesting in its failures to work through aporias or contradictions; it is my contention that *Resignation* works better as a companion poem to *The Sefarer* than the conventional "partner," *The Wanderer*," because it can be interepreted as a more accomplished outcome of liminal activity than the seafaring speaker's sermonizing conclusion; finally, *The Wife's Lament* presents a particularly challenging psychological case study, as it is deeply concerned with patriarchal structure, gendered experience and the form of liminal utterance: like *The Seafarer*, this poem does not quite manage to construct a balanced symbol of self, but nontheless, within the poetic process itself, reveals the complexities of inscribed verse, subjective urgency in the old language of tradition and of repressive patriarchal rule.

Before turning to the Old English elegies, it will be necessary to modify the view of them as ritual processes with a psychoanalytic account of their general poetic dynamic. Since these poems are, of course, verbal acts, rather than dramatic scenes, as are the elements of Turner's rituals, their *rites de passage* operate within the space of language, originating in separation as narcissistic loss, moving through the liminal interval of discursive ambiguitiy and transferential trials, and culminating in various versions of the "Name of the Father," Oedipal resolution, social symbolization and communal reintegration. The function of these psycho-linguistic factors will become clearer in my separate analysis of the poems. At this point, I want briefly to outline a general Lacanian framework for elegy, underpinned by Peter Sacks' exceptionally fine study of poetry, consolation and psychology in *The English Elegy: Studies in the Genre from Spencer to Yeats* (1985).[36] In Sacks' account, the common task of elegies is a project of self-consolation, a *working-through* of the crisis of loss. Thus, elegiac discourse carries with it the mourner's psychological burden as he searches the adequate expression, the fitting system of figures or symbolic register, to represent his grief. Speech, in elegies, is potentially therapeutic because it mobilizes the mourner's social energies, deflecting his narcissistic malaise within dispassionate conventions (1–37).

In order to labor successfully within the consolatory process, the elegist must, in Sacks' words, "withdraw affection from the lost object and reattach it to some substitute for that object" (6). Freud showed, in his essay "Mourning and Melancholia," how this is the process of mourning in general: the detachment of libido from the love object results in healthy grief whereas its continued pathological dependence leads to melancholia, a narcissistic disorder (Freud 152–170; Sacks 155–156).[37] The elegiac utterance crystallizes the "work of mourning" as a process of signification; the healthy mourner improvizes a sustaining consolatory trope, or a system of tropes, which register not only the loss itself but also the awareness that the figure is quite other than the loss, a substitute, a displaced symbol. If an adequate fiction is not construed, the mourner will fall into pathology.

---

36 This section on Sacks, as well as the following analysis of *The Wanderer*, are revised versions of my article, "From Plaint to Praise: Langugae as Cure in 'The Wanderer,'" first published in *Studia Neophilologica* 69(1998), 187–202, reprinted in *Old English Literature*, ed. R. M. Liuzza (New Haven: Yale University Press, 2002), 328–352.

37 Sigmund Freud. "Mourning and Melancholia (1917)." *Collected Papers* Vol 4. Trans. Joan Riviere (New York: Basic Books, 1959), 152–170.

According to Sacks, the narcissistic dilemmas reflected in elegies recapitulate our primal experience of loss and restitution. The theoretical grounding of that view is the Oedipal narrative, told in psychoanalysis as a series of narcissistic conflicts, confrontations between the fantasizing ego and the socialized self, resolved only at the moment of the father's intervention, under the threat of castration, when the *imaginary* yields to the codes of the *symbolic*. In Lacan's account, the Oedipal resolution succeeds the major narcissistic events or crisis, the first occurring at the *mirror stage* and the second during the *fort-da episode*, called so after Freud's descriptions of his grandson's play in *Beyond the Pleasure Principle*.[38]

The first blow to narcissistic integrity occurs in late infancy at the mirror stage when the child perceives the mirror image of himself, or an idealized reflection of himself in the shape of others, before his inner self has developed to any significant degree. As a result of this fantasy of fullness, the child experiences psychic fragmentation, a split within the self and between the self and the world. He can still sense the primary narcissism within, the pull of the early undifferentiated state with the mother, but this sense does not carry with it the same *jouissance*, the blissful oblivion, as it did before. Now, socialized mediation in formalized exterior images dilutes the pleasure principle; narcissistic wholeness is shattered in split desire, in the rise of the conflict between originary, somatic *need* and linguistically coded *demand*.[39]

If the Oedipal resolution is successful, the subject will learn how to supress the fantasizing ego within the nets of signifiers that come to constitute his self-image. The naricissism of the mirror stage will give way to symbolic action, to man's intersubjective experience in culture.

However, as both Freud's discussion of melancholy and Sacks' account of elegiac pathology indicate, an individual's grievous loss, especially in the form of the death of loved ones, can be the occasion of narcissistic regression, the mourner's a-social retreat into the solipsistic reveries of the mirror stage. As Sacks points out – and we will see this as a dominant force in *The Wanderer* – :

> One of the major tasks of the work of mourning and of the elegy is the repair to the mourner's damaged narcissism – but without allowing that repair to have permanent recourse either to the melancholy form of secondary narcissism or to the fantasies of the primitive narcissism associated with the mirror stage. (10)

38 Sacks 8–11; my discussion of the Oedipal narrative here is connected to chapter three above, but oriented more specifically toward the "work of mourning."

39 For a full account of the need/demand/desire sequence, see Anthony Wilden's commentary in Jacques Lacan's *Speech and Language in Psychoanalysis* (Baltimore: The Johns Hopkins University Press, 1968), 185–192.

Sacks goes on to claim that major English elegies such as "Adonais" and "In Memoriam" cannot be fully understood without observance of their intricate work of reparations. In my opinion, the same claim can be made about the Old English poems. Even if *The Wanderer, The Seafarer* and *The Wife's Lament* are conceived in a different idiom from the personal elgies Sacks studies, their consolatory *passion* cannot be fully comprehended without an awareness of the underlying psychological dynamic.

In a general way, the consolatory performance of elegies can be linked to the second major narcissistic event, the *fort-da* episode, described by Freud in *Beyond the Pleasure Principle*. At this moment in a child's life, around the ages of 1–11/2 years, the psychological reactions are more fully socialized than at the mirror stage and reveal more clearly the linguistic aspects of symbolic induction. The expression *fort-da* comes from Freud's account of his grandson's behavior during his mother's frequent absences. In order to compensate himself for the loss of the mother, the child invents a substitute game, playing with a wooden reel, which he alternatively casts away, with the syllable *fort* ("there"; "away") and pulls back, with the sound *da* ("here"). The game soothes the child as he manipulates these signifiers of absence and presence, gaining a sense of self-mastery from submitting his need to their alienating representation (Sacks 10–12).

The *fort-da* phase is a major cultural event, registering not so much the acquisition of language as an understanding of its functioning. The young child's rudimentary language, his consolatory figure, represents his loss, grief and narcissistic desire; at the same time, this figure is at a far remove from an interiorized sense of self: it is displaced, abstract, other. The psychological compromise with the otherness of this code marks the subject's entry into language.

Since the mourner in elegy replays primal grief and the child's narcissistic crisis, and since he strives, as the child, for self-mastery, he must produce a symbol or a symbolic system that overtakes not only his personal desire but the otherness of this desire – its cultural alienation – as well. As Lacan argues in his depiction of the psychoanalytic situation, *true* speech, and thereby the process of healing, can only be generated when the analysand becomes aware of the reply of the other in his own utterance. The therapeutic ground is constituted by an intersubjective matrix, the dialectical relation between self and other. Without socialized resonances, speech either evaporates into cold, functional language or degenerates within the particular fantasy of psychotics.[40]

In great elegies, those that have truly *worked through* mourning, language may alternate between functionalism and pathology, but the final product is always *true* speech, some dispassionate image or sublime sign, which does not impose

40 See Lacan in *Écrits* 85; 179–225.

the burden of passion, but merely evokes it. We will see how this work is carried out in the Old English elegies.

b. *The Wanderer*'s Talking Cure

In recent years, it has become something of a critical commonplace to regard *The Wanderer* as a "Bildung" lyric, a poetic account of spiritual growth. Previous conflicts of interpretation concerning the identity of the speaker, the nature of his utterance (dramatic monologue, meditative dialogue, heroic soliloquy?) and the general ideological thrust of the poem have given way to a common reading of a quasi-didactic figure who, in the idiom of elegy, illustrates the growth of a mind, the way from pagan malaise to Christian comfort. As Robert Bjork points out, critics have come to underscore the poem's self-enclosing structure – its "envelope pattern":"[...] the wanderer develops from an individual focusing on his personal quandary to a wise man, manifesting a broader perspective on the universe." Perhaps we can assume from now on that the genre *The Wanderer* most resembles is spiritual autobiography.[41]

One of the more fruitful results of these conciliatory readings of *The Wanderer* has been a new emphasis upon the poem's dialectical movement between individual and cultural fate. The historical situation in the guise of "Paganism," Germanic culture" and "Christian doctrine," is no longer merely perceived as a static background against which the speaker's interior anguish can be measured but as a complex ideological fabric the individual engages with actively, emotionally and

41 Bjork's article is "Sundor æt Rune: The Voluntary Exile of The Wanderer," *Neophilologus*, 73 (1989): 119–129, esp. 126. Also, see Bjork's summary of critical approaches to *The Wanderer*, 119. The classical criticism of *The Wanderer* is marked by the debate over "voices," speaker's identity" and the poem's religious content. For the major statements, see John C. Pope, "Dramatic Voices in 'The Wanderer' and 'The Seafarer'," in *Franciplegious: Medieval and Linguistic Studies in Honour of Francis Peabody Magoun Jr.*, eds. J. B. Bessinger Jr. and Robert P. Creed (New York: New York University Press, 1965), 164–193, and Pope's later retraction in "Second Thoughts on the Interpretation of 'The Seafarer'," *Ango-Saxon England* 9 (1974): 75–86; W. F. Kein, "Purpose and Poetics of 'The Wanderer' and 'The Seafarer',"in *Anglo-Saxon Poetry: Essays in Appreciation for John C. McGalliard*, ed. Lewis E. Nicholson and Dolores Warwick Frese (London: University of Notre Dame Press, 1975), 208–223; R. M. Lumiansky, "Dramatic Structure of the Old English 'Wanderer'," *Neophilologus*, 34 (1950): 104112. For a synthesis of the "Bildung" paradigm, see Anne L. Klinck, *The Old English Elegies: a Critical Edition and Genre Study* (Montreal: McGill-Queen's University Press, 1992), esp. 107–126.

unreflectively at first, in dispassionate certainty at the end.[42] Clearly, the variety of relationships the speaker establishes and works through within the cultural network is open to diverse analytical positions, and it is precisely here, within the process of self-fashioning, that *The Wanderer*'s chief critical interest lies for us today. Even if the problems of the poem's surface have been solved within the "Bildung" paradigm, the intricacies of its hidden logic, its deep structure, are only just now emerging. In this section, I explore the poem's psychological processes as these echo in the speaker's complex use of the language of elegy.

Traditional Lament

In the past, readers' sense of *The Wanderer*'s disjunctive speech was often formulated as an aesthetic problem, entailing questions about the integrity of the poem's voice, about the number of speakers or characters and about generic class.[43] Even if these questions rarely arise today, there is no reason to disregard the intuitive perception of polyvocality in the elegy. In fact, vocal divisiveness is a defining feature of the elegiac work as the mourner's self-awareness is shattered in narcissistic crisis and then painfully reassembled in the multi-dimensional search for a consoling stability. In *The Wanderer*, this search moves in three major directions which correspond to marked shifts in the poetic utterance. Thus, the first division (1–57) is characterized by the voice of melancholy, filled with sites of self-contradiction or aporias, imaginatively impotent, despite the lexical richness. The second movement (58–100) is spoken by the public voice, which at first hearing sounds entirely other than the private expression that went before. However, as we shall see, these sections are logically linked both sub-structurally, through psychological affinity, and formally, through the poem's aesthetic progress. The third and final section (111–115) borrows its full force from a superbly worked out variation on the poem's beginning lines: its voice, I will contend, is that of the artist, in full, triumphant awareness of his creative skill.[44]

---

42 Two rather recent articles are good exampels of this dynamic historicism: Bjork, 119–129, and Patrick Cook's "The Bonds of Exile in 'The Wanderer'," *Neophilologus* 80 (1996): 127–137.

43 See, for instance, Pope, 164–193; Klein, 208–223; Luminasky, 104–112. For an influential discussion of genre see Rosemary Woolf, "'The Wanderer,' 'The Seafarer,' and the Genre of *Planctus*," Nicholson and Frese, 192–207.

44 Citations from *The Wanderer*, and from the elegies in general, are from the *Exeter Book*, eds. George Phillip Krapp and Elliott van Kirk Dobbie (New York: George

Elaborated upon in a variety of critical idioms, *The Wanderer*'s three-pronged structure has often been noted. For instance, the relatively recent articles on the poem develop their analysis in tune with three movements: Robert E. Bjork traces the conventional pattern or cultural meshes the speaker engages with and then separates himself from, and Patrick Cook focuses on the most abstract version of the three autobiographical stories the poem tells (Bjork 119–129; Cook 127–137). For the purposes of examining the different formal aspects of the poetic utterance, J. E. Cross' generic division in his essay on *The Wanderer* as consolation seems most pertinent.[45]

According to Cross, *The Wanderer*'s achievement is self-consolation in the manner of the Latin stoics, and he points out many affinities, especially rhetorical ties, between the poem's consolatory strategies and the devices of the classical tradition. As in the standard "consolatio," the mourner in *The Wanderer* tests principally three areas for potential solace to his misery – the area of personal lament, an autobiographical solution, the area of public discourse, or philosophical council, the area of the divine, or Christian doctrine. Cross implies that these generic spheres should be considered on a progressive narrative line, as the cultural maxims gain ascendancy over the speaker and his anguish dissolves within the paradigms of ethical moderation and cosmic wisdom (524–26).

What Cross draws attention to is the poem's symbolic register, the realm of social statements or official utterance. *The Wanderer*'s elegiac pathos becomes the more acute as loss and narcissistic desire founder not only within the general signifying strictures of language but within the historically and culturally specific commonplaces as well. As Cross points out, even the first section of the poem – the personal lament – is, no less than the more communally oriented section, saturated with poetic "solacia," with the traditional rhetoric of comfort. The articulation of grief is restricted by the general precepts: silent suffering "is a noble mark of a man ("biþ in eorle indryhten fleaw" 12); the loss of community, of home, of kin, of lord and *comitatus*, may be countered with hopes of new cultural ties, another "sinces bryttan" ("distributor of treasure" 25) who in the mead-hall comforts the friendless wanderer ("mec freondleasne frefran wolde,/weman mid wynnum" 28–29); the memory of former joys or lusty dreams can compensate for bleak reality (34–57). Thus, the details of the wanderer's autobiography are arranged in a general narrative pattern by the consolatory tradition and its dominant stoic precepts (517–19).

Routledge and Sons, 1936). All references to the Exeter manuscript are to this edition. Unless otherwise noted, the translations from Old English are mine.

45 "On the Genre of 'The Wanderer'," in *Essential Articles for the Study of Old English Poetry*, eds. Jess B. Bessinger and Stanley J. Kahrl (Hamden: Archon Books, 1968), 515–526.

Similarly, in this passage of the poem, the speaker's personality as well as the ideology he propounds are cultural and poetic commonplaces. The "anhaga" of the first line, who treads the "paths of exile" ("wadan wræclastas" 5), is an entirely conventional figure, elaborated upon in formulaic diction in a variety of Anglo-Saxon poems. Moreover, Stanley Greenfield's study of exile as an oral theme illustrates how the loners' emotional state is determined by oral-formulaic constraints: expressions of misery, wretchedness, dejection, and so on, never evolve into independent autobiographical passages but cluster in traditional semantic units – "hean" ("dejected") with "hweorfan" ("turn away"; "go"), "geomor" ("sad") with "gewitan" ("go"; "depart"), "earm" ("miserable") with "anhaga," "earmcearig" ("wretched") with "eðle bidæled" ("deprived of native land").[46] The despairing sense of personal alienation is overshadowed by exile as a cultural code and its concomitant routine images of desolate journeys, deprivation and misery.

Also, an aphoristic ideology blunts the force of personal utterance in this section of the poem. The wanderer's narrative of exile, feud, hardships and loss is punctuated by a number of gnomes reflecting pagan fatalism, the trust in mystic causality. Apparently, the speaker accepts without a doubt a fatalistic world-view that leaves no room for individual choice or desire or even for existential questioning. All experience, the most desolate wandering included, is predetermined ("wyrd bið full aræd" 5), and it is not only futile but ignoble as well to bewail that cosmic fixity ("ne mæg werig mod myrde wiðstondan,/ne se hreo hyge helpe gefremman" 15–16). *Wyrd* is the poem's ultimate commonplace, the most banal, and therefore the most oppressive, stricture of its symbolic order.

If *The Wanderer*'s genre, persona and philosophy are stock items in a standard poetic milieu, what is there to prevent the elegy from evolving into either the language of dogma, functionalist and inauthentic, or, in the case of the mourner's unbearable repression, isolated fantasy? The example of *The Seafarer* and *The Wife's Lament*, often designated as companion pieces to *The Wanderer*, shows how a similar elegaic process – loss, narcissistic mourning, therapeutic drive – collapses within the rigid order of the the Anglo-Saxon symbolic. Few readers have overlooked the incongruity of *The Seafarer* where a lengthy homiletic conclusion (66–124) abruptly cuts short the imaginative (and ambiguous) account of exile, grief and spiritual quest.[47] In *The Seafarer*, the work of mourning is overtaken by theological clichés; creative figuration is abandoned in favor of the stock phrases as if the speaker loses faith in his audience, in intersubjective, energetic exchange.

---

46 Greenfield, "The Formulaic Expression of the Theme of 'Exile' in Anglo-Saxon Poetry," Bessinger and Kahrl, 352–362.

47 See, for instance, Klinck's commentary, 139.

The loss of this psychological faith and the alternative adoption of orthodoxy is, in *The Seafarer*, equivalent to both emotional stasis and aesthetic bankruptcy.

The seafaring speaker seems to accept his own exclusion from the symbolic register, to opt for "empty speech" instead of the difficult word, the rich consolatory tropes of successful elegies. On the other hand, the language of *The Wife's Lament* indicates psychological betrayal of a different kind. The thick obliqueness of that poem is not solely due to a lack of reading context or intertextual milieu, as Alan Renoir suggests, but is rather the effect of the speaker's abjection, exactly the kind of narcissistic regression Sacks warns against as hindrance to elegiac recovery.[48] Indeed, the images of confinement in *The Wife's Lament* – "the gloomy cave" ("eorðsele [...] dimme" 29–39), the intractable "forest-grove ("on wuda bearwe" 27), "the looming cliffs" ("duna uphea" 30), the mourner "sick at heart" ("is min hyge geomor" 17) in a "joyless dwelling" ("wic wynna leas" 32) – suggest that *imagos*, fantasies of the mirror state and its imaginary context, have replaced the *symbol*, the communicative, albeit alienating, social signifiers. Like the "seafarer," the "wife" surrenders her place in the chain of signifiers; however, the former erases himself in platitudes whereas the latter disappears in delusional speech.

The Psychology of Plaint

In elegies, it is the mourners' colossal task to position themselves in the alienating codes of official expression. Lacan's psychological semiotics emphasizes the troubling relation between subjectivity and positionality within signification. Because language is structured as chains of differential signifiers, one signifying unit connected to the next one in an anticipatory, linear movement, there exist no stations of subjective transcendence, no conflation of signified and signifier in a pause of full meaning.[49] There is, in other words, no pre-ordained place for the subject in language; consequently, *enunciation* or individual speech, grounded in a-temporal need, is always at odds with – sometimes painfully so – the socialized *utterance*, the language of demand, conditioned by time, place and others.

Again, elegies highlight the barrier between signifier and signified, between the language of grief and the subjective sense of loss. In *The Wanderer*, the mourner

48 Alan Renoir. "A Reading Context for 'The Wife's Lament.'" Nicholson and Frese, eds. 224–241; Sacks, esp. 10.

49 Lacan in *Écrits*, esp. 153–4; there exists, however, as I point out in relation to character construction, a post-transferential, sublime space, which the wanderer does aspire to, not "in a pause of full meaning," but as cultural spokesman, in order to symbolize it.

faces the same dilemmas as the speakers in *The Seafarer* and *The Wife's Lament*, the gap between need and demand and the struggle with symbolic exclusion. Judging from the poem's first section, the speaker's solutions seem similar to those of *The Seafarer*'s conformist, riddled as the passage is with commonplaces, uttered by a stilted persona, framed by a banal philosophy. Still, *The Wanderer*'s beginning is more complex than *The Seafarer*'s homogeneous conclusion. The wanderer's conventionality is like a tattered blanket hurled over the urgency of need. Narcissistic speech, close to the fantasies of *The Wife's Lament*, contradicts and blocks the sterile commonplaces.

As Rosemary Woolf has demonstrated, *The Wanderer* shares many formal affinities with the medieval genre of *planctus* or complaint (192–207). What characterized plaintive speech in Old-English poetry, lyrical, biblical as well as heroic, is a melancholic expression of any kind of painful loss and a so-called "ethopoetic" speaker, a quasi-didactic figure who may originate in personal experience but who tends to evolve into a universalized fictive stance (Woolf 192). Unlike elegy proper, which usually involves a particular death, planctus ranges widely in its perception of loss: in *Beowulf*, for instance, there is Hroþgar's complaint about old age (2105–14), a father's grief for the death of a son (2444) and "the last survivor's" existential lament (2247–66).[50] Thus, the causes of plaintive loss can vary between the concretely physical or libidinal and the more diffusively psychological, even metaphysical. In *The Wanderer* loss appears to emerge from both concrete and abstract causes, the death of loved ones as well as existential alienation.

Woolf indicates that the typicality of the speaker in *The Wanderer* prevents psychological conflict, that the apprehension of loss is entirely conscious and formal from the poem's beginning to its end (199). Still, in the course of her commentary Woolf makes many revealing suggestions about the psychological identity of the speaker, noting, for instance, the strangeness of his split persona, the constant tendency to speak about the self as if it was other. Woolf even claims that the situation in the poem is generally described as if "from the point of view of a thoughtful onlooker" and that it is a "general peculiarity of the poem [...] that the Wanderer most often describes, not how he feels, but how someone in a comparable situation would feel" (200). Surely, it is no longer sufficient to link this poetic peculiarity to the poet's artistic "intention" to typify and stylize human suffering (200). Instead, I want to suggest that this split is a peculiarity of narcissistic speech, of *plaint*, not in the new-critical sense of stylized literary genre, but in the psychoanalytic sense of libidinal speech act. The first part of *The Wanderer* is spoken in the language of melancholia; it is the beginning of the poem's difficult work of mourning.

50 See Woolf's examples, 194.

According to Freud in "Mourning and Melancholia," melancholic speech is first and foremost a profoundly self-contradictory phenomenon (esp. 157–158). Although the state of melancholia may originate in genuine grief, it does not achieve the healthy mourner's detachment but remains locked in dejected lamentations. Freud draws special attention to the strangeness of the melancholiacs' accusations against themselves, which are delivered compulsively and without shame, as if in masochistic delight (157). These outbursts, however, are far from being straightforward self-recriminations but are, in fact, the effects of an intense ambivalence toward the loved and the lost object, which the ego has internalized and identified with in narcissistic fullness. The reproaches against the self are in essence disguised attacks on the other, the ambivalent object of desire. Freud calls the melancholic speech act a *plaint*; "their complaints," he says, "are really 'plaints' in the legal sense of the word" (158). In this connection, it is interesting to note the etymological connection between "plaint" and "planctus": the former carries over some of the originary somatic meaning of the latter as the act of "striking the breast in grief." Indeed, as Freud contends, the melancholiac's expression proceeds from "an attitude of revolt," the violence of this protest muted in semantic contradictions (159).

This delineation of the speech genre of *The Wanderer*'s first section enables us to unfold its strangely evasive logic. The speaker's vacillation between convention and fantasy, between *The Seafarer*'s orthodoxy and the imagos of *The Wife's Lament* is caused by his ambivalent state of revolt, his alternate sensuality and contempt for the world. Several nodal points in this section of the poem, sites of aporias or self-contradiction, illustrate the wanderer's difficult psycholgical dilemma. The following analysis will focus on three such nodal points.

As suggested above, loss in *The Wanderer* is a heterogeneous object, incorporating the death of a particular person, the separation from country and kinsmen as well as a more indefinite experience that can best be characterized as both cultural and existential alienation. As is the case with Anglo-Saxon poetry in general, *The Wanderer* seems to exist in a kind of cultural twilight, within a period of a major historical transition. In his "*Beowulf* and the Origins of Civilization," James W. Earl convincingly argues that the cultural context of the Anglo-Saxon epic is itself ambivalent, caught in the shifts of religious ideologies (Paganism/Christianity) and of communal structures (the tribal/urban; the local/national).[51] Earl contends that *Beowulf*'s response to these transformations is neither conformist nor cyni-

51 James W. Earl, "*Beowulf* and the Origin of Civilization," in *Speaking Two Languages: Traditional Disciplines and Contemporary Theory in Medieval Studies*, ed. Allen J. Frantzen (Albany: State University of New York Press, 1991), 65–89. I would add a shift in cognitive structures affected by the rise of chirographic culture.

cal – nor even objective – but *disillusioned* which, even if it is a "negative" reaction, is nevertheless an affirmative and a constructive one (37).

The speaker in *The Wanderer* will learn how to achieve disillusionment, to move from destructive grief to healthy negativity. However, in the first phase of the work of reparation, in tune with melancholy logic, the ego internalizes both private and communal deprivation – the death of the heroic lord as well as the dissolution within the *comitatus* – and identifies with it in a love-hate complex of associations. On one hand, the cultural injunctions are lovingly maintained; on the other, they are rejected in nihilistic abandon.

The three major nodal areas that foreground the ambivalent blockage are those of the narrative frame itself, of the metaphoric system and of the Oedipal story the poem, at this point, tries to tell. The framer of the wanderer's autobiography is, as we have already seen, the typical heroic exile, thoroughly equipped with his culture's most valuable paraphernalia. The most insistent of these is the virtue of silence, a privileged theme in each of the poem's three sections. The beginning lines of the elegy are almost exclusively concerned with the strange contradiction between poetic desire and the cultural injunction against superfluous speech (8–21). The speaker feels compelled to recite his suffering ("Oft ic sceolde ana [...]/mine ceare cwiþan") even though he has lost his bosom-friends and confidants, exiled from his country and deprived of a lord (8–9). He knows, however, that such compulsion is morally unjustifiable; his heroic education has instilled in him a faith in stoic silence. It is no less than *nobility* in a man "to lock feelings within the breast," "to hoard them, like a treasure, within the mind" ("his ferhð-locan fæste binde/healde his hordcofan" 13–14). True manhood is bought at the price of individual speech. The wanderer knows this intimately and lovingly repeats the stylized maxims; but no sooner has he asserted the gnome than he defiantly breaks it in voluble fantasy, self-indulgent and self-commiserating. The heroic exile turns out to be a rebel. One must, however, be careful not to mistake this narcissistic rebellion for genuine subversion. At this stage in the poem, the ego is still in a state of thoughtless identification with the other: by attacking this other, it attacks itself.

Breaking through the barrier of cultural silence, the self-contradictory poetic voice generates a succession of figurative constructs, each in the form of wish-fulfillment fantasy (19–57). As the mourner elaborates upon loss, his backward movement, his regression, seems to intensify, starting with a lush memory of the heroic milieu, moving into a sensuous dream of the lost lord, concluding with a hallucinatory experience, apparitions and voices of the dead ("maga gemynd mod geondhweorfeð;/greteð gliwstafum, georne geondsceawað/secga geseldan" 51–53). Also, within each fantasy, the language becomes increasingly unsettled;

the relatively conventional epic of the mead-hall and its ceremonies gives way to phantasmagoria, to the mirror-stage *imago* and to the delusional metaphor.

Thus, in his dream (37–49), the wanderer identifies narcissistically with his former master, projecting the circumstances of what psychoanalysis calls the "Ideal Ego," an imaginary relation, unconscious of symbolic positionality.[52] The hallucination that follows comes dangerously close to the uprooted fantasy of *The Wife's Lament*. In a kind of waking dream, the speaker senses the presence of his old companions so concretely that he sees them "watch him intensely" ("georne geondsceawað" 52) and hears them speak "joyfully" ("greteð gliwstafum" 52). Both the dream of the lord and the vision of the departed kinsmen – "fleotendra ferhð" (54) – can be characterized in medieval terminology as "vain illusion" ("vana illusio"), false dreams, produced by desire for what is lost. In his study of "Christianity and Dreams," Jacques Le Goff shows how both pagan and Christian theories of dreams recognized the category of the *phantasma*, the pure illusion, that usually originated in some kind of physical or spiritual lack and might even, in Gregory's the Great elaboration, tempt the dreamer into sinfulness.[53] There can be no doubt that the wanderer's hallucination is caused by his "sore longing" for the irretrievable ("sare æfter swæsne" 50); it is further characterized by what psychoanalysis calls "foreclosure," an expunging of the real world, the realm of signification, through absolute metaphoric substitution. Like the *imagos* of *The Wife's Lament*, the wanderer's *phantasma* tears the utterance away from its symbolic roots, replacing the difficult trope of consolation with "the voices of the dead."[54]

52 In psychoanalysis, both Freudian and post-Freudian, a distinctioon is made between the intrapsychic agencies of "ideal ego" and "ego ideal." Lacan relates these two structures to his orders of the *imaginary* and the *symbolic*. "The ideal ego" is a narcissistic delusion, assumed during the mirror stage; on the other hand, "the ego ideal" is formed after the Oedipal solution, indicating the subject's awareness of "the gaze of the other." Symbolic positions are both identifications and performances: the subject retains the narcissistic drive, but now it is modified within intersubjectivity. See Jacques Lacan. Seminar II, *The Ego in Freud's Theory and in the Technique of Psychoanalysis, 1953–4*. Trans. Sylvana Tomaselli (Cambridge: Cambridge University Press, 1988), esp. Chapter XVII. See also J. Laplanche and J. – B. Pontalis, *The Language of Psychoanalysis*, 144–145; 201–202.

53 Jacques Le Goff, *The Medieval Imagination*. Trans. Arthur Goldhammer (Chicago: The University of Chicago Press, 1985); see especially Chatper 5, 196–229. Also, see an interesting discussion by Andrew Galloway about Gregory's the Great dream-theory and *The Wanderer*. Galloway, however, does not make a distinction between the wanderer's sleeping and waking dreams; in "Dream-Theory in 'The Dream of the Rood' and 'The Wanderer'," *The Review of English Studies* 180 (1994), 475–485. Antonia Harbus argues along similar lines as Galloway in "Deceptive Dreams in 'The Wanderer'," *Studies in Philology* 93 (1996), 164–179.

54 Lacan's major statements about *foreclosure* and the three registrers, the imaginary, the symbolic and the real, in relation to psychosis are to be found in "On a question

The narcissistic regression that characterizes the first part of *The Wanderer* makes partly clear the speaker's desire to abandon his positionality within official signification. The mistaken search for the adequate consolatory figure leads him away from the utterance, from his own symbolic voice to the mirage of narcissistic enunciation. Nevertheless, in spite of this pathological movement, the wanderer is – against need, as it were – brought back to a communicative matrix, eventually, in the poem's next section, to take his place in the Symbolic, fully and triumphantly. How is such recuperative work managed?

Again, psychoanalytic insight provides an explanation. As I indicated above, psychoanalysis considers the Oedipal phase as the culminating moment in the subject's narcissistic drama. The psychic crises experienced at the mirror stage and during the *fort-da* episode, the shocks of self-alienation, are re-ignited, now in confrontation with the *father* himself as the representative of the Law against incest and of the prohibitions, in general, against all the subject's misguided self-identifications. Psychological health depends on the Oedipal resolutions: the child's fantasy of sameness must give way to intersubjective difference.

In her fine essay "Beyond Oedipus: The Specimen Story of Psychoanalysis," Shoshana Felman argues that the major distinction between Freud's and Lacan's reading of the Oedipus myth lies in the latter's structuralist perspective and in his insistence on the myth's significance for psychoanalytic practice.[55] Whereas Freud's interest in Sophocles' play *Oedipus Rex* is mainly theoretical, that is, mainly tied to the discovery of unconscious desire and its general impact on psychic life, Lacan's concern is clinical, joined with the observance of the role of speech in the analytic cure (80–83). Thus, for Lacan, the Oedipal experience, the central event in psychic history, as encountered in the clinical situation, is not crucially about the family's libidinal dilemma but about the subject's confrontation with his own history, and cure becomes the question of *assuming* one's narrative of oneself, of *recognizing* what had been misapprehended, the previous fatal misrecognition ("méconnaissance").[56]

Subjective recovery in analysis happens when the analysand ceases to repeat the old retrospective fantasies, propelled as they are by imaginary fulfillments,

preliminary to any possible treatment of psychosis," in *Écrits* 179–225. Briefly, psychosis is a possible effect of a failed Oedipal task, a delusionary, instead of a healthy/alienated, experience of language. Lacan talks about the "delusional metaphor," an illusory stabilization of signifier and signified, which replaces the "paternal metaphor," the subject's *anchor* to the world of signification. See esp. 217–218. Also, see discussion of "The Name-of-the-Father" below.

55 Shoshana Felman, "Beyond Oedipus: The Specimen Story of Psychoanalysis," *Psychoanalytic Literary Criticism*, ed. Maud Ellman (London: Longman, 1994), 76–102.

56 Lacan, *Le Seminaire II: Se Moi dans la théorie de Freud et dans la technique psychoanalytique* (Paris:Seuil, 1978), 58; Felman 82.

and instead "names his desire" as detached spectator of his own destiny (Lacan, *Le Seminaire II* 267; Felman 82). This naming, this full recognition, is, according to Lacan, equivalent to the Oedipal resolution, which is first and foremost an induction into symbolic knowledge, into the epistemology of the signifier (Felman 83). What is primarily involved in the unravelling of the Oedipus complex is not the cessation of yearning for the mother and the consequent identification with the father; at stake is what Lacan calls "the paternal metaphor," and assumption of the "Name-of-the-Father," the subject's anchorage to the world of signification.[57] In his role as intruder the father does not demand that the child identify with his own reality but that it should displace its wishes unto the split inherent in language, that it should, in other words, know itself as Other.

It may appear that I have strayed far from *The Wanderer*, from its speaker's heavy grief and search for consolation. In fact, the paternal metaphor – The Name-of-the Father – is an essential operation in the recuperative process of the poem. It is precisely a symbolic realization, the detached naming of desire that rescues the wanderer from anchorless retreat into narcissistic fantasy. What I want to argue is that, at the end of the first section, when the speaker is brought back from his hallucination to the icy landscape and the emptiness around him and to his own exile, he is also brought to the moment of recognition, to a kind of creative epiphany, an entrance into truthful signification. From oscillating between cultural dogma and melancholy protest, unable to figure his grief in an adequate name, the speaker is finally empowered to symbolize. The symbol he now constructs is himself as other, his own artistic meditation on the wandering exile and on exile as the human condition.

The Eschatological Artist

The new figuration starts at the opening of the poem's second section (58), a section which is in many editions presented after a break in the text, either to indicate poetic discontinuity or merely to underscore the great difference between part one and two. Indeed, readers have often been hard pressed to explain this difference and have generally wondered at the discrepancy between the private malaise of the first part and the public loftiness of the rest of the poem.[58] However, the sections are intricately connected, both psychologically and formally. The

57 Lacan, "On a question preliminary to any possible treatment of psychosis," *Écrits* 217–218; see also *Écrits*, "The signification of the phallus, 281–291.

58 Such a reading is a commonplace within the criticism. See, for instance, Klinck's textual note, 188.

shifts from the personal and public are effects of the speaker's Oedipal resolution. Because he wakes from imaginary plenitude to the brink of himself, to nothingness, the wanderer can no longer speak an autobiographical language, a language that assumes the subject's identification with himself. Instead, he speaks like a sage or a philosopher who delineates for mankind its true condition, its exiled state on earth. The topics of his speech are no longer the miseries of grief but existential realities – war, violence, destruction and death. Like the language of the first section, this utterance is multi-layered and polyvocal, but it is not fantastic, punctuated with mirror-stage imagos. It is true speech in the Symbolic. Possibly, the best way to characterize the whole latter section is as an eschatology, the articulation of the topic of last things (apocalypse, individual and cosmic death, the last judgment). Compared to the "self-haunted" speech of the former section this is the discourse of self-effacement, infused with otherness, almost vatic in its aphoristic exactness.

Of course, it may be objected that the confrontation with self-alienation is nothing new in the biblically inspired literature of the Middle Ages. After all, the idea of "man's exile on earth," is a Christian cliché, derived from the Old Testament account of Edenic expulsion. In fact, Old English poetry, vernacular as well as overtly religious verse, is saturated with the imagery of "paradise lost" – Grendel in the guise of Cain, the archetypal outlaw, empty mead-halls suggesting the lost idyll of the past, the desolate sea-voyage as life's allegory, the story of the Fall itself, told with didactic fervor in "The Phoenix" and the *Genesis* poems. As Dorothy Whitelock has demonstrated, *The Seafarer* can be interpreted literally as the account of a *peregrinus*, an ascetic exile who celebrates, however ambiguously, existential suffering and alienation as the natural state of being.[59] The ubiquitous diction of an exile has been analyzed by Stanley Greenfield, and we have seen it at work as a restrictive frame in the first part of *The Wanderer* (352–362).

What I have been hinting at throughout this essay, however, is *The Wanderer*'s creative insight into a clichéd theme. At stake in the movement from private to public utterance is an enormous leap of the imagination, a kind of epiphanic glimpse into the operations of discourse, into the epistemological premise of the Name. In his "comitatus"-fantasy the wanderer's drive for self-identification is propelled by a longing not only for psychological stability but for cultural stability as well, for the lore of tradition, "the council of his lord" ("his winedryhtnes / leofes larcwidum" 38), and the familiar sayings of kinsmen" ("fleotendra ferhð no þær fela bringeð/cuðra cwidegiedda" 54–55). It is the mourner's mel-

59 Dorothy Whitelock, "The Interpretation of 'The Seafarer'," Bessinger and Kahrl, 442–447.

ancholy move away from the Oedipal resolution, the unique consolatory trope, towards narcissistic language, the soothing unified gnome.

Like Oedipus in Sophocles' *Oedipus at Colonus*, the elegist in *The Wanderer* is rescued from the misrecognition – the illusory knowledge ("méconnaissance") of himself – and, within a moment of epiphany, is ushered into a recognition, into true knowledge of the symbol, of its difficult, disjunctive, split being and of himself as its capable maker. In her discussion of Lacanian therapy, Shoshana Felman notes that the psychanalytic cure "is radically tied up with language, with the subject's analytic speech-act, and as such, its value is less cognitive than *performative*"; and she goes on to say that "[the recognition] is, itself, essentially a speech act, whose symbolic action *modifies* the subject's history, rather than cerebrally observing or recording it, at last correctly" (Felman's emphasis; 82). Indeed, this kind of therapeutic logic is at work in the wanderer's recuperation. What distinguishes his speech act from that of the ordinary analysand is not an essential difference but a matter of "performative" degree: although both the recovering elegist and analysand come to realize the entrapment of desire by language and learn to disengage themselves from their libidinal scenarios, it is only the former who transforms this decentred knowledge into aesthetics, who dramatizes, *performs*, self-alienation, as an artist.

Thus, *The Wanderer*'s next section, the recuperative speech-act, performs death as the epistemological ground of the human subject. Whereas the first section figured loss nostalgically, driven by logocentirc desire, the second part elaborates an eschatology, a decentred discourse about the end of the world. Within Old English poetry, this passage is a remarkable artistic *tour de force*, a triumph of intertextual sophistication. I will indicate a few of the poem's unusual signifying ways.

As a speech act, *The Wanderer*'s second section is composed of many textual strands, all linked in one way or another to death and to language. The heterogeneous object of loss of the personal lament is now contextualized, submerged within varieties of the Anglo-Saxon tradition. It is as if the elegy has become an encyclopedic genre, incorporating the entire cultural utterance of grief: strains of homily, gnomic wisdom and maxims, "de excidio" ("of ruin") descriptions, images from battle poems, "ubi sunt" nostalgia, Boethian-style "consolatio." This pastiched death-song has often been criticized for what appears to be its associative logic and discontinuous movement.[60] However, the randomness is only superficial, an effect of the sustained artistic work of aligning mirror-stage fantasy with symbolic control. The melancholic protest against cultural bonds in the poem's

60 For an older criticism, see P. L. Henry, *The Early English and Celtic Lyric* (London: Allen and Unwin, 1966), esp. 166. More recently, a reader notes the wanderer's self-directed discourse, "with its haunting mix of associational and persuasive logics" (Cook, 127).

first part has been transformed into a creative display of those bonds. The speaker neither accepts nor rejects the offical codes; what he does is to figure them in his own way, to make of them his consolatory trope.

This imaginative gnomic web does not only contain topics of loss but the highly valued issue of speech and silence as well. After his initial apocalyptic image of a shrinking earth ("swa þes middangeard/ealra dogra gehwam dreoseð and fealleð," 62–63), the wanderer itemizes some of the standard gnomes of wisdom and of silence. This list is suffused with a dispassionate philosophical temper:

> Wita sceal geþyldig,/ne sceal no to hat-heort ne to hrædwyrde/ne to wac wiga ne to wanhydig/ ne to forht ne to fægen ne to feohgifre/ne næfre gielpes to georn ær he geare cunne.
>
> [A man should be patient; he should not be too hot-tempered nor too hasty of speech, nor too weak in battles nor too heedless nor too fearful nor too cheerful nor too greedy for wealth nor too eager to make a boast before he knows the outcome.]

The speaker then elaborates further upon ways of boasting: "A man should wait before he makes a vow,/until he, the stout-hearted one, readily knows/the movement of his heart" ("Beorn sceal gebidan, þonne he beot spriceð,/oþþæt collenferð cunne gearwe/hwider hreðra gehygd hweorfan wille" 70–72). The previous apocalyptic passage had noted that true wisdom could only be achieved by a man long confronted with the destruction of the earth (64–65). Now, balanced speech appears to be the measure of the man, the wise utterance the outcome of apocalyptic knowledge.

As we saw in the first section, the preoccupation with the virtue of silence was dominated by the mourner's narcissism and expressed in the form of a plaint. At that point, the speaker did not understand the trajectory of desire and imagined a state of utopian conflation between *enunciation* (his private woe) and *utterance* (the socialized statement). On the other hand, in the poem's "public" section, the mourner has grown into a kind of "ex-centric" (and eccentric) wisdom: he has learned about the nature of desire as a dissociative force in language and has realized that in order to "assume his history," to be cured, he must speak, symbolize, within the disjunction. The proverbial wise man – gleaw hæle" (73) – simultaneously gazes upon destruction and death and speaks moderately. The juxtaposition is imaginatively unique, the cultural maxims exploited in order to express a profound philosophical insight.

The images of wisdom in *The Wanderer* are thus radical elaborations, at odds with the culture's idealized depictions of personality, whether those originate in a pagan or a pre-Christian world-view. As has often been pointed out, the poem grapples with two ideologies, the pagan ethics of a heroic milieu and Christian metaphysics. Usually, readers of the poem interpret it in the light of these systems of thought, proposing either their successful synthesis or their conflict, resolved, most often, in favor of the Church.[61] In my opinion, these views tend to be reductive because they pay no heed to *The Wanderer*'s psychology and thereby overlook its driving force, the work of mourning. As this work progresses, the poem's aesthetic awareness strengthens and with it a kind of wise detachment, the disillusioned knowledge James W, Earl notes in relation to the perspectives of *Beowulf*. In a way, then, *The Wanderer* can be classified as a "Bildung" lyric, a story of the growth of mind. This story, however, is not conventionally progressive: it neither registers heroic conformity, like so many Norse sagas do, nor religious conversion, an insight into transcendence. Instead, *The Wanderer* is a story of self-creation, generically closer to modernist "portraits" of the artist as cultural exile than to heroic legend or Augustinian autobiography.

Of course, it is not my intention to uproot *The Wanderer* from its cultural milieu and plant it in some superior universal realm, nor do I mean to overextend its artistic precociousness. In fact, the Anglo-Saxon poetic tradition itself, within which *The Wanderer* is embedded, provides a context for understanding the preoccupation with self, language and the artistic symbol. Before examining that relation, it will be necessary to look further at the elegy's figuration of self-alienation and exile.

If a postmodern perspective makes possible an account of radicalized subjectivity and facilitates a celebration of its psychological recovery, how can such a celebratory account be historically justified, especially within a poetic tradition that seems as obstinately a-psychological and foundational as Anglo-Saxon verse? In other words, how can *The Wanderer*'s trope of the wise exile, who surveys transcience and "deeply ponders this dark life" ("þis deorce lif deope geondþenceð" 89), accomplish the consolatory task of elegies and "repair [...] the mourner's damaged narcissism" (Sacks 10)? Does the speaker not, in the end, swerve away from his decentred discourse toward an affirmation of Christian foundationalism, placing his faith in absolute transcendence? Robert E. Bjork notes how, in the beginning of the poem, the wanderer clings to the strictures of social custom in order not to be whirled into the chaos of exile (122). Stability is the ground of consolation: after disengaging himself from pre-Christian conformity, the speaker, according to Bjork, affirms "the superior, heaven-bound, hope-filled exile track of the Christian faith" (126). Also, R. M. Lumiansky, J. E. Cross and others have argued that the wisdom of *The Wanderer*'s second section is Boethian or quasi-Boethian, stoic equilibrium in the face of universal ruin.[62]

61 See, for instance, John C. Pope's commentary in his edition, *Seven Old English Poems* (New York: Norton, 1981), 80–81; see also Bjork, 126.

62 R. M. Lumiansky, "The Dramatic Structure of the Old English 'Wanderer'," *Neophilologus* 34 (1957), 104–12; Cross, 515–526; note S. B. Greenfield's comment that the wanderer achieves "a negative *de consolatione*," in "'The Wanderer': A Recon-

In *The Wanderer*'s third and last section (111–115), the heavenly kingdom is indeed depicted as the ultimate ground of human comfort ("fæder on heofonum þær us eal seo fæstnung stondeð" 115). Nevertheless, a psychological reading of the poem should make clear that the "father in heaven" is neither a theological cliché nor the outcome of religious conversion. Those critical readings that overvalue the Christian implications of the epilogue, closing the poem on the note of dogma, ignore the elegist's deep crisis and his difficult work toward recovery. In fact, the operative words are neither "fæder," "heaven," nor even "fæstnung," but the word *ar* or "mercy"; "It will be well for him who seeks mercy (grace) for himself,/comfort from the father in heaven, where for us all stability stands" ("Wel bið þam þe him are seceð,/frofre to fæder on heofonum, þær us eal seo fæstnung stondeð" 114–5). In the context of *The Wanderer*'s psychological movement, its work of mourning, "ar" sparkles as – what psychoanalysis would call – "the full word," a sign resonating with its own otherness, emerging from the subject's history, conscious as well as unconscious, and from the intersubjective matrix of the Symbolic.[63] In the final stages of analysis, it is the analysand's word of cure, dialectical, suffused with the response of the Other. "Grace" represents the wanderer's cure.

In the poem, "ar" reverberates on at least three poetic and semantic levels: on a structural level, reflecting the speaker's artistic control; on the cultural level, underscoring the speaker's symbolic recovery; on the personal/spiritual level, capping the speaker's fine consolatory trope. First, the mention of God's mercy in the concluding sentence links the end to the beginning, where the lonely exile ("anhaga") waits for this mercy, apparently unsure whether he will receive it; he uses the word dejectedly ("modcearig" 2) as if it were a stock item of his culture, pagan as well as Christian.[64] Indeed, at the beginning of the poem "ar" (1) is an "empty word," cold and functionalist like *The Seafarer*'s dogmatic statements. During the wanderer's epistemological education, his growing insight into the paternal metaphor, the word becomes filled with wise significance, until it is re-stated at the end in artistic triumph.

The recursive movement back to the poem's beginning alerts us to the recuperative work that has taken place, to the transformation of narcissistic grief into

---

sideration of Theme and Structure," *Journal of English and Germanic Philology* 50 (1951), 462. Further, Cross contends that the poem shows that the secular "de excidio" tropes are not sufficient consolations but merely prepare a mourner for the ultimate salvation, the epilogue's *patria* in heaven" (524–525).

63 Lacan in *Écrits*, "The function and field of speech and language in psychoanalysis," 40–55.

64 Klinck notes the two meanings embedded in "gebidan," "to wait" and "to experience." She also notes the element of duration in the word: the wanderer experiences a period of waiting for mercy, 106–107.

detached representation. Also, the semantic store within "ar" strengthens its symbolic function; on one hand, its significance is firmly tied to the wanderer's secular culture as a word of "honor," "dignity," "glory;" on the other hand, it is a Christian word, expressing the "grace/mercy" only God can bestow on believers.[65] Thus, it is an exemplary sign within the poem, registering not only the psychological experience the speaker has gone through but his interaction with both the vernacular and spiritual sides of his culture a well. "Ar" registers the wanderer's intersubjective triumph.

However, if the poem's final appeal is to the "mercy" of "fæder on heofonum," to the Christian God, does that not mean that *The Wanderer*'s triumph is not so much psychological, or even artistic, but religious, the outcome of spiritual conversion? Such a conclusion would be at odds with my interpretation of the elegist's epiphanic moment, his insight into otherness. All the same, I do not think that the poem's Christianizing tendencies necessarily overturn its radical vision. It is not in the power of a traditional singer to cast off the cultural language, unless he retreats into fantasy like the speaker of *The Wife's Lament*. What the wanderer accomplishes after his narcissistic breakdown is a linking of his private mourning with an activity anthropologists call *cultural work* – the construction of images or metaphoric systems that overtake the concerns of both individuals and communities. In his essay "Culture as Identity: An Anthroplolgist's View," Anthony Cohen makes use of this concept and shows how important it is for a culture to possess multivocal symbols that, for instance, in extreme political situations, express ethnicity or some intricate situation of communal identity.[66] It is only the complex, open symbol, that can register both collective identity and autobiography. For instance, when a traditional symbol – some ritual, costume, even the name of an ethnic group – works effectively as protest in some exploitative situation, it is performing both in a representative and a therapeutic manner for the individual as well as the group.

The consolatory trope the wanderer constructs is the outcome of such cultural work. It is the trope of himself as a traditional singer who receives grace. The "snottor on mode" ("the one of wise mind;" "the sage" 111) in the epilogue thus refers neither to a religious recluse nor a Boethian stoic but to a kind of wandering minstrel, a composite of the figures of Caedmon, praising God, and of Widsith, praising himself and his craft. In his account of Caedmon's divine inspiration, Bede demonstrates how the Anglo-Saxons considered poetic skill a gift of God:

65 See definition of "ar" in Joseph Bosworth's *Anglo-Saxon Dictionary*, ed. T. Northcote Toller (Oxford: Clarendon Press, 1992), 42.

66 Anthony P. Cohen, "Cuture as Identity: An Anthropologist's View," *New Literary History* 24 (1993), 195–209.

These verses of his stirred the hearts of many folk to despise the world and aspire to heavenly things. Others after him tried to compose religious poems in English, but none could compare with him, for he received this gift of poetry as a gift from god and did not acquire it through any human teacher.[67]

A more secular version of the glory of song is given in the minstrel poem "Widsith":

> Swa scriþende gesceapum hweorfað/gleomen gumena geond grunda fela,/þoncword spre-caþ,/simle suð oþþe norð sumne gemetað/gydda gleawne, geofum unhneawne,/[...] lof se gewyrceð,/hafað under heofonum heahfæstne dom. (135–143)
>
> [Widely they wander as Fate may guide,/The strolling singers who roam the world/Tell-ing their need, returning their thanks,/And always finding, or south or north,/Some great one skilled in knowledge of song/Who is open-hearted in giving of gifts/[...] He who earns praise/Has under heaven the greatest glory.] [68]

The Wanderer's concluding lines reflect this Janus-faced artistic glory, heav-en-bound as well as rooted in the earth. The speaker is now fully aware of the dual function of his speech as private *passion* and public blue-print and feels confident in his role as poetic sage: "a man should only speak his *passion* when he knows the remedy" ("ne sceal næfre his torn to rycene/beorn of his breostum acyþan, nemþe he ær bote cunne" 112–113). He knows that it is for this speech that he will be praised, that he will be glorious in the eyes of his culture and of his culture's God. He knows this because his speech is true.

c. The Embodied Soul in *The Seafarer* and *Resignation*

Both *The Wanderer* and *The Seafarer* highlight the complexities of Anglo-Saxon textuality as well as the transitional technological, cultural and psychological dynamic which underlies it and shapes it. Inscribed verse, or "visible song," as Katherine O'Brien O'Keefe calls it, is an intricate phenomenon, a multi-layered composition of oral performers, scribes and interpretive communities, a curi-ous mixture of traditionalism and flexibility.[69] Even if this poetry emerges from oral-performative situations and is appropriated by audiences trained in commu-nal listening rather than private reflection, the Old English elegies, in particular,

---

67 Bede, *A History of The English Church and People*. Trans. Leo Sherley-Price (Pen-guin Books, 1955), 245.

68 Charles W. Kennedy's translation from *An Anthology of Old English Poetry* (New York: Oxford University Press, 1960), 60–61.

69 See the discussion at the beginning of this chapter in "Alterior Space."

display a new subjective configuration, a libidinal search in the cultural language for a combination of tropes, within which to speak of *character*, sublime substitutes for multifarious loss. Poems such as *The Wanderer*, *The Seafarer*, *The Wife's Lament*, *Resignation*, and *Deor* evolve according to ritualistic models in pre-industrial societies, involving liminal entities, in the form of poetic speakers, which undergo alienating, often terrifying, experiences as challenges to the roles they seek as cultural authority. As we have seen, the subjectivity of the speaker in *The Wanderer* is put on trial, positioned on the very edge of sanity, and within overwhelming narcissistic desire confronted with the dissolution of language and hallucinatory collapse; like the debased initiate in Ndembu ritual, however, the wanderer emerges triumphant from crisis, imbued with powers to symbolize a new epistemology, a Janus-faced portrayal of himself as both public spokesman and private individual. The entire poem is permeated with the effects of this construction, with, in other words, *character effects*, the tremors of the modern subject within the old language of tradition.

The Seafarer is also best understood as a rite of passage through which passes an initiate seeking cultural authority. Contrary to *The Wanderer*, however, the seafaring speaker does not succeed in harnessing the collisions between imaginary and symbolic structures to the project of constructing himself as character. As I discussed in the preceeding section, both poems reach a point of crisis where the elegist confronts the misrecognitions of narcissistic fantasy and is brought to an Oedipal revelation about the divided structures of intersubjective discourse. Whereas the speaker in *The Wanderer* moves from the destructive identifications of the first part of the poem to a kind of heteroglossic naming of the valuable issues of his culture, to an eschatology, meaningful for both subjective psychology and communal identifications, the seafarer appears to fail in his symbolic quest, in the latter part of his speech, uttering only homiletic banalities and Christian slogans. Although the first part of *The Seafarer* displays the rich and complex condition of a liminal soujourn, the poetic voice in the second part seems incapable of resounding the previous, profound experience, as if the task of mediation, performed so successfully by the wanderer, is not an option for a Christian homilist.[70] Nevertheless, this polarity in *The Seafarer*, the conflict between the identity of a passionate seeker and stereotypical preacher, is even more telling about the nature of Anglo-Saxon inscribed verse, the transitional psyche and character-effects, than is the balanced, authoritative utterance of *The Wanderer*. In fact, the seafarer's strategies to surpass psychological and cultural impasse are more intricate than most readers have given them credit for; because

70 Critics generally agree that the major break in the poem occurs at line 64b; see my discussion below.

the seafarer seeks legitimation not exclusively as a traditional artist or singer, but as religious authority, as Christian speaker, entitled to explicate and offer advice about ultimate, theological truths, the libidinal contradictions here, the collisions between desire and discourse, are more spectacular and more insistent than in the other poems from the elegiac group. In the following discussion, I will concentrate on such contradictions and on the speaker's strategic attempts to legitimize himself as their master.

Desire in Language

Recent theoreticians of oral traditionalism and oral performance frequently stress the qualitative differences between the roles of traditional artist and modern author. In their investigations of Anglo-Saxon manuscripts, both Katherine O'Brien O'Keeffe and Carol Braun Pasternack undercut the resilient conception of modern authorial intention by focusing on the materiality of the verse, revealing layers of construction, reception and interpretation. Pasternack's view of "implied tradition," for instance, is coloured by her assumption that authorship and subjectivity are inextricably linked, and that lacking autobiographical awareness, the verse suggests only collective experiences.[71] Similarly, O'Keeffe contends that the hybridity of Old English poetry confirms its historically conditioned communal nature; in her estimation, the scribe is the displaced Old English poet, a chirographic performer, whose act of inscription, no less than the poetic act in living performance, evokes the whole traditional context, linking audience to its literary heritage.[72] O'Keeffe's interpretation is to some extent built upon John Foley's extensive examination of oral performativity, especially upon his notion of performance as a *metonymic* event, as a suggestive part of the cultural whole, where heroic song or epic, for instance, implies the generic register and is capable of invoking this within an audience. Although Foley is adamant in rejecting mechanistic views of oral poetics and in emphasizing "its wonderfully complex and echoic idiom that can bear the weight of genius," this view of the creative mind in traditional performance is clearly far removed from the interiority of the modern authorial subject (40).[73] Within early medieval scholarship, with the shift of emphasis from the written text to the oral dynamics determining it, there has

71 *The Textuality of Old English Poetry* (1995); as I discussed above, there are contradictions within Pasternack's argument.

72 See especially O'Keeffe's "The Performing Body on the Oral Literate Continuum: Old English Poetry," ed. John Miles Foley. *Teaching Oral Traditions* (New York: The Modern Language Association, 1998), 46–58.

73 "Oral Performance and Oral Text," in Doane and Pasternack, 34–45.

indeed occurred a similarly significant shift from conceptions of authorship to overriding concerns with "implied tradition."

Transitional verse, however, exemplified by Old English varieties, and, in particular by the elegiac group, involves greater cultural, mental and psychic revisions than explained by the displacement of oral performer by scribe or by hybrid textuality. Even if no social histories record the roles of Old English poets, and their literary portrayals are rare and enigmatic, the recurrent concerns and the language itself of some of the major poetry suggests that the cohesive, traditional communities suffered, along with political, cultural and technological changes, a crisis in *representation*: we have seen how *The Wanderer* constitutes a negative *Bildung*, meriting comparisons with modernist autobiographies rather than with contemporary spiritual documents; the images of *The Wife's Lament* are almost impenetrable, unless associated with the metonymic drive within language to recover a lost unity; as Morton Bloomfield has contended, *Deor* works like a magical charm (and I would add, a *sophisticated* charm), constructing character over the abyss of loss, representing a version of the poet in the alienating mirror of transitional subjectivity;[74] in a different idiom, *The Seafarer* is also concerned with poetic authority, although this is variously complicated by the personal experiences and needs of the speaker as exile, as *peregrinus pro amore dei*, as hedonist and as religious authority. Even if it is not entirely successful, the discourse the seafaring speaker desires to establish would culminate in the hybrid symbol of ritual, the construction of *ku-solola*, which empowers the individual to name his condition, to socialize his hidden sense of crisis. I want to maintain that the most complicated, overpowering factor in that task is Christian identity; to a greater extent than *The Wanderer*, *The Wife's Lament* and *Deor*, discourse in *The Seafarer* is permeated with the effects of conflict between the speaker's imaginary and the Christian Symbolic.

In Anglo-Saxon England, the orality-literacy shift was orchestrated to the greatest extent by Christian institutions – Church officials, monasteries and religious education, in the form, for instance, of translation of crucial texts in the vernacular. Acting as Church intermediary, King Alfred, in the last two decades of the ninth century, promoted literate education through his translation project, which consisted of "the core [works] of Latin Christianity": Gregory the Great's *Pastoral Care* and *Dialogues*, Orosius's *History Against the Pagans*, Boethius's *Consolation of Philosophy*, Augustine's *Soliloquies*, and Bede's *Ecclesiastical History* (Howe, 17).[75] The motivation for this deliberate and concentrated educa-

74 Morton W. Bloomfield. "The Form of *Deor*." *PMLA* 79 (1964), 534–541.

75 Nicholas Howe. "The Cultural Construction of Reading in Anglo-Saxon England," in Liuzza, 1–22; see further references to Howe's essay below.

tional reform was to reinstate Christian learning in a climate of sinful ignorance: in a letter circulated to the bishops in England with his translation of Gregory's *Regula pastoralis*, Alfred oulines his view of a threefold renaissance in the country, quickened by his program – of vernacular literacy, Christian faith and unified national identity. As Sarah Foot points out in "The Making of *Angelcynn* : English Identity Before the Norman Conquest," on King Alfred's cultural and political agenda was an appeal to nascent nationalism, bolstered by Christian ideology, and the King's "rhetoric of Englishness," characterized, for instance, by the insistent use of *Angelcynn*, was a conscious extension of Bede's language in the *Ecclesiastical History*, of his use of *gens Anglorum* to name for the first time the Christian English: "while Bede invented the English as a people in the sight of God, they were made one nation by [Alfred the Great]" (66).[76]

The observation that communal identity is constructed through authoritative rhetoric is of paramount importance to an understanding of psychological conflict in *The Seafarer.* A more specific historical instance illustrating the orality/literacy/Christianity conjunction, often referred to as "an originary narrative" of English literature, and by implication, of Englishness, is Bede's account in his *Ecclesiastical History* of the illiterate Caedmon's divine poetic inspiration.[77] Although the authenticity of the event is debatable, since Bede's portrayal of the cowherd-cum-hymnist is the only extant one, the evocation of a transitional cultural moment, the encounter between the oral universe of the common folk and the literate Christianity of a monastic milieu, are undoubtedly firmly tied to a churchman's intimate knowledge of national issues and concerns. As several recent commentators have remarked, Bede's presentation of Caedmon's "conversion" is far from a binary one, privileging repression of the tradition in favor of Christian topics, but a conciliatory narrative of communal border crossings, of the oral and the textual, of the traditional and the institutional, of the laboring class and the powerful monastic rule.[78]

In accordance with the subject matter of Caedmon's hymn, Bede's account in the *Historia Ecclesiastica* assumes both a heroic and a hagiographic shape. The

76 Sarah Foot, "The Making of *Angelcynn*: English Identity before the Norman Conquest," in Liuzza, 51–78. For further information about King Alfred and his reign, see S. Keynes and M. Lapidge, eds and trans. *Alfred the Great: Asser's 'Life of King Alfred' and Other Contemporary Sources* (Harmondworth, 1986).

77 Clara A. Lees and Gillian Overing focus on Bede's *desire* in producing this particular narrative, as well as on critical desire for mythic origin for English culture. See "Birthing Bishops and Fathering Poets: Bede, Hild and the Relations of Cultural Production," in Liuzza, 125–156.

78 See especially Howe's discussion in "Cultural Construction of Reading" as well as Jeff Opland's in *Anglo-Saxon Poetry: A Study of the Traditions* (New Haven: Yale University Press, 1980), 106–120.

common laborer, Caedmon, affiliated with the Northumbrian monastery, Whitby, in the mid-seventh century, through a visionary experience in a dream, is raised from his lowly status as illiterate outsider to a central figure in the missionary project of the Church. From a cowherd who merely attended to his simple duties, and did not even possess the basic skill of playing a lyre and reciting festive songs, Caedmon is, following the miraculous inspiration, transformed into a composite bard, in Jeff Opland's phrase, perhaps the first "crucial transitional figure" in Old English poetry, in that his verse combines traditional/vernacular form with Christian theology.[79] The climactic point of Bede's narrative occurs when, after his dream, the cowherd is transported into the presence "of the more learned men" of Whitby and authenticated as an inspired singer, whom "the Lord had granted [...] heavenly grace" (417). For further confirmation, the learned monks read to him passages from scripture and ask him to turn this into song, a task he dutifully fullfills, returning the next morning, "repeat[ing] the passage he had been given, which he had turned into excellent verse" (421). Bede's simile of the oral poet is a telling one: "he learned all he could by listening to them and then, memorizing it and ruminating over it, like some clean animal chewing the cud, he turned it into the most melodious verse" (419). Caedmon's humble heroism lies in the exquisite mental ability to both retain oral mnemonic technique and the subject matters of Christian doctrine.

In particular, the success of Caedmon as a transitional oral poet crystallizes in his subsequent role as a religious authority, whose former teachers "became in turn his audience" and whose general hearers "were inspired to despise the world and to long for the heavenly life" (421). Bede's description of Caedmon's repertoire makes clear that underlying the harmonious melody was a didactic intent: not only were the songs based on Biblical narrative, on "the creation of the world, the origin of the human race, [...] the whole history of Genesis, [...] the departure of Israel from Egypt and the entry into the promised land, [...] the incarnation, passion, and resurrection of the Lord" (419); they were also homiletic compositions, guiding a lay audience into fear of profane living and submission to Christian doctrine and morality:

> He also made many songs about the terrors of future judgment, the horrors of the pains of hell, and the joys of the heavenly kingdom. In addition he composed many other songs about the divine mercies and judgements, in all of which he sought to turn his hearers away from delight in sin and arouse in them the love and practice of good works. (419)

Together with his "heroic" indoctrination, Caedmon achieves blessed status, as we learn that he took monastic vows, and died as a "religious and pious man,"

79 Opland 119; see Bede's *Ecclesiastical History of The English People*. Bertram Colgrave and R.A.B. Mynors, eds. (Oxford: Clarendon Press, 1969)

uttering his last words in "the praise of the Creator," as he had done so many times in his career as a religious oral singer (421).

The heroic and quasi-hagiographic reversals in Bede's narrative from secular, lowly conditions to sacral authority provide a structural parallel to the movements and transformations of the mental universe in *The Seafarer.* Although nothing specific is said about the speaker's profession in the first part of the poem, there is no reason why the descriptions of the "anti-hall" conditions, the toilsome sea-journey, the "terrible tossing of the waves" ("atol yþa gewealc" 6), the hazardous proximity of the ship to looming cliffs, the freezing cold, as well as the traveller's spiritual anguish ("bitre breostceare" 4), should not be taken at face value as reminiscences of a sailor's career.[80] Whether or not the first thirty-three lines of the poem, desolate depiction of the speaker's *via dolorosa*, are understood as real exploit or allegorical construction, there can be no mistaking the powerful, sensual evocation of the forces of nature as well as the strange fascination for the physical and mental challenges they set the human individual. As Peter Orton has perceptively remarked, the first "seafaring" half of the poem works formally on the lines of running commentary in a *diary*; the speaker's account is autobiographical, not in the sense of retrospectively reconstructing experience, but rather as (almost) simultaneous narration:

> we are given, not just a bare sequence of incidents and episodes, but something like a running commentary by the speaker on their impact on him. The reader must follow the speaker in taking each piece of information [...] just as it comes. (371)[81]

On this reading, the first part of *The Seafarer* is an *empirical* narrative, filled with memorable events, moments of crisis and personal observations; as I will continue to explore, this narrative encompasses the speaker's *rite de passage*, as he is transformed into a liminal quester for his proper communal function. Unlike Bede's presentation of the case of Caedmon, however, the reversals in *The Seafarer* from a secular, even a profane, context to Christian morality are not successful, neither heroic nor hagiographic. The sensuous ambiguity of the empirical section gives way to sterile commonplaces; Christian identity is assumed as empty performance, not as the blessed teaching in harmonious melody, accomplished so smoothly by the celebrated Caedmon.

My focus on creative failure in *The Seafarer* is not meant to undermine the capacitiy of Christian discourse to signify sensuous experience. As became appar-

80 All references to *The Seafarer* are to the edition of the *Exeter Book* in *Anglo-Saxon Poetic Records*, eds. George Phillip Krapp and Elliott Van Kirk Dobbie (New York: George Routledge and Sons, 1936). Unless otherwise noted, the translations from Old English are mine.

81 Peter Orton. "The Form and Structure of *The Seafarer*," in Liuzza, 353–380.

ent in *The Wanderer*, the language of Christianity effectively accommodates the trials of the individual subject, situating the speaker, not unlike Caedmon himself, as both religious authority and traditional artist. Similarly, the devotional poem, *The Dream of the Rood*, from *The Vercelli Book*, often promoted as the most accomplished Christian poem of the ninth century, combines an intense psychosomatic experience, the speaker's visceral sense of Christ's death on the cross, with the verbal iconography and didactic techniques of patristic literature. As S. A. J. Bradley observes, *The Dream of the Rood* masterfully illustrates how aesthetic discourse transforms abstract doctrine into empathetic communication: the Church's theory of *compunctio* ("compunction"; "spiritual empathy"), revolving for the most part around liturgical identifications and defined redundantly in patristic documents (e.g. Defensor's *Liber Scintillarum*), is harnessed by the poem's expert use of the dream vision and prosopopoeia and transposed into a passionate, cathartic encounter with an audience (1995: 158–160). Toward the end of this section, I will examine a companion piece to *The Seafarer*, the penitential poem, *Resignation*, which manages a more harmonious symbolism, a construction of character as a kind of superego, more substanital than in *The Seafarer*, despite the homiletic echoes and interspersed Christian formulas. Whereas in *The Seafarer*, the ascetic strain, the drive toward self-denial and a martyred condition, collapses in dejected rehearsal, in *Resignation* it achieves productive *compunction*, a transferential nodal point for members of its audience.

The Seafarer's creative bankruptcy at the end of the empirical half of the narrative is not so much the effect of the Christian symbolic *per se* as it is the outcome of the enormity of the speaker's libido, of his *desire* to register, in the socialized language of religious teaching, narcissistic pleasure as well as the excess of that pleasure, destructive *jouissance*, which goes beyond the self toward death. During the first part of this book, in the general discussion of psychoanalysis and literary character, I outlined the distinction made by Lacan between alienation and separation in the history of the subject's ascendance. Both conditions, according to Lacan, stake out significant moments in the transitional process from *being* to *having*, that is, from the narcissistic desire to be the mother's phallus to the assumption of the "Name-of-the-Father," a detached position within the divided structures of discourse. Thus, the event of separation is analogous with the Oedipal resolution, which severs the narcissistic illusion of unified desire, and ushers the subject into a revelation of the otherness of its own libidinal apparatus. Whereas alienation occurs at the level of signifiers, merely positioning, or anchoring, the human subject to *the real*, separation fleshes out being, embodies it as a *specific* desiring entity, linked in transferential chains to other such entities. In Lacan's view, after separation, primary narcissism, or "the mOther's desire," is transformed into "object *a*;" the heterogeneous world of others, which, as a result of healthy Oedipal resolution, informs subjectivity about its own permanent constitution in lack. If pleasure, or *jouissance*, is grounded in such an informed sense of negativity, then a special kind of union with the other is possible, what Brian Fink has called, "pure *desirousness*," a paradoxical sublimity, blissful knowledge of the otherness of signification, which it momentarily transcends.[82]

The quest for a sublime epistemology of otherness is not as successful in *The Seafarer* as it is in *The Wanderer* because in the former poem desire in the primary narcissistic state overpowers the demands of the Oedipal trial. In order to examine the vicissitudes and contours of the seafarer's desire, I will, to begin with, concentrate on the poem's autobiographical section, which comprises two phases of a rite of passage, separation and margin or *limen* ("threshold").[83] The narcissistic collapse at "the threshold" produces the last homiletic section, which is analogous to the third and last stage of ritual, aggregation; here, we will see how the seafarer's participation in community is not necessarily an opportunistic stance, but more comparable with strategies of mimicry in colonial and post-colonial texts. The effects of *The Seafarer*'s character construction are just this: the contradiction between *mimesis*, empirical narrative, and *mimcry*, the perfomance of Christian identity.[84]

The seafarer enters the narrative like a participant in ritual, in state of separation from community. Even bleaker and more desolate than comparable situations in *The Wanderer* and *The Wife's Lament*, "the anti-hall," the reverse side of heroic society, in the first thirty-three lines of *The Seafarer*, consists of a voyage "in the paths of exile" ("wræccan lastum" 15) in a storm-tossed ship on the wintry sea, the terrible solitude of the voyager broken only by the inhuman cacophany of wind, water and seabirds. The speaker stresses the excruciating deprivations he undergoes: not only are his feet bound with icy fetters ("calde geþrungen/wæron mine fet, froste gebunden,/caldum clommum" 8–10) and his innards ravaged by hunger ("hungor innan slat/merewerges mod" 11–12), but his mental state and sensory apparatus similarly register the pain of utter nega-

82 This is a brief recapitulation of chapter four; see also Lacan's seminar on the Other in *The Four Fundamenta Concepts of Psycho-Analysis*, esp. 203–230, and Brian Fink. *The Lacanian Subject* (1995), esp. 52ff.

83 Here, I'm using "separation" in the autobiographical sense rather than the specifically psychoanalytic one. On the other hand, rite of passage, as the anthropological structure of *The Seafarer*, encompasses both alienation and Oedipal separation.

84 Although no critic has commented on the ritual structure of the poem, my tripartite line division follows a rather conventional model: separation: 1–33a; margin: 33b-64a; aggregation: 66b-124. See, for instance, Peter Orton, in Liuzza, 353–380. It seems apt to start the last section at 66b, since the "I" here is a public voice, in some respects comparable to the vocal change in *The Wanderer*, at line 58. For terms of ritual, see Victor Turner's *The Ritual Process*, 94.

tion. To an even greater extent than in *The Wanderer*, this section of the poem is characterized by a language of negativity: the speaker's environment is the absolute antithesis of society, the images it invokes, in almost every instance, in geometrical opposition to human communication in cities, boroughs and festive halls. Thus, the speaker almost immediately presents himself as a contrast to the "landlubber," the comfortable man, who lives without care on the fastland ("þe him on foldan fægrost limpeð" 13), and who enjoys urban plenty, "high-spirited and flushed with wine-drinking" ("se þe ah lifes wyn,/ gebiden in burgum [...] wlonc ond wingal" 27–29). On the other hand, the seafarer is the "anti-hall" archetype, inhabiting only *cearselda fela* ("abodes of care" 5), where, instead of the mead- drinking ("medodrince" 22) and the laughter of companions ("hleahtor wera" 21), the rule of the day is anxiety, bitter cold, labour, and the inhuman cries of the seascape.

The contrast elaborated upon between sea and land produces an image of a *no man's land*, the more terrifying for the co-presence of pleasurable memory. In a way, it is as if the seafarer has traversed the terrible chasm the speaker in *The Wanderer* confronted after awakening from his "vana illusio," his false dream of narcissistic fulfillment among the ghosts of the past. From a psychoanalytic perspective, however, the latter poem works through the psychic challenge of this moment as an Oedipal experience, assuming a place for its speech within the intersubjective matrix of the Symbolic; *The Seafarer*, on the other hand, appears to have crossed the terrifying border of human community, without anchoring that crossing within the Oedipal resolution and the consequent assumption of the "Name-of-the Father": what the first section of the the poem primarily registers is an *imaginary* experience of death, originating perhaps in a real ordeal, but magnified within the speaker's narcissistic fantasy, to the extent that the desire for bliss, for the paradisal hall, extends into pathological *jouissance*, the desire for death. Again, viewing the poem as an anthropological structure which incorporates the individual's quest to obtain cultural authority, this first phase of the seafarer's rite of passage strips him of his social being, of heroic life on land, the *comitatus* and the festive hall, and confronts him with the basic facts of existence – with danger, hunger, pain, labour and the raw indifference of the natural world – in order to prepare him for the liminal state of egalitarian community as well as an aggregation into social structure as authorized speaker. In other words, this harsh, unprotected experience of nothingness is potentially an initiation into wisdom, where speech will be infused with the neophyte's humbling experiences in ritual performance. On the highest semantic level, in *The Seafarer*, rite of passage is an existential trial, educating a potential eschatological artist, an expert in acts of communal consolation. The seafarer plunges into the ritual experience, acquiring profound knowledge of last things, but unable to detach his desire from their reality. Hence, during the phases of separation and liminality, his speech is richly imaginative, whereas the last section, often referred to as a homily, fails as socialized eschatology. The homily is also concerned with the facts of existence and with mortality, but, as I have already indicated, it is functionalist speech, without the compunction of genuine aesthetic insight. As it turns out, the languages of Christianity cannot contain the *The Seafarer*'s enormous desire.

There have, of course, been several critical speculations about *The Seafarer*'s preoccupation with death. Especially, earlier views of the poem as an allegory interpreted the sea-voyage as *peregrinatio*, as the wanderings of the Christian exile on a hostile earth, seeking the heavenly home. Here, quite influential was G. V. Smithers' contention that the poem reflects ecclesiastical tradition as elaborated by St Augustine in *De Civitate Dei*.[85] Accordingly, Smithers considers the seafarer's alienation to represent the predicament of good Christians generally, whose sojourn in the world is marked by the search for the city of God, named, in the poem, *elþeodigra eard*, the home of worldy aliens (151). The prevalent presence of the "landlubber," as the second category of citizens, the *cives*, comfortable inhabitants of human communities, strengthens Smithers' allegorical view as does a crucial passage depicting the speaker's spirit depart from the body and fly like a bird over the ocean, in anticipation of life after death ("Forþon nu min hyge hweorfeð ofer hreþerlocan,/min modsefa, mid mereflode,/ofer hwæles eðel hweorfeð wide" 58–60) (Smithers, e.g. 137; 151). Further, Smithers' controversial emendation in line 63a, the reading of *wælweg* – "the road taken by the dead" or "the road to the abode of the dead" – instead of *hwælweg* – the conventional *kenning* for the sea, "whales' road" – clinches the argument that the seafaring theme is an allegory of the Christian's preparation for death (151).

Generally, more recent criticism has contested allegorical interpretations, giving credit to the powerful realistic component in the poem and variously agreeing with Nora Kershaw's estimation that *The Seafarer*, and the Old English elegies as a group, are characterized by their concreteness, that they are, in fact, "studies of situation or emotion applied to imaginary and nameless persons who are detached from any definite associations of time or place" (6).[86] *The Seafarer*, of course, may have ecclesiastical connotations, but is, first and foremost, an investigation of a highly personalized experience. Although no critics have specifically examined the speaker's psychological attitude to death, there have been a few studies interested in the ascetic strain in the poem and in tracing a logic, which integrates the

85 G. V. Smithers. "The Meaning of *The Seafarer* and *The Wanderer*." *Medium Aevum* 3 (1957), 137–53.

86 Nora Kershaw, ed. and trans. *Anglo-Saxon and Norse Poems* (Cambridge: Cambridge University Press, 1922). See also I. L. Gordon's problematizing of the allegorical view in the introduction to her edition of *The Seafarer* (London: Methuen, 1960).

sensuous and the spiritual, the autobiographical and the homiletic. Thus, Peter Orton, in a close, careful structuralist analysis of *The Seafarer* demonstrates the speaker's Christian compromise with his devastating experiences as an exile, linking the eschatological dissection in the homily to psychological trauma.[87] Even if the nature of this trauma cannot be concretely established, it is clear that "the seafarer's experiences cannot be encompassed within the framework of conventional life, and this alienates him from the values and priorities prevailing among his fellow-men" (359). According to Orton, the last part of the poem resolves its human dilemma, since both Christian doctrine and practice, especially in the ascetic dimension and in the monastic ideal, provide a *Weltanschauung*, which matches the speaker's sense of personal crisis (esp 374–375). In an earlier essay, Stanley Greenfield comes to a similar conclusion about the form of *The Seafarer*, that it, in fact, embodies a "psychological-religious sequence of experience" and that "the juxtaposition of the seafaring and homiletic halves [...] can [...] be viewed as the objective correlative for the speaker's experience" (207).[88]

As will become clear, my consideration of the poem's last part as functionalist performance, not genuine conversion, does not gainsay its integral structure. However, even to a greater extent than Orton, I examine the poetic process as a ritualistic *trial*, undertaken by a neophyte questing in the language of his culture for symbolic authority; in other words, the trial is an *elegiac* task, hurling a speaker into a second narcissistic crisis, challenging him to negotiate his *jouissance*, to substitute his desire for what is lost with creative naming. In *The Seafarer*, the object of loss is not as heterogeneous as it is in *The Wanderer*, where the elegist grieves for his departed kinsmen, his lord, the heroic past, as well as for transcience in general; as the first section of the poem so dramatically illustrates, existence itself initiates the seafarer's crisis. In the remainder of this section, I aim to show that the task of the speaker in *The Seafarer* is to name his desire as *uncanny* character, as mirror of alienation, a displaced symbol for death.

The next liminal phase (33b-64b) in *The Seafarer* thus aims at ritualizing desire, constructing a figure, grounded in trauma, and at the same time surpassing it in sublimity. Whereas in the first part of the poem, the speaker's seafaring experience seems unique and isolated, the perspective in the second part has widened to include relationships within a community. As in ritual, the neophyte speaker is situated within a transitional cultural zone, where normative social structure – class, rank, hierarchies of generations and gender – has given way to *communitas*, to "undifferentiated *comitatus* [...] or even communion of equal individuals"

87 Orton, in Liuzza, 353–380.

88 Stanley Greenfield. "*Sylf*, Seasons, Structure and Genre in *The Seafarer*." *Anglo-Saxon England* 9 (1981), 199–213.

(Turner 1977: 96). What the seafarer primarily grapples with here is compunction, the connection between his personalized trauma and human existence, between his "moment of being" and temporality as such. Consequently, as many critics have variously pointed out, the key expression here is "elþeodigra eard," "the land (or dwelling-place) of exiles (or strangers; foreigners)" (38). At the start of his liminal plunge, the seafaring speaker powerfully imagines a community of strangers, of singular human beings, as it appears, united only through their spiritual quest, born of existential crisis. As he names this far-away shore he longs to visit, the speaker's "I," his personal pain, merges with a collective vision: he now knows that all men are travellers on the sea of life, that stripped of their accoutrements, their generous riches, their bold youth, their courageous deeds, their loyal lord, they are without rank or status, equal in their mortal bodies and limited time on earth ("forþon nis þæs modwlonc mon ofer eorðan,/ne his gifena þæs god,/ ne in geoguðe to þæs hwæt,/ne in his dædum to þæs deor, ne him his dryhten to þæs hold,/þæt he a his sæfore sorge næbbe" 39–42). The eventual community of existential questers will have nothing in common with the comfortable life of the "landlubber," of normative, essentialist society: "the blessed man on land knows nothing about the trials of those who travel on the paths of exile" ("þæt se beorn ne wat,/sefteadig secg, hwæt þa sume dreogað/þe þa wræclastas widost lecgað" 55–57). The *home* the seafarer desires, which his "mind's lust" urges him toward ("monað modes lust" 36), is *unheimliche*, an uncanny dwelling-place for a community in transition.[89]

In *The Ritual Process*, Victor Turner notes how within pre-industrial societies, there exist liminal structures of *communitas* in actual organizations and figures, such as conquered aborigines, cult associations and jesters. For instance, in the societies of the Ndembu and Lamba of Zambia, members of cults gain entrance through shared experiences of misfortune, disaster and trauma, thus acquiring "magico-religious properties," their very weakness imbuing them with the power of healers, "with regard to such common goods of mankind as health, fertility, and climate" (109). What primarily distinguishes such cult types and other quasi-mythical groups from the dominant social structure is what Turner, following Henri Bergson, calls "open morality," a fluid, outsider status, in creative contrast to, and often conflict with, the closed, normative, routine world of the insider (110–111). Just as the *rite de passage* of a prospective tribal chief prepares him for moral responsibility by confronting him with the *degree zero* condition of humanity, stripping him of status, wealth and power, so marginal figures and out-groups,

89 Peter Orton's explication of "elþeodigra eard" seems to me to be one of the most reasonable ones; he translates it literally as "the dwelling-place of exiles *(or)* foreigners" and is critical of allegorical interpretation, such as Smithers' (362).

at times, infiltrate, upset and renew the central, static world-order. "In closed or structured societies," say Turner, "it is the marginal or 'inferior' person or the 'outsider' who often comes to symbolize what David Hume has called 'the sentiment for humanity,' which in its turn relates to the model we have termed 'communitas'" (111).

In the liminal phase of *The Seafarer*, the speaker elaborates a figure of a community of outsiders – *elþeodigra eard* – in order to initiate a process of imaginative ethical contrasts to rigid social identity. Since the quest in the poem is that of a marginalized *speaker* seeking cultural authority, it is of paramount significance to weave an intricate web of self-divided tropes, chains of *ku-sololas*, which reflect as alienated mirror to potential cult members. In fact, this middle section of *The Seafarer*, so concerned with articulating personal trauma in a communal idiom, culminates in a moment of sublime revelation, where the speaker sketches an image of himself as an embodied soul. Having imagined *communitas*, the temporal bond between human bodies, and coming to a profound understanding of his outsider status, his difference from the "homebody," the seafarer is inspired to envision an integral image of body and soul, an individualized *psychomachia*, I want to contend, based to some extent on contemporary psychological conceptions, but for the most part revelatory, the outcome of the singular, inventive mind.[90] As the seafarer gives vent to his longing for the "foreign shore," he is transformed into a composite organism where mind, body, spirit and heart act in unison, attempting to constitute the desire of this new subjectivity, this member of uncanny community:

> Forþon nu min hyge hweorfeð ofer hreþerlocan,/min modsefa, mid mereflode,/ofer hwæles eþel hweorfeð wide,/eorþan sceatas; cymeð eft to me/gifre ond grædig, gielleð anfloga,/ hweteð on hwælweg hreþer unwearnum,/ofer holma gelagu; (58–64)
>
> [Therefore my mind now, my spirit, moves beyond my body, travelling with the sea-tide, across the haunt of whales; it ranges widely over the expanse of the earth; it comes back to me, eager and greedy, the bird-soul cries out to the willing heart to depart on the whale's path, over the waters of the sea.][91]

90 Peter Clemoes has shown remarkable similarities between *The Seafarer*'s conception of the flying mind and Alcuin's philosophical and poetic elaborations on the relation between body and soul. "*Mens absentia cogitans* in *The Seafarer* and *The Wanderer*", in A. Pearsall and R.A. Waldron. *Medieval Literature and Civilization: Studies in Memory of G.N. Garmonsway* (London: The Athlone Press, 1969), 62–77.

91 Literally, "anfloga" translates "solitary fier," and there have been speculations within the criticism about its referring to the "sumeres weard," "the warder of summer," the cuckoo of elegy, mentioned a few lines above as harbinger of sea-journeys. Gordon, Whitelock and Orton, for instance, view it in this way; Charles W. Kennedy's translation, however, accords with mine: "Eager, desirous, the lone sprite returneth;/It cries in my ears and it urges my heart," in *An Anthology of Old English Poetry* (New York: Oxford University Press, 1960).

The psychomachia, the moral performance of self, enacted here is that of divided faculties, which nontheless constitute an integral subjectivity, an enlightened "I." Despite the seafarer's sense of trauma and his almost obsessive preoccupation with mortality, at this point in the poem, he almost achieves the elegist's task of self-surpassing, of displacing a visceral sensation of death onto sublime trope. The mortal body communicates passionately with the transcendent soul, which is presented in almost physical terms, "eager and greedy," an ally of the mind and the heart, not their binary opposite. "The bird-soul" is a consolatory image, articulating death as a part of life in the language of both individual and community. It is, as was *The Wanderer*'s "grace," eschatological sublimity.

Mimesis versus Mimicry

Unlike *The Wanderer*'s symbolic activity, however, the seafarer's creative aspiration does not extend into cultural work. Instead of an exploration of the new psychological dynamic the speaker has envisioned, the next statement presents a blunt contradiction of it, an image, in fact, of the conformist Christian subject, not of uncanny character. No longer does the speaker's pscyhomachia stage an integral dialogue between body and soul, but almost perversely turns into a depiction of conventional morality: "because the joys of the lord are more enticing to me than this dead, transitory life on land" ("forþon me hatran sind,/dryhtnes dreamas flonne þis deade lif,/læne on londe" 64–65). Subsequently, as in *The Wanderer*'s last section, the first person narration in the poem – the "Ic" – broadens into a public voice, disquisitioning now on contemporary values and issues, in contrast to the previous autobiographical fixation. On the other hand, whereas vocal transition in *The Wanderer* follows a genuine psychological and aesthetic logic, because *naming* here implies Oedipal displacement, the Christian "homilist" in *The Seafarer* sounds like an illogical intruder, connected only in the most superficial terms to the previous voluble voice. The seafarer's psychomachia, his embodied soul, can be understood as the last threshold, as the crucial *limen*, in his rite of passage, through which he passes into the last phase of aggregation, assimilation with social structure. Why is the seafarer's passage conformist, not heroic or hagiographic to the same extent as is Caedmon's, who expertly combined the older secular knowlegde with Christian ideology? Why does it lead to functionalist composition and not to the wanderer's creative figuration?[92]

92 The sense that the structure of *The Seafarer* is disjointed has persisted in the criticism, with early readers, in particular, contending that the "homiletic section was an interpolation; especially, W. W. Lawrence was certain lines 103–24 were a later

As I suggested previously, the major reason for *The Seafarer*'s flawed structure is the movement within the poem of *pathological* desire, of destructive *jouissance*. In the ritual phases of separation and liminality, traumatic experience was recollected and re-imagined in an extended narcissistic narrative, without traversal through the Oedipal juncture, and the concomitant renunciation of the mOther's desire and assumption of place in the intersubjective matrix of the Symbolic. In other words, the entire structure of *The Seafarer* is narcissistic: like Ovid's Narcissus, the seafaring speaker is fixated on his desire for self-presence, unable to surmount the realization of subjective lack, instead mourning the "very plenty [that] makes [him] poor," wishing only for death.[93] The curative function of *communitas* in the liminal phase, the transferential context it provides the traumatized speaker does not cover his libidinal excess, his drive for death. Although he strives to displace this drive unto a consolatory image – the embodied soul – his narcissistic regression overpowers his elegiac impulse. It is as if the weight of his own body is too heavy, too much of a materialistic obstacle, to be sublimated into a renewed espistemological symbol. As it turns out, Christian ascetic morality, the binary view of the human subject as sinful body versus redeemable spirit offers the seafarer a more apt system of representation than does his own vernacular psychology and newfound sense of modern interiority.

A fruitful psychoanalytic explanation for *The Seafarer*'s narcissistic structure is "the compulsion to repeat," adumbrated by Freud in many of his metapsychological writings, especially in *Beyond the Pleasure Principle* (1920). Here, Freud comments extensively on primarily three phenomena, encountered both in analytic practice and outside it, which cause much marvel for actively deviating from the pleasure principle proper, that is, from that mental principle which "tend[s] towards stability," toward regulating the balance between pleasure and unpleasure in the human organism (9).[94] In the first case, traumatic neurosis, a psychological illness prevalent after World War I, appears to negate the theory of dreams as wish-fulfillment, since traumatized patients repeatedly dream of the initial frightful accident; even if they consciously avoid harmful memories, it is as if the unconscious propels them again and again toward pain. In the second instance, familiar to Freud from the analytic situation, in the first stages of therapy, analysands are more inclined "to *repeat* the repressed material as contemporary experience instead of, as the physician would prefer to see, *remembering* it as something belonging to the past" (18; Freud's italics); the acting out of painful

addition, "*The Wanderer* and *The Seafarer*," *Journal of English and German Philology* 4 (1902): 460–80.

93 See my discussion of the Narcissus episode in the *Metamorphoses* in chapter two.

94 The quote is G. T. Gechner's from *Einige Ideen zur Schöpfungs-und Entwichlungsgeschichte des Organismen* (Leipzig 1873).

situations occurs primarily in the transference, the patient, as it were, compelled by some "'daemonic' force" to re-visit and to re-live the traumatic events of the past (esp. 21; 35). Freud's third strange phenomenon of repetition occurs in the "normal" context of children's games: here, the major example is the one-and-a-half year old grandson, who with a wooden reel, cast back and forth, accompanied by the sounds *fort* (gone) and *da* (there), stages the disappearance and return of his mother. Whereas Freud acknowledges the "child's great cultural achievement," his feat of symbolic substitution, he also marvels at his willingness to undergo distress (15).[95] Does the propensity of children in general to repeat unpleasant experience point to an impulse in the mind, working "independently of the pleasure principle," yet yielding a kind of negative satisfaction?(16).

Indeed, Freud's major conclusion in *Beyond the Pleasure Principle* is that the compulsion to repeat is born of negative libido, a mental agency poised in a state of tension within the constitution of the ego. The fact that not only traumatized subjects and patients in psychoanalysis, but normal childhood itself, register an almost "daemonic" desire to return to situations of pain runs counter to the previous monistic view of the pleasure principle as ruling force in the psyche. As so often basing his investigation on interdisciplinary evidence, on biology, philosophy and myth, Freud affirms the *dualistic* nature of instinctual life, the tension within the human subject between constructive and destructive drives. In other words, pleasure – *jouissance* – is a double force, aspiring, on one hand, to an enhancement of life, to sublimation, on the other, to destructive inertia, to death (36).

The tension between retrograde narcissistic desire and creative production is a dominant force in *The Seafarer*. As we saw in the liminal phase of the poem, the speaker works toward displacing his sense of trauma unto a consoling vision of an alienated, yet vital, human body, bound to other bodies in a land of the future. The compulsion to repeat, however, the desire to return to the source of pain in the past overrides the work of restitution. Instead of elaborating on his newfound knowledge of self, the speaker re-visits death in the language of Christian doctrine. The terrifying experience in the first part of the poem, the naked encounter with nothingness, is recapitulated in the last part in the rhetorical patterns and motifs of homily.

According to the psychological law or logic of ritual, an initiate crosses the last *limen* into social aggregation as a result of revelation. For instance, in *Isoma*, the women's ritual of the Ndembu tribe, investigated by Victor Turner, psychosomatic illness, such as infertility, is partially cured in a quasi-psychoanalytic situation, where the repressed is made visible to the patient, "grasped by the mind, made

95 The "fort-da" episode is central to Lacan's interpretation of Freud in "The agency of the letter in the unconscious or reason since Freud."

capable of being thought about, [...] dealt with, mastered" (Turner 26). Also, in the liminal phases of initiation rites, the participants' insight into *communitas*, the essential mortal bond between human beings, ensures their successful re-integration into social structure as figures of authority (Turner esp. 95–102). What happens at the seafarer's threshold, however, his social re-entry, is the outcome of functionalist conversion, not genuine revelation. Because the trial of the subject in the poem is within language, a process of authorization through speech, the pre-requisite for mastery is the Oedipal resolution. It should be clear by now that, unlike the speaker in *The Wanderer*, the seafarer bypasses the Oedipal task, persisting in the narcissistic pattern of acting out painful events, not working through them.

Although I admire Peter Orton's discussion of *The Seafarer*'s "diary" structure and of its symbolic techniques, and find many of his psychological observations penetrating, I do not perceive the poem in the same terms as a controlled entity, where the alienating experience of the first half smoothly motivates the Christian view in the last section (esp. 367–376). It is true that the speaker's divided sense of self reverberates to some extent in the Christian view of religious exile, especially in the conception of *peregrinatio*, of ascetic voyage toward the heavenly home. In this respect, Orton contends that the abrupt conversion to ascetic morality "in the scheme of the seafarer's personal development represent[s] [...] the remedy for the alienation from life on land that he has been describing so feelingly" (367). In the Christian religion, the seafarer discovers a "positive" social identity as opposed to his former isolation and outcast status (368). The drive of the poem, however, especially in the middle section is toward a kind of visionary existentialism, an open morality, based on the integrated human body, mortal as well as imaginative. The seafarer expresses this vision through an original psychomachia, a starting point, perhaps, for a new, materialistic morality. In fact, the Christian discourse the seafarer opts for is a stark contradiction of his "negative" identity. In the form of the Anglo-Saxon homily, the seafarer's major concerns – time, mortality, community and the social self – are deprived of their vitality and transformed into static binaries. Thus, the prevalent juxtaposition of the poem's final speech is *ruin* versus the heavenly home, a negation of the earlier dynamic vision of "elþeodigra eard," the uncanny community of embodied souls.

Because he bypasses the Oedipal resolution, the seafarer's authority as religious spokesman is diminished; his aggregation into social structure is semblance only, a short-cut for his narcissistic compulsion. Indeed, in the Christian formulations of Anglo-Saxon homily, the speaker recovers a rhetoric of death, exemplified by the expression, "þis deade lif, læne on londe," "this dead, transitory life on land" (66–67). In various guises death rules the earth as "sickness or old age" ("adl oþþe yldo" 70), as "violence of war" ("ecghete"), as "fading looks" ("onsyn blacað" 91), as "the laments of greybeards" ("gomelfeax gnorrað" 92). The genre of *plaint*, a melancholy speech act, which obstructs cure in *The Wanderer*, is the prevalent style of homily. Nothing avails the decaying, sinful body, neither riches, joy, nor the company of friends (97–100). Unless self-indulgent materialism is rejected, at the end of life, only the cold grave welcomes the helpless flesh; in the homily, the stark confrontation with elemental nature, presented in the first part of the poem, is transformed into grotesque display:

> He who loses his life has no use for the body,/nor can he swallow sweet things, nor feel pain,/ nor move his hand nor think thoughts with his mind. (94–96)
>
> [Ne mæg him þonne se flæschoma þonne him þæt feorg losað/ne swete forswelgan, ne sar gefelan,/ne hond orhreran, ne mid hyge þencan.]

The trials of existence which initiated the seafarer's quest and prompted him to tell his "true tale" – "soðgied" – are, in the last part of the poem, abandoned in favor of a moral doctrine which not only minimizes their significance, but ridicules them as aberrations in the life of the virtuous.

The seafarer's abrupt adoption of a rhetoric of death is a symptom of his persistant, even pathological, narcissism. In her investigation of so-called "border-line" patients in relation to Freud's conception of narcissism, Julia Kristeva characterizes their psychic constitution as *empty*, and their often voluble, fashionable discourse as "a screen for emptiness" (21).[96] In one of her fascinating case studies, on "John, the ferryman," Kristeva follows the patient's slow recovery from incomplete separation from the mother, through what she calls *abjection* toward the Oedipus complex proper, the triangulation eclipsed in infancy. Like the pscyhotic, the borderline case suffers from a pathological relationship with language, although here foreclosure of the paternal signifier does not entail retreat into hallucinatory fantasy, but rather compulsive repetition of a "castrated" discourse, of barren signs, without subjective significance.[97] In a way, the border-line patient's language can be described as "post-modern," because

> for these patients nothing is taboo because nothing seems meaningful: all their utterance lacks depth, and their stream of words, far from repressing anything simply seem to be masking a void. (Moi 1986: 239)[98]

The analytic situation, especially the transference, reveals the source of John's, the ferryman's, pathology to be the *phallic* mother, that is, a pre-Oedipal situation dominated by maternal desire, pre-empting identification with a father. Following to some extent Freud's discussion in *Group Psychology and the Analysis of*

96 Julia Kristeva, "Freud and Love: Treatment and its Discontents," in *Tales of Love*. Trans. Leon S. Roudiez (New York: Columbia University Press, 1987), 21–56.
97 See my discussion above in chapter three of foreclosure in Lacanian analysis.
98 Toril Moi. *The Kristeva Reader* (New York: Columbia University Press, 1986)

the Ego, Kristeva stresses the developmental role of just such an *archaic* father, who functions for the child as a magnet of sublimated love, of *agape*, as opposed to the mother's desire, the eroticized attachment to the maternal body. The child's deprivation of the pre-Oedipal purification forms and prolongs his narcissistic character, his impotence in love, his love-hate attitude to the mother and his overwhelming sense of abjection (esp. 48–51).

The relevance of Kristeva's case history to *The Seafarer* lies precisely in the connection made between narcissistic structure and abjection. In the homiletic section of the poem, the speaker's compulsion to repeat existential trauma registers a kind of nauseous, disgusted attitude toward the trials and tribulations of the body. Whereas in liminal space, a creative effort was made to displace narcissistic loss unto a sublime sign – the embodied soul – the entry into Christian discourse reactivates retrograde desire, *Thanatos*, the drive for death. The seafarer's rite of passage, the voyage toward visibility, toward the Janus-faced symbol, the uncanny home of individual and community, turns back on itself in ascetic *peregrinatio*, the binary rhetoric of homiletic morality. In the concluding lines of the poem, the *home* envisioned, the heavenly habitation ("Wuton we hycgan hwær we ham agen/ond þonne geþencan hu we þider cumen" 117–118), severed from "this dead transitory life on earth," presents a stark negation of "elþeodigra eard," the uncanny company of strangers; in psychological terms, as an outcome of the work of mourning in the poem, it is best understood as a space of abjection, harbouring the empty landscape of the narcissitic subject.

In her lucid explication of Kristeva's conception of the *abject*, Toril Moi notes that it is "neither subject nor object [but] may be defined as a kind of 'pre-object' or, perhaps as a *fallen* object" (1986: 238; Moi's emphasis). As psychic Imaginary space, the abject preceeded ego formation at the mirror stage, "represent[ing] the first effort of the future subject to separate itself from the pre-Oedipal mother" (238). Because of the archaic ingredients of this arena of struggle, the domination of (im)pure corporeality, the "pre-subject" establishes itself through "radical revulsion," through "nausea, distaste and horror" (238). On parallel lines of development to the later Oedipal resolution, only an *imaginary* father's intervention can interrupt abjection and channel drives toward healthy identification. Thus, this pre-phallic father functions as a sublimating ideal for the child, analogous to the role of analyst in transference. Kristeva emphasizes the distinction to be made, even at the incipient narcissistic stage, between types of identification: on one hand, the child identifies *metonymically* with the mother as erotic body; on the other hand, the relation between archaic father and child is *metaphoric*, an instance of *agape*, of love in a purified state (246–248).

The analogy Kristeva establishes here between the imaginary father and the psychoanalyst coincides with my elaboration of the role of literary character as post-transferential authority. In general, in the Old English elegies, mourning works toward constructing a new epistemological figure or metaphor, as we have seen, in both *The Wanderer* and *The Seafarer*, potentially compounded of individual desire and communal concerns. The fact that the seafarer's creative figuration eventually collapses is, as I have suggested on several occasions, due to his excessive libidinal fantasy, to the desire for (maternal) presence at the origin of traumatic loss. The destructive eroticism of this *metonymic* drive eclipses metaphoric identification in the poem: instead of the uncanny – full, integral subjectivity – *The Seafarer* constructs character as an abject, Narcissus as "a screen for emptiness." Because it eventually bypasses all symbolic intervention – the imaginary father as well as the Name-of-the-Father – the abject constitutes an *empty* subjectivity, born along with the death drive and the longing to extinguish self; in contradistinction, the uncanny represents character proper – the proper name for the fullness and ethical consistency of new narcissistic being.[99]

The conclusion that *The Seafarer* partly fails as a creative figuration of character does not, in my estimation, undermine its powerful lyricism nor its greatness as a Christian poem.[100] Even if the outcome of the poetic work is a stale version of Christian identity, the imaginative contradiction between the last performance and the autobiographical trial in the first part also results in a powerful sense of *ambivalence*, which acutally exceeds, and subverts, closure. From liminal exploration, the seafarer turns into a hyperbolic homilist, miming the Christian rhetoric of death and, with reformist zeal, advocating its binary moral logic, the severance of sinful body from repentant spirit. At the same time, instead of clinching the speaker's conversion, this extravagant, almost ridiculous turnabout, *inadvertently* exposes the hegemonic tendencies, moral control and repressive limits of the Christian religion.[101] Viewed retrospectively as a complete aesthetic ritual – a rite of passage of the imaginative mind – *The Seafarer* represents an ambivalent discourse where *mimicry*, the repetitive imitation of a dominant rhetoric or ideology, is posited against *mimesis*, the "diary"-like, empirical account of subjective desire and its vicissitudes. Even if the cultural/historical situation of Anglo-Saxon Chris-

99 See especially Kristeva's discussion of abjection as self-expulsion in *Powers of Horror*. Trans. Leon S. Roudiez (New York: Columbia University Press, 1982), esp. on "the improper/unclean," 2–4.

100 Note Jerome Mandel's statement: "*The Seafarer* is a completely unified and coherent poem. It is a Christian poem. It is also a great poem because, and not in spite of, the Christian design and conception" (95), *Alternative Readings in Old English Poetry* (New York: Peter Lang, 1987). Despite conflicting arguments, most recent readers of the poem would agree.

101 I want to emphasize that such exposure is not the automatic outcome of Christian literature. As I will continue to examine, *Resignation* operates as a more authentic instance of Christianity, as a teaching of humility and repentance.

tianity is different from problems of empire and colonialism in the nineteenth and twentieth centuries, Home Bhabha's analysis of mimic textuality helpfully explains the primary contradiction in *The Seafarer*.[102]

Bhabha's major contention is that colonial texts, especially those authored by spokesmen for empire, such as Charles Grant's "Observations on the State of Society of Great Britain" and Maculay's *Infamous Minute* (1835), present instances of self-contradiction, or self-subversion, because their articulation of the historical circumstance is *double*; despite themselves, these texts cast a divided gaze upon the Other, the colonial subject, as both racially inferior and a duplicate British citizen. Charles Grant, for instance, expresses an ambivalent attitude toward Indian colonials; as Christian emissary, he desires to refrom them morally, and, at the same time, for political reasons, fearful of native rebellious tendencies, he suggests that this reform should be an indoctrination in British manners only, "a 'partial' diffusion of Christianity." Thus, Grant advocates a divided colonial subjectivity, an "'*imitation* of English manners'" as well as a cultivation of native traditions and community (Grant's emphasis; Bhabha 382). Bhabha comments on the inadvertent mockery of Grant's project, how he "violates the evidences of Christianity – a central missionary tenet – which forbade any tolerance of heathen faiths" (381–2).

The idea in this and other colonial texts of reform as mimicry undermines their essentialist pretentions: "the figure of mimicry [...] problematizes the signs of racial and cultural priority, so that the national is no longer naturalizable" (383). Because a *partial* subject is envisioned by the colonial author(ity), "a gaze of otherness" is introduced into the text, returning "the look of surveillance [...] as the displacing gaze of the disciplined" (383). The hegemonic text's self-contradiction lies in this almost perverse logic that "the observer becomes the observed and 'partial' representation rearticulates the whole notion of *identity* and alienates it from essence" (Bhabha's emphasis; 384).

Just such a logic operates in *The Seafarer*'s assumption of Christian identity in the face of the empirical adventure of otherness. Despite – or perhaps because of – the hyperbolic conversion in the last part of the poem, the speaker's partiality, the alien mark of his being, ruptures the seamless discourse he appears so effortlessly to promote. Just as colonial essentialism is undermined by the mimic men it perversely fosters, the "Anglicized," but not English, subjects, so the foundational message of Christian homily is interrupted by its form of mimicry, the screen of repetitions assumed by the abject speaker, Christianized, but not Christian. It is significant that in order to define the psychodynamics of mim-

102 Homi Bhabha. "Of Mimicry and Man: The Ambivalence of Colonial Discourse." *October* 28 (1983), 125–33; reprinted in *Modern Literary Theory*, ed. Philip Rice and Patricia Waugh (London: Arnold, 1989), 380–387.

icry, the way it articulates partial difference – "*almost the same but not quite*" – Bhabha turns to "a Freudian figure," to fantasy, "caught *inappropriately* between the unconscious and the preconscious" (384; Bhabha's emphasis). In his essay on "The Unconsious" (1915), Freud speculates on this mixed, slippery origin of fantasy, comparing it to

> individuals of mixed race who taken all around resemble white men but who betray their coloured descent by some striking feature or other and on that account are excluded from society and enjoy none of the privileges. (Bhabha 384; Freud 190–1)[103]

The appearance of exclusionary features, of the aberration which divides identity, in hegemonic texts, is, according to Bhabha, not an instance of "the return of the repressed," but of the *metonymy of presence*, the ambivalence of desire in discourse, which in approaching presence, or essence, succeeds only in displaying the force of difference (384).

In *The Seafarer*, the metonymy of presence registers in the speaker's overwhelming desire for a *home*. In the beginning of the poem, separated from community, the seafarer is confronted with the terrifying facts of existence as a state of homelessness, a revelation which motivates him to forge his own alienated vision as a cultural spokesman, The second section, analogous to the liminal phase in a rite of passage, takes the form of a quest toward a creation of an *uncanny* home of outsiders, where a new materialistic ethics is glimpsed in a sublime image of the human subject as embodied soul. Metonymic desire, however, overpowers metaphoric identification; the compulsion to repeat the originary event of trauma diffuses the elegaic work toward restitution. The final section, composed of the Christian rhetoric of death, provides the seafarer with a mimic home, which he delineates, with reformist zeal, to an audience of potential converts:

> Wuton we hycgan hwær we ham agen/ond þonne geþencan hu we þider comen,/ond we þonne eac tilien þæt we to moten/in þa ecan eadignesse/þær is lif gelong in lufan dryhten,/hyht in heofonum. (117–121)
>
> [Let us consider where our home is/and then consider how to get there/and then we will always strife to achieve in that place/bliss for eternity,/where the source of life is within the love of God, high in heaven] .

Within the context of *The Seafarer*'s pscyhological work, this conventional Christian home is, despite (or because of) the avowal of a single origin, an impure fantasy, merely resembling, not matching, the speaker's existential adventure. Nevertheless, in that fissure, opening up between reality and semblance, truth breaks forth in uncanny measure.

---

103 Sigmund Freud. "The Unconscious" (1915). *SE* XIV (London: Hogarth Press, 1957).

Superego in *Resignation*

Poems such as *The Wanderer*, *The Seafarer* and *Resignation* present landscapes of the mind rather than fully fledged realistic stories or allegorical elaborations. In the previous section on *The Seafarer*, I contended that the speaker's sudden advocacy of Christian moral doctrine is mimic speech, not genuine conversion, inadvertently rupturing the logic of homily and undermining the closure it so ardently desires. Even if an end to journeying and to exile is envisioned in the Christian heaven in the concluding lines of the poem, the tension between that conventional image of home and the uncanny community of the preceding section, born of trauma and the work of mourning, persists as *The Seafarer*'s hallmark; the effect of character construction is *partial* subjectivity, a Christianized screen, not Christian identity proper.

Like the seafaring speaker, the penitent in *Resignation* seeks a remedy for his experience of devastating misery on earth.[104] The poem operates, in the manner of the major elegies, according to a principle of mental ritual, moving through phases of separation, liminal initiation and aggregation into social structure or discourse. Psycholinguistically, it is also an elegiac work, striving toward sublimating restitution for primary, or narcissistic, loss. Again, parallel to its companion pieces, *Resignation* is marked by effects of character construction, the speaker's travail in language toward uncanny figuration, which will match his newfound sense of self as an ex-centric (and ec-centric), a self-divided being. Even if *Resignation* is less than an aesthetically satisfying poem to modern readers, in my estimation, it accomplishes restitution more successfully than the narcissistic seafarer.[105] In this section, I will argue that the penitential speaker achieves mental balance, which is most fruitfully examined from the perspective of Freud's anatomy of mind, as outlined, in particular, in *The Ego and the Id* (1923), *Group Psychology and the Analysis of the Ego* (1921) and *Civilization and its Discontents* (1930). At the forefront here is the agency of the superego in the contstruction of Christian character.

104 All references to *Resignation* are to Krapp's and Dobbie's edition of the *Exeter Book*. Unless otherwise noted, all translations from the Old English are mine.

105 In an early influential assessment of *Resignation* – calling it *The Penitent's Prayer* – E.G. Stanley compares it unfavorably to *The Seafarer*: "Unlike *The Seafarer*, the manner of exposition in *The Penitent's Prayer* is confused" (494). "Old English Poetic Diction and The Interpretation of *The Wanderer*, *The Seafarer* and *The Penitent's Prayer*, in *Essential Articles for the Study of Old English Poetry*, eds. Jess B. Bessinger and Stanley J. Kahrl (Hamden: Archon Books, 1968), 488–514. In general, critics discuss the merits of *Resignation* with reservations; see especially Alan Bliss and Allen J. Frantzen. "The Integrity of *Resignation*." *The Review of English Studies* 27 (1976), 385–402, and Anne L. Klinck. "*Resignation*: Exile's Lament or Penitent's Prayer?" *Neophilologus* 71 (1987), 423–430.

Within the criticism, the view of *Resignation* as a unitary, balanced, structure is less than a common one. An influential contestation is Alan Bliss' and Allen Frantzen's article "The Integrity of *Resignation*" (1976), where quite convincing material is gathered to make a case for a missing folio in the *Exeter Book*, between lines 69 and 70, and consequently for the fragmented disposition of the poem. Bliss' and Frantzen's rather radical claim is that *Resignation* is not a complete poem at all, but parts of two generically different poems, which they designate as "*Resignation* A" (ending with folio 118b) and "*Resignation* B" (beginning with folio 119a). The sense of former critics that poetic unity, despite their best efforts, remains problematic, reflected, for instance, in a proliferation of titles – *Gebet*, *A Prayer*, *Klage Eines Vertriebenen*, *The Exile's Prayer*, *The Penitent's Prayer*, *Resignation* – is vindicated by the missing leaf, which also brings into purview disparities in genre, style, dialect and theme between the two halves of the poem.[106] In the thrill of discovery, Bliss and Frantzen even go so far as to read "*Resignation* B" as a unique piece, "not at all like any other Old English poem" (401), a psychological study of a morally dissolute man "who never succeeds in any of his enterprises, and who blames everyone but himself for his failure" (397). Further, the critics sever any relation to the companion pieces, *The Wanderer* and *The Seafarer*, established, in particular, by Stanley, emphasizing that the speaker in "*Resignation* B" is not an exile at all, but a man fallen on hard times, feeling sorry for himself (26–27).

As Karma Lochrie observes, Bliss and Frantzen go to interpretive extremes in their arduous attempt to debunk previous "unitarian" readings of *Resignation*.[107] Nontheless, in her essay on a thematic group in the *Exeter Book*, Lochrie accepts the *hypothesis* of a missing manuscript leaf as a fact, a basis for her analysis of *Resignation* as separate poems, albeit with a shared concern, the influence of divine *wyrd* upon human existence. John Pope also considers Bliss' and Frantzen's argumentation as equal to evidence, terming it "the most interesting discovery" within the field of *Exeter Book* paleography (28–29).[108]

---

106 Earlier commentators such as P. L. Henry and E. G. Stanley argue for a unified *Resignation* but generally find it more difficult to combine the confessional mode with the narrative of exile than in *The Wanderer* and *The Seafarer*; see Henry's chapter on *The Penitent's Prayer* in *The Early English and Celtic Lyric* (London: George Allen, 1996), 176–180, and E. G. Stanley's essay, "Old English Poetic Diction and the Interpretation of *The Wanderer*, *The Seafarer* and *The Penitent's Prayer*."

107 Karma Lochrie. "Wyrd and the Limits of Human Understanding: A Thematic Sequence in the *Exeter Book*." *Journal of English and Germanic Philology* 85 (1986), 323–331; n7, 324.

108 John Pope. "Paleography and Poetry: Some Solved and Unsolved Problems of the Exeter Book," in *Medieval Scribes, Manuscripts, and Libraries: Essays Presented to N. R. Ker*, eds. M. B. Parkes and Andrew Watson (London: Scholar, 1978).

On the other hand, Anne Klinck has shown that Bliss and Frantzen examine only the *possibility* of a missing leaf whereas the situation they describe – a single sheet in lieu of the more regular double sheet – is not so unusual in a manuscript setting: "it is only on a basis of discontinuity in the poem that they regard the loss as certain" (423). Klinck's aim is to re-establish connections within the poem, based on co-ordinates of the journey motif, which, despite disparate poetic modes, are articulated in both parts as the speaker's desire for a *home* (424). As in *The Seafarer*, and to a lesser extent in *The Wanderer*, journeying in *Resignation* implies both an autobiographical experience and an allegorical dimension, the speaker's ascetic lifestyle, for instance, as well as his spiritual yearning. The binding element between the two parts of the poem, according to Klinck, is the word *ferðweg* (72) – soul's road – which occurs midway and links the previous penitential prayer to the actual exile's journey (427). In part one, the speaker prays that he may reform his earlier wicked ways and learn how to prepare the spirit for the heavenly kingdom (41–46); just before the shift to autobiography his wish is re-stated, echoing both its previous urgency and verbal choice: in both cases, the soul is on a penitential quest toward the bliss of heaven.[109] Klinck claims that there is no sharp division between the mode of prayer and the exile's narrative, whereas Bliss and Frantzen assign lines 72–75 to "*Resignation B*." Thus, the literal voyage contemplated in the concluding lines is associated with "the soul's road" embarked upon in the speaker's mood of meditation. Klinck suggests that perhaps the most suitable title is the older *The Exile's Prayer*, capturing as it does the integrity of the poem's utterance, the expression of its desire in language for a (heavenly) home (424).

Clearly, the poetic patternings here, generic, verbal and psychological, invite close comparisons with *The Seafarer* whose speaker, as we saw, was propelled by metonymic desire to devise closure to a quest initiated by traumatic loss. In fact, in both poems, not only are there parallels between dualistic utterance, at one point in personalized, "diary," style and at another in a Christianized genre, but between the concrete situation of the speaker as well: in *The Seafarer* a devastating experience, involving fundamentally a confrontation with pure negativity alienates the protagonist from his own nativity, from country, kinsmen, "the joy of life in cities" ("lifes wyn,/gebiden in burgum" 27–28) and the landlubber, the man "blessed with bounty" (esteadig secg" 56), "proud and flushed with wine" ("wlonc and wingal" 29); not matching the intensity of the seafarer's ordeal, the penitent in *Resignation* also laments a loss of origins, a dissociation from a native community ("eþle"), and

109 Compare these lines from part one and part two: "nu ic fundige to þe […] / feroma me þonne/wyrda walend, in þinne wudordream" (41–45); frætwian mec on ferðweg ond fundian/sylf to þam siþe þe ic asettan sceal,/gæst gearwian ond me þæt eal for gode þolian/bliþe mode" (72–75).

the fate of the "friendless exile" (91). As is the case with the *Exeter Book* elegies in general, the precise cause for sorrow is not given in *Resignation* although there are hints that some sort of feud or malicious slander drove the speaker away, turning him into an outcast, a poor wretch, dependant on the "kindness of strangers" ("þonne ic me to fremþum freode hæfde,/cyðþu gecweme" 114–115) and hoping only for remedy in the life hereafter ("Is seo bot æt þe/gelong æfter life" 110–111).[110] In both *The Seafarer* and *Resignation* the destitute speaker concludes his travails by displacing existential misery onto the Christian faith, its ascetic morality, penitential doctrine and stoic philosophy. Whereas the seafaring speaker, however, abruptly, and, in my interpretation, unconvincingly shifts from liminal exploration of an earthly home to hortatory speech about the afterlife, the penitent in *Resignation* achieves a balanced discourse, a smooth transition between empirical alienation and Christian vision. How is such balance obtained?[111]

In the first place, the *reversed* ritual process in *Resignation*, where social discourse precedes separation, creates a therapeutic context, within which the speaker, on the model of psychoanalytic transference, is guided away from a compulsion to repeat to active remembrance. In fact, the beginning section of *Resignation*, a mixture of confession and prayer, would have worked admirably, with slight alterations, as the concluding speech of *The Seafarer*, because what underlies aggregation here is the curative principle of ritual – *ku-solola* – the naming of the hidden or repressed. As I pointed out in the discussion of *The Seafarer*, the regressive desire in the poem, its narcissistic form, elides the Oedipal resolution, so that social entry is marked by the abject subject, not authentic character. In contrast, at the start, the speaker in *Resignation* has crossed the *limen*, the threshold to the Symbolic, from the state of miserable outcast, he recalls at the poem's end. As almost all the Old English elegies, *Resignation* assumes processual form; unlike *The Wanderer* and *The Seafarer*, however, it does not follow a chronological *Bildung*, but depicts an image of mind in the synchrony of rehabilitation. The situation is similar to the alterior space-time unit of psychoanalysis: conventional progressive time is suspended in favor of the complex psychic *chronotope*, where relations between past, present and future are performed and revised for the sake of regenerative memory. Although the mind in *Resignation* belongs to a rather

110 Klinck makes a comparison with family feud as the reason for exile in *The Wife's Lament* (1987: 425).

111 I want to make clear that my focus is upon menta/psychological balance, not aesthetic harmony. The *tension* in *The Seafarer* is aesthetically much more productive than the rather static equilibrium in *Resignation*.

conventional Christian framework, it is particularly instructive about the mode of being of character in literature.[112]

Christian character intersects in illuminating ways with Freud's model of mind, especially with the delineation of the agency of the superego. Psychic constitution presents, according to Freud, the outcome of a series of substitutions. Within the type of psychoanalytic psychomachia, the dynamic interrelations between psychic agencies, conscious and unconscious, Freud is concerned with outlining in *The Ego and the Id*, the superego functions first as vehicle of infantile identifications with the primary, or archaic, father and secondly as "the heir to the Oedipal complex," the representation of the "father complex" as a general principle in the human mind (38). It is important to note that Freud's mental anatomy is not hierarchially constituted and that the superego, because of its derivation from the most archaic object-cathexis, reaches deeper into unconsious territory than the ego and combines "the lowest part of the mental life" with its function as an ego ideal, a substitute father function (26–27). As the term implies, the *super*-ego stands in a position of superiority to the ego, watching it, restraining it and judging it; it is set up as a sublimating *ideal* by the ego as a resolution to the conflicts at the Oedipal phase. At the same time, this higher moral faculty "is always close to the id and can act as its representative *vis-à-vis* the ego" (39); the mastery of the Oedipus complex results in an ideal which persists in entanglement in that very complex "and thus [...] is also the expression of the most powerful impulses and the most important libidinal vicissitudes of the id" (26). The superego is a contradictory force in the mind, repressing the libidinal substance which drives it.

In chapter two above, "Narcissus: From Ovid to Freud," I discussed in some detail Freud's critique in *Civilization and its Discontent* of the predominance of a strict superego in the moral mentality of Western culture. Whereas in "On Narcissism," Freud envisions a harmonizing role for the ego ideal, especially as it

---

112 The *chronotope* is M. M. Bakhtin's conception of temporal-spatial relations in the novel. By tracing the evolution, and generic variations, of chronotopes, Bakhtin aimed at writing a historical poetics, with emphasis on the relaltivized "image of Man" in literature. Thus, the chronotope is significant for a discussion of literary character, in the case of the elegies, especially "the chronotope of the threshold": it is "highly charged with emotion and value [...] the chronotope of crisis and break in life" (248). See "Forms of Time and the Chronotope in the Novel," in *The Dialogic Imagination*, ed. Michael Holquist, trans. Caryl Emerson and Michael Holquist (Austin: University of Texas Press, 1981), 84–258. See an interesting application of the threshold chronotope to two of Henry James' novels, *The Portrait of a Lady* and *The Golden Bowl*: Lisa Eckstrom. "Moral Perception and the Chronotope: The Case of Henry James," in *Bakhtin in Context: Across the Disciplines*, ed. Amy Mandelker (Evanston: Northwestern University Press, 1995), 99–116. Below, I will have occasion to return to Bakhtin's chronotope, especialy in the analysis of *The Wife's Lament*.

evolves intersubjectively, within a situation of love, in the later post-war essay, this ideal is analyzed almost exclusively in its prohibitive function, it its position as a guilt-inducing, tyrannical father. The possibility that the individual subject may transform paternal identification, and subsequent repression, into healthy self-regard, into a balanced agency, weighing pleasure and guilt on scales of ethical concerns, dissolves in the pessimistic outlook of human destructiveness advocated in *Civilization and its Discontents*. Here, the relationship between ego and superego is described entirely in terms of aggression, whereby a punishing conscience produces *guilt* as the dominant state of mind of the modern individual. In Western culture, the moral mind-set. the psychomachia of the day, is in a state of war:

> Civilization [...] obtains mastery over the individual's dangerous desire for aggression by weakening and disarming it and and by setting up an agency within him to watch over it, like a garrison in a conquered city. (124)

Internalized aggression in the form a defenseless, guilt-ridden supplicant, in bondage to paternal conscience might constitute the essence of character in Christian civilization. My analysis of *The Seafarer* indicates that at the poem's conclusion the Christian *rhetoric of death* enhances the speaker's pathological narcissism, his compulsion to repeat; by adopting a moral doctrine, based on aggressive psychomachia, the speaker compromises his rich existential vision of a community of strangers in harmony. An aggressive morality can also be said to characterize *Resignation*. In the first section – the prayer – the pentential speaker is presented as a dejected seeker after God's forgiveness, whom he has incorporated as stern, watchful superego, wielding punishment for sins and adamant in demanding absolute renunciation. The penitent seems wrecked with a sense of guilt: he accuses himself for not having listened to God's word before now ("þeah þe ic scyppendum/wuldorcyninge waccor hyrde,/ricum dryhtne, / þonne min ræd wære" 16–18); although hoping for restitution, he feels unworthy, "meriting few mercies in earlier times" ("ic ær on fyrste lyt/earnode arn" 48–49); the expression is often tinged with fear, the sinner, at one point, foreseeing punishment on a par with the banished fallen angels (52–26). The dominance of superego as a vengeful father-substitute is perhaps most forcefully reflected in the proliferation of names for God: "god," "dryhten," "wundorcyning," "leohtes hurde," "tungla hyrde," "meotud," "cyning," "halig heofoncyning," "fæder moncynnes." In "*Resignation I*", lines 1–69, repetitions of, and variations on, the name of the Christian God number no less than thirty! In this speaker's mental universe, the "Name-of-the-Father" is overdetermined.

Despite these conventional features of repressive morality, I maintain that *Resignation* is a therapeutic piece, depicting a healthy balance in the psychic constitution, not "a garrison in a conquered city." In fact, elegiac techniques in *Resignation* bear resemblance to the poetic process in *The Dream of the Rood*, which S. A. J. Bradley has described as "artistry [...] designed to engage the audience in vicarious participation in this [poetic] experiencing and enlightenment" (1995: 158). The patristic tradition, which fostered most early medieval religious writers, elaborated a theory of ritual, in relation to both the liturgy and the Corpus Christi drama, the central tenet of which is Aristotelean *catharsis*, psychological cleansing through empathetic identification with ficitonal imitation of spiritual events (158). As Bradley points out, the early Church fathers – Jerome, Isidore and Gregory – were particularly interested in defining *empathy – compunctio –* and although their perspective, of course, is primarily spiritual and mystical, it encompasses psychological, as well as aesthetic, dimensions. In Defensor's *Liber Scintillarum*, a popular compilation, most likely known by Anglo-Saxon poets, the forms and workings of *compunction* are listed according to the major religious authorities:

> 'Compunction of the heart is humility of the mind arising in tears out of the remembering of sin and the fear of judgment' (Isidore). 'When compunction is poured forth [...] a way appears in our heart through which we come at last to the Savior' (Gregory). [...] 'Compunction is the remission of sins. Compunction attracts to itself the Holy Spirit. Compunction causes Christ the only-begotten to dwell within it' (Epharaim of Syria). (Quoted in Bradley 158)

The formal complexity of *The Dream of the Rood*, its tripartite level of narration, intimately linking the perceptions of implied author, the Dreamer and the Cross, implicates an audience profoundly in the event of the Crucifixion and in the suffering of Christ. Especially, through the portrayal of Christ as tragic hero, a composite of "almighty God" ("god ælmihtig" 39), "young warrior" ("geong hæleð "39), "strong and unflinching" ("strang ond stiðmod" 40) and sacrificial body, members of the audience experience spiritual, as well as psychological, enlightenment. It is a process of identification Gregory the Great compares to love: at first, the penitential viewer or reader feels fear at the thought of his or her own sinfulness; as emotional experience, however, expands and deepens, "fear subsides through prolonged sorrow [...] [and] a feeling of security emerges from an assurance of forgiveness"; in interaction with the spiritual text, the weeping penitent is transformed: "the soul begins to burn with a love for heavenly joys," and finally "the compunction of fear [...] leads the soul to the compunction of love" (*Dialogues*; quoted by Bradley 159).[113]

113 My discussion of *The Dream of the Rood* is to a large extent based on S. A. J. Bradley's introduction to the poem in *Anglo-Saxon Poetry*, 158–160. Citations are from *The Vercelli Book*, ed. George Philip Krapp (London: George Routledge and Sons, 1932).

Not as expertly crafted as *The Dream of the Rood*, *Resignation* contains similar features of a *spiritual exercise*, penitential speech directed at an audience on the threshold of transformative experience. Because of the subtle ways in which the moralizing superego is incorporated into the fundamentally narcissistic constitution of the speaker of the poem, this exercise is quite effective, and, for my purposes, instructive about the formation of character and its role in culture. In a subdued, yet significant way, *Resignation* demonstrates how the aggressive, guilt-inducing superego of Christian morality, internalized as normalizing ideals by medieval subjects, is, in the encounter with literary character, within compunctious indentification, transformed into a more radical agency, an enlightened *conscience*, which lovingly balances the forces of the mind. Whereas the speaker in *The Seafarer* persists in narcissistic lamentations, hidden in the abject rhetoric of homily, *Resignation* achieves a post-transferential state of revised Narcissus, purified of destructive desire and regarding the self with love. Here, in a delicate way, the speaker performs the role of character in *The Wanderer*, in *Hamlet* and in *St Mawr*: a consolatory trope, empowered to act as cultural authority.

In the poem, this empowerment is effected within the transferential context of Christian morality which activates *memory*. Because of the reverse ritual structure, aggregation, or social discourse, preceeding autobiographical separation, the speaker's "soul's road" to enlightenment is from a situation of transference – his prayer, as well as confession, to God – to a vision of himself as an individual worthy of the compunction of love. As Krapp and Dobbie have noted the mood of *Resignation*, at least in the first part, is one of "spiritual dejection" (lx), the penitent projecting an image of himself as prostrate sinner, in fearful anticipation of forgiveness.[114] However, in the manner of the penitential process, as delineated, for instance, by Gregory the Great, in the *Dialogues*, within the context of confession, penance and prayer, the speaker's fear evaporates and turns gradually into sympathetic acceptance, into "love for heavenly joys" (quoted in Bradley 159). In other words, within a situation resembling that of transference in psychoanalysis – in the dialogue with Christian traditions – the speaker's resistance to self-knowledge is broken, and he is guided, not only into a vision of heavenly glory, but into a new image of self. In fact, Bliss' and Frantzen's contention that the last section, "*Resignation B*," "is not at all like any other Old English poem" (1976: 401), in my opinion, applies only if it is seen as an integral part of the poem: the image of the exile here constitutes a moment of revelation – *ku-solola* – whereby the repressed is brought to light like an artifact, amenable to creative cure.

114 "Introduction" to *Resignation*, in the *Exeter Book*, eds. George Philip Krapp and Elliott van Kirk Dobbie (London: George Routledge and Sons, 1936).

Although S. A. J. Bradley, in his suggestive introductions, does not make specific comparisons between *The Dream of the Rood* and *Resignation*, he characterizes both as "spiritual exercises," and with regard to the latter, observes that "the dramatic I-persona is doubtless chosen for the intensity of realization it helps the audience to achieve" (387). In the movement toward revelation, experience in *Resignation* does indeed intensify in the last figure of the exile, which, as Bliss and Frantzen claim, is quite unique, both within the conventional context of penitential literature and of oral-formulaic genres.[115] Even in comparison with the more accomplished companion pieces, *The Wanderer* and *The Seafarer*, the "anhoga" in *Resignation* is in some respects more fully realized, a miserable outcast, "driven in wretchedness from home ("ic afysed eom/earm of minum eþle" 88–89)[116] because of malicious plotting or calumny ("for tæle" 106), living like a beggar, resenting the handouts of strangers ("ond him ælce mæle men fullestað;/ycað his yrmþu" 93–95). Homesickness is more realistic here than in the other elegies, since not only spiritual alienation prevents a return, but material deprivation as well; the speaker is too poor to buy a boat: "because of poverty I cannot fulfill my desire" ("fore minum wonæhtum willan adreogan" 103–104). Social marginality, lonlieness and material destitution appear to be the speaker's doom. Like the wanderer, the seafarer and the female speaker in *The Wife's Lament*, the penitent in *Resignation* recounts this "sad tale" – "þis sarspel": he will "never dwell on earth in the light but always suffer hardships, a destitute man" ("Ic on leohte ne mæg/butan earfoðum ænge þinga,/feasceafthæle, foldan wunian" 110–113). Notwithstanding this depiction of almost unrelieved spiritual and physical misery, the figure of the exile in *Resignation* constitutes *sublime* character, created in a moment of revelation, after loss, fear, dejection and penance.

In a manner analogous to Freud's female patient whose transference-love, at first, a misguided product of resistance, during analysis, becomes a means for self-discovery, the penitent in *Resignation* experiences an interior turn from an overdetermined superego to sublime image of self.[117] With the figure of the wretched outcast, the aggressive morality implied by the poem's "prayer" section is softened, balanced now with an existential vision of elemental humanity. Although this portrayal lacks the intensity of tragic character, as adumbrated, for instance, by Lacan, in his essay on Antigone, it *reveals* a truth, brings to light what is hidden in Christian morality: the materiality of the spirit, the body that

115 On the oral theme of exile, see especially Stanley B. Greenfield's "The Formulaic Expression of the Theme of 'Exile' in Anglo-Saxon Poetry." *Speculum* 30 (1955): 200–206.

116 This is Mackie's translation, reproduced by Klinck, 1987, 425

117 See my discussion above, in chapter five, of Freud's essay, "Observations on Transference Love."

encloses a soul. In a way, the exile in *Resignation* functions as one of the cult types described by Victor Turner in *The Ritual Process*, an outsider to the normative Christian community, whose very being on its fringes upsets and re-defines the dominant *Weltanschauung* (Turner e.g. 110–111). In the synchronic situation of the poem, as an expression of mind in meditation, this individual is the *limen* itself, the threshold into the truth of existence, into Being. By remembering himself as a poor, friendless vagabond, doomed to eternal homelessness, the speaker in *Resignation* balances the Christian superego with the "open morality" of the existential outcast.[118] The poem remains a spiritual exercise in the penitenital tradition. However, unlike *The Seafarer*'s hortatory closure, it calls for an audience's active participation, for compunctious identification with *difference* itself; repentance in this poem is an act of transvaluation, potentially turning aggressive psychomachia into the harmonious relations of an embodied soul.

d. Maternal Form in *The Wife's Lament*

Specializing in proper names, literary character should perhaps be baptized *Alter*, the position of "being for the other."[119] As magnetic textual node, which draws to itself the energies of both fiction and audience, character does not, as the realistic tradition claims, reflect social essences, but re-casts identity as constructed integrity, based on the libidinal drama of loss and restitution. Thus, in literature, character represents the outcome of a transferential relation, within which psychic re-organization has taken place: retrodgrade desire for narcissistic wholeness is transformed into healthy conscience, a third "eye," which surveys self-division, mourns it and repairs it in revelatory substitution. In different ways, the Old English elegies, I have examined so far, exemplify this fundamental aesthetic activity, *The Wanderer* excelling in its powerful trope of existential alienation, *The Seafarer*'s profound insight into negativity cut short by the stilted Christian discourse of death. Although *Resignation* does not carry an equal magnetic force as these two poems, it illustrates particularly well the consolatory function of character, infusing the strict morality of the medieval subject with genuine repentance; in the encounter with the uncanny outsider, the psychomachia of the day, ruled by an aggressive, unrelenting superego, is readjusted to dramatize mental balance, effected by *compunctio*, or in psychoanalytic parlance, by transference love.

---

118 "Open morality" is Henri Bergson's coinage, quoted by Turner, 111.

119 This is how Leon S. Roudiez translates Kristeva's "un être altéré," in *Powers of Horror*, vii.

A fundamental component of literary character, powerfully elucidated by the *Exeter Book* elegies, is its revelatory condition, its coming-into-being in a moment of creative rapture. In the first part of this book, especially in chapter four – "The Other's Desire" – I suggested that characters are versions of the psychoanalytic conception of object *a* – the permutation of primary loss, the narcissistic object, inundated with the mOther's desire – and that one of the most relevant parallels between transference in analysis and aesthetic interactions is the staging of individual fantasy in relation to such objective substitutions. In the analytic situation, cure consists of the production of conscientious pleasure, or *jouissance*, through the movement from pathological attachments to an experience of *agalma*, of desirousness in its pure state. Similarly, reading for character in literature involves an enlightenment in the realm of pleasure: a previously static insistence on self-presence, on the ideal conflation between the knower and the known, perceiver and the perceived, form and meaning, is shattered in the confrontation with the uncanny, with the reflection of self as castrated psyche. The subsequent creation of a new epistemological metaphor is the special joy evoked in the transferential relation which is character.

As the elegies also make clear, especially in terms of their processual form, is that character construction is a trial in language, only on rare occasions consummated in cathartic tropes. What is significant is that without the fundamental quest for substitution for the lost object, literary fictions turn into static, closed entities, projecting only monologic figures, without psychological claims on an audience. Textual movement, desire in language, generated by narcissistic loss, carries the reader, and the reading community, with it in the transferential activity, which ideally leads to the revelatory moment of character; even if, as happened in *The Seafarer*, this moment is not worked through, only glimpsed, the mobilization itself, what I previously referred to as the *effect* of character, cracks open normative structures, rupturing the Symbolic with sublime visions. In *The Seafarer*, the desire for the lost object overrides the liminal insight of otherness, thus trapping the language of the poem in repetitions, in "thanatic" libido. Nevertheless, the poem's pervasive ambiguity, the oscillation between object *a* – the consolatory trope – and retrograde narcissism – the drive for death – reveals the transformative potential of literary character; the failure of the seafarer to sustain its power replicates the failure in psychoanalytic transference to re-position subjective fantasy as the libidinal origin of substitute objects. In Lacanian analysis, the successful appropriation of the analysand's life-story equals his or her constitution as the *cause* of the Other's desire. In literature, such spacing of self, in a moment of blissful discovery, effects the third "I" (and "eye"), the new knowledge we call character.

Like the seafarer, the speaker in *The Wife's Lament* urgently quests for a new relation to object *a*, but fails to position herself as substantial ground for the Other's desire.[120] As many recent critical studies have emphasized, it is on account of the uniqueness of this speaker as female subject that this elegy offers no consolation, neither in terms of wise experience nor religious comfort.[121] In the following discussion, I will be concerned with what Pat Belanoff calls "the differentness" of *The Wife's Lament* as a "woman's song" (1990: 194), but less in terms of social power than psychological constitution. As should be clear by now, my estimation of the uniqueness of the Old English elegies resides in genre rather than gender. The alterior space these poems stake out within the dominant oral-traditional structures temporarily marginalizes them, but at the same time opens up vistas to enduring explorations of the human subject. *The Wife's Lament* participates in the elegies' project of self-exploration; what sets it apart, I will argue, is the particular form it assumes of home for the exile. If in *The Seafarer* and *Resignation*, stability is finally conceived of as the Christian heaven, in *The Wife's Lament*, it is as the maternal imagination. Whereas *The Seafarer* concludes with an abject speaker, trapped within the Christian *Weltanschauung*, *The Wife's Lament* outlines the situation of female abjection, the "prison-house" of the pre-oedipal mother. Below, I will investigate this strange space in the poem and how its configurations determine language and character.

---

120 All references to *The Wife's Lament* are to Krapp's and Dobbie's edition of the *Exeter Book* in *The Anglo-Saxon Poetic Records*. Unless otherwise noted, all translations from the Old English are mine.

121 In two articles on *The Wife's Lament* and *Wulf and Eadwacer*, Patricia A. Belanoff focuses on "women's songs," on their essential difference from both the conventional elegiac utterance of male lyrics and from the codes of heroic society, in "Women's Songs, Women's Language: *Wulf and Eadwacer* and *The Wife's Lament*," in *New Readings on Women in Old English Literature*, eds. Helen Damaci and Alexandra Hennesey Olsen (Bloomington: Indiana University Press, 1990), 193–203; and "*Ides ... geomrode giddum*: The Old English Female Lament," in *Medieval Woman's Song: Cross-Cultural Approaches*, eds. Anne L. Klinck and Ann Marie Rasmussen (Philadelphia: University of Pennsylvania Press, 2002), 29–46. Helen T. Bennett also telescopes gender as the differential element in the Old English poetry of exile, "Exile and the Semiosis of Gender in Old English Elegies," in *Class and Gender in Early English Literature*, eds. Britton J. Harwood and Gillian R. Overing (Bloomington: Indiana University Press, 1994), 43–58. Although the most recent essay on *The Wife's Lament* is not feminist, John D. Niles' assumption is that the powerlessness of the speaker is the effect of her female gender; her only recourse as revenge is cursing, the methods of a witch," "The Problem of the Ending of *The Wife's Lament*," *Speculum* 78 (2003), 1107–1150. For an excellent overview of the critical literature on *The Wife's Lament*," see Anne L. Klinck's *The Old English Elegies*, 49–54.

Character as Symptom

In critical history, *The Wife's Lament* is marked by a concern with its riddling quality. Almost all levels of the poem, grammatical features, plot, narrator, setting, historical background and context, prompt controversial interpretations, on occasion resembling ingenious guessing-games or competitions in critical showmanship.[122] Although not all readings go as far as Faye Walker-Pelkey's designation of the poem as a riddle proper, belonging to the group of riddles it borders on in the *Exeter Book*, several curiously literalist suggestions have been made especially about the nature of the plot and the identity of the speaker.[123] For instance, the longstanding debate about gender in the poem and the critical resistance to a female voice in Old English poetry resulted in a variety of suppositions about its nature: the lament of a male retainer, of a heathen deity, of a revenant, of the Church, yearning for Christ.[124] Even if some straightforward information is given about elements of plot, problems remain on the level of chronology and of the action and relationships of participants: does the poem give an account of one married couple or is there a third party involved, a male intruder?; what exactly has caused the narrator's present misery, the husband's betrayal or the feuding of hateful kinsmen?; what is the wife's, a friendless stranger's ("wineleas wræcca" 10), aim in seeking retinue ("folgað" 9) – the assistance of her lord, of her husband's household, of any kindly disposed *comitatus*?[125]

Despite the critical complications, the most recent scholarship has to a great extent accepted the argument, first advocated by Kemp Malone in 1963, that *The Wife's Lament*, together with *Wulf and Eadwacer*, belong to the Germanic, vernacular tradition of *Frauenlieder*, or women's song.[126] Also, as John D. Niles points out, as is the case with the Old English elegies in general, the consensus nowadays

122 John Niles describes the task of writing about *The Wife's Lament* thus: "part of the ritual of writing about *The Wife's Lament* seems to be that one first picks one's way through the various critical controversies that beset this poem, exposing other critics' follies for what they are, and then, as a long-awaited gesture of resolution, one offers a new translation that embodies a 'true' reading fo the work" (2003: 1144). Niles himself "solves" the problem of the ending, arguing convincingly that its speech act is a curse, angry and aggressive, not an indication of passive resignation; Niles, however, is wary of the "truth" of his interpretation: "I regard my version of those lines as no more than yet one more offering on the smoky altar of this poem" (1144).

123 Faye Walker-Pelkey. "'Frige Hwæt Ic Hatte': 'The Wife's Lament' as Riddle." *Papers on Language and Literature* 28 (1992): 242–266.

124 See Niles for a brief summary of critical positions (1107–1108); for a more extended overview, see Klinck's *The Old English Elegies*, 49–54.

125 Again, see Niles (1109) and Klinck for summary overviews.

126 Kemp Malone. "Two English *Frauenlieder*, in *Studies in Old English Literature*, ed. Stanley B. Greenfield (Eugene: University of Oregon Press, 1963), 106–117; Peter

appears to be to discard allegorical readings in favor of the concrete circumstances within the poetry (1109; 1112). Thus, the situation of the speaker in *The Wife's Lament* is sufficiently outlined by the language of the poem itself to provide the rudiments of her experience and to patch together a chronology of plot. The speaker's present misery is caused by feuding among her husband's kinsmen, who have managed to separate the couple, ostracizing them, expelling the wife to a desolate place in the woods, where her dwelling is a grave-like barrow (eorðsele (29); eorðscræfe (28)), beneath an oak-tree, and where her doom appears to be to mourn the past and utter lamentations for her longing. Before arriving in this "no-man's-land," the wife roamed around on "the paths of exile," "a friendless outcast" ("wineleas wræcca" 10), seeking the comfort of strangers, not unlike the wretched penitent in *Resignation*, miserably enduring the absence of home ("leodwynna leas, leng drohtian,/wineleas wrecca" 90–91). The painful nostalgia of the poem is reiterated in memories of happier times and especially of her love, glimpsed in the concluding lines in a mental image of the husband, suffering a similar fate to her own, far from native land, in a dreary, dismal hall, beneath a cliff, "always remembering a happier home" ("he gemon to oft/wynlicran wic" 51–52). As John D. Niles discusses, two strands of critical thought dominate views of the last lines of the poem (42–52a), the "genteel" versus the "vindictive" school, the former considering them as resigned speech, offering some consolation, the latter as a curse, a "passionate, vengeance-driven cry," the powerless female speaker's only recourse to action (1115; 1150). My examination of *The Wife's Lament* will make clear that I do not consider the last speech act as resigned comfort nor as an empowering curse. As I have underlined with regard to the elegies in general, literary consolation constitutes a complex psycho-cultural phenomenon, involving an individual's quest for cultural authority in the rite of passage of language. Because *The Wife's Lament* displays the vicissitudes of desire in the search for the lost object, it effects *catharsis*. In the poem, character construction establishes a transferential relation with an audience, bringing its members to the brink of transformative insight.

In *Reading (Absent) Character* (1983), Thomas Docherty proposes to account for the paradoxical nature of fictional character, its lifelikeness as well as its absence, or intangibility, through a revision of psychological theories of motivation. Basing his argument to some extent on neo-Freudian conceptions, as well as on Heideggerian existentialism, Docherty replaces conventional views of desire, as primarily an erotic force, seeking satisfaction, with a Lacanian inspired model of the constitution of drives: characters which quest for fulfillment, for stasis, are motivated by *need*, by, for instance, erotic longing, or pathological versions,

Dronke makes a similar claim in his influential *Medieval Lyric* (New York: Harper and Row, 1969).

such as the death drive; on the other hand, genuine *desire* is the hallmark of the post-modern novel, Docherty's favored form, the terrain of characters, who move beyond centered, static selves to *kinetic* subjects. In literary history, the realist novel, as well as most modernist literature, express the need for self-identity, for an end to libidinal quests, whereas the works of Beckett and Kafka, which verge on post-modernism, generate desire in the form of *agape*, motivation which introduces the "possibility of Romantic transendence of an identity or of a centred and unified self" (224). Need drives characters "homewards," to a point of conflation between experiencing and speaking subject; *agape*, on the other hand, prepares the ground of exile, staking out Derridean *différance*, the otherness of Being itself.[127]

Docherty's categories of character, static "homebodies" versus kinetic exiles, approximate my elaboration of the contrast between inauthentic self and the uncanny subject, which condition character construction in literature. However, as my examination of the Old English elegies has hopefully shown, "homeward" drives do not necessarily forfeit the transferential relation text establishes with audience, nor the transformative potential such a relation makes possible. *Agape*, the transcendence beyond home into difference, is, in my view a transhistorical force, a motivation for characters in all periods of history, for the Anglo-Saxon elegist, as well as the modernist innovator or post-modern experiementalist.[128] The following chapters on medieval romance as well as on the modernist and contemporary novel will in some detail investigate character as a transhistorical structuration, a creative force in the mind. At this point, I want to emphasize that in the Old English elegies, the movement between home and exile constitutes a libidinal ambiguity which defines character: in *The Wanderer*, the elegist surpasses this movement in the powerful creation of himself as differential metaphor; even if such surpassal is defeated in *The Seafarer*, the desire to attain it persists, rupturing the smooth Christian discourse, by merely mimicking its version of home. Of all the elegies, *The Wife's Lament* exemplifies most succinctly narcissistic conflicts, the tug-of-war between fixity and alienation, as a *symptom* of character. In fact, the lament analyzes this symptom: searching for "a talking cure," a way to channel private pain into the language of culture, the female speaker remains fixated in a state of abjection. It is as if she is the prototype for Kristeva's abject analysand, from the section, "Catharsis and Analysis," in *Powers of Horror*, whose *wound*

127 These ideas are aired primarily in chapter seven, "From Motivation to Mobility," 217–243. See my chapter one, "Situating Character," for a brief account of Docherty's book.

128 In fact, I must object to Docherty's proposition that early modernism's quest for the centered self "reaches it peak [...] in Lawrence" (231). On the contrary, Lawrence dramatizes the contrast between realist figures, such as Rico in *St Mawr*, and complex visionaries, such as Lou in that novella, or Ursula Brangwen in *The Rainbow*.

must be kept open – "a wound that the professional establishment, along with the cynicism of the times and of institutions, will soon manage to close up" (27). The wife's lost object, the home of the past, defines her wound, invisible within the institutional Symbolic, expressible only in the opaque speech of the Imaginary. Unlike Kristeva's hypothetical patient, who comes out of the analytic situation, an "unstabilized subject [...] – like a crucified person opening up the stigmata of its desiring body to [structuring] speech" (27), the wife remains locked in abjection, the form as well as the substance of her utterance.

In fact, as a gendered product, *The Wife's Lament* distinguishes itself in terms of form. As several critics have pointed out, in comparison with the mobile processes of *The Wanderer*, *The Seafarer*, and even *Resignation*, *The Wife's Lament* is, despite the outbursts of passion, a confined, ultimately self-defeating, expression. For instance, both Helen T. Bennett and Pat Belanoff contrast the social and physical mobility of the wanderer and the seafarer with the circumscribed spaces of the female elegies, *The Wife's Lament* and *Wulf and Eadwacer* (Belanoff 2002: 29–46; Bennett 1994 43–58). Even if the desolate condition of exile colours all these poems, male speakers are, in a sense, more at liberty to come to terms with it, as we have seen in the wanderer's majestic assumption of cultural authority and, to a lesser extent, in the seafarer's transition from private sphere to public pronouncement. Negotiations with official codes, such as the language of tradition or the Christian *Weltanschauung*, are less arduous for an exile such as the wanderer because, no matter how intense his present isolation, his history is that of the warrior, at home in the *comitatus*, mourning now "the lost stability and security of the lord-thane relationship" (Bennett 44). On the other hand, the speaker in *The Wife's Lament* does not recall belonging to a communal heritage against which to harmonize her present pain. Thus, what she mourns most profoundly is not loss of communal cohesion nor of social position, but of the contact with a lover, most likely her husband, to whom she was devoted, dependent and subordinate. The *personal* nature of loss emerges more powerfully in *The Wife's Lament* than in the male elegies, at the same time as it delimits the poem formally. Because she is doubly marginalized as a female exile, the wife is incapable of re-creating herself as rich cause for object *a*, of assuming the Name-of-the-Father and, in the manner of the wanderer, of injecting her private passion into patriarchal codes. As a result, speech in *The Wife's Lament* remains locked in the pathology of plaint, obsessively rehearsing loss, not repairing it.

In the section on *The Wanderer* above, I investigated the psychology of plaint and do not intend to retrace that discussion here. Nevertheless, I want to focus attention on the plaintive mood, on *melancholia*, as the symptom of female subjectivity in Anglo-Saxon culture. In Freud's understanding, psycho-neurotic symptoms comprise libidinal replacements, compromise formations, which operate in the ambiguous manner of dream symbolism, both hiding and expressing an unconscious wish.[129] As formative elements of culture, symptoms obliquely refer to the "return of the repressed," creating a kind of pathological language within the normative structurations of the Symbolic register. As a predominate mood of Old English women's song, as well as of female representation in the literature, in general, melancholy ruptures traditional male symbolism with the repressed material of the semiotic, of the archaic carnality of pre-Oedipal space.[130] Although Patricia Belanoff in "Women's Songs, Women's Language" (1990), does not examine symptomatic aspects in *The Wife's Lament*, she makes rewarding use of Kristeva's linguistic theory, making a strong case for the "polysemy" of the poem as a complex instance of "the presence of the incommunicable" within the oral act of immediate communication of emotion (1990: 196; 197). Also, relying on psycho-linguistic theory, I want to elaborate on a version of the semiotic, which Kristeva in *Powers of Horror* calls "analytic speech," the return of the repressed as *abject* in the psychoanalytic situation (1982: 29–31).

In the first part of *Powers of Horror*, Kristeva outlines what she calls a "phenomenological" survey of abjection, considering its appearance in the discourses of religion, philosophy and literature (1–31). In the latter sections, in particular, "With Plato and Aristotle" (27–29) and "Philosophical Sadness and The Spoken Disaster of The Analyst" (29–31), a brief historical overview is given of the vicissitudes of *defilement* in philosophy, running from Plato's purism through Hegelian dualism (defilement as "the negative side of consciousness" 30) to Freudian transference. It is primarily the last situation which "takes us away from purity" (29) and creates a fertile condition for heterogeneous speech, "a poetic unsettlement" of normative utterance, a cohabitation of "'knowledge' of abjection" with analytic interpretation. Kristeva emphasizes that even if the analyst's listening presence is infested with the "sadness" that comes with sane repression, his point of view, through transference and countertransference, also encompasses the analysand's libidinal articulation. In fact, such impure exchange is the mark of psychoanalytic catharsis:

> analytic speech is one that becomes 'incarnate' in the full sense of the term. On that condition only, it is 'cathartic' – meaning thereby that it is the equivalent, for the analyst as well as for the analysand, not of purification but of rebirth with and against abjection. (31)

---

129 See especially Freud's *Inhibitions: Symbol and Anxiety* (1926); see also my discussion of *St Mawr* above.

130 Note this "melancholy" statement by Helen T. Bennett on Anglo-Saxon women: "Women in this warrior society have the non-roles of (failed) peaceweaver and mourner for the dead produced by feud" (45); also, the title of Belanoff's article, culled from the characterization of Hildeburh in *Beowulf* – "Ides … geomrode giddum" (2002; "the lady lamented with songs") – indicates the typical literary roles for women.

It is exactly such cathartic potential I envision for the audiences of *The Wife's Lament* as their members confront what resembles Kristeva's analytic speech, the abject female becoming a mirror of alienation, casting back, in transference, a knowledge of themselves as others. As Pat Belanoff notes, contemporary poetic performance would be a particulary amenable situation for such a connection between listener and speaker, resulting in an emotional education for the oral community (196–7). It is, however, important to keep in mind that the establishment of a consolatory context for *The Wife's Lament* does not diminish the force of the poem's pathology, its status as a symptom of female subjection. In other words, the poem's speaker assumes the role of an analyst, benefiting the audience with new knowledge, through a transferential relation, but receives no counter-transferential benefits herself, because of the nature of contemporary patriarchal culture, whose only outlet for the female subject is in symptomatic melancholy song.

Thus, as was the case in *The Seafarer*, character construction in *The Wife's Lament* is incomplete, does not achieve the fullness of the uncanny, but nevertheless, through the *effect* of this construction reveals the authenticity of the process. During the remainder of this section, I will examine how the speaker's abject status overtakes the elegiac drive toward substitution for loss. In the first part of *Powers of Horror*, Kristeva's reading of extracts from several modernist writers makes clear that abjection figures variously, depending on the underlying psychic structuration (26). Antonin Artaud's texts, for instance, articulate abject borders most conspicuously in terrifying images of the corpse, obsessed "with the death that 'I' am" (25). Also, positing the body as the ground of human subjectivity, James Joyce is a more cathartic writer than Artaud, performing the abject in the spectacular rhetoric of his novels: "The abject lies, beyond the themes, and for Joyce generally, in the way one speaks; it is verbal communication, it is the Word that discloses the abject" (23). For the other writers Kristeva examines, the abject persists variously as transgression, infringement of normative rules and law: in Dostoyevsky's novels, abject characters are often criminals, expressing their nihilistic vision in the "*ecstasy* of [...] ego" (Kristeva's emphasis; 18); Proust's abjection is more domesticated, constituting nontheless a scandal within "the realm of 'one's own clear and proper'" (20); Borges narratives of infamy capture the heterogeneous composition of the abject, fallen object, "vertiginous and hallucinatory" (23). For Kristeva, contemporary literature performs a similar cultural function as analytic speech, conveying knowledge of abjection, not obtainable in other fields of the symbolic, and thereby "becom[ing] a substitute for the role formerly played by the sacred, at the limits of social and subjective identity" (26).

Operating in the liminal zone between ritual and manuscript culture, Old English poetry, especially two of the *Exeter Book* elegies I investigate here, *The*

Seafarer and *The Wife's Lament*, display states of abjection to a much greater extent than the more conventional literature of the time, such as biblical verse or heroic battle song.[131] The different psychic structurations grounding these elegies determine their abject forms. The seafarer's obsessions are perhaps close to Artaud's terrifying corpse, the thanatic drive propelling him toward the origin of trauma, stripping his final authority as Christian speaker of genuine compunction. On the other hand, in *The Wife's Lament*, abjection is *erotic*, appearing in the poem in primarily two patterns, the relationship with a lover and *imagos*, the specular images of the mirror stage.

The differentness of *The Wife's Lament* as an exile's elegy lies in the speaker's conflation of the desire for a lover with the desire for a home. Usually, with the individual subject, it is crisis, some disastrous upheaval or threat of disorder, which precipitates an experience of abjection, the encroachment of archaic, pre-Oedipal sensations upon symbolic positionality. Because of the violent separation from the man she calls her "lord" ("min hlaford" 6), the wife's secure place in the Symbolic is undermined, and her definition of herself as an ego collapses. In the beginning lines of the poem, the female speaker claims that the present moment is the climax of her troubled life, that never before has she endured such hardship ("Ic þæt secgan mæg/hwæt ic yrmþa gebad siþþan ic up weox/niwes oþþe ealdes, no me þonne nu" 2–4). The departure of her lord over the "expanse of waves" ("over yþa gelac" 7), hurled her onto the exile's path of torments ("A ic wite wonn minre wræcsiþa./Ærest min hlaford gewat heonan of leodum" 5–6). She has now become what Kristeva calls "a stray," an outcast who cannot find her psychological or social bearing, who has, with the lost object, lost the sense of self (1982: 8). Like the *Exeter Book* elegies in general, and especially *The Wanderer* and *The Seafarer*, the speaker's journey in *The Wife's Lament* assumes the form of a quest for replacement for grievous loss. However, unlike the male elegies which re-figure the object in a language of substitutions, the female speaker discovers no-thing, the fallen object, the abject.

From a psychoanalytic point of view, it is extremely significant in *The Wife's Lament* that the descriptions of the lover, in the first half of the poem, at a certain point give way to a lengthy delineation of place (26–41). Within their theory of subjectivity, both Lacan and Kristeva underscore the processes of separation – primary repression, narcissistic crisis, the Oedipal resolution – for human individuation. Individual identity, the sense of self as a bounded entity, is to the greatest extent dependent on the subject/object dialectic, on, as Elizabeth Grosz states so well, "the ego and the object [as] correlates, supporting and providing each other

131 For there to be "analytic speech," there must be awareness of psychological interiority, which is lacking in purely orhodox literature.

with stability" (72).[132] Demarcation of a subjective zone in relation to another is surety of rootedness, a kind of home. On the other hand, the abject is an ambiguous no-thing: it is "neither the subject nor the object. It is a recognition of the impossible untenable identity the subject projects unto and derives from the other" (Grosz 72). In particular, during crisis in love, there is consciousness of the instability of the ego, of its excessive dependence on identification with an other. Building upon Lacan's disquisition of *objet petit a* in *The Four Fundamental Concepts of Psycho-Analysis* (1977), Elizabeth Grosz graphically depicts the dissolution of love as abjection: in order to physically delimit themselves, lovers experience the erotegenic zones – "mouth, anus, eyes, ears, genitals" – as a rim, an open field "seek[ing] a satisfaction in which the object ideally stops up the lack" (72). If there is a dialectic of response, subject and object become absorbed and expelled, within the intersubjective rhythm, special to (erotic) love. With grief in love, however, abjection overwhelms identity: "the object does not fill the rim: a gap emerges, a hole, into which the subject, through lack of an anchor in the object, is propelled" (Grosz 73). This hole or *abyss*, the constant threat to subjective identity, is further characterized by Kristeva as pre-Oedipal space: it marks both the "genesis *and* the obliteration of the subject" (73; Grosz' emphasis); "it is a space inhabited by the death drive, Hegelian negativity, the indistinct space occupied by mother and child in symbiotic dependence" (Grosz is summarizing Kristeva here, 73).

In *The Wife's Lament*, after the dissolution of love, the female speaker falls into abject space, articulated in the poem as a fantasy landscape, gloomy and cavernous, suggestive of an ancient burial site.[133]

132 Elizabeth Grosz. *Sexual Subversions: Three French Feminists* (Sidney: Allen & Unwin, 1989).

133 The critical commentary on the landscape in *The Wife's Lament* is profuse. See Anne Klinck for and overview (1992: 49–54) and pertinent observations by Niles (2003: 1109). Many see a connection between the narrator's dwelling and her identity, without, though, interpreting this in psychoanalytic terms; for instance, both Elinor Lench and Raymond P. Tripp hypothesize that the *eorðscræfe* is a literal grave inhabited by the revenant who speaks the poem; Elinor Lench. "*The Wife's Lament*: A Poem of the Living Dead." *Comitatus* 1 (1970): 3–23; Raymond P. Tripp. "The Narraor as Revenant: A Reconsideration of Three Old English Elegies." *Papers on Language and Literature* 8 (1972): 339–61. Still, as Joseph Harris notes, *eorðscræf* does not necessarily denote grave, but more generally an underground habitation, such as the dragon's den in *Beowulf*, "A Note on eorðscræfe/eorðsele and Current Interpretations of *The Wife's Lament*." *English Studies* 58 (1977), 204–8. In this respect, note also Niles' apt remark: "Much of the pathos of the speaker's condition is that she lives a kind of 'living death' in a place as cheerless as the grave, but she is not therefore to be regarded as a revenant" (n7, 1109). As we shall see, the depiction of the wife as a "living dead" is psychologically particularly appropriate.

In this ominous place, the woman's dwelling is an underground cave of some sort (eorðscræf 28; 36; eorðsele 29), beneath an oaktree ("under actreo" 28), surrounded by lofty hills, overgrown with briars ("duna uphea [...] brerum beweaxne" 31–2). Layers of enclosures descend upon the only human figure in this terrifying scene: the abysmal cave in a dark hollow, trapped within looming hills. It is, indeed, not surprising that critics have tended to decode this as a site of graves, inhabited by a ghost.[134] On a less literal level, according to the poem's psychological logic, this is the abject speaker's psychic space, the abyss she fell into after loss in love; it is ambiguous, pre-Oedipal space, suggesting both a return to the womb and descent into the grave. As Elizabeth Grosz defines the pre-objectal abyss: "[it] marks the place of the genesis *and* the obliteration of the subject, for it is a space inhabited by the death drive, Hegelian negativity, the indistinct space occupied by mother and child in symbolic dependence" (73).

Thus, it is particularly appropriate to characterize the narrator, as several critics have done (albeit not with a psychoanalytic aim), as "the living dead."[135] Being neither subject nor object, the abject is unspeakably ambiguous, "attest[ing] to the impossibility of clear borders, lines of demarcation or divisions between the proper and the improper, the clear and the unclear, order and disorder, as required by the symbolic" (Grosz 73). Without an anchor in the object which defines her identity symbolically, socially and psychologically, the female speaker of *The Wife's Lament* becomes an indistinct creature, half dead/half alive, half animal/half human, at the break of dawn ("on uhtan" 35) roaming around her equally ambiguous dwelling, bewailing her loss, without hopes of restitution: "because I will never be able to rest from the griefs in my heart/nor from this intense longing, which I have been assailed with in life" ("forþon ic æfre ne mæg/þære modceare minre gerestan,/ne ealles þæs longaþes þe mec on þissum on life begeat" 39–41).

At the conclusion of *The Wife's Lament*, the female speaker is trapped within her own poetic form, the abject maternal space of the mind. As I indicated in the section on *The Wanderer*, the riddling intersections of the wife's speech are not solely due to the lack of reading context or intertexual milieu, but are effeced by the poem's fantasy mind-set, its anchorless signification. Although generated by loss, the spatial images – "the gloomy cave" ("eorðsele [...] dimme" 29–39), the shady "forest-grove" ("on wuda bearwe" 27), "the looming cliff" ("duna uphea" 30), "the oppressive surroundings, overgrown with briars" ("bitre burgtunas brerum beweaxne" 31) – reflect a mirror-stage scenario and do not achieve the status of the detached symbol. Keeping in mind the speaker's abjection, these are archaic images – or *imagos* – produced within a movement of narcissistic regression. In

134 See previous footnote.
135 See footnote 133.

fact, critics' conflation of speaker with site, for instance, revenant with grave, or deity with sacred grove, seems intuitively true, because place here appears as an extension of the woman's body, abysmal and empty as her abandoned erotogenic zones.[136] The intractable forest-hollow in *The Wife's Lament* is influenced by a kind of pathetic fallacy whereby desire infiltrates dwelling: "the earth-hall is old; and I am seized with longing" ("eald is þes eorðsele; eal ic eom ofongaþ" 29); the wife's pacing back and forth beneath the oak-tree brings to mind the bliss of lovers, sharing a bed ("Frynd sind on eorþan, leofe lifgende leger weardiað,/þonne ic on uhtan ana gonge/under actreo" 33–36); in this place, she is again and again seized with the irreparable loss of her lord ("Ful oft mec her wraþe begeat/fromsiþ frean" 32–3). The abyss the speaker fell into after loss in love merges with the gaping wound of her body.

The pathological dependence of libido upon the object of loss bypasses the work of mourning and leads to melancholia.[137] The tendency of most criticism to view the last lines of the poem (42–53) as a resolution, in terms of the "genteel" and "vindictive" schools, as either stoic acceptance of fate or as a curse, a passionate revenge upon the husband, appears to me to be misplaced because it neglects the discursive logic, the development of melancholia as a symptom of character. The thoughts of the lover in these concluding lines indicate that the order of *imagos* – of specular images – persists in the speaker's mind. In her state of pre-Oedipal regression, the wife identifies narcissistically with the husband, internalizes his situation to the extent of seeing it as the mirror reflection of her own: the lover too is an outcast in a far country ("sy ful wide fah/feorres folclondes þæt min freond siteð" 46–7), "dejected and sad" ("werigmod" 49), imprisoned in a "wretched cell [...] under rocky cliffs" 50; 48). He is ruled by the same libido as herself, equating their love with the home of the past ("he gemon to oft/wynlicran wic" 51–2). If, as both Barrie Ruth Strauss and John D. Niles claim, the speech act here consists of an energetic curse then it is a melancholy one, a plaintive pronouncment upon that indistinct creature – the Anglo-Saxon female abject.

136 A. N. Doane has suggested that the speaker is a heathen deity, addressing a priest, "Heathen Form and Christian Function in *The Wife's Lament*." *Medieval Studies* 28 (1966): 77–91.

137 See Freud's "Mourning and Melancholia"; also, see my discussion above of *The Wanderer*. I read the last 10–12 lines of the poem (42–53) as an outcome of its psychological logic and do not take sides with either the "genteel" or the "vindictive" schools (see Niles 1115–1120).

Ethical Chronotope

Character in literature is the building of a poetic home for both the individual subject and community. Thomas Docherty's contention that motivation of characters in narrative occurs either in forms of need or of desire, and that only *agape*, propelling the self beyond its illusory stable core, toward the radical differentness of subjectivity, casts a revealing light on such processes in fiction in general (1983: 217–243). However, Docherty privileges the experiments of the postmodern novel, and of avant-garde cousins, as playgrounds of *différance*, juxtaposing the static characters of realistic and modernist fiction to mobile figures such as Beckett's Watt and Kafka's Jacob in *America* (e.g. 227; 240–3). Although this contrast works as a heuristic model, it threatens to reduce subjectivity in literary history to the post-Enlightenment novel only, as if characters do not exist in other genres or other periods. On the contrary, I want to suggest that the grounding of character in literature is *originary*, in Heidegger's sense of the word, and that as a consequence *agape*, or the desire to transcend the known self to difference, is a transhistorical force, an immutable structure of the perceiving mind.[138] Nevertheless, within diverse historical contexts, such a structure is modified and articulated in complex ways, depending on epistemological formations or, as Roland Barthes says, "ideologies of the person." In my opinion, a more productive model than Docherty's construct of contrasts, one that accounts for both identity and difference, is a combination of Heidegger's conception of the *poetic home* and Bakhtin's view of the literary *chronotope*. Below, I will attempt to show the relevance of such a combination for character in the Old English elegies.

There can be no doubt that desire for a home defines subjectivity in the *Exeter Book* poems I have discussed here – *The Wanderer*, *The Seafarer*, *Resignation* and *The Wife's Lament*. The major figures in all poems are exiles on a journey, mourning loss and questing for its substitution. Because these are philosophical elegies, only peripherally related to the more recent personal elegy, such as Shelley's *Adonais* or Tennyson's *In Memoriam*, the questers ultimately confront not only their special misfortune but the condition itself of ontological homelessness. Through a trial of authority, comparable to a *rite-de-passage* in pre-industrial societies, the speakers of the different poems move from almost pathological nostalgia to a rejuvenating ambition to build a new home. This process is remarkably complex and most fruitfully analyzed from a psychoanalytic perspective as cre-

138 Character is *orginary* because it has ontological priority to any conceptual enquiry. Scientific study or theorizing, a Lacanian one, for instance, thus configures ontic quests into ontological presuppositions. See Stephen Muhall's "Introduction," in *Heidegger and Being and Time* (London: Routledge, 1996), esp. 4.

ation of a regenerative sign in language. The most successful is the wanderer, who harnesses the *Name-of-the-Father* to represent himself as the culture's mirror, as its differential dwelling. The seafaring speaker is also tested in a ritualized process of language, at one point glimpsing a powerful version of home as hospitable land of existential strangers; the vision, however, gives way to the dominant *Weltanschauung*, the Christian view of heaven as man's true habitat and essentialist destination. A less accomplished poem, *Resignation* nevertheless aspires to revise the oppressive Christian superego, depicting an uncompromising image of homelessness as its ontological ground. The speaker in *The Wife's Lament* is also called upon to devise a home in language for the individual subject after exile; because of the double marginalization of the female outcast, her building, a dark, narrow hole, in a landscape of enclosures, appears almost incomprehensible. Still, the generic connection of this lament to the other elegies suggests that similar energies are at work here as in *The Seafarer*: the wife envisions an originary abode for the differential subject. That her efforts fail does not diminish the passion which initiates them.

What the *Exeter Book* elegies reveal is the emergence of character in literature as an uncanny (*unheimliche*) dwelling for a culture in transition. In a recent, lucid exposition of Heidegger's post-war writings, Charles Bambach correlates the philosopher's critique of modernity with a revisionary ecology, stripped of the older nationalistic passions and politics.[139] Especially, in works from the late 1940s and the 1950s, such as "Fieldpaths" (1949), *Woodpaths* (1950), and the lecture, "Building Dwelling Thinking" (1951), a topos of the homeland is developed, generating various kinds of relations with humanity and with the earth itself. A particular significant conception is *Bodenständigkeit* – "rootedness" or "autochthony" – which Heidegger explicates as not just a geographic/national/regional sense of belonging but as

> a profoundly *metaphysical* relation to the earth as a place of dwelling, to the landscape as one's indigenous home, and to language as the expression of one's rootedness in both. (268; my italics)

Bambach makes quite clear that in the sense used by Heidegger, rootedness has nothing to do with ownership or technological mastery, but does, in fact, constitute a politicized critique of hegemonic thinking. To be rooted in the earth, to dwell in it as a native, involves an openness to "the gift-giving powers of being," that is, to what in *Being and Time* (1927) is referred to as the realization of the potential for *Being-a-whole*.[140] Bambach shows how Sophocles' *Antigone* served

139 Charles Bamback. "Heidegger, Technology, and the Homeland." *The Germanic Reiview* 78 (2003): 267–282.

140 Bambach, 268.

as an inspirational source for the philosopher's juxtaposition here between an exploitative attitude toward the land as merely a resource and an ecological relation, – a juxtaposition exemplified by the central conflict in the play between Creon's Cartesian subjectivity and Antigone's religious humility: Creon's idea of community, of the *polis*, is "out of touch with the powers of the earth"; "he becomes a model for the kind of untrammeled Cartesian self-assertion and volunteerism of the modern subject armed with *techne*" (269). On the other hand, Antigone grasps the connection between the question of Being and dwelling in and on the earth: for her, *Bodenständigkeit* is a kind of "poetic dwelling," "an integrative play of earth and world, humans and the sacred" (274); it is a conception of space as *physis*, not as *techne*, an "understanding [of] the earth as the originary source of all being and as the space within and against which human beings confront their limits" (269). Building one's proper dwelling, staking out one's human ground, leads to the question of the subject's ecological relation to the otherness of things in the world. It is an activity which dispels hegemony, or what Heidegger called *Erdherrschaft*, "'dominion over the earth'" (Bambach 270). It is a matter of a new home for both the individual and the *polis*, a new *ethical* relation, in fact, originary, "'neither theoretical nor practical [but what] comes to pass [ereignet sich] before this distinction'" (quoted in Bambach 277, from *Wegmarken* (1967)).

Significantly, with the revision of Heidegger's former nationalist agenda emerges a new conception of ethics, in its pre-Socratic meaning of a primal relation between the human subject, dwelling, ecological milieu and language. For my purposes of arguing that authentic (literary) character culminates in a radical epistemological metaphor, this defamiliarization of ethics is particulary relevant as it replaces the understanding of *ethos* as normative value, or habitual conduct, with "our originary dwelling place on earth" (277).[141] Thus, character is *ethos*, a place in literature to realize a different relation, an originary home – "a strange [...] uncanny relation to being by a human being who allows for the dispossession of the self and the abandonment of control, mastery, and dominion" (277).[142] The motivation for character building in literature is the preparation of just such ethical ground: a place within which to rehearse a different kind of being.

If character as uncanny home constitutes a transhistorical force, then the literary *chronotope* as conceived by Mikhail Bakhtin, a relativized space-time unit historicizes the contours of this structure. In his prolegomenon to a historical poetics, in "Forms of Time and Chronotope in The Novel" (1937–1938), Bakhtin traces modifications of temporal perception in fictional texts and the relation-

141 Bamback cites Richard McKeon for the conventional view of ethics: "Moral virtue comes about as a result of habit" (281; n11), from *Introduction to Aristotle* (New York: Random House, 1947), 331.

142 Bambach is here referring to Heidegger's radical conception of ethics.

ships of those to genre as well as to "the image of man in literature" (*The Dialogic Imagination* 85). Bakhtin's historical overview spans centuries, starting with pre-novelistic forms such as the Greek romance in antiquity and concluding with the novel proper, emphasizing, in particular, the influences of Rabelais and the Dostoevskian chronotope. The philosophical premise for this sort of investigation is Immanuel Kant's definition of space and time as *cognitive* categories, shaping factors in human perception and mental processes. However, it is important to note that Bakhtin differs from Kant in considering chronotopes as relativized, concrete features – images, devices, forms – not transcendental inclination. The chronotope is, according to Bakhtin, "a formally constitutive category of literature" (85), an artistic visibility of both time and space, a representational catalyst:

> We cannot help but be strongly impressed by the *representational* importance of the chronotope. Time becomes, in effect, palpable and visible; the chronotope makes narrative events concrete, makes them take on flesh, causes blood to flow in their veins. (250; Bakhtin's italics)

In art and especially in literary fictions, this almost tangible corporeality of time, its embodiment within spatial configurations, is determined by historical reality, primarily by the dominant *episteme*, or normative conceptions about the cognitive constitution and experience of the human individual. In varying degrees of technical facility, literary works "assimilat[e] real time," and grapple with "the problem of assimilating historical reality into the poetic image" (251). Thus, Bakhtin's focus is to a large extent on "the chronotopicity" of the human image in literature, ranging from its exteriorized composition and ties to adventure narrative and the rhetoric of the public square to the development of interiority and the depiction of the autonomous character in the novels of Fyodor Dostoevski. Of particular relevance for my readings of the Anglo-Saxon elegies is the section on "Ancient Biography and Autobiography" (130–146), where a distinction is made between early classical forms, especially the Greek type, their conflation between the public and the private, and proto-modern life writing, such as Plutarch's biographies, Cicero's letters to Atticus and what Bakhtin calls *stoic* autobiography, or the "consolationes" of St Augustine, Boethius, Petrach and Marcus Aurelius. The most conspicuous difference between the early and the later (auto) biographical genres is that the latter develops a sense of "a singular self-consciousness," both an awareness of a detached, interiorized mentality and an urge to ponder and elaborate upon this detachment. Bakhtin stresses that at this stage there persists a connection with the public utterance and that the separation between an inner core and a surface role is a rudimentary one, even in Marcus Aurelius' private ruminations (esp. 145–6). Nontheless, self-consciousness fosters an existential sense of time, a visceral experience of earthly transcience and human limits; as a consequence, the Roman genre of stoic consolation, exemplified in Cicero's

Consolatio, expresses tragic emotion, evoked by the death of a loved one and supplemented by ruminations upon "the theme of personal death" (145).

Although the historical reality giving rise to Anglo-Saxon elegiac utterance is at great variance with the Roman context, there occurs within the poetry a similar transition from public exteriority to self-conscious inwardness. As I noted at the beginning of this chapter, the *Exeter Book* elegies constitute, within contemporary culture, an "alterior space," a libidinal, as well as a reflective, zone, energized by a movement from loss to restitution, from crisis to authority, from alienation to community. On the model of pre-industrial cultures, investigated, in particular, by Victor Turner in *The Ritual Process* (1969), poems such as *The Wanderer*, *The Seafarer*, *The Wife's Lament* and *Resignation* reveal a *subject-on-trial*, experiencing and articulating a new spatio-temporal configuration. Depicted powerfully in *The Seafarer*, all poetic speakers confront and journey through a no-man's-land, challenged to transform existential devastation into meaningful language. In liminality, the questers explore – what Victor Turner calls – a "limbo of statuslessness" (97), a realm stripped of all accoutrements of civilization: in *The Wanderer* and *The Seafarer*, individual and cultural collapse is figured most vividly in the landscape of the *anti-hall*, the dark, cold and empty reverse of the rich, voluptuous bonds of *comitatus*; less concretely envisioned, in terms of poetic setting, *Resignation* nontheless projects with compunctious skill the figure of an *antihero*, a kind of exemplary stray, deprived not only of friends and family, but of native land, home and possessions; the female speaker in *The Wife's Lament* also strays, figuring her deprivations both as actual homelessness and as abject mentality. Generally, the Old English elegaic voice is propelled from multivalent loss of home toward an uncanny dwelling, an authoritative restitution within imaginative discourse. The *chronotope*, the historicized spatio-temporal perception, anchoring the elegies' revelatory sense of loss is, I want to maintain, *ruin*, an apt sign for fundamentals of Anglo-Saxon culture, as Bakhtin would say, of great "*representational* importance," making events, impressions and ruminations "palpable and visible" (250; Bakhtin's italics).

As in some types of classical life writing, examined in "Forms of Time and Chronotope in the Novel" (130–146), for instance, Plutarch's biographies, stoic autobiography and Cicero's *Consolatio*, the awareness of ruin in Old English literature fosters inwardness and self-conscious, detached modes of reflection. It is noteworthy that Bakhtin focuses on character as embodiment of changing perception: the increasing privatization of life, the "breakdown of [the] public exteriority of a man," crystallizes in the human figure in literature, in ancient times culminating in incipient autobiographical genres (143). Whereas Plutarchian biography is influenced by models of pre-determination, especially Aristotle's doctrine of *entelechy*, that is, the conflation between causality and purpose in individual development, later Roman forms, such as philosophical "consolationes" and

Marcus Aurelius' *Meditations*, emerge as midwives to the genre of the novel: in Plutarch's works, "biographical time [...] is specific" and does not intersect with historical reality in the fluid representation of being; on the other hand, a new temporal dimension saturates later Roman *Consolation*, telescoped in self-conscious characters, pondering "the transitoriness of all that is good, man's mortality" (141; 145). In the latter instance, there is awareness of interpenetration between biography and historical time, so that Aristotelean finality gives way to a proto-modern sense of human *becoming*; in Bakhtin's view of literary history, this birth of mobile consciousness founds and shapes the future discourse of the novel.

In Anglo-Saxon times, the *Exeter Book* elegies articulate in images of *ruin* a similar transitional sense of individuality, grappling with human *becoming* as opposed to older forms of pre-determination. In the poems I have discussed so far – *The Wanderer, The Seafarer, Resignation* and *The Wife's Lament* – the autodiegetic speakers project themselves as temporally saturated agents, acutely self-conscious about their separation from the fixed mentalities of the past. The hallmark of the poems is an exploration of a *new* consciousness and a search within language for an apt epistemological metaphor to represent it: the knowledge each quester acquires is of a real, existential time, in contrast to the ideal time of epic or the transcendences of the Christian religion. What I have wanted to show in the previous discussion is the elegistis' original spatio-temporal perception in diverse versions of (literary) character: the wanderer, the seafarer, the penitent in *Resignation*, the female speaker in *The Wife's Lament* and, as we shall see, the minstrel in *Deor* are unique figures in Anglo-Saxon culture, born within the chronotope of *ruin*, marked by both intense meditations upon death and future visions of the integrated individual. They dwell in language in uncanny, ruinous homes, inviting audiences to participate in re-building them, within the perimeters of alterior minds.

Throughout the discussion in this chapter, I have suggested that the Old English elegies be considered as the products of eschatological artists. Although that proposition is most viable in the exquisitely developed *The Wanderer* and (as we shall see) *Deor*, as a group the *Exeter Book* elegies bear the mark of – what Julia Kristeva calls – *death works*, the individual subject's creative exploration of, and energetic compromise with, the conditions of human mortality. In her penetrating explication of Kristeva's theory of violence, Martha J. Reineke notes in particular a vital variance within psychoanalysis between the conceptions of death-drive and death-work (1997:25; 49–64). Citing Kristeva's 1983 essay, "Within the Microcosm of the 'Talking Cure,'" Reineke demonstrates that the subject's *death-work*, even if it is anchored in the unconscious economy of drives, implies a "capacity for autonomy and active engagement in [the] world" (25).[143] The general human trauma of

143 Reineke's book and Kristeva's article are referred to in my introduction.

confronting negativity, of acknowledging and mobilizing an originary lack – a "being-at-a-loss" – does not exclude agency, the individual subject's constructive potential, "labor [...] on behalf of creativity and productive excess" (25). Whereas Freud's theory of drives, especially of *thanatos* as a destructive force in both culture and subjective psychology, tends to foster a pessimistic outlook on change and renewal, Kristeva asserts the regenerative features of death-work, the impulse, for instance, to transgress, to traverse bounded categories, to re-create spaces for new modes of signification. In almost all her work, and especially in her book about depression and melancholia, *Black Sun* (1987; 1989), Kristeva advocates aristic practices as exemplary for "revolution in poetic language," fields within human discourse, within the Symbolic, where new ethical mentalites emerge.[144] The propensity within contemplative minds to mourn absence, to internalize it and nurture it like a wound in the manner of melancholiacs, is, in some forms of art, transformed into signifying regeneration. If the "black sun" of Kristeva's title, culled from Gérard de Nerval's poem, "El Desdichado," suggesting the paradoxical nature of the death drive – the sustenance and growth of a mortal mind, – paralyzes viewers with narcissistic depression, it is also a source of positive energy, the prime mover of creative consciousness.

In the Old English elegies, *ruin*, a consolidation of the paradoxes of mortality, mobilizes poetic minds to quest for restitution, autonomy and cultural authority. As we have seen, the latter sections of *The Wanderer* exemplify such a quest, intertwining retrograde death-song with imaginative eschatology. In fact, *The Wanderer*'s affinities with spiritual autobiography, its mental *Bildung,* resemble modernist life-writing, especially portraits of artists, not epic indoctrination nor the Augustinian account of self. What I have, following Lacan and Peter Sacks, called *consolatory tropes*, the outcome of the work of mourning in the Old English poems, incorporate character as structure of both narcissistic depression, the inner wound, and of cultural authority, the poet as healer. Thus, the awareness of ruin in the *Exeter* elegies generates an authorial consciousness, outlined and articulated in specialized tropes of character.

In the last section of this chapter – "*Deor*: Poet as Healer" – I will investigate in some detail this incipient bond between author and character in Old English poetry. At this point, I want to emphasize the proto-modernity of that bond, what can be designated, with certain reservations in mind, the aesthetics of impersonality: the creation of authentic character in literature entails a dualistic mind-set, a perception of authorship as both autonomy in language and intersubjective prac-

144 Julia Kristeva. *Black Sun*. Trans Leon S. Roudiez (New York: Columbia University Press, 1989).

tice. It is an ethical stance, the preparation for the building of the uncanny dwellings of literature.

In her 1966 essay, "Word, Dialogue and Novel," a presentation and development of Mikhail Bakhtin's central ideas, Kristeva provides a fascinating account of the aesthetic dynamic I am attempting to establish within the author-character pair.[145] Focusing on ancestors of the genre of the novel, Kristeva is interested in exploring poetic meaning as a zone of dialogue and ambivalence in contrast to the preoccupations of traditional linguistics with the one-dimensional/monologic utterance in speech and writing.[146] An important precursor to the polyphonic writings of, for instance, Rabelais, Swift, Lautréamont and Bataille is the ancient Greek type of Socratic dialogue, a mode both of pedagogical exchange, practised by the philosopher himself, and *écriture*, a field of ambiguous authorship, of intertextual movements and relations. Kristeva emphasizes that even if "speech *is* man and his activity" in the Socratic interchange (Kristeva's itialics), a work such as Plato's *Apology*, recounting Socrates' last days, his trial and his waiting for judgment, illustrates "the exclusive position of a subject of discourse that provokes the dialogue" (1986: 51). Authorial *and* impersonal, the situation in the *Apology* exemplifies the other logic of literature:

> Socrates' trial and period of awaiting judgment determine his discourse as the confessions of a man 'on the threshold'. The exlusive situation liberates the word from any univocal objectivity, from any representative function, opening it up to the symbolic sphere. Speech affronts death, measuring itself against another discourse; this dialogue counts the *person* out. (Kristeva's italics; 51–2)

Poised at the edge of self – in Plato's halls of blind justice, in the icy landscapes and dark, empty caves of Old English verse, in Hamlet's "rotten state of Denmark," and in Anigone's cold sepulchre – speakers metamorphize into impersonal mediators, whose strategies of self-surpassing endow them with cultural power. Like the wanderer's post-Oedipal restitution, his self-creation after existential trauma, the author-character couple in general reflects the logic of "being-at-a-loss," not self-identification. In fact, authorship, as it is born in the Old English text, and propelled as a creative force in literary history, equals the insight into

145 Julia Kristeva. "Word, Dialogue and Novel" (1966). *The Kristeva Reader*, ed. Toril Moi. Trans. Alice Jardin, Thomas Gora and Léon Roudiez (New York: Columbia University Press, 1986), 34–61.

146 Also, in *Revolution in Poetic Language*, Kristeva is critical of modern linguistic theories in general for considering language "strictly as a 'formal' object – one that involves syntax or mathematicization" and for neglecting an *other* logic, and opaque logic, issuing from the *subject of enunciation*, inundated with semiosis as well as with the laws of the Symbolic (1984): 21–23.

language as uncanny ground for the subject and the reflection of this insight in epistemological metaphors.

The ethical chronotope as habitat for character in Old English poetry takes the palpable form of ruin, as an initial image of nothingness, which the thinking mind fills with meaning. In the *Poetics*, in a section on the elements of tragedy, Aristotle uses the ancient Greek term for character – *ethos* – to indicate a quality, distinct from action, thought and diction, assumed in literature at moments of crisis.[147] An agent becomes character within circumstances of moral choice, as when Oedipus sacrifices happiness and reputation for truth or Antigone opts for inner conviction in confrontation with the laws of community. Although Aristotle does not develop in great detail his definition of character, the separation of tragic elements makes clear that *ethos* is a specialized mode of cognition, not realistic representation. Bearing in mind the Greek philosopher's elliptical comments here, I want to underline their significance for the new epistemological configuraion emerging in the *Exeter Book* elegies: their death work generates the ethical subject.

An interesting variation on the work of mourning is a poem from the *Exeter Book* – *The Ruin* – usually classified as a close kin to *The Wanderer*, *The Seafarer*, *The Wife's Lament*, *Resignation* and *Deor*.[148] Despite textual problems and interpretive enigmas, the former caused by fire damage to the manuscript, the second by the vagueness of place, or setting, *The Ruin* appears to be more straightforward than the other elegies, as Klinck notes, unencumbered by "ambiguities [...] puzzels [...] allusions and [...] moral complexities" (61). On the surface, the poem presents a realistic depiction of, what it calls, "the work of giants" ("enta geweorc" 2), a city in ruins, "the roofs of buildings tumbled down, towers collapsed, gates missing, hoar-frost on the mortars" ("hrofas sind gehrorene, hreorge torras,/hringeat berofen, hrim on lime" 3–4). Subsequently, the camera-eye perspective moves from close observation of decayed buildings to a mental visualization of former inhabitants, the builders themselves, the feasting warriors in the grand halls, and the burghers, victimized by plague. The last survivors, who might have repaired the crumbling city, "fell in battle [...] returned to the earth" ("betend crungon,/hergas to hruron" 28–9). Mesmerized by the empty, ruined dwellings, their majestic desolation, the speaker becomes increasingly preoccupied with the vision of the past; the provisional conclusion of the poem, sug-

147 "Character in a play is that which reveals the moral purpose of the agents, i.e. the sort of thing they seek to avoid, where that is not obvious – hence there is no room for Character in a speech on a purely indifferenct subject" (*Poetics* Chapter 6 1460–1465).

148 References to *The Ruin* are to Krapp's and Dobbie's edition of the *Exeter Book*, in *Anglo-Saxon Poetic Records*. Unless otherwise noted, all translations from the Old English are mine.

gesting perhaps an elaborated historical scenario, transposes ruin and the former glorious inhabitants:

> Hryre wong gecrong,/gebrocen to beorgum, þær iu beorn monig,/glæmod ond goldbeorht, gleoma gefrætt wod,/wlonc on wingal, wighyrstum scan;/seah on sinc, on sylfum, on searogimman,/on ead, on æht, on eorcanstan,/on þas beorhtan burg brad rices. (31–37)
>
> [The structure lies fallen/shattered in ruins where before many a warrior/joyous and bright with gold, clothed in splendours,/proud and wanton with wine, feasted in shiny armours;/he gazed upon treasure, on silver, on riches of pearl and precious stones,/on property and wealth/ and on this shining city of the broad kingdom.]

Furthermore, the last description of the stone-court baths, "with a gushing spring of boiling water" ("stream hate,/widan wylme" 38–9), suggests human ingenuity, sensuous living and rich beauty, at absolute odds with the desolated emptiness evoked in the first part of the poem.[149]

In her introduction to *The Ruin* in *The Old English Elegies*, Anne Klinck observes that in the last section, the poet "loses himself in admiration of the city as it once was" and that here the elegiac mood it shares with *The Wanderer* and *The Seafarer* gives way to the celebration of "the triumph of the human imagination" (63). More elevated in tone and more involved with sensuous pleasure than its fellow poems, *The Ruin* perhaps does not sustain a disconsolate attitude; it seems to me, though, that a similar poetic dynamic is at work here as in the other elegies: *The Ruin* is a death work, productively exploring human temporality in order to signify it in a rich and complex verbal structure, in, to be more precise, *ethos*, the vital cognition of *being-at-a-loss*. Because of its impersonal perspective, its lack of an ethopoetic speaker, of "I," *The Ruin* articulates more fully the nature of melancholic meditation than the authobiographical poems. Observing nothingness in the form of ruin, the speaker invests the object with the powers of mind, in the course of meditation filling empty structure with beautiful significance. The crescendo of *jouissance* within which this reconstruction takes place is as palpable as the concrete image of "shining city," "þas beorhtan burg" (37), which it effects toward the poem's end. As Klinck notes, *The Ruin* turns toward celebration of "the triumph of the human imagination" (63); however, in doing so, it does not abandon melancholy, but weaves knowledge of absence into fullness, of ruined city into *ethos*, the creative mind in the act of building.

149 After the detail of the warm baths (38–41), the manuscript is too severely damaged to leave room for speculation about the sequel.

e. *Deor*: Poet as Healer

Without a social history delineating the role of the Anglo-Saxon poet, it is near impossible to give a coherent account of such a figure. Throughout the above discussion of the *Exeter Book* elegies, I have suggested that a poetic function can be traced in consolatory speech, that certain authorial patterns – crisis, liminal soujourn, social aggregation – can be construed on a par with the therapist's impact in the psychoanalytic situation. The language of the traditional poet, part oral performance, part transitional text, develops into an intricate transferential artifact – a *ku-solola* – bringing to light the unsaid, private grief transformed into public utterance. As Pat Belanoff has noted, elegies such as *The Wife's Lament* are polyvocal, the way they harbour "the presence of the incommunicable," implicating listeners in therapeutic rituals (1990: 196; 197). Thus, it is possible to speculate about a role for the Old English poet analogous to that of the Freudian/Lacanian analyst: consequent upon processes of transference, the analyst embodies a hybrid cure, a detached involvement in the self-exploration of others. What I have wanted to underline is the intimate connection between poet and character, the former's Janus-faced troping of the latter as both autobiography and public blueprint.

In this section on *Deor*, I will elaborate futher on the author-character couple, in order to illustrate both a transhistorical textual dynamic and a specific cultural situation. As the most fully evolved "protrait of the artist" in Old English poetry, *Deor* exemplifies this phenomenon admirably: the poet-character – "deor" – constructed within the elegiac patterns of loss, grief and restitution, combines in concise form the functions of (Lacanian) analyst and Old English minstrel. Character in *Deor* serves as an instance of the psychoanalytic "naming of desire" as well as of a specialized, historically circumscribed authorical consciousness. Before turning to post-Freudian interpretations of literary authorship, I will examine some of the most significant contributions to a historical portrayal of the Anglo-Saxon *scop*.

The Singer and the Hearer of Tales

If aesthetic balance was askew in *The Seafarer*, especially discordant in the gap between imaginary explorations and Christian ideology, *Deor* superbly achieves an integral presentation of the poetic mind, oral-traditional, steeped in both popular lore and Christian knowledge, and transitional, exploring the capabilities of the new culture of writing. At the start of this chapter on the Old English elelgies,

I referred to the recent scholarship on orality – especially, to Katherine O'Brian O'Keeffe's and Carol Pasternack's work with the so-called *inscribed* text in its manuscript context – noting the tendency here to deflate resilient, a-historical conceptions of literary authors, which still dominate medieval studies. O'Keeffe, in particular, revised such conceptions by foregrounding the collaborations of oral poet, scribe and audience, and Pasternack further historicized poetic creation in Anglo-Saxon England by substituting ideas of implied tradition for the figures of post-Romantic authorship.

As invaluble as these studies are, in their polemical zeal, they risk a denuding of the powers of the traditional artist, even a stereotyping, depicting him or her simply as a channel for communal lore, stripped of hermeneutic desire and interiorized probings.[150] The critical heritage of Old English elegies shows, without a doubt, their psychological specificity, even if readers have hesitated to claim this as a central feature.[151] My analysis of the major poems – *The Wanderer*, *The Seafarer*, *Resignation* and *The Wife's Lament* – has centralized their libidinal investments, and has aimed at interlinking them as avatars of the psychoanalytic work of mourning. Because of the intense and, more importantly, *originary* experience of narcissistic loss, crisis and restitution, the tropings of character in the Old English elegies reflect a new epistemology of the subject. As will become clearer in the following section, *Deor* demonstrates particularly well the cultural role of character as a transferential node, a point of re-visionary encounter between (the oral-performative) artist and (the traditionally trained) audience. In fact, the *Exeter Book* elegies in general, and *Deor*, in particular, justify "the rebirth of the author" in a traditional setting, albeit as a specialized professional, not the private individual, intending the plots and puzzles of modern fiction,

Even if scholars cannot avail themselves of a concrete portrayal of the Anglo-Saxon *scop*, comparative oral traditions, especially in rural Serbia (former Yugoslavia) and in South Africa, contribute to an understanding of the communal

150 In my examination of Pasternack's *The Textuality of Old English Poetry*, I pointed out contradictions in her argument, especially in positing a Lacanian view of a de-subjectivized text.

151 As T. A. Shippey has pointed out, the grouping of *The Wanderer*, *The Seafarer*, *Deor*, *Wulf and Eadwacer*, *The Wife's Lament*, *The Husband's Message* and *The Ruin* as a genre is a rather arbitrary gestur, based on critics' intuition rather than precise formal and thematic analysis (*Old English Verse* esp 54). Although Klinck's generic definition is helpful, it builds upon broad, manifest patterns rather than psychic latencies (1992: 246). My proposition, of course, is that self-explorations are the generic keys to these Old English poems. Their verbal dynamic is motivated by the desire to fill the chronotope of the *ruin* with human content. The resulting figures, or tropes, are more or less successful versions of *ethos* – *character*.

functions of ancient and early medieval poets.[152] The seminal work in this area, the instigator of the so-called Oral Theory, Milman Parry's and Albert Lord's ethnographic research in the countryside of former Yugoslavia, to a great extent sets the terms of the debate, but as pliable source, not as prescriptive wisdom.[153] Here, Lord's *The Singer of Tales* (1960) carries a particular relevance because of its analysis of tradition as a multiform and fluid phenomenon and of the oral singer as creative artist, spontaneous inventor as well as mouthpiece of an epic heritage. Throughout the discussion of the training and performance of artists within the South-Slavic regions under investigation, Lord makes clear that conceptions of poetic creation in an oral-performative context bear little resemblance to the work

152 The groundbreaking fieldwork of Milman Parry and his student Albert Lord among epic singers in the countryside of former Yugoslavia constitute the touchstone of most subsequent investigations into oral traditions, past and present. Lord's *The Singer of Tales* (1966), in particular, provides a point of departure, because, even though its major claim is "this book is about Homer. He is our Singer of Tales" (xxxvi) (Cambridge: Harvard University Press, 2000), it elaborates, in the first part, a flexible theoretical frame, focusing upon tradition, not as monolithic entity, but as various, complex and open to creative improvizations.
Scholars working amidst living oral traditions in South Africa, especially Jeff Opland (*Anglo-Saxon Oral Poetry: A Study of the Traditions* (Cambridge: Cambridge University Press, 1980)) and Ruth Finnegan (*Oral Poetry: Its Nature, Significance and Social Context* (Cambridge: Cambridge University Press, 1977); *Literacy and Orality: Studies in the Technology of Communication* (Oxford: Basil Blackwell, 1988)), stress generic diversity, and Opland, for instance, points out how praise poetry (the eulogistic traditions) dominates the Xhosa canon, not the epic model, privileged by Parry and Lord.
In recent years, fieldworkers interested in interdisciplinary methods – John Foley (*The Singer of Tales in Performance* (Bloomington: Indiana University Press, 1995)), Dennis Tedlock (e.g. *The Spoken Word and the Work of Interpretation* (Philadelphia: University of Pennsylvania Press, 1983)) and Del Hymes (e.g. *"In vain I tried to tell you": Essays in Native American Etnhopoetics* (Philadelphia: University of Pennsylvania Press, 1981)) – incorporate both ancient and contemporary traditions into their rich and inclusive perspectives. Here, ethnopoetics and the ethnography of speaking are major influences (see esp. Foley 1995: 1–28).

153 Parry's fieldwork in the former Yugoslavia was conducted first in the summer of 1933 and then during a longer stay from June 1933 to September 1935. On a second occasion, his student, Albert B. Lord, joined him. Because of Parry's untimely death in December 1935, the burden of the work fell on Lord's shoulders, who continued collecting and recording material in the South-Slavic regions, yielding particularly rich findings in the early 1950s. The major publication that grew out of these efforts is Lord's *The Singer of Tales* (1960), still a vital, even controversial, document.
Milman Parry's own writings were collected by his son, Adam Parry, in *The Making of Homeric Verse : The Collected Papers of Milman Parry* (Oxford: Clarendon Press, 1971), the latter giving a rather misleading picture of the collaboration with Lord in the introduction: the son minimizes the father's interest in Homer as an oral poet.

of the literate/literary imagination. Unlike the continuous mental effort a written poem generates, typically circumscribed by silence and solitude, oral poety exists only in the performance arena, a highly complex phenomenological act, involving the background of tradition, the compositional powers of the artist and the impact of audience.[154] Lord underlines *the difference* of this situation, especially the multiformity of the artistry involved:

> We must eliminate from the word 'performer' any notion that he is one who merely reproduces what someone else or even he himself has composed. Our oral poet is composer. [...] Singer, performer, composer, and poet are one under different aspects *but at the same time.* Singing, performing, composing are facets of the same act. (13; Lord's italics)

It is important, Lord further suggests, to realize that not only is the oral singer a different figure from the literate poet, but a much more intricate and profound individual than the "folk" stereotype allows: "It is sometimes difficult for us to realize that the man who is sitting before us singing an epic song is not a mere carrier of the tradition but a creative artist making the tradition" (13). The first part of *The Singer of Tales* – "The Theory" – is concerned with dissecting the many facets of the oral-performative situation, especially the apparatus of the singer – his apprenticeship, techniques (such as use of formulas and themes), his communication with audiences and with the traditional heritage itself.[155] Lord's flexible intellectual frame and his broad perspective in the second part of *The Singer of Tales*, not only upon *The Iliad* and *The Odyssey* but upon Medieval epic as well, has ensured the vitality and longevity of his version of The Oral Theory. However, as successive scholars within various discipline – classicists, Old English/ Medieval scholars, students of native traditions in America and Africa – applied the findings of Parry and Lord to their respective fields, often as test-cases of the "orality" of older texts, the tendency was for these findings to becoome encrusted into a binary couple, "The Great Divide" between the oral and the written.[156]

---

154 In *The Singer of Tales in Performance*, John Miles Foley elaborates on the idea of performance arena, from an ethnopoetic perspective (13–138). Below, I will return to Foley's ethnography of performance.

155 Using the feminine pronoun would be inappropriate here as South-Slavic epic singers are always male. However, as Foley has shown, female genres, performed by women, exist in the oral culture.

156 This was certainly the case with early applications to Old English poetry. See especially the "divide" between Francis P. Magoun's "The Oral-Formualic Character of Anglo-Saxon Narrative Poetry." *Speculum* 28 (1953), 446–67) and Larry Benson's "The Literary Character of Anglo-Saxon Formulaic Poetry." *Publications of the Modern Language Association* 81 (1966), 334–41.
Both Foley (esp. *Immanent Art: From Structure to Meaning in Traditional Oral Epic* (Bloomington: Indiana University Press, 1991) and Ruth Finnegan (1977) propose alternatives to "The Great Divide," with emphasis on cultural transition.

Ironically, such apparently opposed views emerge from what Richard Bauman had called a "text-centered" bias, a conception of the verbal artifact as circumscribed by its visible structure and linguistic patterns (1977: 8).[157] Despite the development of effective methods for investigating the traditional utterance, the scholarly focus within The Oral Theory remained on a microscopic level, on cataloguing formulas, mapping themes and narrative patterns, graphing "elaborate 'grammars' of phraeseology" (Foley 1995: 3). Only within the last two decades or so, with the rise of interest in sociological and anthropological approaches to traditional verbal art, has the impasse of "the great divide," the false dichotomy between the mechanical skill of oral poets and the meaningful artistry of written texts, been traversed by broad cultural spectra, involving, along with the segment of utterance,[158] larger units such as *tradition, cultural performance, situated speech events, communicative economy* and *folk poetics*.[159]

As a synthesizer of the variegated work done in the fields of sociolinguistics, ethnography, and the ethnopoetics of speaking as well as in ancient and medieval "orature,"[160] John Miles Foley, particularly in *The Singer of Tales in Performance* (1995), refines, broadens and elaborates upon four "extratextual" components of verbal art, which complicate the oral poet's expression and endow it with specialized meaning. In the first place, Foley rescues *tradition* from its denigrated milieu, re-instituting it as a vital, dynamic matrix, a mobilizing cultural catalyst for artistic discourse within oral communitites, ranging from the Homeric epic to the contemporary South Slavic pluralist scenario, involving, for instance, the *guslar* ("singer of talels") as well as a variety of folk performers such as the teller of folktales, the female lyric composer and the *bajalice*, the speaker of charms. One of the ironies resulting from text-centered appropriations of verbal art was that Milman Parry's ambition to rediscover Homer's traditional holism, that is, to trace the often iterative and formulaic features of the poem to extratextual worlds of larger significance, fade into the localized interests of twentieth-century scholars in strictly the mechanics of oral compositions and the conventional density within the utterance (Foley 1995: 5). Instead of giving only "lip service" to the surface patternings of a text, noting only the recurrence of, for instance, noun-ep-

157 Richard Bauman. *Verbal Art as Performance* (Prospect Heights: Waveland Press, 1977).

158 "Word" in folk poetics denotes a different entity than in contemporary linguistics, for instance, combination of lines, speech, scene or even a whole song (Folely 1995: 2).

159 The major scholar in these areas are Bauman (1977); Finnegan (e.g. 1977; 1988); Foley (e.g. 1991; 1995); Hymes (e.g. 1981); Tedlock (e.g. 1983). See also Doane's and Pasternack's edition of influential essays, *Vox intexta: Orality and Textuality in the Middle Ages*.

160 "Orature" is preferred by many scholars to the oxymoronic "oral literature."

ithets such as "grey-eyed Athena" and "Hector of the glancing helm," Foley proposes that larger questions should be asked of the traditional formulations:

> What if traditional came actively to indicate extratextual? What if it came to refer to a reality larger even than the entire individual performance, or group of performances? [...] Under the aegis of such a reconception, "grey-eyed Athena" would serve as an approved traditional channel or pathway for summoning Athena not just of this or that particular moment, but rather of all moments in the experience of audience and poet. (5)

In Foley's exposition, the focus here upon the "channel or pathway" criss-crossing the traditional artifact, broadens into a concern for "tradition as the *enabling referent*" for individual speech acts, for, in fact, an aesthetic differential: highlighted in its holistic referentiality, tradition constitutes the *metonymic* base of oral art; it motivates and mobilizes the variegated forms of speaking and saturates them with meaning.[161]

The task of the oral poet as a link between the traditional organ and the evocative potential of the verbal artifact is not unlike that of a performing musician, whose expert knowledge of an idiomatic repertoire combined with a singular insight into and technical mastery of a musical intsrument create arenas of extraordinary cultural power. Influenced by the interventions of sociolinguistics and anthropology into folk traditions, Foley's second largest extratexutal category is the event of the performance itself, the *enabling* occasion for the articulation of verbal art. Founding the crucial import of performance within cultural studies in general and folk aesthetics in particular, Richard Bauman's *Verbal Art as Performance* (1977) is concerned with the oral artifact as a form of communication, as *situated speech* circumscribed by specialized performative frames. Objecting to strands of speech act theory, especially J. L. Austin's propositions in *How to Do Things With Words* (1962), which juxtapose the criterion of "serious" ordinary language and "parasitic" language games of artistic utterance, Bauman affirms the situatedness of all speech events, emphasizing the need to be aware of cultural framing, of "the notion of frame as a defined interpretive context providing guidelines for discriminating between orders of message" (9).[162] Throughout *Verbal Art as Performance*, Bauman's examples from a variety of social arenas – the "everyday talk" versus

---

161 Throughout, Foley articulates his two major points proverbially: "*Tradition is the enabling referent, performance the enabling event*" (for instance, xiii, n6).

162 J. L. Austin. *How to Do Things With Words* (Oxford: Oxford University Press, 1962). Bauman's conception of framing relies on two seminal sociological studies from the 1970s, Gregory Bateson's *Steps to an Ecology of the Mind* (Chicago: University of Chicago Press, 1972) and Erving Goffman's *Frame Analysis: An Essay on the Organization of Experience* (New York: Harper&Row, 1974). As against the multivalent situations of spoken language in social life, Bauman's study is critical of "the notion of a strictly referential, 'literal' meaning" (50, n1).

"ceremonial speech" of the people of the Malagasy Republic, the "three major speech styles" of the Ilongot of the Philippines, Japanese professional storytellers, verbal behavior among Cahmuals of the Chiapas Highlands of southern Mexico – should be viewed not from a binary perspective, but as a spectrum of intensity, ranging, for instance, from the old South Slavic singer in his living-room suddenly "breaking into performance" to the ceremonial "pure speech" of the Maya Indians (esp. 12–24).[163] Partly, the nature of performance can be gauged, according to Bauman, by analyzing, in the first place, the role of performer, and in the second place, the *keying* techinques of the performative event, the features it highlights as cues to the kind of communication being framed.

What is particularly relevant here for an investigation of *Deor* as an event of performance, which enables a certain specialized communication to take place, is the understanding of the traditional artist as a powerful cultural agent, assuming "responsibility to an audience for a display of communicative competence" (11). Not only do listeners expect a certain performative fluency and an "enhancement of experience, through the present enjoyment of the intrinsic qualitites of the act of expression itself," but they progressively yield to the magnetic pull of the performer, who "*binds* the audience [...] in a relation of dependence that keeps them caught up in his display" (11; 16; my italics). To make a perliminary comparison with the psychoanalytic situation, as I noted in the section on "*The Wanderer*'s Talking Cure," following Shoshana Felman's observations in "Beyond Oedipus: The Specimen Story of Psychoanalysis" (1994), the analysand's cure evolves within an arena of performance, where assumption of symbolic codes takes precedence over resolutions of libidinal dilemmas, where fluency within the field of "the paternal metaphor" yield creative potential, bestowed by the *word-power* of the analyst, who as a type of specialized performer, spellbinds the participants "in a relation of dependence that keeps them caught up in his display."[164] Before examining *Deor* more specifically as an avatar of the psychoanalytic situation, I want to connect Bauman's version of social performance to John Miles Foley's ethnographic investigation of Serbian charms, as this has a direct bearing on an understanding of *communicative economy* and *word-power*, both in the proper cultural context and in the transposition of this context unto the character-zone in the verbal artifact.

Emerging more closely than tradition and performance from linguistic textures, Foley's remaining "extratextual categories" are summed up in the *economies of*

163 See also Gary H. Gossen's supplementary essay in Bauman's volume, "Chamula Genres of Verbal Behavior" (81–115). Gossen's essay was originally published in *Towards New Perspectives in Folklore*, eds. A. Parades and R. Bauman (Austin: Texas University of Texas Press, 1972), 145–167.

164 I will return to the role of the analyst below in the more specific analysis of *Deor*.

communication and the powers which the dynamics of performance, with metonymic links to the traditional organicism ("tradition is the enabling referent, performance the enabling event"), bestow upon the spoken *word*. The latter part of *The Singer of Tales in Performance* is concerned with the ethnography of oral traditions in a South-Slavic setting as well as with ancient and medieval "tradition-dependent" texts.[165] On the spectrum of performance intensity, highlighted by Bauman, the speech event of the Serbian charm (*bajane*), despite the mundane staging, most often in the conjurer's living room, constitutes a particularly well defined arena, underscoring the nuances of communication, enabled by the traditional conglomerate – the historical transmission of oral genres, the dedicated idiom of verbal art, the competence and the accountability of the performer.[166] In Foley's account, the aesthetic differential of orality, the theory of *word-power*, is concretized within the circumference of the magical cure, where the patient, suffering usually from a physical ailment, succumbs willingly to "the subject-supposed-to-know," becomes, in fact, "spellbound" to the conjurer's powerful utterance.[167]

That the healing potential of *bajane* is a product of the intensity of the performance arena becomes clear in the contrast Foley sets up between his own and his co-fieldworker's westernized preconceptions about the archaic, even romantic, context of magical charms and the mundane realities within the peasant communities of contemporary Serbia.[168] Instead of "a fairy-tale hag or crone, who plied her liminal trade strictly behind closed doors, employing all manner of ritual objects [...] well away from polite village society," the researchers encounter an ordinary household, where the *baba*, or "granny," occasionally, prompted by village demand, assumes the function of a conjurer, mobilizing her latent knowledge of the charm register, and, often among a casual crowd of visitors, in her own

165 Generally, in his work, Foley has refined early scholars' "Great-Divide" model, by conceptualizing, along with pristine orality and textuality, the "tradition-dependent" artifact. See, in particular, "Tradition-dependent and -independent Features in Oral Literature: A Comparative View of the Formula." John Foley, ed. *Oral Traditional Literature: A Fest-schrift for Albert Bates Lord* (Columbus: Slavica Publishers, 1981), 262–81.

166 See chapter IV in *The Singer of Tales in Performance*, "Spellbound: The Serbian Tradition of Magical Charms," 99–135. For a helpful prolegomenon to the study see Foley's "Epic and Charm in Old English and Serbo-Croatian Oral Tradition." *Comparative Criticism* 2 (1980), 71–92.

167 "Subject-supposed-to-know" is one of Lacan's nominations for the analyst, who constitutes an authoritative source for both the symbolic and imaginary registers. See especially *The Four Fundamental Concepts of Psycho-Analysis*.

168 Foley's field research was carried out with the anthropologist Barbara Kerewsky-Halpern in the village of Orasac in central Serbia.

kitchen or living-room, whispering the pregnant words of the charm into the client's ear (esp. 108–110).[169] Thus, despite the manifest ordinariness of the situation, the speech event carries a latent intensity: because performance here is a dedicated way of speaking, metonymically calling upon the traditional whole and thereby charging each integer, the word as a morpheme, with connotative surplus, the conjurer "harnesses the singular communicative economy of the charm genre – as terse and yet as reverberative an idiom as one is likely to encounter – in order to initiate a highly focused discourse, in order to banish the disease and bring about a cure" (136). In short, because the communicative economy involves more than the transmission of a message from a sender to a receiver, but is honed as a *pars pro toto* of a complex cultural entity, the concluding word of the *bajalica* – "out of my *speaking* has come the cure" – empowers the individual participants in the act, effectively assigning them roles as healer and beneficiary.[170]

As my intention is to underscore the *communicative economy* of the Serbian charm arena, this brief sketch of the *bajalica*'s work does Foley's thick description scant justice. What does emerge, however, is a problematization of the apparatus of communication as a friction-free delivery of a message from a sender to a receiver, revealing how a specialized, framed utterance carries within it residual layers, a latency of meaning, built up as in a *montage*, activated as word-power, when speaker and hearer enter the perfomance area, experiencing facets of language which reach "far beyond its nominal, superficial semantics" (Foley 1995: 135). Further elucidating the usage of "economy" to outline oral-traditional communication, Foley stresses that what is at stake is the relationship between "the dedicated, focused [...] register and its [...] performance-centered array of meanings," a pathway between tradition as a metonymic catalyst and the responsive indexes, or nodal points, within the verbal artifact (53: footnote 58; 54). Hence, it seems apt to depict the creative work done within this "enabling event of performance" as a kind of communal *montage*, in the sense that in the hands of a competent player, a musical hodgepodge, combining odds and ends of styles, achieves integral harmony. In fact, in the figure of the performer – the singer of tales, the ceremonial speaker, the trickster, the elegist, the *bajalica* – the multivalent word

169 Foley draws attention to the practice of whispering the charm, noting the deviating circumstance of field research where a tape recorder is used (102–4).

170 In *The Singer of Tales in Performance*, see the libretto of Deskansas', the *bajalica*'s, two performances, 117–120. It is interesting to note that the ailment the cure is aimed at is vaguely diagnosed as the disease of "the nine winds." Foley characterizes it thus: "Villagers perceive these illnesses as both borne on and caused by the powers of the wind (*vetar*), which can blow them from their right and proper place in the 'other world' to a destabilizing and threatening presence in the world we know" (115). Because symptoms of the disease are not specifically described, what is at stake could be no less psychic than physical.

is made flesh, is, to use Kristeva's expression, transubstantiated, imbued with the potential to heal.[171] In the next section, I will examine character in *Deor* as just such a magnetic site.

The Charmed Circuit

In this chapter on "the psychological tradition in Old English poetry," the preceding sections have, to some extent, attempted to trace *Bildung* within the elegies as both a psychic and a cultural process, culminating most successfully in *The Wanderer*'s talking cure, the speaker's assumption of the Name-of-the-Father, his self-fashioning as a consolatory trope for a community in a state of crisis. Even though the other major elegaic poems, *The Seafarer* and *The Wife's Lament*, do not succeed in mobilizing their speakers as cultural authorities, their very errors are instructive about character-making from a psychoanalytic point of view: even though libidinal excess overtakes the work of mourning in these poems, the subjects' desire erupts into the discourse of tradition, in the seafarer's case, stitched into the Christian commonplaces as an uncanny vision of "the dwelling-place of exiles," and registered by the abandoned wife in the visualization of strange, pre-Oedipal space. Because these three Old English poems, in particular, within their processual structure, grapple with the *subject-on-trial*, the task of articulating *being-at-a-loss*, they shed a light on the figurations of character within literature as a quest for an authorial pose, a space wherein is inscribed both crisis and sublimity, collapse, trial and superior knowledge.

Within the psychological tradition, *Deor* may appear as an anomaly, because its dense, lyrical form does not seem to involve *Bildung*, the psychological process of an eschatological artist. Instead of the wanderer's travails in language, the speaker in *Deor* assumes an authorial, disillusioned position from the very start of the poem, presenting loss as the human predicament, moving through accounts of historical catastrophes, on both the personal and communal level, concluding at last with a reference to his own professional crisis, the transferral of patronage, the protection and generosity of a lord, to a more accomplished singer, to Heorrenda, "leodcræftig monn," "a man skilled in song" (40).[172] Thus, even though autobi-

171 Julia Kristeva. *Powers of Horror*, e.g. 27.

172 All references to *Deor* are to Krapp's and Dobbie's edition of the *Exeter Book* in *Anglo-Saxon Poetic Records*. Unless otherwise noted, the translations from the Old English are mine.
Although the rivalry between *scops* here appears to be fictitious, Heorrenda is a reputed figure, and is, according to Kemp Malone, alluded to in the Old Icelandic

ographical desire mobilizes the poetic voice, unlike the Oedipal narrative in *The Wanderer*, at issue here is not the ritualistic process from crisis to sublimation. Instead, in *Deor*, the situation, I want to suggest, is post-transferential, staging character as a (Lacanian) analyst, the subject purified of narcissistic pleasure, not struggling to articulate a cure, but subtly indicating, what Lacan calls, "the analyst's desire," that is, a state of animation, which has traversed the personal, an impersonal will, which directs the analysand into a recognition of and accommodation with absolute difference.[173]

In order to fully grasp the specialized force of the character construct in *Deor*, it is necessary to be aware of the complexities of the communicative speech act in psychoanalysis as well as of transference as an ethically motivated relation. As Anthony Wilden notes in "Lacan and the Discourse of the Other," object relations within the Lacanian *oeuvre* contain multivalent layers, taking their point of origin from British psychology (as inflected by the theories of Melanie Klein), evolving in the later work, through structural linguistics and "the return to Freud," as radical epistemology, centering on the "logic of the signifier" (*une logique du signifiant*), where the *function* of the object takes precedence over its concreteness in, for instance, familial or institutional contexts:

> [t] hus there is a significant difference in the nature of the objects involved: in the early works it is "*l'autre (petit a)*"; in the later ones it is "*l'objet a* ," which is a much more primordial relationship, a relationship to objects which is anterior to the child's relationship to a person as an object. (163)[174]

---

saga, *Bósasaga*, Saxo's *Gesta Danorum* and the Middle High German *Kudrun*. Heorrenda has also been identified as the Old English Widsith, the prototypical minstrel of Germanic culture. See Kemp Malone's edition of *Deor* (New York: Appleton-Century-Crofts, 1966), 39.

173 Lacan elucidates "the analyst's desire" in, for instance, the seminar on transference in *The Four Fundamental Concepts of Psycho-Analysis* and in Seminar VII, *The Ethics of Psychoanalysis* (1959–1960). Trans Dennis Potter (London: Routledge,2008). Note also Dylan Evans' helpful definition in *An Introductory Dictionary of Lacanian Psychoanalysis* (London: Routledge, 1996), 39–40, and Bruce Fink's depictions of Lacanian psychoanalysis as primarily clinical work in *A Clinical Introduction to Lacanian Psychoanalysis: Theory and Technique* (Cambridge: Harvard University Press, 1997).

174 Antony Wilden's essay is found in his edited translation of Lacan's *Discours de Rome*, here titled *Speech and Language in Psychoanalysis* (Baltimore: The Johns Hopkins University Press, 1981). The French title in *Écrits* is "Fonction et champ de la parole et du langage en psychanalyse," translated by Alan Sheridan as "The function and field of speech and language in psychoanalysis" (New York: Norton, 1977), 30–113. The *Discours de Rome* is discussed in this book in chapter three: "The Mirror of Alienation: Jacques Lacan's Theory of the Subject."

Wilden adds nuances to Lacan's later understanding of *l'objet a* as a "partial object," implying a desire for unity with another within pre-Oedipal space, symbiosis with the mother's breast, for instance, a psychic movement which exists on a different level than the drive for identification within specular, ego-motivated contexts, nontheless operating as the same "object relation [...] when one moves from the genetic to the structural level" (163). In analysis, retrospection, especially prompted by the Freudian *Nachträglichkeit* or "deferred action," the excavation of a past event from the temporal space of the unconscious, may be directed by the subject or analysand only to the interaction between specific objects, ignoring the primal origin, *object a* as cause of desire. Multivalent object relations must be taken into account as vital constituents of analytic communication: with regard to the transference, the analyst's responsibility is to assume a position of the subject-supposed-to-know, not in terms of mastery or of an advisory role, but as trigger of unconscious processes, as a configuration of *object a*, a reflector of the analysand's alienating desire.

As Foley's model of the performative arena in oral-traditional communication, Lacanian analysis operates within an *economic* field of relations, quite at odds with conventional delineation within linguistics of the speech act as static and transparent, "as subject to the mechanics of articulation and to time in a non-essential way" (Wilden 1981: 164). Quite the contrary, as Wilden notes, what is significant for Lacan is "the question of the *movement* of discourse, [the view of] speech as a movement toward something, an attempt to fill the gaps without which speech could not be articulated" (Wilden's emphasis; 164). From the perspective of the "logic of the signifier," the art of listening in the clinical situation is primarily dependent on deciphering the speaker's messages as *demands*: they do not exclusively address the analyst, but are veiled intimations of the language of the unconscious, actually oblique statements aimed at the sender himself. As Dylan Evans lucidly explains,

> [w] hen speaking to the analyst, the analysand is also addressing a message to himself, but is not aware of this. The task of the analyst is to enable the analysand to hear the message he is unconsciously addressing to himself; by interpreting the analysand's words, the analyst permits the analysand's message to return to him in its true, unconscious dimension. (26–7).

Underscoring the primacy and the dupliticitous nature of the signifier, in *The Four Fundamental Concepts of Pscyho-Analysis*, Lacan compares the transference to the discourse of love. Unlike the model construed by ego psychology, with the analytic goal of adapting a deluded self to an essentialist reality, communication in a Lacanian setting is premised within "the domain of possible deception": in analysis, Lacan says, "the danger is that this Other is deceived" (133). Like the unworthy lover who, through amorous rhetoric, assures the loved one of the splendid constitution he, in fact, lacks, and thereby misleads himself, the analysand's speech is riddled with blind spots, with misrecognition: "in persuading the other that he has that which may complement us, we assure ourselves of being able to continue to misunderstand precisely what we lack" (133).[175] Here, Lacan is working from an understanding of the distinction between *need* as a potentially exhaustible biological craving and *demand* as an irreducible speech phenomenon, presupposing an Other, avatars of the mOther, whom the subject appeals to, not in order to be fulfilled, but in order to elicit a response of love. In fact, according to Lacan, what distinguishes the Freudian field of transference from other forms of psychology is the highlighting of demand as a polyvalent signifier, not as need in the form of affects or instincts:

> The fact is that the transference is also a suggestion, but one that can operate only on the basis of the demand for love, which is not demand arising from any need. [...] this demand is constituted only in so far as the subject is the subject of the signifier. (*Écrits* 270)

Indeed, this significant attention paid to the symbolic contours of the analysand's discourse characterizes Freud's explorations of the transference in, for instance, "Remembering, Repeating and Working-Through" (1914) and "Observations on Transference-Love" (1915). As I discussed in Chapter 5, in the latter essay, Freud, as if in anticipation of Lacanian *jouissance*, emphasizes the genuineness of the female patient's erotic attachment, even though, in a sense, it is a deception, a lie, and encourages analysts, encountering similar cases, to enchance the love as an artifact, the symbolic product of analytic work. The challenge here is to listen to the patient's demand, or as Lacan would say, to mark the pulsations of "sexuality in the defiles of the signifier," so that the *cause* of desire emerges, effected by the staging of fantasy and its intersubjective traversal, cure in the form of post-transferential "mental freedom."[176]

On analogous lines to the psychoanalytic transference, *Deor* produces a consolatory trope, a communicative field, where the analyst's desire is brought to bear upon the audience's misrecognition, directing it to authentic subjectivation, to a state of accommodation with absolute difference. In the figure of the poet-character, Deor, *word-power*, understood as both the metonym of tradition and the Lacanian signifier, consolidates, opening up a space for new knowledge to emerge within the movements of desire. Essentially, a global process within the character

175 In a section called "The Presence of the Analyst, "this passage occurs just after a severe critique of an an article on transference by a proponent of American psychoanalysis, Thomas S. Szasx, who is bereft of the insight that "truth is based only on the fact that speech, even when it consists of lies, appeals to it and gives rise to it" (133).

176 Lacan discusses "Sexuality in the Defiles of the Signifier," in *The Four Fundamental Concepts of Psycho-Analysis*, 149–160.

construct crystallizes in *Deor*: the analyst's desire as purified libido, an impersonal will, aimed at the relief of suffering, through subjectivation, registers a trajectory from ontology, from, for instance, excavations of unconscious "deferred actions," to ethcis, to the psychoanalytic admonition, "have you acted in conformity with the desire that is in you?" (*The Ethics of Psychoanalysis* 314).

As analytic authority, the speaker in *Deor* is superior to *The Seafarer*, because he has become accommodated with the death drive and is able to direct an audience into a similar disillusioned stance.[177] In distinction from the miniature epic structure of the Old English elegies in general, *Deor* manifests lyric form, in the manuscript divided into six strophes, each elliptically narrating suffering, the first five (1–27) referring to mythic, folkloric and national catastrophes, the last one (28–42) depicting Deor's own personal crisis, his loss of patronage and place as a court minstrel with the royal family of the Heodeningas.[178] A particularly unique feature of the poem is the last line of each stanza, a repetition or a refrain, a kind of a wise aphorism, expressing what appears to be a consoling insight, that the recounted misfortunes passed away and that as a consequence, present woe will be alleviated: "Þæs ofereode; þisses swa mæg!" – "that passed; so will this!"[179] A significant point here, which I will return to below, is that until the statement of Deor's private grief, "þisses" – "this," "regarding this," "with references to this"[180] – remains an open-ended, hybrid verbal node, the audience's objective correlative, accumlating semantic layers, in the final stanza, operating like a *charmed* utterance, in both Foley's and Lacan's understanding of communciative ecomomy within "the enabling event of performance" on one hand and psychoanalytic transference on the other.

---

177 "Accommodation" as the aim of analytic treatment is the term used by Lacan, indicating that transference effects a complex cure, involving not at all adaptation and popular notions of happiness. I want to maintain that "literary consolations" operate in the same way as the Lacanian "accommodation." This will become clearer in the analysis of *Deor.*

178 This six-part division is by no means without controversy as, for instance, Kemp Malone's edition of *Deor* divides the poem into seven stanzas, and both Charles W. Kennedy's and S. A. J. Bradley's translations follow Malone's example. Charles. W. Kennedy, trans. *An Anthology of Old English Poetry* (New York: Oxford University Press, 1960); S. A. J. Bradley, ed. and trans. *Anglo-Saxon Poetry* (London: Everyman, 1982). I will come back to the problematic last fifteen lines (28–42).

179 The translation "that passed; so will this" captures the gist of the refrain, although variations are found in the formulation of *mæg*. Klinck's comments are particularly pertinent: "*Mæg*, then, in the *Deor* refrain, expresses something stronger than possibility; it indicates what is desired and expected" (1992: 161).

180 Both "þæs" and "þisses" are genitive forms, apt impersonal expressions of the purified singer.

In fact, the series of cryptic narratives within the first five stanzas of *Deor*, ranging from the legendary sufferings of Weland and Beadohild, the master craftsman and the woman he ravished as an act of revenge, through the love-pangs of Mæðhild, enamoured of a water-demon, to oppression on the national level in the form of the exiled Þeodric and the tyrannical Eormanric, function as both the metonyms of tradition and Lacanian tragedy.[181] Although many of the poem's cultural allusions remain indecipherable for a modern audience, the extensive recent scholarly investigations of oral traditions, which John Foley synthesizes, especially in *The Singer of Tales in Perfomance*, corroborate the claim that within the performance arena a specialized reciprocity is enabled between singer and listener, so that an apparent opaqueness or trite formula resonate with *word-power*, with semantic richness, mobilized through the competent rehearsal of the traditional heritage. Above, in the discussion of the traditonal communicative mechanism in a Serbian context, I noted that holism here can be experienced as musical *montage*, the assemblage of disjunctive styles, in the hands of a skilled player, into melodic continuity. In order to understand psychic reality in *Deor*, I suggest that one approach the poem as just such a *montage,* as the harnessing of the psychic drives, by the pure desirousness of the analyst, into a confrontation with *jouissance*, with the inscription of the death drive into the pleasure principle as human destiny. Viewed in this way as a type of death-work, in Kristeva's conception, the detailed reconstruction of the elliptical content of the poem's stanzas becomes less important than the *leitmotif* of *eros* and *thanatos* which runs through them. Each of the stanzas, the personal one included, can, in this sense, be interpreted as Lacanian tragedy, as a kind of negative vitalism, as, in fact, an affirmation of *negativity* as the indestructible principle of life.[182]

In *Lacan's Medievalism* (2006), Erin Felicia Labbie traces important connections between the psychoanalytic theory of desire and medieval philosophical and literary discourse, especially concerning conceptions of sovereignty, the singular subject, animality and human sexuality. In a nexus of comparisons between Old French romances, troubadour texts, Freud's case histories and Lacan's analysis of

181 These allusions to legend and history are by no means clear-cut, and most scholars express reservations about their own reconstructions. The briefest and most enigmatic stanzas, number three and four, are still being debated: Kemp Malone's explication of Mæðhild's situation, based on Scandinavian ballads, seems at present the most credible one (8–9); the two-line reference to Þeodric in stanza four is difficult to gauge, especially as the meaning of "ahte" is ambiguous – "Þeodric ahte þritig wintra/Mæringa burg; þæt wæs monegum cuþ" (Þeodric *ruled* over Merovingians for thirty years; this was known to many" or Þeodric *dwelt* for thirty years in the city-fortress of the Merovingians") (18–19). In the poet's mind, is Þeodric an oppressor or victim?

182 I will come back to a consideration of character as a sign of this principle.

courtly love in *The Ethics of Psychoanalysis*, focusing upon the study of the Wolf Man, Labbie comments upon the ambivalence of the scoptophilic drive, how, for instance, the desire of the young child to see the naked female body persists in a state of conflict "with a sense of repulsion and a fear of what might occur if the wish is fulfilled" (85). Thus, according to Freud, eroticism emerges as a dualistic drive, constantly in "revolt against" its own attachments (*Three Case Histories*, 24; Labbie 85).[183] The Wolf man's case is particularly instructive because the witnessing of the "primal scene," the actual or fantasized display of the parents' sexuality, triggers in the subject's psyche a simultaneous sense of "pleasure and repulsion, holiness and scatology" (91).[184] Subsequent formation of sadistic fantasies within masochistic identifications with the suffering Christ, oscillations between cruel treatment of animals and phobic reactions, and, in general, a "twofold ambivalence," a "lovehate" saturation within all object relations reflects the empty fullness of desire, a dualistic dynamic which, as Labbie states, "takes on a specific discursive and scientific form as Eros/Thanatos in [...] *Beyond the Pleasure Principle*" (238, n33). More profoundly than is possible to investigate at this point, Lacan's theory of desire builds upon a revision of Freud's insight into the ambivalences of sexuality. At the risk of simplifying, here, it is sufficient to note that in Lacan's conception, the sexual drives, as manifestations of unconscious desire, – oral drive, anal drive, scopic drive and invocatory drive – move in dualistic circuits ("What is fundamental at the level of each drive is the movement outwards and back in which it is structured" (*The Four Fundamental Concepts*, 177)), unamenable to satisfaction, communicating not as a biological whole, but in "the mode of a headless subject, [having no other] relation to the subject [than] one of topological community" (181). As Dylan Evans notes, this surrealistic terrain of the the human organism brings *dualism* to the fore as "an opposition between the symbolic and the imaginary" (48); moving through "the defiles of the signifier," the drives, as partial manifestations of the libido, exhibit the condition of *lack*, the effect of the structure of signification upon subjectivity. As in the case of Narcissus, subjectivation entails coming to terms with one's own "poor plenty," the "want-to-be" (*manque-à-être*) at the core of *jouissance*. The consolatory task of

183 Sigmund Freud. *Three Case Histories*, ed. Philip Rieff (New York: Collier Books, 1963).

184 As Lars Sjögren points out, Freud's (re)construction of the Wolfman's primal scene, in turn, based on the four-year old child's dream of the white wolves, occurs at a transitional point in psychoanalytic thinking, the abandonment of the so-called "trauma theory," with roots in positivistic assumptions about the relation between material fact and psychic reality, in favor of explorations of the unconscious as the space of subjective truth. See Lars Sjögren. *Sigmund Freud: Mannen och verket* (Natur och Kultur, 1997), 202–207.

Deor consists of this suturing, this stiching-in, of transformed Narcissus into the montage of the ambivalent drives.[185]

It is possible to contend that Lacan's "medievalism" has a bearing on the *exempla* of suffering in *Deor*, especially in the concern, within the theory of desire, for the singularity of an ethical stance, which flourishes as a consequence of ontological speculations. In the "death-work" of *Deor*, with the assumption of the analyst's desire to conduct subjects into a confrontation with the circuitous drives, the psychic proclivity for both Eros and Thanatos, each stanza depicts a tragic scene, where what Kristeva refers to as *sacrifical economy* erupts into violent acts, causing extreme mental and physical suffering.[186] In the first two stanzas, alluding to the legend of Welund the master smith of, for instance, *Völundarkvida* and *Þidrikssaga*, and Beadohild, king Niðhad's daughter, *Deor* singles out the act and effects of torture, the king's hamstringing of the craftsman, enslaving him to the royal court. As a consequence, in the tormented manner of revenge tragedy, Welund murders Niðhad's two sons, turning their remains, their skulls, eyballs and teeth, into ornamented jewelry, and after offering these as products of his smithy to the royal family, raping and impregnating Beadohild (1–13). An economy of sacrifice is also hinted at in the remaining four stanzas: animality threatens subjectivity in the cryptic tale of Mæðhild, the wife of Geat, who insomnolent laments her "sorrowful love" – "seo sorglufu" (16) – for a water-demon or a merman, who, in an analogous ballad, lures her into his watery abode;[187] as Jerome Mandel contends, political oppression characterizes stanzas four and five, the rather ambiguous status of Þeodric in "the strong-hold of the Mærings" (20) most likely referring to enforced exile, lasting thirty years and the "wolfish intentions" ("wylfenne geþoht," 22) of Eormanric implying the cruel excess of a tyrant king (1977, 6);[188] finally, at first sight seeming a less grievous case than the previous ones, the destitute *scop* in the last stanza deepens the insight into the ambivalent drives, in foregrounding the *fragility* of the human subject, intimating how the tragic fall, in the specialized medieval interpretation of it as subjection to

185 I will return to a discussion of the Lacanian version of the drives in the next chapter.

186 Basically, the psychological underpinning of Kristeva's theory of sacrifice is the Lacanian subject, who having invested in mirror-stage images, suffers a crisis when the repression sustaining that misrecognition fails, threatening "to return the subject to the incohate chaos of their origin" (Reineke 1997: 27). Such "boundary failure" often leads to sacrificial violence, a perverse compensation for subjective lack. See Reineke's development of Kristevan theory, primarily within a feminist context.

187 See Malone's discussion of the sources for the Mæðhild tale in Scandinavian ballads, 1966: 8–9.

188 Jerome Mandel. "Exemplum as Refrain: The Meaning of 'Deor'." *Yearbook of English Studies* 7 (1977), 1–9.

the whims of Fortune, is the lot of everyman, rulers and the ruled, warlords and retainers, lovers and loved ones, poets and patrons.[189] As I will return to below, the fictional name of the poet-character – "Deor" ("the dear one," "animal," "the bold one") – can be interpreted as the incarnation of the *leitmotif* of the poem: the fragile subject, divided by the destructive drives, boldly assumes his tragic destiny.[190]

With regard to the composition of the six *exempla*, in my opinion, Jerome Mandel's approach in "The Meaning of 'Deor'" (1977) does the poem great justice in that he considers the sentiment of suffering more meaningful than the reconstruction of material fact, which is, in every case, bound to be partly conjectural (esp, 1–2). However, while I agree with Mandel's analysis of the lyrical design as a consolatory pattern of spiritual and physical misery, appealing first to an audience "on a primal level, that of one's first experience with the poem" (9), and subsequently leading them into disillusioned reflection, the assumption that this higher-order position is reached through *identification*, through mimetic recognition and stoic acceptance, is contrary to my understanding of the poem as essentially an *examplum* of transference, of the communication between the analyst's desire and potentially ethical subjects. By, as Mandel says, appealing to the audience "on a primal level," the poet-analyst does not so much elicit their sympathy as, in the manner of psychoanalytic transference, create unconscious space, which subverts analysands' mirror-stage identifications, substituting those with the fragile subject, with the "poor plenty" of narcissistic reflections. According to a psychoanalytic reading, the design of *Deor* embraces Lacanian tragedies, patterning its *exempla* as instances of the death drive, moving from economies of sacrifice, from victimization of individuals, to affirmation of *jouissance* in the singular subject. Whereas *The Seafarer* failed to imagine the alterior community, *Deor's* analyst succeeds in troping literary character as a consolatory node for the (potential) psychic re-organization of the audience. In order to demonstrate how "Deor" functions as such a consolatory node, it will be necessary to re-examine the last stanza, attending particularly to the substitution of singular subjectivity for the processes of identification.

An area of scholarly contention, *Deor*'s last stanza, on a superficial reading, appears incongruous in form and subject-matter. Concluding with the refrain – "þæs ofereode, þisses swa mæg," – the jar between the general Christian/Boethian reflections of the first seven lines (28–34) and the following personal vignette,

189 The world-view of Chaucer's *Troilus and Criseyde* is informed by Boethian fatalism: "What other thyng bywayen the cryinges of tragedyes/but only the deedes of Fortune, that with unwar strook/overturneth the realmes of greet nobleye? (Book II, Prose ii). *Chaucer's Translation of Boethius's De Consolatione Philosophiae*, ed. Richard Morris (Kessinger Publishing, 2001).41

190 See especially Klinck's gloss on the name, "Deor," 1992, 167–8, n37b.

Deor's *exemplum*, has nevertheless led some critics to dismiss either part as an interpolation, and has prompted Kemp Malone, one of the more authoritative editors of the poem, to suggest that lines 35–42 are actually a postscript, added by the poet as an afterthought (1966: 16).[191] Despite the disparity, most editions and translations of the poem follow the manuscript divisions in printing the last fifteen lines as a complete stanza, although, again, Malone's edition adheres to his idea about the two endings.[192]

Even if Malone's comparison between the two endings in Chaucer's *The Clerk's Tale* and *Deor's* seemingly incoherent last strophe can be taken as far-fetched (16), in my opinion, a fruitful way to approach the problem is to focus on the jar, to conceive the stoicism of the first part as at odds with the account of the poet's misfortunes in the last lines. Whether or not the poetic source is Boethius's *Consolatio of Philosophiae*, King Alfred's Christianized translation, or, as Harris (1987) contends, general knowledge of the Old Testament, there can be no doubt that lines 29–34 express a sentiment of stoic adjustment to the instances of breavements of the sacrifical economy catalogued in previous stanzas.[193] In an abrupt transition, the disillusioned speaker of the poem, its libidinal directive, abandons the aim of subjectivation through transference, submitting to ego-driven identification with the Christian God. Contemplating the deprivations of joy, the gloomy prospect of misfortune without end, the all-knowing Lord comes to the mourner's mind, depicted in the Christianized guise of Boethius' Lady Philosophy:

> He who sits apart, troubled by sorrow, deprived of joy, becomes gloomy in the mind, thinks that misfortune is without end; but may he then bring to mind that throughout the world, the wise Lord frequently causes change, endowing many a man with glory, granting joy to some, sorrow to some. (28–34)
>
> [Siteð sorgcearig, sælum bidæled,/on sefan sweorceð, sylfum þinced/þæt sy endeleas earfoða dæl./Mæg þonne geþencan, þæt geond þas woruld/witig dryhten wendeþ geneahhe,/ eorle monegum are gesceaweð,/wislicne blæd, sumum weana dæl.]

---

191 Although debates persist about the Boethian connotations of the verse, critics generally agree that the sentiment expressed in the first seven lines accords with Christian consolation. In recent commentaries, the "interpolation theory" holds little sway. See Mandel (1977) and Klinck (1992) for brief reviews of critical histories.

192 Note also that two translators, Kennedy (1960) and Bradley (1982), divide the poem into seven stanzas.

193 On the Boethian/Alfredian connections, see Murray F. Markland. "Boethius, Alfred, and Deor." *Modern Philology* 66 (1968), 1–4, and W. F. Bolton. "Boethius, Alfred and 'Deor'Again." *Modern Philology* 69 (1972), 222–227. Joseph Harris contends that stoic pessimism rules the poem, based on the axiom from *Wisdom* 5:9: *transierunt omnia illa*. "*Deor* and its Refrain: Preliminaries to an Interpretation." *Traditio* 43 (1987), 23–53.

As opposed to the tragic ontology of previous scenes, triggering the movement of psychoanalytic accommodation, what is advocated here is patient adaptation to transcendent authority, a *Weltanschauung* bound to systems of ideas propagated and fostered by sacrificial economies. In a reading of Chaucer's *The Clerk's Tale*, with ties to Boethius and Judaic interpretations of the story of Job, Erin Felicia Labbie makes pertinent observations about the stoicism of the suffering Griselda, whose loyal and obedient love is tested in a display of horrid ordeals by her sadistic husband, King Walter, "struggl[ing] to maintain sovereignty over his subjects" (2006: 50). Debating Griselda's patient convictions, Labbie refers to Shadia Drury's critique of stoicism, pursued in her reading of Alexandre Kojève and Leo Strauss: stoicism, according to Drury, "allows the slave to convince himself that he is free simply by thinking he is free, or by having the abstract idea of freedom" (Drury 143–60; quoted in Labbie 59).[194] Further pondering the role of repression in Griselda's behavior, Labbie refers to Drury's commentary that

> Stoicism tries to deny the conflict between the ideal of freedom and the reality of slavery by relegating the actual world to the status of nonbeing. In this way, Stoicism becomes an exercise for inaction. It convinces people that there is no need to change the world or the state in order to realize the abstract idea of freedom. It insists that man is free even though he is everywhere in chains. (Drury 31; Quoted in Labbie 59)

Especially, as a female, inhabiting the imaginary site of submissive stoic, within the misogynistic economy of *The Clerk's Tale*'s realm, Griselda's situation parallels the poet-analyst in *Deor*, who, despite his (Lacanian) desire and transferential aim, is, within the mental process of the poem, abruptly lured away from his radicalism to assume the place prepared for him in the sacrifical economy, he has previously both acknowledged and subverted. Thus, the Boethian lines represent a kind of psychological crux, as well as an aesthetic cross-roads, not unlike *The Seafarer*'s moment of revelation, which that poem's speaker dissipated in mimic recitals of Christian dogma. At this crux in *Deor*, I maintain that the speaker falls from his position as *object a*, as cause of the audience's desire, to the level of mimicry, to a pre-transferential indulgence in what Lacanian psychoanalysis refers to as *the fundamental fantasy*. What is significant, though, for an understanding of the character construct is that after this regressive lapse, the analyst mobilizes himself as a singular subject, inscribing or suturing that singularity into a *Weltanschauung* which seeks to deny the reality of desire. By again, incarnating the cause of the analysands' desire, the analyst enables "the crossing of the

194 Shadia B. Drury. *Alexandre Kojève: The Roots of Postmodern Politics* (New York: St. Martin's Press, 1994).

plane of identification," preparing the ground for the new knowledge of ethical subjects.[195]

With regard to an ontology of character, what is significant toward the end of *Deor* is the connection between public and private fantasy, how the very ambivalence of *jouissance* creates this juncture where the pscyhe is either manipulated by the identity politics of the public realm or is subjectified, responsibly accommodated to absolute lack. In Lacanian psychoanalysis, "the fundamental fantasy" connotes a kind of myth of creation, a psychical elaboration of being-in-the-world, a staging of the scenario of "the subject com[ing] into the world as the object of desire of its parents, who incarnate [the] Other" (2).[196] The opaqueness of the Other's desire, intimated in the subject's demand, in the cry of the infant, for instance, fuels fantasy, which in its fundamental modality contains both global and particular features as responses to the enigma: "What am I in the Other's desire?" Sean Homer captures what is at stake in the hybrid conception of the fundamental fantasy:

> fantasies are never a purely private affair but circulate in the public domain through such media as film, literature and television. Fantasies, therefore, are at once universal and particular. There are a limited number of themes or primary narratives that consistently reappear in fantasy scenarios, but these can be endlessly reworked through the contingent material of a subject's everyday life. (85)

In the Christian consolation *Deor*'s speaker momentarily succumbs to, the circulating fantasy represses the circuit of the drives, the destructiveness at the core of *jouissance*, substituting an imaginary screen, mirror-stage identification with symbolic law. In such a scenario, what is appropriated is the subject's propensity to fanasize as protective mechanism, as an escape route from the terrifying encounter with the real. In *Le Séminaire. Livre IV. La relation d'objet* (1956–7), Lacan emphasizes the immobile quality of fantasy scenes and likens them to frozen images on a cinema screen: "just as the film may be stopped at a certain point in order to avoid showing a traumatic scene which follows, so also the fantasy scene is a defence which veils castration" (119–20; summarized in Evans 1996: 60).[197] What happens in *Deor*'s sixth stanza, is a momentary trans-

195 The reference to "crossing the plane of identification" is culled from Lacan's *The Four Fundamental Concepts of Psycho-Analysis*, e.g. 273.

196 Genevève Morel. "Fundamental Phantasy and the Symptom as a Pathology of the Law." *The Center for Freudian Analysis and Web Journal*, Summer (www.cfar.org.uk, 2008). The author makes use of Lacan's unpublished seminar of 1966–1967, *The Logic of Phantasy*. My explication of the fundamental fantasy relies also on Sean Homer's *Jacques Lacan* (New York: Routledge, 2005), esp. 60–63; 82–94.

197 Jacques Lacan. *Le Séminaire. Livre IV. La relation d'objet*, 1956–57, ed. Jacques-Alain Miller (Paris: Seuil, 1994).

formation, by the consolatory ideology, of subjective *jouissance* into masochistic fantasy about the inevitability of suffering. However, through the mental powers enabled by the poem's perfomance arena, the transferential process of knowledge is re-assumed in the last eight lines. As abruptly as ideology took hold, the singular name – Deor – asserts itself; *character* overtakes deceptive consolation as the aesthetic version of psychoanalytic accommodation:

> About myself, I will tell that, for a while, I was the bard of the Heodeningas, dear to my lord; Deor was my name. For many a year I had a good position and a kind provider, until now Heorrenda, a man skilled in song, received the land-right, which my lord had earlier given to me. That passed; so will this. (35–42)
>
> [þæt ic bi me sylfum secgan wille,/þæt ic hwile wæs Heodeninga scop,/dryhtne dyre. Me wæs Deor noma./Ahte ic fela wintra folgað tilne,/holnde hlaford, oþþæt Heorrenda nu,/ leoðcræftig monn londryht geþah,/þæt me eorla hleo ær gesealde./þæs ofereode, þisses swa mæg!]

Rupturing stoic discourse and offering the audience his own private *exemplum*, the speaker *traverses* the fundamental fantasy and sutures singularity into the official codes, which attempt to suppress it. The frozen image of masochistic subjection is substituted by *character*, a consolatory trope in the psychological tradition of Old English poetry, subverting the cultural fantasy of imaginary identification with a transcendent sovereign. As Sean Homer explains, in Lacanian psychoanalysis, "traversing the fantasy involves the subject subjectifying the trauma of the real. […] the subject takes the traumatic event upon him/herself and assumes responsibility for that *jouissance*" (89). The ends of fictional character as the "end of (Lacanian) analysis" pursue this libidinal directive: to position the subject in an ethical relation to desire, to elicit in him or her the "mental freedom" to never "give ground relative to one's desire" (Lacan *The Ethics of Psychoanalysis* 319).[198]

The aesthetic differential of character, imprinted upon the Old English elegies in various forms, crystallizes in *Deor* as a traditional poem, performed within a communal arena, which, in Foley's understanding, empowers the *word*, drawing to it like a charm the variegated interests of audiences. In this respect, there are relevant speculations within the criticism about the nature of *Deor* as a generic variety, Norman Eliason proposing it as a *begging poem* and Morton W. Bloomfield as a sophisticated *charm*. In both cases, there are assumptions about a self-aware poet, who constructs his artifact with a certain practical aim, to win a new patronage through the display of skill and to overcome misfortune through the appro-

198 The full sentence, as translated by Dennis Potter in *The Ethics of Psychoanalysis*, is: "From an analytic point of view, the only thing of which one can be guilty is of having given ground relative to one's desire" (319). In subsequent chapters, I will have occasion to come back to this statement.

priation of a traditional magical genre.[199] Urging readers to penetrate "the nature of [*Deor*'s] emotion" (541), Bloomfield detects in the poem a sophisticated charm pattern, a reliance on a homeopathic incantation of characters and events as well as the use of a repeated command. What Bloomfield is particularly interested in is the shape-shifting speaker, who in a quasi-magical gesture "tak[es] up the mask of a mythological or heroic character" (who probably overcame grievous misfortune) and thus effects a cure through the powerful refrain: "That passed; so will this" (540). To strengthen his claim about the emotional intensity of *Deor* arising from the elegant aesthetization of primeval *word-power*, Bloomfield concludes, "lyric poems were probably originally cult-songs and addressed to the gods. Lyric poetry has kept ties throughout much of its history with primitive incantation and prayer patterns" (540).

It seems to me that in trying to understand the poetic emotion in *Deor* through the oral-traditional charm genre, Bloomfield touches on the very verve of the aesthetic differential of character. In the poem, character can, indeed, be viewed as a mask, post-tranferentially subsuming the division inherent at the core of human identity. Deor is a tragic figure, in the Lacanian sense, eliciting from the audience cathartic accommodation with the death drive. According to the logic of tragedy, which Peter Sacks has, for instance, traced in *Hamlet*, despite the singular assumption of trauma, what typifies literary character is a remarkable faith in the restorative powers of language.[200] In this sense, *Deor*'s understated refrain – "þæs ofereode, þisses swa mæg" – captures the dynamic of the character construct, its aesthetic differential as an integral combination of post-transferential desire and poetic utterance. The contours of character, emerging from the psychological tradition of Old English poetry, crystallized in the elegantly crafted *Deor*, can thus be defined as *sublimated ambivalence*: absolute difference is gauged, affirmed and woven into *word-power*.

199 Norman Eliason. "*Deor* – A Begging Poem?," in Pearsall and Waldron, eds, 55–61. Morton W. Bloomfield. "The Form of *Deor*." *PMLA* 79 (1964), 534–541.

200 See the discussion of *Hamlet* in chapter four.

Chapter 8: "We Have Never Been Modern": The Libidinal Machine in Graham Swift's *Last Orders*[1]

The Category of Character

One of the most valuable aspects of Erin Felicia Labbie's *Lacan's Medievalism* is the demarcation of an interface between psychoanalytic thought and the medieval scholastic debate about the possibility of the existence of universals. Anticipating tensions within twentieth-century philosophy and critical theory between (post) structuralism and humanism, involving the supremacy of the signifier and the status of the human subject, the quarrel in the Middle Ages between realists and nominalists, catapulted by Boethius' quest for the realm of the sovereign good, is characterized by "a belief that language refers only to itself (nominalism) and creates the world of things, or that language signifies a greater category outside of itself (realism)" (Labbie: 6). In an important passage, comparing the different attitudes of Derrida and Lacan toward the animality of desire as they respectively respond to Heidegger's conception of the Thing, *Das Ding*, as the possible dimension "beyond-of-the-signifed," Labbie contends that in perceiving an absolute split between the inaccessible *beyond* and the speaking subject, the philsopher exhibits a nominalist preference whereas the psychoanalyst's position is realist, designating the foreignness of the "other scene" as a universal category.[2] In Derrida's account, what is not named encloses a sort of animalistic "benumbedness," excluding ambivalence, the "access to the difference between the open and the closed" (*Of Spirit*: 53–54; quoted in Labbie: 76);[3] Lacan, on the other hand, understands ambivalence as the effect of the split subject, the incorporation of unnamable animality within the human psyche (Labbie: 77).

In the development of her thesis that Lacan is a realist "in dialogue with the scholastic debates about the existence of universals" (xii), Labbie, in particular,

1 *We Have Never Been Modern* is the title of Bruno Latour's book, referring to an investigation of pre-modernity and modernity in terms of anti-periodicity. *We Have Never Been Modern*. Trans. Catherine Porter (Cambridge: Harvard University Press, 1993).

2 During the discussion of the unconscious in *The Four Fundamental Concepts of Psycho-Analysis* (1973; 1977), Lacan remarks, the unconscious must "be apprehended in its experience of rupture, between perception and consciousness, in the non-temporal locus, […] Freud calls […] another scene" (53).

3 Jacques Derrida. *Of Spirit: Heidegger and the Question*. Trans. Geoffrey Bennington and Rachel Bowlby (Chicago: University of Chicago Press, 1989).

investigates the connections between poetic language and the field of the unconscious as a trans-individual/trans-historical category. In the history of subjectivity, in Labbie's words, "no one, single discovery marks a historical moment or an epistemological break where, suddenly, an unconscious appears," and it is quite incorrect to maintain that, for instance, "Epicurus discovered the unconscious, that Teresa of Avila discovered the unconscious, or that Freud discovered the unconscious" (9). It is, however, as Lacan himself and several commentators emphasize, of utmost importance to distinguish the *Freudian* subject of the unconscious from other versions such as the primal unconscious, "the romantic unconscious of imanginative creation" or the Jungian conception of the unconscious as resevoir of mythic traces and archetypes – versions which fail short of the ambitious intention of pscyhoanalysis to establish itself as "*the conjectural science of the subject*" (Lacan 1977: 43; Lacan's italics).[4] The key expression here is *conjectural* as Lacan, in Seminar XI (1977), works toward integrating the Freudian field into his own conceptualizations of unconscious processes. In the history of thought, according to Lacan, it is René Descartes' formulations of the rational subject which initiated developments leading to Freud's outlining of the split psyche, that is, to be more precise, Cartesian certainty, originating in scepticism, but concluding in the self-assured *cogito*, facilitates the emergence of the subject of the unconscious, as an extension of the other side of rationalism, first surmised, but subsequently elided in the French philosopher's *Meditations* (1642). As Sean Homer observes, both Descartes and Freud set out "from a position of doubt, but, whereas Descartes moves from a position of doubt to the certainty of a conscious mind, Freud moves the opposite direction and places the emphasis on the *doubt* that supports certainty" (67; Homer's italics). Thus, the premise of uncertainty, the doubting thought that grounds conscious life, subverts the Cartesian assurance that "*I am, I exist*, is necessarily true, everytime I express it or conceive of it in my mind," replacing this by the radical assertion that "*one does not exist*," that a kind of thinking absence modulates subjectivity.[5] On this point Lacan is quite adamant, depicting the unconscious as a *gap* or *rupture*, not sceptical intellection itself, but "the *unrealized*, the unknown of Cartesian doubt" (Homer 67; Lacan 1977: 29–41).

It is this pre-ontological status of the unconscious which defines it as a global, or universal, phenomenon, transecting history as well as individual space. Showing the convergences between the subject of certainty and the subject of doubt,

4 Lacan marks this distinction in several places in *The Four Fundamental Concepts of Psycho-Analysis*, especially in the seminar on "Of the Subject of Certainty" (29–41) and "Presence of the Analyst" (123–135).

5 Descartes' statement is from *Meditations* (1642), qutoed in Homer, 67; the explanation is my shorthand for Homer's discussion, 66–67.

Lacan refers to Freud's understanding of dream thoughts in *The Interpretation of Dreams* (1900), singling out his predecessor's therapeutic mandate – "*Wo es war, soll Ich warden,* " – translating it provocatively "*Here, in the field of the dream, you are at home*" (1977: 44). Lacan's objection to the "execrable [French] translation, [...] "*Le moi doit déloger le ça* (the ego must dislodge the id)" proceeds from his critique of "Ich" as the normative ego and the authentic roots of psychoanalysis in structural linguistics:

> It is not a question of the ego in this *soll Ich werden*; the fact is that throughout Freud's work – one must, of course, recognize its proper place – the *Ich* is the complete, total locus of the networks of signifiers, that is to say, the subject, *where it was*, where it has always been, the dream. (1977: 44)

The Freudian/Lacanian subject is ruptured, is, one can maintain, criss-crossed by the pulsations of the unconscious, its truths gleaned through coded formations, dreams, parapraxis (accidental slips of the tounge), jokes, symptoms, of a more or less pathological nature, free associations as well as poetic sublimations. The unconscious erupts in the interstices where meaning is blocked, where "it fails and stumbles," where signification betrays its excesses and where, as is Lacan's point about interpretation, "irreducible signifiers" arise, the play of "non-sensical" letters belonging to the other scene (1977: 250).[6]

In this chapter, focusing on Graham Swift's *Last Orders* (1996), my aim is to investigate literary character as a real (universal) category, which emerges from the irreducible play of signifiers in the unconscious and which sublimates in transhistorical patterns the libidinal effects of symbolic structures upon subjectivity. In the previous discussion of the Old English elegies, certain fundamental features of the character construct came into view, especially its eschatological function, pinpointed most powerfully in *The Wanderer* and *Deor* as sublimated utterance of the ambivalences of desire. The operations of literary character in Swift's novel demonstrate the persistance of such a function, revealing to a greater extent than the medieval poems the connections to the subject of the unconscious. The main aspects to be considered are the death drive as a conduit for the (Lacanian) real as a connective between the psyche and the social body; modernist eschatology as scatology in assuming the trauma of the real; and the inscription of singularity into national myths.

---

6 See in chapter three, my inspection of Lacan's crucial essay about langugae and psychoanalysis, "The agency of the letter in the unconscious or reason since Freud."

Anecdote of a Jar

In both literary criticism and psychoanalysis, the concept of character plays a prominent role, although it is only in recent years that the latter has made productive use of it. In an outlining of what he calls "new character analysis," Bjørn Killingmo draws attention to the clinical advantages of integrating an understanding of character as a structure, as a stable organization, into the variable, mobile situation of analysis, dominated by "narratives and affects [that] change from one session to the next" and where "even within a single session, an oscillation from one extreme to another may take place" (77).[7] No less than psychic object-relations, energized by the drives and opaque infantile scenarios, an analysand's character may constitute a pathological mechanism, often revealed in strategies of defense against repressed material. Killingmo states that in extreme cases, "the character structure can be like an impenetrable shield blocking any experience of affect" (77). Paying heed to such resistances, to structural aspects no less than to the patient's narratives and transferential projections, the analyst listens within a broad scope, "tuned in towards the most subtle nuances in [...] language and style" (78). In Killingmo's interpretation then, marks of character such as stale, repetitive language, for instance, passive constructions which elide the self or "small words and empty phrases" (82), delineate symptom formations, which, just as insistently as the energies of transference, realize unconscious processes:

> Thus, these resistances can be seen as persistent messages from the unconscious of the patient, and this challenge has to be sensitively received by the analyst, often for a long time, till the patient himself can hear the call embedded in his own style. (81)

Although Killingmo's position is not strictly Lacanian, taking its cues from "the British Freud" and Kleinian object-relations pscyhology, the observation about character as a *message* from the unconscious, a potentially multivalent symptom, amenable to interpretation and transformation, is a fruitful one with regard to literary figurations. As will become clearer in the following discussion of *Last Orders*, the global, transsecting patternings of literary character foreground its emergence within the subject of the unconscious, expressed in poetic language as the more or less successful sublimation of the real of desire. The Old English elegies telescoped the processes of this aesthetization: *The Seafarer*, for instance, bares the defense mechanism of an inadequate character and *The Wife's Lament* articulates abjection, not subjectivation; on the other hand, *The Wanderer* and *Deor* stake out character as the field of the (Lacanian) analyst, assuming pure

7 Bjørn Killingmo. "Relational-oriented Character Analysis: A Position in Contemporary Psychoanalysis." *Scandinavian Psychoanalytic Review* 30 (2007), 76–83.

desirousness, a cathartic directive for the potential pscyhic transformation of audiences. In the poetic processes, resistances occur, on one hand, "like an impenetrable shield blocking any experience of affect" (Killingmo 77), and on the other hand, traversed by post-transferential knowledge.

In this section, I will, in Swift's novel, concentrate on the characters' resistances as they retrospectively, through memory, interpret their desires, in the process subverting imaginary identifications with paternal authority figures. As we will see, a certain pathology of the Law, impels the four protagonists, Ray, Vic, Vince and Lenny, to undertake a "sentimental journey" from Bermondsey in south-east London to Margate, in response to their dead friend's, Jack Dodd's, last wish, found handwritten on a piece of paper after the funeral, to have his ashes scattered out at sea.[8] On the road, in Vince's, the car-dealer's, fancy Mercedes, Dodd's memorial, the urn, most often referred to as a "jar," functions as a catalyst for the friends' infantile scenarios, mental representations in various guises of unresolved family matters. What I want to draw attention to is that through the characters' introspection, their filial sense of obligation to father figures, their resistances, in fact, to the subject of the unconscious, are broken by poetic signification itself, which ruptures the phallic signifier, returning messages to the speaker, so that he "can hear the call embedded in his own style" (81). Indeed, what each uniquely discovers is the tragi-comic nature of the symbolic; this realization brings them closer to the social body, turns them into carriers of analytic discourse, which infiltrates and (potentially) transforms the language of the masters.

In order to trace this process of transformation, it will be helpful to examine, from the point of view of the desire of the Other, a remarkably telling infantile scenario, depicted toward the end of Doris Lessing's *Love, Again* (1996).[9] As if Lacan-inspired, Lessing's sixty-year old protagonist. Sarah Durham, who, during the course of the novel, has experienced, what she calls, "The Calamity," "love, again" in its variegated forms, erotic, platonic, obsessive, ecstatic, in the last chapter, witnesses a kind of primal scene of love, as she rests on a bench in a London park, thoughtfully "submerged in the *why* of something" (331; Lessing's empahsis). Just before the episode, the narrator's commentary makes clear that the coincidental encounter with this love scenario, composed of a young mother with her two children, an infant boy of ten months and a four-year old girl, to some extent answers "the *why* of something," or at least facilitates Sarah's search for the cause of desire.[10] In short, the three individuals Sarah watches are ruled

8 "Sentimental journey" is the nice subtitle in a section on *Last Orders* in Jakob Winnberg's *An Aesthetics of Vulnerability: The Sentimentum and the Novels of Graham Swift* (Gothenburg: The University of Gothenburg Press, 2001).

9 Doris Lessing. *Love, Again* (London: Flamingo, 1996)

10 Watching the mother and children, Sarah uses the expression "love scene" (332).

by the law of the Other's desire, as formulated by Lacan in the sequence need/demand/desire. Clearly, the mother here is capable of fulfilling the children's biological needs, feeding their hunger, slaking their thirst, clothing and housing their immature bodies. However, such friction-free communication is complicated through the symbolic register these human beings of necessity inhabit: what *Love, Again* focalizes are the toddlers' modes of articulating their needs in the language of demand, suggesting that, especially in the case of Claudine, the little girl, *something* – a libidinal surplus, an excess of desire – remains in suspension, goes beyond the concrete acts, gestures and words. Through her feeble attempts at singing lullabys for her little brother, then asking for orange juice, when she isn't thirsty, desparately murmuring "Mummy, Mummy, Mummy," and finally sobbing, "let[ting] out a single loud hopeless wail," what Claudine demands is the mother's love, to be proof of the Other's love (333; 334). In Sarah's observation, the way in which the subject identifies with the signifier of the mOther's desire becomes acutely apparent when the four-year old girl showers affection on the favored love-object, the infant boy, singing to him blissfully in her mother's voice, "Darling, darling, darling, I love you, I love you my Ned, my darling Ned" (334). With psychoanalytic acumen, Sarah silently addresses the little girl:

> you believe that this is what life is and must be: you will always be disliked, and you will have to watch her love that creature you love so much because you think that if you love what she loves she will love you. (335)

In the final pages of *Love, Again*, this scene of love reverberates in Sarah's mind, and she ponders whether at a certain point "a door will slam shut inside" Claudine, releasing her from the pain of childhood, setting her free so that "one day you'll know it doesn't matter what you do and how hard you try, it is no use" (335). Again, the comment has psychoanalytic relevance, indicating that despite the intractability of the mOther's desire, through separation, the subject is empowered to harness libidinal forces and constitute him/herself as "*being of desire*," as a singularity, imaginatively sustaining "*manque-á-être*," the "*want-to-be*."[11]

The identification of the four "pilgrims" in *Last Orders* with, what I want to designate as, a pathology of the Law, with the desire of the Other, signified in their filial relations with Jack Dodd, their dead comrade, and transferred to his memorial, the urn carrying the ashes, is during the journey re-enacted in each character's memory as infantile scenario, operating on lines similar to the primal scene in Lessing's account. Within the novel's multiple narrations, which, besides the voices of the four friends, include those of Mandy Dodds, Vince's wife, Amy Dodds, Jack's widow, and even a short speech by the deceased himself on the "art

11 See my discussion of alienatioon and separation in chapter four.

of butchery" (285), the problematic father-son bond is conveyed with particular urgency by the fourty-year old Vince, whose pressing "urscenario" is the discovery that he is the Dodds' adopted son, his own biological parents killed in a bomb raid, during the World War II London blitz.[12] As Bjørn Killingmo observes in his discussions of the "new character analysis," disturbed object relations from early years stay lodged within the psyche, pregnant with the child's interpretations and fantasies, providing the background to the adult's representations of them in the analytic situations. The ferociousness of some memories coming to the fore in transference, often "demonic, annihilating and merciless" (78), owe their strength to infantile investments, and are not to be grasped as realistic copies of past events, but as adults' defenses against painful repressed material which controls them. In Vince's recollections, the idea of adoption functions as a psychic knot, weaving together strands of half-understood childhood inductions into the fundamentals of life: the intimations of puberty and sexual difference; the uncanny relation between birth and death; the ambivalences of affects, causing him both to love and hate his adopted parents and treat cruelly the young woman, Sally Tate (Lenny's daughter), whom he is attracted to.

Of particular relevance for the events of *Last Orders* are Vince's thoughts about how Jack and Amy bungled up their account to him of the "facts of life," of love, fertility, pregnancy and birth. With distant echoes of the archetypal infantile scenario, the Wolfman's observations, as a one-and-a-half-year old child, of his parents' sexual intercourse, in a scene set in the vicinity of Wick's Farm in Kent, "the Garden of England," Jack attempts to tell the young boy about his origin by euphemistically associating this with his own and Amy's youthful love-making in a pastoral landscape replete with apple-trees, grazing sheep and hop-picking, revealing in the process the shocking fact that the child born of this first love is a kind of living dead, a severly mentally handicapped girl, and Vince himself is without parents, a pitiable orphan. During the course of the novel, it becomes clear that this primal scene forms the background of the adult character, determining to a large extent his course of life, for instance, his choice not to go into the butchery business with Jack, his joining the Foreign Legion instead of settling down with Sally, his quasi-incestuous marriage to Mandy, a runaway, taken in and cared for deeply by the Dodds. In short, a perverted pastoral scene, a traumatic "want-to-be" constitutes Vince's psychic landscape, his libidinal machine. On the road to Margate, such an unconscious drive steers the pilgrims' Mercedes, with the adopted son at the wheel, into a detour to Wick's Farm, where latent agressions erupt, Lenny is beaten to a pulp, and Jack's jar itself is in danger of splitting open,

12 Graham Swift. *Last Orders* (Picador, 1996). All further citations from the novel are from this edition.

spilling out "what's inside" or it "could bounce back and start rolling all the way down the steep slope of the hill" (147). Ray, who focalizes the incident, notes how "it's like [Vince] wants us as witnesses" (147), and then shows us:

> He delves in the jar and he throws quickly, spluttering, once, twice. It looks like white dust, like pepper, but the wind blows it into nothing. Then he screws the cap back on and turns, coming towards us.
>
> 'This is where,' he says, wiping his face. 'This is where.' (151)

Thus, from a psychoanalytic point of view, it becomes apparent that the character here is inadequately separated from the Other's desire, that he has not, it is possible to surmise, assumed with full force the effects of the Oedipus resolution in *castration*, understood as confrontation with being as absolute lack. In fact, Vince's pursuits in the novel, as well as those of Ray and Lenny, are motivated by imaginary identifications with a father figure, realized as an interpellating agency, what Freud termed the "ideal ego," a narcissistic modality, deriving from the mirror stage.[13] Supporting such an orientation is the sense at the beginning of the journey that the travellers are under the surveyance of Jack's watchful eye, that in Ray's formulation, "they're watching, the dead uns [...] they're all watching us, even now, the old man, and Charlie Dixon and Vince's mum and dad, and Duke, and Jack here, peeping through the cardboard" (77). It is in this sense of an ambivalent, love-hate devotion to phallic authority that the characters are, to begin with, driven by a constituent pathology of the law, pinpointed by Morel as "turn[ing] away from the problems of the polis and from politics in order to devote oneself to the law inherited from one's father, one's family, and one's race" ("Fundamental Phantasy and the Symptom as a Pathology of the Law" 6). In other words, the self-knowledge that shapes these characters can be defined as a form of resistance to the subject of the unconscious, as the aporia of meaning, as the absent thinking within. However, as memory of the dead triggers a generalized thinking about loss, they are catapulted to *the other scene*, tapping into the logic of the signifier, within which they are inscribed as split subjects. The new knowledge that emerges can best be illustrated by a change in perceptive modes from the interpellating look to the creative gaze.

In terms of resistant character structures, on a lesser scale than Vince, the other co-travellers, especially Ray and Lenny, are symptomatically bound to Jack as a censoring father figure. On account of his boyishness and vulnerable physique, considering himself chosen as Jack Dodds' protégé during their time of war service in the Egyptian desert, Ray has developed strong filial, even Oedipal, ties to his friend, whom he thinks of, in a way, as is the case with Vince, having brought closer the facts of life – eros and thanatos in the form of the first sexual experience

13 See Freud's essay "On Narcissism" as well as my discussion in chapter two.

in a bordello in Cairo and of the savagery of war. Also, in Ray's memory, especially after his own father, Frank Johnson, unexpectedly dies, Dodds acts as a substitute caretaker, "baptizing" him "Lucky " and in the desert, "plac[ing] himself between me and the bullets" and in general serving as "shield and protector" (279). Later, a brief love affair with Amy Dodds seems to oppress Ray with Oedipal guilt and shame, assuaged to some extent through acts of penance – an enormous win at the races which helps Jack (and Amy after his death) pay off a large debt and this last pilgrimage to Margate, fulfilling the deceased's last wish. No less than Ray, Lenny Tate works through unresolved "father-son" issues, which mostly center around the Dodds' near adoption of his daughter Sally, resentful memories of the many summers his own meagre earnings from the fruit-and-vegetable trade could not match what the butcher's family offered his child, entertaining trips to the seaside in the meat van. As an outgrowth of such resentments, Lenny blames Vince Dodds for impregnating Sally and then abandoning her, making them all sinful accomplices in, what was at the time, illegal abortion. Less insistent in his thoughts than Vince, Ray and Lenny, Vic Tucker, the undertaker, nevertheless harbours guitly sentiments towards Jack, especially comparing his lucrative family business, passed on from father to son, to the demise of the butchery trade, the end of *Dodds&Son*.

During the course of *Last Orders*, these networks of filial obligations, symptomatic of imaginary self-reflection, encouraged by paternal politics of identification, in other words, these *resistances* to the subject of the unconscious, are ruptured by the transformation of habitual vision into the pscyhoanalytic gaze. At first, sensing themselves oppressively controlled by the "eyes of the fathers," by a generational law, the four men progressively, through their often free-associative inner speech, in fact, through "hearing the call embedded in their own style," access not a confirmation of their male identities but the big Other, knowledge of the Symbolic as a force field, constituted in its very operations by a lack, by subjective splitting. The transition that occurs then is from the conscious seeing, or (mis)recognition, of Jack, to a kind of creative distortion, expressed in the novel, I want to contend, as *anamorphosis*, on lines similar to Lacan's presentation of the "the split between the eye and the gaze" in *The Four Fundamentals of Psychoanalysis* (67–90). In a section on anamorphosis as a painterly device, in particular, in Hans Holbein's *The Ambassadors*, Lacan's interpretations form a corrollary to the travellers' perceptions of the urn, carrying their dead friend's ashes, the central piece, of course, on their Margate pilgrimage. From both perspectives, the emphasis is upon the plurality of significations embedded in the Other, apprehended as the field of the Symbolic, no longer as object, as imaginary counterpart of ego.

At first, a memorial object, in the course of *Last Orders*, Jack's receptacle, the urn itself, turns into a multivalent signifier, in fact, into a version of the phallic signifier, The-Name-of-the-Father, which the four perceivers improvize, destabilizing the fixity of meaning. From the first scene in the Coach and Horses, the Bermondsey pub, to the last magnificent ritual in Margate, the funeral urn metamorphizes into a variety of shapes, ranging from "a plain brown cardboard box" (3) to a precious toy, bandied about by the four "big boys," from a plastic container looking like "a large instant-coffee jar" (3) to a *Rochester Food Fayre* carrier-bag, sitting forlorn at a table in the Bull Hotel, from a rugby ball in the hands of Lenny and Vince as they take punches at each other, during the detour to Wick's Farm, to the ceremonial container of human remains, embraced lovingly by Ray ("cradling the jar in my arm" (292)) at journey's end. In the first Coach and Horse scene, Vic having rather clumsily placed the jar on the bar counter, like any other "pint glass" (10), Bernie, the bartender, surprised by its presence, asks "'What's that?'," an almost fearful interrogation, which, in a sense, can be taken as the catalyst for the ensuing playful metaphoric production. At the start of the journey, expecting a rigid, "solemn" signifier, "a little oak casket with brass fittings" (3), this way of conventional seeing is, during the course of the novel, transformed into a tragi-comic gaze, comparable to Salvador Dali's surrealistic representations of the phallus as "soft watches."[14] In fact, as I will examine in futher detail below, the four working-class comrades' appropriation of phallic discourse, their playful improvization of the paternal signifier, implying not only their filial ties to a father figure but the field of the symbolic as ego-driven interpellation, involves a substitution of the cock for the phallus, of the analytic cock-ney for the legislative master.[15]

During the pilgrimage to Margate, hearing the Cockney call embedded in their own style, the rich tragi-comic speech of their working-class culture, the poetic vernacular, the four male mourners construct characters as consolatory tropes, in the sense that they are transformed into carriers of *the (Lacanian) analyst's desire*, into directives for the audience to accommodate itself with absolute lack. As Dylan Evans observes, in Lacan's topology, unlike the look (ocular vision), the *gaze* is on the other side of subjective division ("of the Other"), the object of the scopic drive, an always-already condition of being looked at (72). Contemporary film theory, in particular, makes productive uses of Lacan's conceptions, for

---

14 The example of the soft watches is taken from Lacan's interpretation of Holbein's Painting, *The Ambasadors*, in *The Four Fundamental Concepts in Psycho-Analysis* (88). In the question and answer session at the end of the seminar on anamorphosis, asked to elaborate on the structure of the gaze, Lacan jokes in a "cockney" fashion: "I said that the gaze was not the eye, except in that flying form in which Holbein has the cheek to show me my own watch" (90).

15 In the Mandy section, "Cockney" is considered a "giggle word": "Cockney. Cockneys. Cock. Knees. Why do men from London get stiff in the legs?" (161).

instance, exploring the uncanniness of the filmic gaze, how an object can transfix the viewer, without the latter's conscious awareness. Basing his illustration on Slavoj Zizek's analysis of Hitchcock's *Psycho* in *Looking Awry: An Introduction to Jacques Lacan through Popular Culture*,[16] Sean Homer focuses on the scene toward the end of the film where "Lilah climbs the hill to the old house where Norman and his 'mother' live": the central point here is that the gaze belongs neither to the objective shot of the house nor to Lilah's subjective viewpoint, but to the uncanny aura of the Thing, an ominous sense of foreboding, associated with the human residence, of course, but emanating from it like a transfixing grasp, never consciously known. Homer comments, "In other words, the gaze is not something that can be seen, as by its very nature it is that which escapes the field of vision, but it is something that can be represented in the form of the *objet a*" (125–6). Because it can be *represented*, the almost sinister hold the gaze has on subjectivity can be pluralized in intersubjective interaction. In *Last Orders*, the watchful eye of paternal signification is metamorphized into such an intersubjective gaze, the Thing, the funeral urn as *objet a* and then in the final scene, into collective character, performing rites of death, as pure desirousness.

The aesthetic device which most helpfully illustrates the structure and dynamics of the gaze is anamorphosis, a central topic in Lacan's seminar on the "Split Between The Eye And The Gaze" and "*Objet Petit a* " (*Four Fundamental Concepts* 67–119). Because it shares features with the Cockney gaze in *Last Orders*, I want to focus on the *jouissance* of Lacan's interpretations of Hans Holbein's *The Ambassadors*, of the "strange, suspended, oblique object in the foreground in front of these two figures" (88). Viewing the representative renaissance picture, replete both with male authorities, "stiffened in their showy adornments," and "the symbols of *vanitas*" of their time, collections of objects from "the sciences and arts as they were grouped at the time in the *trivium* and *quadrivium*" (88), Lacan's questioning resembles Bernie's, the bartender's, catalysing query, directed at the strange thing on his counter: "'What's that?'" In both cases, there is a sense of a transfixing presence that cannot be consciously known, but that can be represented through imaginative interpretation. Warning his audience that in approaching the inverted use of perspective in Holbein's painting, Lacan "will dwell, as in *some delicious game*, on this method that makes anything appear at will in a particular stretching" (87; my emphasis). Indeed, a jubilant unpacking of the anamorphic distortion follows as the lecturer, referring to Baltrusaïts' *Anamorphosis*, first gives instructions on how to grasp the essence of the image: don't turn away, Lacan tells his listeners, "thus escaping the fascination of the picture,"

16 Slavoj Zizek. *Looking Awry: An Introduction to Jacques Lacan through Popular Culture* (Cambridge: MIT Press, 1991).

but "begin by walking out of the room [...], turning around as you leave [...] [and] you apprehend in this form [...] What? A skull" (88). The realization that "Holbein makes visible to us here something that is simply the subject as annihilated" (88), in other words, that lodged in the pictorial gaze is the structure of symbolic castration, triggers Lacan's interpretative game, and the empty center is enveloped in a phallic shape, which sometimes "appears to be flying through the air" or from other angles to be "tilted [...] in a flying positions in the foreground of this picture" (88). In turn, this ghostly phallus is a shapeshifter: whereas Baltrusaïts likens it to a "cuttlebone," the psychoanalyst lifts it into a surreal dimension, spotting not only Salvador Dali's soft watches but also "that loaf composed of two books which Dali was once pleased to place on the head of an old woman" (88). During the question and answer session concluding the seminar on anamorphosis, Lacan actually displays Cockney humour: asked to elaborate on the structure of the gaze, the gamster responds,"I said that the gaze was not the eye, except in that flying form in which Holbein has the cheek to show my own soft watch" (90). The nothingness at the center of signification, the tragic abyss, does not instill solemn silence but generates the laughter of the "Cock-ney," the *jouissance* of the Other.

As developed in *Last Orders*, the distorted image of the funeral urn, the physical comedy and the often hilarious language games associated with it, jolts the four male characters' imaginary understanding of phallic signification, transforming this "knowledge of the ego" into, what Lacan designates as *savoir*, symbolic knowledge of the subject.[17] Through the often free-associative memories, jokes and puns associated with "Jack-in-the-box," perception extends to a generalized sense of the *pathos* of the field of the symbolic itself, of the joys and sorrows and of the absolute lack stitched into human representation. In the domain of vision, what gazes back at the travellers constitutes, as it does in Holbein's wedge-like shape, hiding a skull, symbolic castration, that center around which gather, in Lacan's conception, "the whole organization of the desires through the framework of the fundamental drives" (*Four Fundamental Concepts* 89). Undertaking this pilgrimage across the English landscape, the encounter with the *real* of desire, with negativity itself, binds the characters as singular psyches to the social body. The nature of that bond will be the topic of the next section, expecially in the form of the Cockney appropriation of the master signifier, its metamorphosis into the discourse of the analyst.

17 The distinctions made between *connaissance*, as imaginary knoweldge, and *savoir*, as symbolic knoweldge of the subject, are especially in Seminar 17, *L'envers de la psychanalyse* (1969–70). Jacques-Alain Miller, ed. (Paris: Seuil, 1991).

(E)sc(h)atolgy

The title of Swift's novel, *Last Orders*, captures to a great extent the "delicious game" of the Cockney, the Bermondsey form of punning, the interlacing of late-night revellry at the local pub, with the solemnity and finality of rites of death. In "Graham Swift and the Mourning After" (1999), Adrian Poole notes the conflation between the jocular and the mournful in Swift's writings, expecially how joking is not simply "a distraction from pity and terror" but a vital ingredient in "complex fables of breavement in which mourning takes forms that are spirited, heartening and sociable" (151).[18] Here, Poole puts his finger on the cathartic process inscribed in literary character, the creation of an accommodating discourse, which, oddly, is both representative or "sociable," a cultural token, plugged into experience itself, and subtly subversive, deconstructing those master signifiers which regulate models of identification. As we will see, in *Last Orders*, character as such a dual, Janus-like, entity is achieved on the journey to Margate through the comic appropriation of monuments of the tragic in British history. What is brought into play is the death drive as latency of the Symbolic: as Joan Copjec states in *Read My Desire: Lacan against the Historicists* (1994), "*it is the real that unites the psychic to the social*, [and] this relation is ruled by the death drive" (39; Copjec's emphasis).[19]

In her semiotically derived considerations of the (psychoanalytic) subject, focusing on Lacan's position within contemporary theory, constructivist historical views, poststructural critiques of totalities as well as resilient evolutionary philosophies, Joan Copjec concludes that the paradoxes that harass deconstructive thought, in particular, – "that *undecidability notwithstanding*, decisions are *in fact* taken, power *in fact* exercised, traces *in fact* instituted" – proceed from a reluctance to confront *closure* itself, that the infinity of desire depends upon the discursive limits within which it is fated to dwell.[20] Because the psychoanalytic subject, trapped within symbolic structurations, is finite, is humanized through speech, aware of its own temporality as an effect of symbolizations,

18 Adrian Poole. "Graham Swift and the Mourning After," in *An Introduction to Contemporary Fiction: International Writing in English since 1970* (Polity Press, 1999).

19 Joan Copjec. *Read My Desire: Lacan against the Historicists* (Cambridge: MIT Press, 1994).

20 The quote here, and the italics within it, are culled from Samuel Weber, "Introduction," in *Demarcating the Disciplines* (Minneapolis: University of Minnesota Press, 1986), ix. Weber's essay "Closure and Exclusion" (*Diacritics* 10 (1980)) is Copjec's starting point for the exposure of blind spots within Derridean deconstruction. See Copjec's chapter three, "Cutting Up," 39–63. The prominence given to the real in Copjec's analysis is the starting point of a paradigm shift within contemporary critical thought, especially within film theory.

the libido insistently strives to exceed these limitations, substituting "one thing [...] for another in an endless chain only because the subject is cut off from that essential thing that would complete it" (Copjec 61). An exemplary figure in Copjec's analysis is the hysteric, whose pathology ensues from a sense of being cut off from social representations, appearing often in psychosomatic symptoms of "inert limbs" and "facial paralysis," "testimonies of a cut too often ignored by those who would turn Lacan's theory into a linguistic or cultural deteminism" (51). In Copjec's account, hysteria performs the paradoxical situation of the death drive: constructed by language, the subject is driven to exceed its strictures to the point of reducing itself to nothing, to "the cutting up of [its] movements and the *reduction ad surdum*, that is, the reduction to infinite series of its replaceable objects" (52). Furthermore, Beckett's "hysterical" fictions belie the *jouissance* inscribed in the drive for annihilation; in *Murphy* (1959), the eponymous protagonist exclaims:

> 'And it would not surprise me if the great classic paralysis were to offer unspeakable satisfactions. To be literally incapable of motion at last, that must be something! And just enough brain intact to allow you to exult!' (18; quoted in Copjec 51)

The subject in language is driven to exceed the closure of its images, to be transported to an extradiscursive realm, where its humanity, fated in its symbolic stature, quests for its own annihilation. However, as Beckett's exclamation unearths, a remarkable pleasure is the motor force, the jubilantly mobile sequence, integral to – in ambivalent deadlock with, one can say – the deathly inertia the absolute closure fosters. As Copjec so succintly phrases it, "the death drive does not negate the pleasure principle, it extends it" (54).

Last Orders showcases with particular relevance the mode of being of character, within its aesthetic matrix, dwelling in language, as a conveyor of this ambivalent condition, as sublimation of the *jouissance* inherent in the death drive. In its comic eschatology, the creative distortion of the inertia at the heart of all signification, Swift's novel attempts to articulate a visceral sense of the resistant real which prompts the paradoxical condition of mobility within inertia. In this respect, in a manner reminiscent of Swift's third novel, *Waterland* (1983), where the nothingness beyond, symbolized by the monotonous East Anglian Fenlands, is brought into play in the *jouissance* of History, of narrative in all its forms of representing the past, despite that past's destruction, *Last Order*'s *leitmotif*, the journey, operates on several levels to highlight the narrative pleasure of *the delay*, which often is quite explicitly staged in confrontation with closure. Indicating the ambivalence the characters will increasingly come to represent, in the novel's second section, set in the past during Vince's forty-year birthday celebration, with the four friends present as well as Jack Dodds himself, Ray repeatedly comments on the name of the Bermondsey pub they frequent as if it were the very embodiment of Zeno's paradox of the arrow: "'They calls it the Coach and Horses but it aint never gone nowhere'" (6); disproving the possibility of motion, the ancient Greek Eleatic philosopher Zeno claimed that the trajectory of an arrow in flight contained innumerable points of rest in space and as a consequence confirmed the law of stasis, and at the start of narrative, obsessed with this "'daft name to call a pub," Ray Johnson allegorizes the pilgrimage to come.[21] Thus, as will be returned to below, the very last Margate chapter expresses the same contradictory principle on a higher metaphysical plane, as this "*Dreamland*," this resort of the retired and fairground of the young, the conjunction of birth and death, stages the performance of the last orders. *The delay* between these two points, though, constitutes mobility itself, elaborated upon by the four tavellers in a variety of concrete and metaphoric ways, woven into, what I want to call, analytic discourse, – a discourse pregnant with the hermeneutic pleasure which is the mode of being of character in literature.

A significant scene, set in Ray's memory in a World War II Cairo bordello, captures in a nomination many strands of the Bermondsey perspective which dominates the narrative. Introduced to the facts of life by the father surrogate, Jack Dodds, "Lucky" Johnson loses his virginity during a quick encounter with a prostitute, who speaks broken English, for instance, asking her client, after taking off her clothes, "'[do] you lick me?'" (91) and then "after I shot my jollop, quick as spit" (92), causing laughter and merriment in the common room, responding to Dodds' question, "'well how was it Ray?,'" with, 'very good, very good. Little man, big cuck'" (92):

> '*Cuck*?' Jack's laughing and the girls are giggling and the sappers in the yard are looking up and laughing too, and we're in Cairo, in Egypt, in Africa, in the middle of the war.
>
> 'Well, Raysy, that sounds like just about everything rolled into one.'
>
> Including luck. (92)

The recollection here of the summary nature of the *cuck*, how it encompasses all things – the multi-cultural Egyptian setting, the co-presence of eros and thanatos, "fuck" and "cluck" (the little hooker's word for "clock"), male and female, destiny and luck, determined meaning and its playful collapse – telescopes the analytic discourse of the Cockney, which is both anchored in and subversive of "the Name-of-the-Father." Even though phallic signification, as Lacan notes in "The signification of the phallus" (1958), operates, as it did in the ancient mysteries, similar to a veil or a "simulcrum" (*Écrits* 285), covering absence, it conditions the hermeneutic pleasure involved in anamorphosis, word-play and semantic ambivalence. Cockney discourse assumes tragedy in comic distortions.

21 Lacan often resorts to Zeno's paradox to make the claim about infinity within limits; see e.g. Seminar XX, *Encore* (1962–3), ed. Jacques-Alain Miller (Paris: Seuil, 1975).

In order to suggest tragi-comic mobility, *Last Orders* harnesses the connotations of the journey motif, especially in the proliferation of vehicles the four friends are associated with. Besides the stationary "Coach and Horses" in Bermondsey and the "royal blue Merc" that carries the travellers (as well as the jar, a vehicle of sorts) to Margate, a variety of mobile forms takes centre stage: at the start of the journey a jocular dialogue occurs between Vic and Vince, concerning the pro and cons of a hearse vis-à-vis a Mercedes; Vince's thoughts often reveal anxiety about his used car-dealer's business, and his childhood and adult recollections involve the (adopted) father's meat van and Ray's camper respectively; the latter's "dormobile," bought to placate the discontented wife, Carol Dixon, but failing that, is turned into a "travelling home" for one, and then a love-nest, the locus of *rendez-vous* with Amy Dodds; of course, Ray is not only connected to women and campers, but primarily to another form of mobility, namely the horse races, his felicity in betting equal to the nickname, "Lucky"; the thought sections of Amy, Mandy and Vic also include vehicles, a panegyric to bus travel, (228–230), a hitchiker's ride in a butcher's van from Blackburn to London (153–164), a Navy man's reflections that "you joined the Navy to see the sea but what you saw were the giddy innards of a ship" (123).

In addition to functioning as social signals, as integral to the working-class male characters' habitat, the engines, both natural and mechanical, suggest a condition of *vehicleness*, – "motorvation," as Vince calls it (71) – linking these travellers with other historical voyager, with "everyman" of the eponymous medieval play, making his way along the road of life, with the "wanderer" and the "seafarer" of their repsective Old-English poems, striving for pure literary desiriousness, Chaucer's Canterbury pilgrims riding their often well-introduced steeds along the Old Kent Road and Thomas Pynchon's Oedipa, from *The Crying of Lot 49*, motivated by her dead lover's enigmatic wish to quest in her Impala across the California landscape. In Swift's novel, the most significant feature of this "motorvated" libido is its enhancement of the pleasure principle: not only Amy celebrates bus routes as "the arteries, bleedin arteries, and veins" of London (230), but a whole section is devoted to Vince's praise of cars, a poetic incantation of the motor as man's prosthetic, an empowering extension of the human:

> There's nothing finer, if you ask me, there's nothing that shows better that you're alive and humming and living in this present day and age than when you squeeze the juice and burn up road and there are the signs and the lights and the white lines all so it can happen and everything's moving, going. (71)

The *jouissance* of the language here matches Ray's later rapturous evocation of the races, after he bets Jack's one thousand pounds on *Miracle Worker*, the "rank outsider, twenty-to-one the field" (232). Not only are images conjured of the scents, the speed, "the rush and roar of the race," but of Eros itself, the principle of life:

> I stood at the window. Back end of Bermondsey. And the track at Donnie a wide, flat gallop. You'd have to be a fool. I felt the flutter in my ribs and the luck in my veins. What you do it for in the first place, why you're in it in the first place. I opened the window like I was short of breath. I felt the air and the smoke in my nostrils and the life in my limbs and Jack's money burning a hole against my rear.
> *Miracle Worker.* (233)

Throughout the narrative, from the inert start in the Bermondsey "Coach," the poetic discourse of mobility directs readers toward the rites of death in the last Margate section, which, on account of the accumlated tragi-comic discourse, exemplifies character as post-tranferential sublimation. In order to explain how character functions thus as both subversive and representative, it will be helpful to examine the progression of Swift's novel from the vantage point of psychoanalytic *extimacy*, a Lacanian portmanteu word, combining *ex* (exterior) with *intimacy* (interior; an internalized condition).[22] The main emphasis will fall on how analytic discourse problematizes and blurs the boundaries between inside and outside, between the unconscious subject and the Other. The way in which nation and character interact here is particularly instructive.

In a manner comparable to one of Lacan's topological structures illustrating *extimité*, progressively, in *Last Orders*, analytic discourse overtakes and subsumes the discourse of the master. Related to mathematical figurations within topology such as *the moebius strip*, *the torus* and *the cross-cap*, developed by Lacan in psychoanalytic terms primarily during the last phase of his work in the 1970s, in *The Four Fundamental Concepts of Psycho-Analysis*, an image culled from Maurice Merleau-Ponty's posthumously published *Le Visible et l'invisible* (1964), suggests the interlacings of perceptual fields, how the visible and invisible, the conscious and the unconscious, inside and outside entangle and overlap: drawing attention to Merleau-Ponty's unfinished manuscript notes, Lacan singles out a reference to "the turning inside-out of the finger of a glove," with an aside to the seminar audience: "note the way in which the leather envelops the fur in a winter glove" (82). This "inside-out" structure seems particularly relevant for the narrative progression in *Last Orders*, not least because of its phallic connotations as well because of the hollow interior, the emptiness, which sustains the upright shape.[23] On the road to Margate, the discourse of the "cuck" is folded into master signifiers of

22 The French word is *extimité* coupled with *intimité* (Evans 1996: 58). Note Lacan's statement in *The Ethics of Psychoanalysis*; the Other "is strange to me, although it is at the heart of me" (71).

23 The major introduction to Lacan's use of topology is Jeanne Granon-Lafont's *La topologie ordinaire de Jacques Lacan* (Paris: Point Hors Ligne, 1985).

the nation, especially historical monuments the travellers come into contact with, assimilate and distort through scatological seeing.

The subversive significance of the detours Ray, Vince, Vic and Lenny spontaneously take to the naval memorial in Chatham, Wick's Farm in Kent and Canterbury Cathedral ensues not least from their several recollections about the nature of the master's discourse they are subserviant to. In particular in Seminar XVII, *L'envers de la psychanalyse* (1969–70), Lacan elaborates upon and formalizes the features of the "Four Discourses," – the Discourse of the University, the Discourse of the Master, the Discourse of the Hysteric and the Discourse of the Analyst – social exchanges, which are mappable according to *real* and regulating structures, in fact, in algebraic formulations depicting the communicative dynamics at work.[24] Among the discourses, that of the Master has a privileged position and functions as the primary field of signification, the foothold of subjectivation, "the fundmental matrix of the coming to be of the subject through alienation" (Fink 1995: 130). In the four alogorithms, as many positions are in operations, divided among the master signifiers (S1), the systems of signifiers and of knowledge (S2), surplus value, in the form of fantasy and *jouissance* (a), and the divided subject ($), split between mirror-stage identifications and "the jouissance that it sacrifices in assuming that [symbolic] identity" (Bracher 1993, 53).[25] The Master's discourse is characterized by the dominance of S1, an unquestioned *doxa*, which elides ontological speculations, generating meaning and interpellating subjects according to totalitarian principle, not sensible logic. Because mastery subdues, the knowledge the paradigm produces merely enhances the status quo, constitutes an end in itself, perpetuating signifiers with strangleholds on the "slaves," which underpin its functioning. Thus, in the alogorithm of the Master, the subject of the unconscious, and its potential articulation of a new epistemology, occupies a subordinate, "invisible" position:

$$\frac{S1}{\$} \rightarrow \frac{S2}{a}$$

In dupliticious twists, both anchored in and splintering this totalizing paradigm, literary character signifies the *extimacy* of discourses, the analytic undermining of the unreflective *doxa*, which steers subjects toward new knowledge of them-

24 Jacques Lacan. Seminar XVII, *The Other Side of Psychoanalysis* (1969–70). Trans. Russell Grigg (New York: Norton, 2007).

25 My very summary outline of the discourses relies on both Fink's *The Lacanian Subject* (1995), esp. 129–137, and Mark Bracher's *Lacan, Discourse and Social Change: A Psychoanalytic Cultural Criticism* (Ithace: Cornell University Press, 1993), esp. 53–80.

selves as split beings. In *Last Orders*, national history in the form of, what appear at first as, monolithic, even blatantly phallic, structures, dominating the landscape the travellers cross, the "white and tall" obelisk at Chatham and the cathedral towers hovering over Rochester ("like some big old bird sitting on a nest" 122) and Canterbury, operates as signifier of mastery no less than the figures of authority Vince Dodds, most conspicuously, comes into close contact with, first in the principal's office as a tormented school boy and in adulthood at Jack's deathbed in St Thomas Hospital, enduring the condescending pomposity of the surgeon, "that geezer Strickland" (185). The clash with the headmaster, Mr Snow, taking place shortly after the young boy has been informed aobut his orphaned state, is particularly instructive, telescoping for Vince what defines mastery and subjection, the humiliation of the meeting reverberating "when I went in to see the surgeon," remonstrating how "life's a process of going before geezers who want to see you crawl" (96). Also, at the heart of the scene, is the defacing of subjective desire, the motor force of the Master's discourse: in suffering, thinking about "accidents of birth," his own orphanhood, as well as the disaster of the mentally retarded June, whom the Dodds "never meant to have," Vince is obligated to respond to the headmaster's daft question, "What do you want to be, Vince? What are you going to be?" (96–9). As Vince reflects, impotent to encompass difference within its significations of self-identity, the headmaster's "to be" represses the young man's ontological doubt ("but the point is I aint even sure what I am in the first place" 96), his singularity as a fantasizing individual, as well as the "hysterical" reaction against totality:

> But maybe June doesn't think at all, she aint got a thought in her head, and supposing what you want to be is not like anything. Supposing what you want to be is a driveshaft. (96)

Similarly, surgeon Strickland's mechanical, technical language, his "giving the facts straight" and punctuating his speech with words such as "inoperable" and "symptom control" (187), not only excludes compassionate understanding, but betrays the incapacity to imagine the other side of discursive domination. As an extension of these repressive representatives of the educational and medical establishments, the historical discourse of the nation, tokened, as I pointed out above, in monumental remembrances of the dead, in structures linked to war and to religion, appear at first as rigid master signifiers, phallic simulacra, which veil the truth of subjective division. However, during the journey to Margate, as is the case with "the anecdote of the jar," these monuments to the past are appropriated by the scatological viewpoint of the travellers, are transformed into "extimatic" structures, which both retain and undermine the logic of totality.

In contrast to authority figures who suppress multivalence, the four pilgrims, especially in confrontation with national memorials, excavate what it means to *be*, the fragility of Being. In an interview with Catherine Bernard in *Contemporary Literature* (1997), Graham Swift contends that in his fiction, he seeks a kind of impersonal authority, a stance comparable to Virgina Woolf's quest for a dualistic voice, articulating both formal expertise and vulnerable openness to an audience (229–30).[26] During *Last Order*'s journey, the accumulated thought processes of the characters, a discourse most succinctly depicted as *analytic*, acquire just such two-sided impersonality, rooted in fragile experience as well as directing the audience to a state of transformative valuation. A poignant summation of the characters' function in the novel, made by Ray Johnson as they enter Canterbury Cathedral, looking like "a strange bunch," after working out their tensions on the road, both mentally and physically, is "it's like we aren't the same people who left Bermondsey this morning, four blokes on a special delivery. It's like somewhere along the line we just became travellers" (194). It is this transformative process that is traceable in the character construct: within a realistic habitat Being itself is contemplated; personal purpose evolves into existential teaching.

As analytic authorities, the four pilgrims link their private recollections to loss in the national consciousness, presented, in particular, in the naval memorial at Chatham and in Canterbury Cathedral. It is noteworthy that the characters observe these structures with fresh, virginal eyes, as they visit them for the very first time, and that, instead of being guided by tourist signs and instructions, they spend considerable effort looking for the landmarks. Following Vic Tucker's, the navy man's, lead, the group loses its way in Chatham, unable to spot the "white tower" (119), struggling up a wooded hill along a muddy path, "leading up through it to where the memorial ought to be, except you can't see it because of the trees, no signs, no nothing" (120). The fact that the memorial is hidden is repeated a couple of times ("we can't see no memorial" 121) as if to underscore that Ray's first sighting of it is a discovery, an original interpretation:

> Then we come out of the trees and we can see the memorial all of a sudden, like it's been waiting for us all along, expecting us, sticking up tall and white against the sky, though the base of it's hidden behind the brow. There's a word for it. [...] The sun's shining from under a bank of cloud across the pale grass and it's as if, though we're still climbing, we've entered an easier, kinder, cleaner zone. It's as though the tower of the memorial is pulling us toward it. (121–22)

The word Ray searches,

> it's an obelisk, that's the word, obelisk. The sun's shining on it. It's white and tall. It looks like it's floating, because you can't see what it's attached to, like when you get near it, it might shift off somewhere else. There's still no signs to tell you, just the rough grass, ruffled by the wind. (122)

26 Catherine Bernhard and Graham Swift. "An Interview with Graham Swift." *Contemporary Literature* 38 (1997), 217–231.

The absence of public signals is amply compensated for by Lucky's poetic evocation, which assimilates this symbolic structure into cockney speech, blurring the edge between the master signifier "obelisk" and the polyvocal "cuck." Further, as the travellers make their way up the hill, an emphasis is placed on the paradox of the apt unsuitability of this "sight-seeing" tour: having drunk one too many brews in the "Bull Hotel" in Rochester, at the start of the climb, Ray and Lenny "need again to piss badly," and the subsequent account focuses on the latter's comic travails, coughing and spitting, "his chest going like a pair of bellows," prompting his friend to worry that "Lenny [might] peg out before we've said our last goodbye to Jack" (121). Ray himself admits that "I don't feel so A-1 myself" (121).

Nevertheless, "pulling [the four mourners] up towards it" (122), the obelisk assumes the function of Merleu-Ponty's glove finger, shaping the character's meditations on Being, not only specific remembrance of the dead, but ontological explorations as well. Thus, the spotting and description of the Chatham memorial is followed by Vic's, the undertaker's, free-associative reflections on his grandfather's death at Bexhill-on-Sea ("that's where people go when" 124), his service as "disposing of the dead" in the navy, fishing corpses out of the North Sea, only to sink them, folded in canvas, into the water again, his own professional knowledge, culminating in impersonal directive; the personal experience of the sea as burial ground is extended into existential metaphor: "even on land we're all at sea, even on this hill high above Chatham where I can read the names. All in our berths going to our deaths. Floating coffins" (125). Next in line to Vic, Ray's section can be likened to the exchange between responsory and soloist in church ceremony, the list of names on the stone wall around the obelisk sounding the anthem to the solitary's thoughts on contingency, fate and the difference between survival and life. Like Vic's meditative logic, Ray slips from intimate knowledge of insurance houses, where he works as a clerk, the horse races and gambling and World War II service in the army to a position of existential neutrality: "man is just a name. Which means something to him it attaches to, [...] but it don't mean a monkey's beyond that. [...] it all goes on when you're gone and you don't make a blip" (128). Also, in the vicinity of the obelisk, the least reflective of the friends, Lenny turns into an interpreter: amid images of the Bermondsey neighbourhood – "Dodds and Tucker, steaks and stiffs" (131) – irreverently mixed with observations of "that tower thing" (131), the former boxer glimpses his own mortality, wondering whether the daughter and the wife will pay their respects at his funeral. Despite the often grotesque humour, Lenny's section, no less then those of his friends, teaches an ethical attitude:

> it's a question of duty. There's a soldier's duty, a sailor's duty. Heligioland. Jutland. But if you ask me, that aint duty as much as orders. Doing your duty in the ordinary course of life is another thing, it's harder. (132)

Although Vince's voice is less prominent than usually in the Chatham episode, his affectionate comment on Ray, Lenny and Vic captures their essence as incongruous interpreters: "Old buggers" (130). These fragile indiviuals are worthy to be listened to as impersonal conduits for the vicissitudes of existence.

Like the Chatham memorial, Canterbury Cathedral functions as an extimatic structure, interlacing in tragi-comic distortions the private life of the four pilgrims with the national past. Interestingly, the approach to the building resembles the ascent to the obelisk, the cathedral tower not immediately visible, but "like it's playing tricks with us" (193), glimpsed here and there, then ducking out of sight. Also, a revelatory moment follows the circuitous approach, Ray given the privilege of assimilating the sight:

> suddenly there is nothing in front of us except the cathedral itself, and a few bits of chained-off lawn and cobbles and people walking. It's a big building, long and tall, but it's like it hasn't stretched up yet to its full height, it's still growing. [...] it makes you feel sort of cheap and titchty. Like it's looking down at you, saying, I'm Canterbury Cathedral, who the hell are you? (194)

Once inside, in its proper spiritual environment, the exchange between historical repsonsory and soloist text, begun in the Chatham episode, continues, images of fourteen centuries, of "pillars and arches" (200), "stone and space and oldness" (207) and tombs of royalty ("all these geezers made of stone, lying face up, flat out, out for the count" 203) interpsersed with Ray's, Lenny's, Vic's and Vince's specialized eschatology. In fact, Ray's interpretation of the naval memorial situation captures that of Canterbury: "It's like it was only half meant to be here and so were we, but here we are, together, on the top of this hill" (122). The essence of these encounters between the fragile individual and the national past is their very unsuitable suitability.

In the Canterbury episode, the strangeness of the "old buggers" as interpreters is highlighted by singling out Lenny Gunner as the initiator of the visit to the Cathedral and by developing his thought sections here to a greater extent than those of the others. In the early pages of the novel, Ray called Lenny a "stirrer" (55), referring to his provocative manner, especially the way his resentment toward Vince stays close to the surface, exploding in the scuffle at Wick's Farm. These shock-tactics of Lenny, this habit, to use Slavoj Zizek's phrase from his eponymous book, of "looking awry" at entrenched phenomena, are foregrounded in the Cathedral as he both thinks of private "sins," his responsibility for Sally's abortion, and jokes blasphemously about the aristocratic dead, "this Black Prince feller [who] don't look like he ever smiled" (208), about the thin line between "live meat" and "dead meat," as in the case of June Dodds and about his own sexual fantasies about Amy Dodds:

> You shouldn't ever have wicked thoughts in church, but you do, you want to have 'em, like it's an encouragement. You shouldn't think such things when you're an old man of sixty-nine with no breath in your lungs and nothing but a penny whistle between your legs, but I do, I am, like I'm free to, seeing as Jack's in the bag. (209)

As Zizek's points out about previous philosophers' mode of "looking awry," of, for instance, staging in a concrete, subjective way, certain fixed theoretical motifs, "otherwise hidden inconsistances" are revealed and "aspects that would otherwise remain unnoticed" are rendered visible (1991: 4). Hegel's *Phenomenology of Spirit* serves as one of Zizek's examples, where the *mise-en-scène* of "an existential subjective attitude (that of asceticism, that of the "beautiful soul,"etc.)" undermines the "positive contents" of philosophical master signifiers (4). In his scatological interpretations of prohibitive monuments, Lenny Gunner similarly inscribes his energetic fragility into the commonplaces of history. It can be no coincidence that Lenny closes his sections with recollections of Cock Lane, Smithfield. Thinking back on Vince's fourtieth birthday in the Bermondsey pub, echoes of Jack Dodd's speculations about this "giggle-naming" of a thoroughfare resound in the old geezer's mind:

> 'Cock Lane, Smithfield, famous for it once. You wonder how they think up the names. Cock Lane off Giltspur Street. We've all been there, aint we, Raysy? Cock lane, cock alley, cock passage, we've all driven the coach up there.' (210)

Like Raysy's assimilation of the "obelisk" into his poetic evocation, Lenny here, through Jack, sums up the collective goal of *Last Orders* to sublimate in the discourse of the "cuck" the paradox of mobility in closure. As we will see more clearly in the Margate section, character focalizes such discourse as a signifer of hermeneutic pleasure.

In his fiction, always attuned to the symbolism of place, it comes as no surprise that Swift chooses plebeian Margate over aristocratic Canterbury as the pilgrim's final destination. Surveying the geographical features of the "land's end," sometimes referred to as "the limb" of Dover, Ray divides his attention between "the elements" – the North Sea, the strong wind, the grey sky threatening rain – and the resort structures on the waterfront, the "poor men's palaces" (273), most of them closed in April, before the start of the holiday season, looking ruinous and tacky, "like a troop of tired old tarts" (273).[27] In fact, Ray's evocation of this favorite vacation spot for working/lower-middle class Londoners resembles the notorious practise, especially during the forties and fifties, of devising lists of "Englishness," exemplified by the poet's, John Betjeman's, enumerations in a wartime broadcast

27 In the fifteenth century, Dover was added to a historic series of coast towns, comprising Hastings, New Romney, Hythe, Sandwich. The association was called the *Cinque Ports*. See www.wikipedia.

(1943): the staples of English character include "'oil-lit churces, Women's Institutes, modest village inns, [...] the poetry of Tennyson and branch-line trains.'"[28] As Dominic Head points out, in *The Cambridge Introduction to Modern British Fiction, 1950–2000*, because of the arrogant self-assurance and untheorized premises, such lists are often mockingly improvized and parodied, as, for instance, in Jeremy Paxman's addenda of "'punk, street fashion'" and "'drinking to excess'" (22–3; quoted in Head, 123) as well as in Julian Barnes' satirical "false metonymy," in *England, England* (1998) of "'Fifty Ouintessences of Englishness' ranging from 'ROYAL FAMILY' to WHINGEING' and 'FLAGELLATION'" (83–5; quoted in Head, 124).[29] Besides singling out the drabness of the Margate establishments, Ray appears to call into being their resilient Englishness by parading their exotic names: "*Flamingo. Tivoli. Royal. Grab City.* [...] *Mirage, Gold Mine, Ocean.* [...] *Dreamland*" (269; 273). However, as becomes clear when the four mourners approach the end of their mission, if Margate provides the apt habitat for the English Cockney, what is revealed is the contingent, transient nature of human habitation, the accidental bond between the native land and the communites which cultivate it. Thus, in the final sections of *Last Orders*, the strength of the discourse of the "cuck" lies to a great extent in its weakness, in its awareness of its own fragility as it evokes in lyrical speech the severance between ordinary life and *being* in the world. In the Margate sections, the development of the novel's *extimatic* structures culminates in the *jouissance* of the Other, conveyed by character as a collective impersonality.

During the staging of the last scenes, the drive from Canterbury, the approach to the vista of the seaside, the "sight-seeing" tour around the resort town, the slow, deliberate hearse-like movements of the Mercedes, the ceremonial procession along the Pier, the scattering of the dead man's ashes to "the sky and the sea and the wind" (294), a gradual, climactic dissolution of borders takes place as subjectivities merge, unconscious rhythms erupt into consciousness, the natural elements, water, earth, air and human substance, intermix and speech turns into attentive listening. In contrast to the Master's discourse, which promotes the unreflective *doxa* and blocks the conduits of new epistemologies, the discourse of the (Lacanian) Analyst privileges the subject of the unconscious, enabling the production of revisionary signifiers. In the analytic algorithm, agency is assigned to *a*, to fantasy and excess *jouissance*, displacing the self-identical conflations of authoritative paradigms with knowledge in the form of the split subject. Here, the

28 The example is taken from Dominic Head. *The Cambridge Introduction to Modern British Fiction, 1950–2000* (Cambridge: Cambridge University Press, 2002), 123. The broadcast was on BBC Home Service, 25. February 1943.

29 Jeremy Paxman. *The English: A Portrait of a People* (London: Michel Joseph, 1998). Julian Barnes. *England, England* (London: Jonathan Cape, 1998).

communicative structure indicates the successful outcome of a psychoanalytic session, that the analysand is guided toward a confrontation with absolute lack and that within the process of assuming it he is accommodated with the otherness of pleasure:

$$\frac{a}{S2} \rightarrow \frac{\$}{S1}$$

In Mark Bracher's words, in this situation, epistemological guidance moves toward "mak[ing] subjects more capable of accepting and nurturing otherness not only in themselves but also in other subjects" (100). Ideally, the psychological reconstitution, post-transferential reconfiguration of identity, culminates in the transformation of analysand into analyst. In aesthetic terms a consolatory trope ensues, a trope that obstructs the narcissistic desire for identification, triggering instead the potential for the nurturing of *the-want-to-be*, for the *jouissance* of the Other. As my investigations throughout this book aim to show, literary character figures such an analytic entity, registrering the passage from narcissistic libido to the pure desirousness of the analyst. It is, however, important to note that in accommodating lack, character does not generate a discourse of comfort, a mode of stoic acceptance of existential vicissitudes; rather, its consolations imply an ethical directive: Lacan's dictum that "the only thing of which one can be guilty is of having given ground relative to one's desire" (*The Ethics of Psychoanalysis* 319) construes the responsible subject, the one whose self-knowledge is tragic, transvaluative and actively revisionary.

The self-exploratory journey of *Last Orders*, with the incessant weaving of a tragi-comic discourse, transforming monolithic master signifiers into Cockney fluency, concludes in the Margate rites of death, which telescope hermeneutic pleasure in the face of inevitable finitiude. What dominates in these last scenes is harmonic accommodation, where dwelling is staked out in language despite the paradoxes of Being the four travellers reflected on in Chatham and Canterbury. The directive for the audience here is quite different from, for instance, the consolation offered in Keats' "To Autumn," where images of transcience and mortality are beautified to the extent of gratifying narcissistic longing for immaculate cosmic unity. In his expert analysis of Keats' ode, Mark Bracher reveals its hidden ideological force which subtly nourishes readers' fundamental fantasies of "full being," sustaining those by "a jouissance or a sense of being that is greater than life," enabling one to "contemplate death with equanimity and accept it calmly" (178). As is made clear throughout *Last Orders* via the characters' dismantling interpretations of the Master's discourse, such imaginary plenitude is not the novel's goal; the dissolution of borders during the Margate rites of death, rather than performing cosmic wholeness, suggest a situation of ethical flourishing, an attentiveness to the singularity of the other's desire.

Especially, what marks analytic agency in these last scenes is a kind of synaesthetic *listening*, a sphere of silent perception, in the manner of the "cuck," encompassing all, but now attuned to Being, not to scatological detail. Although the Margate sections are narrated in Ray's voice, they *show* rather than *tell*, conveying the collective drama of the mourners, not autobiographical reflection. What at first overwhelms the teller are the sights, sounds and smells of the ocean, the waves "jostling and squirming like animals at feeding time" (286), the "niff of the seaside: tarry and bilgy and mucky, same as it's zingy and clean" (297). As the travellers assemble, ready to proceed along the Pier to the very edge to scatter Jack's ashes, they move as if directed from outside, in speechless harmony, prompting Ray to wonder about "a part of me's taking charge of me, telling me what to do, telling me how to act" (290). Nature itself seems an accomplice and instigator of the ritual, the strong wind and the rain, "push[ing] us to it, like the elements aren't so much against us as behind us" (288). As the ceremony itself begins, the four men scoop the ashes out of the jar in musical rhythms, as if at one with each other and the natural elements, "the sky and the sea and the wind" (294), attuned to both the biomusic and the silences of their own bodies. Although the poetic evocation of this harmonious community beautifies the act of the last orders, it does not interpellate an audience into stoic acceptance; instead of gratifying images, Ray attends to the paradox of Being by, in the novel's very last paragraph, interlacing the other scene, Vic's "that's where people go when" (124), with the "poor men's palaces" (273), the edge of Margate's Pier with Dreamland. In fact, Ray draws special attention to how even the ocean contains the remains of human history, as the old Jetty, destroyed in a storm in 1978, is spotted in the water, "a rusty mass of old iron-work" (292). Again, in these last sections, another extimatic structure takes precedence: Being itself is Merleu-Ponty's glove finger; radical otherness is inscribed within it, sustaining it as present absence.

That a kind of deep musicality dominates the characters towards the end of *Last Orders* is supported by Graham Swift's own comments on levels of voices in his fiction, and on how crisis may activate a truthful expression. Asked by Catherine Bernhard, in the interview cited above, whether his novels can be understood as "akin to a sort of musical score," Swift asserts that "pace and rhythm" underly his compositions and that his storytellers often rupture their own superficial voice in order to access the buried truth within (220). Because during their interior journey, Ray, Vince, Lenny and Vic have assumed their own interpretative voices, have heard "the call embedded in their own style," as literary characters they function as ethical directives, potentially triggering in the audience a desire to do good. It is therefore fitting that one of the central conflicts in the novel, Ray's inner debate about whether to pay back to Vince the thousand pounds the latter had in filial love lent his dying father, having to borrow the money to do so, and Jack in turn handed over to the lucky gambler, is spontaneously solved within the Margate ritual: in a scene on Margate Pier, the four men moving in elegaic procession, Ray, as if listening to the psychoanalytic prerogative that one is only guilty of "having given ground to one's desire," whispers the truth into Vince's ear. It is also noteworthy that instead of dwelling on his own motivation, Ray attends only to "the look in Vince's face":

> like simple plain relief, like light's suddenly splashed across it. It's like he can wait for the full story but right now he's shot of some little nagging side-problem and he can give the matter at hand full attention. (290)

This joy in the situation of the other's desire as well as the loving care the four friends, in a kind of impersonal ecstacy, bestow on the remains of their friend stake the ground for genuine ethical flourishing, a persistant trait of that dweller in literary language we call character.

Chapter 9: Myths of Creation in *Sir Gawain and the Green Knight*

Didactic Desire

In *Last Orders*, through scatological play, the character construct, equivocally anchored in master signifers, makes visible certain pathologies of the Law, especially the guilt-inducing filial bonds it fosters and the elision of the desiring subject from the historical discourses it generates. From a psychoanalytic point of view, the novel highlights the development of the analyst's hermeneutics, which transforms the rule-bound signifier into ethical directive. Through the node of literary character, consequent upon self-exploration, fragility interlaces with authority to impel audiences not to give ground to their desire. Thus, the *impersonality* Swift's novel quests for is that of the post-transferential collective, which accommodates itself to the otherness of pleasure, not that of deontological morality, which legislates behavior according to economies of sacrifice, hegemonic systems of rewards and punishments.

The following discussion of the fourteenth-century medieval romance, *Sir Gawain and the Green Knight*, will claim that, as in *Last Orders*, character mobilizes a transvaluative ethical discourse, registrering *jouissance*, which goes beyond and undermines narcissistic identifications. In contrast to the contemporary novel, however, the pathologies of the Law in the medieval narrative are not concretized in paternal demands, but elusively operate the very ideological fabric which composes it. L.O Aranye Fradenburg's *Sacrifice Your Love* (2002) focuses attention to how, within the history of the signifier, the Law reveals itself in a dual capacitiy, as both impersonal and personal, as an opaque body of rules, an insentinent signifier, on the one hand, and the living, often capricious, authority figure, the "father of enjoyment," on the other (24–28).[1] Further, Fradenburg characterizes this interdependence between formal, non-substantial codes and actual governing bodies – the church, the royal court, military groups, secret societies – as a feature of moral obligation: the opacity of directives which both exist beyond and impinge upon the human libido (the unconsicous is, after all, "structured like a language," *Four Fundamental Concepts of Psycho-Analysis* 24) imbues cause with an ora-

1 L. O. Aranye Fradenburg. *Sacrifice Your Love: Psychoanalysis, Historicism, Chaucer* (Minneapolis: University of Minnesota Press, 2002). "Father of enjoyment" is Slavoj Zizek's phrase from *Enjoy Your Symptom!: Jacques Lacan in Hollywood and Out* (London: Routledge, 1992), 149.

cle-like fixity, leading to unquestioned submission and obedience. What is more, as Fradenburg discusses with penetrating acumen, subjective life strategies, often in the form of *ascesis*, of physical and mental discipline, abnegation of pleasures and preparedness for self-sacrifice, intertwine with regulating moral codes, highlighting a libidinal reciprocity, how, in fact, the Law "is inseparable from desire because it designs the drives," a propellor of heightened sensibilities (28). Basing her reconfiguring of morality upon Elaine Scarry's analysis of the conception of *sentience* in *The Body in Pain* (1985),[2] Fradenburg assesses the effects of signification upon the human organism as the painful sense of insentience within aliveness. Because a confrontation with the absolute lack in the Other would be too traumatic to assume, subjects devise "techniques of living" in order to enhance the principle of vitality within spectra of *jouissance* (esp. 12–24). In other words, it is possible to understand such compromises with the signifier as inharmonious sublimations where more or less intense "modes of enjoyment" overtake the tragic working-through full knowledge of finitude entails.[3]

These observations are relevant for literary character in general whose discursive directive carries the enabling of mourning for the otherness of desire, leading to potential psychic transformation and transvalued ethical connections. Also, Fradenburg's problematization of the opposition between morality and pleasure, her claim, indeed, that the Law, "sometimes jubilantly," perpetuates desire, that "desire is in part *for* the law" (6; Fradenburg's emphasis) provides an entrance point into the world of *Sir Gawain and the Green Knight* where the chivalric world-view, with its attendant moral strictures, religious idealism and matters of courtesy, generates operable modes of enjoyment, filtered at first through Sir Gawain, the representative knight, but within progressive, albeit subtle, underminings of libidinal bonds, realigned within the character construct as sublimation proper – vitalism engendered from tragic awareness. Before an integral ethos is achieved, though, the narrative contends with several ontological models, proposing, what I want to call, contrasting *myths of creation*, which in broad outline can be seen as imaginary construction versus *savoir*, new knowledge about the enjoyment of the symptom.[4] During Sir Gawain's adventure, the imaginary whole-

2 Elaine Scarry. *The Body in Pain: The Making and Unmaking of the World* (New York: Oxford University Press), 195.

3 Again, Slavoj Zizek provides a useful phrase (in *The Sublime Object of Idelogy* (New York: Verso, 1989), 114–16): as Fradenburg points out, "'modes of enjoyment' […] designate any organized relationship to *jouissance*, including pleasure and methods of avoidance" (n2, 253).

4 The enjoyment of the symptom is Zizek's formulation, partly based on Lacan's neologism *sinthome*, coined to account for James Joyce's *jouissance* in language. Later in the chapter, I will discuss the *sinthome* in greater detail. See Slavoj Zizek. *Enjoy Your Symptom!: Jacques Lacan in Hollywood and Out* (London: Routledge, 1992).

ness of the pentangle knight breaks down into hybrids, into nonhuman as well as intersubjective structures, concentrated on the highest level of the romance as a call for the *jouissance* of the Other. In order to show how character functions in this narrative patterning, the chapter will begin with a consideration of didactic desire within the narcissistic realm of the Arthurian court.

Although numerous critics have remarked, either appreciatively or sceptically, on the lengthy depiction of the pentangle, component of Sir Gawain's arming ritual at the start of the romance's second fitt (619–669),[5] as an emblem of essentialist identity, no specific links have been made between that paradigm and the initial contours of the Arthurian court, the narcisisstic revels preceding the Green Knight's challenge.[6] In fact, the integral unity of the five-pointed star, "depaynt of pure golde hwez" ("painted in colours of pure gold" 620) on the protagonist's shield, the interlacing of its properties into a seamless – "endelez" (629) – thread, its nomination ("bi tytle þat hit habbez" 627) as a "token of truth" ("in bytoknyng of trawþe" 627) and its fusion with the "fautlez" ("without flaw" 640) carrier, the Christian knight, project, what Julia Kristeva, calls, "a unifying circularity" (110), conflating form and content, law and action, in the Plotinian One. In *Tales of Love* (1987), in her considerations of the geneology of Narcissus within Western thought, especially of Plotinus' version in the *Enneads*, Kristeva outlines psychic space which, even if it verges on insanity, on "infantilism and perversion" (115), mystifies its inner workings, transforming autoerotism into the splendors of self-re-

5 Malcolm Andrew and Ronald Waldron, eds. *The Poems of the Pearl Manuscript: Pearl, Cleanness, Patience, Sir Gawain and the Green Knight* (Berkeley: University of California Press). All further references to *Sir Gawain and the Green Knight* are based on this edition. Unless otherwise noted, all translations are mine.

6 Earlier critics tended to applaud the "endeles knot" (630) as a model of the ideal knight (see, for instance, J.A. Burrow. *A Reading of Sir Gawain and the Green Knight* (London: Routledge, 1965); A.C. Spearing. *The Gawain Poet: A Critical Study* (Cambridge: Cambridge University Press, 1970); J.R. Tolkien's "Introduction" to his translation of *Sir Gawain and the Green Knight, Pearl and Sir Orfeo* (London: George Allen&Unwen, 1975), 14–17) whereas recent commentators prefer to dismantle, even deconstruct, the idealistic portrayal. For the latter, see, in particular, Geraldine Heng. "Feminine Knots and the Other in *Sir Gawain and the Green Knight*." *PMLA* 3(1991), 500–14. Heng's feminist reading is to an extent built upon A. Kent Heatt's structuralist "*Sir Gawain*: Pentangle, Luf-Lace, Numerical Structure." *Papers on Language and Literature* 4 (1968), 339–59, as well as R.A. Shoaf's semiotically inflected "The 'Sygne of Surfet' and the Surfeit of Signs in *Sir Gawain and the Green Knight*," in Christopher Baswell and William Sharpe, eds. *The Passing of Arthur: Essays in Arthurian Tradition* (New York: Garland, 1988), 152–69. In *Language and Imagination in the Gawain Poems* (Manchester: Manchester University Press, 2005), J.J. Anderson presents an intermediate opinion of the protagonist as failing to meet the Christian standards suggested by the pentangle, but fulfilling its courtly mandate (esp. 178–189).

flection, "sublime hypostasis of narcissistic love" (111). In Kristeva's account, the tragic banality of the Ovidian youth's infatuation with his own mirror reflection, its illusoriness, is overtaken by neo-Platonic idealism, which sublimates narcissistic desire into Oneness, into an inner landscape of the soul in love with itself:

> The One "is simultaneously the *loved one* and *love*; He is *love of himself*; [...]". That *autou eros* that I see as sublime hypostasis of narcissistic love was to constitute the decisive step in the assumption of inner space, the introspective space of the western psyche. God is Narcissus, and if the *narcissistic* illusion is for Myself a sin, my ideal is nonetheless *Narcissan.* (111, Kristeva's italics: the citation is from the *Enneads*)

Here, Kristeva's discussion clarifies how, in *Sir Gawain and the Green Knight*, character as imaged in the pentangle knight can, in the early stages of the romance, be profitably understood as a symptom of a narcissistic group mentality, where primary, infantile libido reciprocates with a Law, which both hides its "sinfulness" and enables it to function within various modes of enjoyment. In the first part of the poem, the smooth operation of the Arthurian court is presented in terms of holiday cheer, festivities and society games, almost as if in a perpetual golden age of youth, innocence and luxorious living. The effort expended on authorizing this realm, on normalizing it, on imbuing its operations with a moral value, can be seen in the first two stanzas, which place Arthur's reign in an epic-historical perspective, as descending from "Ennias þe athel and his highe kynde" ("the noble Aeneas and his renowned kindred" 5), and which elaborate upon the myth of national origin, listing the Roman Brutus' fortunate arrival in Britain among the foundational acts of Romulus in Rome, Ticius in Tuscany and Langaberde in Lombardy (1–19).[7] At the very beginning of the romance, the narrator appears to valorize an introspective, homogenizing lineage for the tale he will tell: its creation is triggered by the national heritage he has respectfully traced, legitimized by courtly traditions and interests. Thus, imaginary identifications with leader, nation and a Grand Narrative underpin poetic creativitiy in the early stages of *Sir Gawain and the Green Knight*; however, as I will continue to trace in this section, the didacticism such a stance fosters dissolves in a progressive interest in an otherness which infiltrates and modulates narrative constructions.

A narcissistic fantasy of wholeness and closure marks the poem's festive Arthurian realm, where modes of enjoyment are expressed in courtly decorum, sumptuous banqueting, a show of etiquette and controlled amourousness, "With rych reuel orygt and rechless merþes" ("conducting their rich revels and carefree merriment

7 As Andrew and Waldron note Langaberde and Brutus are well known in medieval legend as founders of their respective territories, whereas Ticius may be a scribal error for the recognized names of either Tuscus or Tirius (n11).

in a proper fashion" 39). Despite a fifteen-day long Christmas celebration, "with daily rejoicing and dancing at night" ("Dere dyn upon day, daunsyng on nygtes" 47), accompanied by variable games, which range from jousting to "caroles" (ring dances with singing), gift-giving to flirtatious guessing games (65–70), ritualistic courtesy reigns, what might be designated as *stylized* subjectivity, the individuals reduplicating group identity, fashioning themselves in the regulated spectacle.[8] Especially, narcissictic interiority is telescoped in the portrayal of this group "in her first age" ("in their youth" 209), in its primary, imaginary phase, led by King Arthur as permutation of the ideal-ego, the psychic drive toward preoedipal unification:

> Bot Arthur wolde not ete till al were serued;/He watz so joly of his joyfnes, and sumquat childgered./His lif liked hym lygt; he louied þe lasse/Auþer to longe lye or to longe sitte,/So bisied him his gonge blod and his brayn wylde. (84–89)
>
> [But Arthur refused to eat till all had been served;/He was so lively in his youthfulness, and somewhat boyish./He preferred an active life; he did not care to stay late in bed nor to sit still for long;/His young blood boiled and his mind did not rest]

The king's customary New Year's behavior, resembling that of an impatient child, who demands the soothing bedtime story ("an uncouþe tale/Of sum mayn meruayle þat he mygt trawe" 93–4) or a challenging playmate ("sum segg [...]/To joyne wyth hym in justyng" 96–7), clinches the specular exchanges of the group: at Camelot, courtly society operates according to a Law of repetitions, sameness, order, hierarchy and exlusiveness.

To readers of the entire *Pearl Manuscript*, containing, in addition to *Sir Gawain and the Green King*, *Pearl*, *Cleanness* and *Patience*, now almost without exception considered the work of a single author, such fantasies of unity most likely seem a connecting narrative thread.[9] At the risk of simplifying, in the four narratives, it is possible to detect a Plotinian/Christian morality which valorizes passive exclusivity, perhaps most succinctly conveyed through the title of the most overtly homiletic piece, *Cleanness*. As Andrew and Walrdon observe, it is difficult for a modern audience to fathom the intricacies of the middle-English word *clene*, which echoes throughout the stories in the manuscript in a variety of concrete and metaphorical guises, always connoting *cleanliness* and

8 In the introduction to *Sacrifice Your Love*, Fradenburg discusses court spectacle as a mode of enjoyment, where the impossibility of full *jouissance* is mitigated in a fantasy of group identification: "group identification [...] melancholically reworks the split in the subject by passing difference unto the other" (32).

9 Note, in particular, Andrew's and Walton's comments; after listing similarities on almost all levels of narrative – structure, style, character and theme – they state: "the persuasiveness of these similarities as evidence that the hand of one man was responsible for the poems is enhanced by their range and variety, by the complete absence of any counter-evidence of multiple authorship, and by the sheer number of instances" (1978:16).

purity in our senses of these words, but overtaking much broader social and psychological registers. Thus, as Andrew and Waldron show, the semantics of *clene* include the physical realm ("not dirty," "healty," "wholesome"), morality and psychology ("pure," "clear," "righteous," "innocent," "decent," "proper"), communication, behavior, manners and the matter of courtesy ("'"splendid," "elegant," "excellent," "complete," "perfect," "discerning," "skilful") (1978: 21). Moral hyperbole accompanies all of these expressions, insisting on perfection, in the case of Jonah in *Patience*, on absolute obedience, in the case of the speaker in *Pearl,* on submission to ideality and, in the case of Gawain, on chivalric integrity, the inseparable join of the knighlty virtues: "fraunchyse" (liberality), "felagschyp" (brotherly love), "clannes" (cleanness, purity), "cortaysye" (courtesy) and "pité" (compassion) (652–653). As Kristeva discusses in *Tales of Love*, the problem of otherness in Plotinian doctrine becomes dissipated within the motion toward Oneness: unlike gnosticism, which relegated "the Creator's other [...] to the realm of evil," narcissistic inwardness elides the morbid negativity of the autoerotic Narcissus: in Plotinian theory, the "sinfulness" of the death drive is transformed into "the blending-love of the One," which eliminates otherness (119–120).

If contradictions frequently are detected within the *Pearl Manuscript's* ideology of idealism, then in *Sir Gawain and the Green Knight* the inviolable inwardness of the Arthurian court is conspicuously disrupted by a traumatic strangeness, at first, taking over the entire Camelot spectacle, but eventually centering within character as its binding element, Sir Gawain as the carrier of both the representative and the subversive.[10] One of the few critics to seriously consider the *Gawain* poet's perusal of the romance genre, Ad Putter, in *An Introduction to The Gawain Poet* (1996), analyzes the sustained, deliberate combination of "the verisimilar and the marvellous" (47) throughout the poem, claiming, in opposition to earlier, influential views, purporting that the author displays "a contempt for romance," that the fantastic most often merges disturbingly with the literal, effecting a realm of the "in-between," not an antithetical stand-off (60).[11] According to Putter, the "outtrage awenture" ("extraordinary adventure" 29) *Sir Gawain and the Green*

10 Although *Pearl*'s status is that of a didactic dream-vision, it is permeated by subjective desire which "corrupts the formal beauty of logical argument." See Margrét G. Champion. "Reception Theory and Medieval Narrative: Reading *Pearl* as a Novel. *Neophilologus* 76 (1992), 629–637; 635. Also, note Andrew's and Waldron's observation about the paradoxical quality inherent in all four narratives: "through all four works (even, intermittently, in *Cleanness*) there breathes a spirit of sympathetic identification with human frailty besides a zealous dedication to ideal virtue" (29).

11 Ad Putter. *An Introduction to the Gawain Poet* (London: Longman, 1996). "Contempt for romance" is from W.P. Ker. *Medieval English Literature* (London: Oxford University Press, 1912; 1955), 55.

Knight narrates – the Green Man's challenge, the Beheading Game, the travels of the *errant* Knight, the dangerous parlour game at the second court, Bertilak's Hautdesert, the final countdown at the Green Chapel – deviates in signficant ways from the stock adventure of Arthurian romance, where such motifs are taken at face value, implying no problematization of the boundaries between fiction and fact. For instance, in contrast to *Sir Gawain*'s ambiguous version of the Green Knight, who at first appearance oscillates disturbingly between monstrousness and elegant courtliness, the source for that challenging figure, the *First Continuation* of Chrétien de Troyes's *Perceval*, presents the intruding knight in straightforward terms, rehearsing the supernatural circumstances without wonder, as part and parcel of a popular literary genre, firmly lodged within the audience's horizon of expectations (41–2). Similarly, in their focus upon *errant* knights, wandering through landscapes of adventure, both French Arthurian romance and Thomas Malory's adaptations are self-contained mythical settings, "consisting largely of forests, glades, castles, and hermitages, [...] possess[ing] none of the contents that would persuade a reader it could exist anywhere else but inside Malory's fiction" (50). By comparison, *Sir Gawain*'s "ryalme of Logres" (691), legendary Arthurian England, extends beyond the conventions, both recognizable as an ordinary Northern Welsh itinerary and *terra incognita*, a wild, uncanny territory, resisting definition (49).

In drawing attention to the *Gawain*-poet's problematization of genre, Putter paves the way for a psychoanalytic investigation of the transition from imaginary identifications, within a realm of didactic idealism, to the *imagination*, a mode of meditation within symbolic space, anchored in the Law of fiction. Unlike *Pearl*, *Patience* and *Cleanness*, which, in spite of inherent contradictions, tend to exhibit an instrumental view of language, a morally instructive intent, *Sir Gawain and the Green Knight*, as Andrew and Waldron perceptively note, commits itself more fully to "fictional 'objectivity'," (36) to the use of the "mervayles," "wonders," and "outtrage awenture" of romance to explore the meaning of identity. As a consequence, in the course of the narrative, the initial exclusive Plotinian unity, symptomized in the figure of Sir Gawain as the flawless pentangle knight, becomes shadowed by an otherness, a subversive poetics, which in the first fitt is intimated by the irruption of the Green Knight, the dynamic of the *negative*. In my reading, which I will attempt to support below, *Sir Gawain*'s awareness of an existential substratum emerges because the serious preoccupation with romance forces a confrontation with the insentient quality of the object its maker desires to forge and

Also, Ad Putter's *Sir Gawain and the Green Knight and French Arthurian Romance* (Oxford: Clarendon Press, 1995) sheds an illuminating light on the literary and social function of medieval romance.

possess. The Green Knight can be understood as a momentous articulation of such a confrontation, a new myth of creation, within which the initial idealism is repositioned as an ingredient in a hybrid structure. Before specifically examining the hybridity of Sir Gawain, it will be helpful to give a brief account of the Green Knight in the role of the psychoanalytic Thing, *Das Ding*, the uncanny reminder of our own existential inaccessibility.[12] Within the self-enfolding courtly realm at the beginning of the romance, modes of enjoyment appear fetishistic, if not in a precise clinical sense as perverse, then as tainted with pathological excess. As I discussed in chapter four, the substitutive strategies characteristic of fetishism proceed from inadequate separation and concomitant fantasies about the retention of infantile pleasure despite loss. Exemplifying the logic of the existential/narcissistic fetish, rather than erotic perversion *per se*, especially in ritualizing Ophelia as a substitute for castration, Hamlet's case is instructive for the situation at Camelot, where disavowal of self-divison takes the form of an infantile dream about timeless festive harmony. In fact, as with Hamlet's paralysis, this sumptuous company of lords and ladies, who "with all þe wele of þe worlde [...] woned þer samen" ("who dwell there together in exquisite bliss" 49), is trapped within the narcissistic hour, acting in obscene submission to the mOther's libidinal Law, ceaselessly rehearsing childish unity.[13] In the romance, this temporal entrapment is underscored by a holiday chronotope, the ritualistic time-space the Arthurian court inhabits. Even after the Green Knight intrudes, the timeless hour dominates as again, at the beginning of the second fitt, the lords and ladies of Camelot are presented within a festival setting, celebrating All Saints' Day, "with much reuel and ryche of þe Rounde Table" ("with the revelry and the riches of the Round Table" 537), in spite of their sympathy for Sir Gawain and his dismal fate, banqueting, laughing and jesting.

However, after the Green Knight's challenge the otherness of temporality itself irrupts into the narrative, marking the start of Gawain's adventure as well as transforming and transvaluing courtly ideology. In contradistinction to infantile thought, which is either ignorant or unaware of mutability, as if in admonition to the dominant drive for purity, the narrrator, in the first verse of the second fitt, announces a maxim of change, "a year passes quickly and never returns in the same guise" (498) – "þe forme to the fynisment foldez ful seldan" ("the beginning seldom matches the end" 499). As several critics have rightly remarked, the fol-

12 In the following, I will be relying on chapters four and five in Lacan's *The Ethics of Psychoanalysis* (London: Routledge, 1992), as well as A.O. Aranaye Fradenburg's concise explication in *Sacrifice Your Love*, esp 20–24.

13 Group submission to a law which senselessly prolongs pleasure is, according to Slavoj Zizek, "obscene." See *The Sublime Object of Ideology* (New York: Verso, 1989), 81–2.

lowing lengthy lyrical description of the passing of the seasons (499–534) constitutes not only the rehearsal of a familiar *topos*, a version of the medieval *memento mori*, but functions significantly as a critique of the chivalric lifestyle, which either ignores the world of nature or exploits it for its own merriment, in sports activites, shows of horsemanship and hunting.[14] A psychoanalytic view interprets the switch of gears from the *cleanness* at the beginning of the narrative to the impure world of nature, with its transitory goods, the "soft wyndez" (516) and the "brygt sunne" (520) of summer giving way to a harsher autumn, which warns the sun "þe wynter to wax ful rype" ("that winter soon alone will ripe" 522), driving "wyth drogt þe dust for to ryse/Fro þe face of þe folde to flyge ful hyge" ("with the cold drought the dust, causing it to fly from the face of the earth" 523–24) – it interprets this sudden awareness of the paradoxes of time, of creative decay, as attendant upon the fragility of social reality, in this case, of Arthurian constructions, which disavow the *real* of desire. In *Sir Gawain and the Green Knight*, the profound engagement with fictionality, in the form of the romance genre, enables a transition from the fetishization of objects to the dignity of the Thing (*das Ding*). The figure of the Green Knight outlines the proportions of such a phenomenon, as well as suggests its relevance for an understanding of literary character.

In a passage from *Looking Awry*, demonstrating the ingredients of fantasy space, Slavoj Zizek analyzes a movie by Fritz Lang, *Woman in the Window*, which effectively showcases Lacan's dictum that "truth is structured like fiction," that, in fact, unconscious formations such as dreams stage *the real of our desire* (16–18).[15] In schematic summary, Lang's movie concerns a lonely professor, who becomes infatuated with the portrait of a *femme fatale*, falls asleep after glancing at it, appears to be awakened, acutally encountering and having an affair with the woman in question, becoming jealous of her lover and killing him in a fight. In the final scene, informed about his upcoming murder trial, the professor decides to commit suicide, drinks poison, but abruptly awakes, revealing the whole dream scenario of the film. Zizek points out that this seemingly fortunate end is not "an accommodation to the codes of Hollywood," but the truth of fantasy: "*in our unconscious, in the real of our desire, we are all murderes*" (16; Zizek's empha-

14 J.J. Anderson provides a very good estimate of the role of nature in *Sir Gawain*, noting that together with the passage of the seasons, the figure of Morgan Le Fey as old and fading, despite her magical power, may serve a *memento mori* warning (184–89); see also comments on the rhetorical import of this passage, Alain Renoir. "Descriptive Techniques in *Sir Gawain and the Green Knight*." *Orbis Literarum* 13 (1958), 126–32; Derek Pearsall. "Rhetorical *Descriptio* in *Sir Gawain and the Green Knight*." *Modern Language Review* 50 (1955), 129–34.

15 Zizek paraphrases Lacan's dictum, which is taken from *The Ethics of Psychoanalysis*, "every truth has the structure of fiction" (15).

sis). What the looplike progress, the near conflation of end with beginning, of *Woman in the Window* telescopes is the stage of unconscious emanation, "another scene," a fictional space "where alone the truth of our desire can be articulated" (18).

Zizek's observations have a bearing on the "meruayl" in *Sir Gawain and the Green Knight*, the marvellous intrusion of the Green Man into the regulated reality of Camelot. As I noted above, what is involved in the conception of the colorful intruder, is a transition from imaginary constructions to the aesthetic imagination, anchored in the symbolic register, colliding with the indifference – the very *insentience* – of signifying laws. What Zizek's example from popular culture helps to outline is the vulnerability of social reality to incursions of the *real*, in Lacan's sense of an undifferentiated absolute beyond the meaningful, as an *impossible* domain, which even as it resists symbolic activity conditions its articulations and libidinal designs.[16] In his explorations of the ethics of psychoanalysis, in seminar VII, Lacan asserts that contrary to standard moral enquiry, "Freud's position constitutes progress here, [leading to] the question of ethics [being] articulated from the point of view of the location of man in relation to the real" (14). Availing himself of Freud's preoccupation throughout his *oeuvre* with the orchestration of the pleasure principle and the reality principle within the human organism, Lacan refers to a telling letter (no 73), written by the older psychologist as an instance of auto-analysis. Here, Freud, in contrast to the comforting availability of psychic experience in general – "it is as if [...] one had only to reach into a larder and take what one wanted" – encounters an "unpleasant" blockage in the approach to "*die Wirklichkeit*," the reality, he attempts to assimiliate, as if the "*Stimmungen*," the moods and the feelings, mask it and defend the entrance to it. Lacan observes that against expectations Freud's *Stimmungen*, in "a most unpleasant experience," do not lead toward reality, but rather intimate it as an indeterminate, anxiety-invoking psychic stratum: "Freud's experience begins with the search for the reality that is somewhere inside himself. And it is this that constitutes the originality of his point of departure" (*The Ethics of Pscyhoanalysis* 30).

The unpleasant impenetrability Freud intimates within himself suggests in a basic way the psychological dynamics inscribed within *the real of desire*, the trauma that potentially opens up at the limit of the impossible, and evokes how the libidinal apparatus, "the moods or feelings" (30), assemble in a defensive activity to stall the insuf-

16 Although in Lacan's work, the conception of the *real* underwent modifications, the association of impossibility was a constant feature: "the *real* is the impossible" (*Four Fundamental Concepts of Psycho-Analysis*, 167). Note Evans' comments, "[the real] is impossible to imagine, impossible to integrate into the symbolic order, and impossible to attain in any way. It is this character of impossibility and of resistance to symbolization which lends the real its essentially traumatic quality" (160) (Dylan Evans. *An Introductory Dictionary of Lacanian Psychoanalysis* (London: Routledge, 1996).

ferable encounter. In *Sir Gawain and the Green Knight,* the imaginative conception of the green giant operates on lines similar to Freud's auto-analysis, articulating a jarring brush with the insentient real; however, unlike the fetishistic disavowal of courtly ideology, the narrative performs, what I want to call, *poetic denial*, a sublimated response to the indifferent, absolutely inapproachable, substrata of existence. What ensues in the form of the green knight is the very viscerality of literary character, its lifelike, magnetic force, which paradoxically intimates its conditioning in a real beyond meaning. It is henceforth possible to understand the interlacing of the terrible and the beautiful in this intruding figure as a modality of the Lacanian Thing, the dignified object, which harbours loss in gestures of ethical *jouissance*.

In response to the limits of the impossible, *Sir Gawain* rejoices in the plasticity of the creative act, conceiving an encyclopedic figure, which even if it embraces a paradox, suggests a more sublime hybrid assemblage. Referring to Lacan's account of courtly love in *Ethics of Psychoanalysis*, L.O. Aranye Fradenburg makes the important observation that the Lady in troubadour lyric, in particular, is "rais[ed] to the dignity of the Thing" (2002: 21). Contrary to the role of medieval women as mere items in systems of exchange, as family members, wives, mothers and caretakers, the dignified Lady assumes an uncanny significance, transcending her mundane reification to a realm of the secrets of *jouissance*; not only, says Fradenburg, is this noble elevation linked "to her status as *jouissance* […] but to her *access to jouissance* (22; Fradenburg's emphasis). Interestingly, not only women are accorded such adoration, but men also as *finamen* in courtly love lyrics come to represent the eroticized other, the radiant Thing, the embodiment of both pleasure and the *jouissance* beyond. What is at issue in the courtly love dynamic is not primarily the sexual relation, but the poetization of the *real of desire*: "A mortal discourse – courtly love – says that there is something valuable in 'being-as-signifier': in being, as well as articulating, 'the sign of a gap, *a beyond relative to every law of utility*'" (Fradenburg 22; citation is from Lacan, *Ethics of Psychanalysis* 81).

The loving descriptions of the green knight's hybridity suggest the eroticized veneration of the Lady in courtly love lyric. From the moment he enters the Arthurian hall in the first fitt, no effort is spared to catalogue this spectacular character's physical features as well as his accoutrements, his costume, his horse and harness, as well as the smallest detail of the only weapon he carries, "a hoge and unmete" ("a huge and monstrous" 208) ax. As several critics have remarked, what is striking in these descriptions is the mix of the monstrous and the elegant, the ugly and the beautiful, the peaceful and the warlike, the supernaturally strange and the naturally masculine.[17] Appearing at the sound of "anoþer noyse," the colossal figure is

17 J.J. Anderson's section on "The Green Knight" (172–4). based on previous critical opinion, is devoted almost entirely to the knight's ambiguity. Jeffrey J. Cohen puts

at first described as "aghlich," ("fearsome" 135), a word from "monster vocabulary," cognate with the Old-English "egeslic," recalling the terrors of the damned Grendel in *Beowulf*, but subsequently, in the manner of the plastic rhetoric of these early passages, turning into a portrayal of an elegant "mayster" ("lord," "knight" 135), despite his giant bulk, exhibiting the fashionable physique of a courtier: "Both his wombe and his wast were worthily smale,/And alle his fetures folgande in forme, þat he hade,/ Ful clene" ("his belly was tight and his waist beautifully small, and all this features were perfectly proportioned" 144–6). As I intimated above, it would be almost reductive to focus merely on the paradoxical quality here, as a larger kaleidoscopic entity is imagined: in fact, it is possible to perceive the green man as the literal toy kaleidoscope, a shape-shifting pattern viewed through a tube-like opening. Being covered all over with green, from head to toe, simultaneously giving the impression of ugly creature and refined knight, rude manners and elegant courtliness, this figure is both indeterminate and miniscule, almost a formless form, not so much paradox itself as the condition of its making.

This plasticity of the green figure does not only pertain to appearance but to his overall function in the narrative. At first, challenging Arthur's court, the "aghlich mayster" appears to wield the powers of destiny itself, binding Sir Gawain to the terms of a contract, which commit that loyal knight to future action, involving no less than certain death. Also, the Exchange of Winnings and the concomitant temptation scenes at Hautdesert, the poem's second court, as readers find out retrospectively, seem, in the guise of the Host, orchestrated by an omnisicient force, a higher tribunal, testing the virtues of the pentangle knight, and by implication, the moral integrity (*trawþe*) of the chivalric *Weltanschauung*.[18] In the last fitt of the romance, at the Green Chapel, the mysterious control of the supernatural is again evoked as the gigantic knight is presented as an integral feature of the natural landscape ("he keuerez bi a cragge and comez of a hole" ("he climbed past a crag and came out of a hole" 2221)), as the avenging Challenger of the Camelot setting, carrying a terrifying battle-ax, and then surprisingly, as a form of benevolent justice, pardoning Sir Gawain's breach of loyalty, because "As perle bi þe quite pese is of prys more,/So is Gawayn, in god fayth, bi oþer gay knygtez" ("As a pearl is

his finger on the green man as a sublimated Thing in his observation that the poem explores "the lack of a firm boundary between manhood and monstrousness. [...] The giant is not a force to be overcome and banished [...] but rather an interior Other, foundational rather than antithetical to chivalric identity" (159). In *Of Giants* (Minneapolis: Minnesota University Press, 1999).

18 The five virtues of the pentangle – "fraunchyse" ("liberality"), "felawshyp" ("brotherhood"), "clanness" ("cleanness," "purity"), "cortaysye" ("courtesy") – unify in *trawþe*, the integrity of chivalric knighthood (651–3). See Andrew's and Waldron's gloss on this passage in their edition of *The Poems of the Pearl Manuscript* (1978). *Trawþe* can also refer to single qualities such as "honour," "loyalty," "righteousness."

superior in value to a white pea, so is Gawain of rarer quality than any gallant knight" 2364–5).

This paradigm of power, though, shifts shapes as kaleidoscopically as the Green Knight's slippery demeanour. If during the challenge to the Arthurian court, warlike aggression dominates, then the monstrous ax, carried by the intruder in one hand, is offset by a token of peace and natural beauty, the holly branch, held up in the other hand as a perennial symbol of organic life.[19] Similarly subversive of fearful control is the elusive style and tone of the green man's speech, the address to the courtly gathering displaying, what M.M. Bakhtin designates as, *centrifugal* tendencies, that is, a fluid, decentralized combinatory of genres and linguistic registers:[20] in contrast to the mannered and polite tones of Arthur and Gawain, the giant's expressions are often rude and irreverent, although the line between offense and childish good humour is sometimes difficult to detect. For instance, even though the distinguished company is contemptuously referred to as "berdlez chylder" ("beardless children" 280), the subsequent boyish challenge, calling for "a Crystemas gomen" (283), and daring one "so bolde in his blod, brayn in his hede" to "stifly strike a strok for anoþer" ("bold and reckless enough" to "strike one blow for another" 286–7), blunts the threatening edge. Overall, the phrasing of the incitement is a curious mixture of the serious and the humorous, the stern and the childish (even using a dialect word – "barley" ("bags I," I claim the first blow" 296) – from children's games), the outrageous and the legally precise.[21] An interesting comment is made upon this semantic fuzziness by Arthur Lindley, who criticizes the general editorial tendency to emend multivalent words and expressions in *Sir Gawain and the Green Knight*, to "pin Gawain down," instead of allowing for the natural mobility of meaning, that "meanings should bleed into

---

19 J.J. Anderson observes that the evergreen quality of the holly is stressed in the poem: "Þat is grattest in grene when greuez ar bare" ("it is greenest when the woods are bare" 207).

20 On the centripedal and centrifugal in language, see M.M. Bakhtin. *The Dialogic Imagination*, ed. Michael Holquist. Trans. Caryl Emerson and Michael Holquist (Austin: University of Texas Press, 1981), esp 272–3.
That the presence, manner and language of the Green Knight have a dispersing effect within the courly hierarchy of Camelot is made clear by David Baker in his illuminating analysis of paradox in *Sir Gawain and the Green Knight*." "The Gödel in *Gawain*: Paradoxes of Self-Reference and the Problematics of Language in *Sir Gawain and the Green Knight*." *The Cambridge Quarterly* 4 (2003), 349–366. The article is adapted from Baker's prize honours examination essay.

21 See Andrew's and Waldron's gloss on "barley" (n277). Ad Putter discusses the significance of contracts and the vocabulary of legal and commercial arrangments in *An Introduction to the Gawain Poet* (66–8).

one another" (1997: 279).[22] Despite supernatural powers and agressive mastery, the Green Knight can not be pinned down, but disorients readers in his hybrid plasticity. Besides examining the participation of Sir Gawain in the green man's sphere, the next section will further pursue the ethical imperative of character as hybrid.

Hybrids

In the modality of dignified Thing, the Green Knight, first and foremost, foregrounds the confrontations and interactions between primary, formal, arbitrary Law and secondary, substantive signifying codes, generated from the indifferent signifier. As the very first parts of the romance showcase, courtly society operates according to narcissistic exclusion, enhancing group enjoyment through hierarchical stylizations – etiquette, rank, centripetal speech, "luf-talkyng," – fetishizing their life-style at the expense of *the real of desire*, the *meruayl* of life and death. Both in these early scenes and, in altered form, during the adventure at Hautdesert, games function in a variety of ways to draw attention to rigid rules of behavior, mechanistic contracts and regulated *eros*, bringing to light, what Zizek has called, "obscene enjoyment," an unquestioning submission to insentient law (1989: 81–2). As opposed to Bertilak's and the Lady's motivated play, a feature I will investigate below, Camelot stages frivolity: "this fayre folk in her first age" (54) indulges a boyish leader, who, at every New Year celebration, refuses to sit down at table, until his whim to experience "of sum auenturus þyng" (93) or hear "an uncouþe tale" ("a strange tale" 93) is satisfied; before banqueting, during the Christmas season, the youthful males play at being chivalrous warriors, jousting in tournaments, with "rechles merþes" ("carefree mirth" 40); in the evening the company of knights and ladies dance, sing, laugh and exchange gifts in a form of guessing game, with kissing stakes, where "ladies laged ful loude þoz þay lost haden" ("ladies laughed even though they lost" 69), and "he þat wan watz not wrothe" ("he that won was not sorry" 70). Within the context of other, more probing exchanges in the romance, this last escapade appears falsely innocent, thoughtlessly rehearsing the ethical potency of sexual relations.

Upon this theatrical arena, the Green Knight's beheading game erupts as the uncanny unmasking of all group activity, laying bare the impossibility of the *real* and challenging the audience to assimilate this new knowledge into its imaginary realm. However, as Erin Felicia Labbie notes, in a symptomatic manner, concen-

22 Arthur Lindley. "Pinning Gawain Down: The Misediting of *Sir Gawain and the Green Knight*." *Journal of English and Germanic Philology* 96 (1997), 26–42.

trated in Sir Gawain as the pentangle knight, the courtly community resists the infiltration of unconscious territory.[23] Having witnessed the traumatic marvel, Sir Gawain's blow, the headless knight and "þat ugly bodi þat bledde" ("the gruesome, bleeding body" 441), the talking green head, confirming the terrifying contractual terms, the court resumes its merry ways ("at þat grene þay lage and grenne" "laughing and grinning at the green man" 464), fantasizing the whole experience as a fetish, hanging up the giant ax as a trophy "þer alle men for meruayl mygt on hit loke/And bi trwe tytel þerof to tell þe wonder" ("so that all men might view this wonderous object and by it tell the magnitude of the adventure" 479–80). Thus, Gawain, in offering himself as a sacrifice to chivalric ideology, at the start of the quest, binds himself to an obscene law, upholding its modes of subjectivation as stylized group dynamic; clearly, the pentangle knight is ready to risk his life not only in order to rescue Camelot's reputation, but also for pleasure's sake, in order to maintain his own narcissistic inwardness:

> In chivalric ordinances and romances, this "subjectivation" works clearly on the level of the group as well as the individual subject. The nobleman is to re-create himself as a rescuer and defender of the faith, the Eucharist, his *patria*, his lord, widows, and orphans. As Foucault writes, "the work of oneself and communication with others were linked together." (Fradenburg 2002: 29; citation is from Foucault's *The Care of the Self*, 42–3)

Primarlily, what I want to examine in this section is how a perspective outside the group dynamic, in the case of the Green Knight, that of the Thing, as exponent of the *real* of desire, of matters of life and death, overtakes the narrative, creating contact zones with the protagonist in the form of unconscious territory. Here, Erin Felicia Labbie's remarks about "the obviousness of the presence of the unconscious during the Middle Ages by way of *Sir Gawain and the Green Knight*" are pertinent, and her tracing of latent desire within Gawain's resistances, especially in the game of courtly love with Bertilak's Lady, are conducive to an understanding of narrative as psychic terrain (esp. 193–194). However, as I hope preceeding chapters have suggested, a Lacanian theory of character would not be concerned with the protagonist as analysand, as, in short, a mimetic person, but would seek to undermine and go beyond narcissistic identifications to instate the discourse of the analyst, an impersonal textual node, which functions as an ethical directive and catalyst of potential psychic transformation. My reading, then, does as Lab-

23 In *Lacan's Medievalism* (Minneapolis: Minnesota University Press, 2006), Erin Felicia Labbie discusses Gawain as a paranoiac and compares his reactions to Freud's famous case study of Daniel Paul Schreber (190–215). What is particularly interesting here is the use of Lacan's conception of *knotting* in the unconscious to argue that "hysteria, paranoia, and mysticism are discursive forces that are bound together in the discourse of analysis" (192). Thus, it seems to me that Labbie is pointing to Sir Gawain's hybridity, although she does not use that term.

bie's conceive of the Hautdesert adventure as the pentangle knight's entrance into a shadow knot, into, that is, the unconscious itself, but is not so much concerned with individual repression as with showcasing how the symptom of the narcissistic One is tested, probed and transformed into *savoir*, into post-transferential symbolic knowledge.[24]

Increasingly, throughout the narrative, the Green Knight, as alterior knowledge, merges with the figure of Gawain, after the experiences at Hautdesert, functioning as an alienating mirror, reflecting back to the Camelot knight the otherness of desire. In *Sir Gawain and the Green Knight*, within Bertilak's realm, the poetic task and challenge is, as Labbie remarks about Lacan, the struggle to "articulate the unconscious" (196), to intimate that the unknowable is real and accessible in narrative formations conceived as psychic space. In its various dualistic structures, the *Gawain* poet works toward hybrid dimensions, which dispel the narcissistic unity of Arthurian/pentangle identity. The mirroring relation between Camelot and Hautdesert is profitably understood as a *parodic* relation, in Linda Hutcheon's postmodern formulations of parody as both reflection and subversion. Based to an extent upon formalist definitions, Hutcheon develops the aesthetic dimensions of parody, rejecting views of it as merely mocking imitations, claiming instead an exploratory, synthetic potential: "it is wrong to see the end of [the parodic] process as mockery, ridicule, or mere destruction" (1980: 25). Rather this process involves a dialectical assimilation of the older, decaying form, laying bare, exlploring and revitalizing its elements and devices: parody, in fact, effects the "creation of new fiction through the rewriting of the old [...] [it] is, therefore, an exploration of difference and similarity" (25).[25]

In this revitalizing function, the Hautdesert zone as parody both absorbs and evacuates the Arthurian realm, foregrounding its static artifice, and simultaneously suggesting the rich latency of the "other scene." In its general contours, the second court echoes the Christmas season and its festivities at the beginning of the romance, replete with banqueting, parlour games and refined conversation. However, if the interiority of the first setting fostered a narcissistic didacticism, symptomized in the pentangle knight, then Hautdesert undermines all exclusivity, enabling a transvaluation and reconstruction of moral codes. For instance, even if the Host, Bertilak de Hautdesert, recalls King Arthur's boyish courtliness, this reflection also brings to mind a fun-house mirror, distorting courteous speech

24 Labbie says this about the entrance to Bercilak's castle:

The baroque description of the castle with its interwoven stones, harmonic pinnacles, and "chalk-white chimneys" and their gothic complexity demonstrate the folds of strength of the unconscious realm of desire that Gawain is about to enter. (198)

25 Linda Hutcheon. *Narcissistic Narrative: The Metafictional Paradox* (New York: Methuen, 1980).

through the occasional risqué expression (for instance, proposing the bargain of exchanges to Gawain, by the use of the ambiguous word "chek" ("checkmate," "a false stoop" "bad luck" 1106), coming close to offending his virtue), exhibiting a hedonistic excess of joy during the festivities ("þe lorde let for luf lotez so myry/As wyz þat wolde of his wyte, ne wyst quat he mygt" ("for the love of that man, the lord was beside himself with merriment, like one out of his mind, hardly knowing what he meant" 1086–7)), and especially, during his hunting activities, enganging in a brutal version of Camelot games, jolting chivalric images of stylized tournaments and elegant horsemanship. Most significantly, in almost all his actions, Bertilak, again, in a distorting mirror, evokes the ominous situtation of the Beheading Game: after dinner on Christmas eve, the Host laughingly mimics the fetishization of the Green Knight's ax by using his hood as a trophy in a frivolous parlour game; the lighthearted proposal of the Exchange of Winnings to Gawain, of course, evokes the archetypal contract of the Camelot scenes, not least in the way, Bertilak, at the end of day, repeats the terms, stressing, in various guises, the word *contract* – "statut" (1060), "forwarde" (1105), "swap we so" (1108), "bargayn" (1111). Also, in the juxtaposition of death and dismemberment in the hunting scenes with the latent sexuality of the three Temptations, the unconscious import of the entire psychic space of the romance is brought into play. Within this parodic rejuvenation, the zone of Hautdesert enables a testing of a static moral system, bringing to light the ethical potential of hybrid fictions. As I will return to below, the substitution of the green girdle for the symbol of the pentangle at the end of Gawain's "trial" attests to the emergence of new configurations of knowledge.

Within the Hautdesert zone, a further proliferation of dual structures elucidates the testing and destabilization of the narcissistic One. Indeed, it is possible to describe that entire narrative space as a hall of parodic mirrors, where difference is explored within sameness: for instance, during the festivities, a subtle undermining of courtly hierarchy occurs, as pride of place at table is given to "þe olde auncian wyf" (1001) (as is revealed at the end, the very old Morgan le Fey), the lord "lufly her by lent" ("courteously sitting down beside her" 1002); unlike the uniform assembly at Camelot, Bertilak's guests are an indeterminate group, apparently a combination of the English gentry with French influence, "frenkysch fare" (1116);[26] in contrast to the silent Guinevere and, in general, the decorative presentation of women in Arthur's court, Bertilak's Lady as well as her "auncian" companion play conspicuous roles, both at the festivities and behind the scenes; interestingly, what, at first glance, seems to be the self-contained splendor of the

26 See also Andrew's and Waldron's gloss on the Host's use of French terms, such as *honour*, *enbelyse* and *bele chere* (1033).

Lady becomes diluted in a dual portrayal, which juxtaposes youthful beauty with the decaying Morgan le Fey:

> Bot unlyke on to loke þo ladyes were:/For if þe gonge watz gep, golge watz þat oþer;/Riche red on þat on rayled ayquere,/Rugh ronkled chekez þat oþer on rolled. (951–3)
>
> [But these ladies did not resemble each other/for if the younger was youthful/the elder was yellow;/a rosy hue covered the visage of one of them/whereas rough and wrinkled cheeks marked the other]

Although the conventional rhetoric of the comparison, rooted in "the homiletic theme that old age is a mirror of the frailty of flesh" has been pointed out (Andrew and Waldron 1978: 243), this evocation of mutability interlaces with the general concern with divided subjectivity, which marks parodic explorations within the zone of Hautdesert.[27]

I have dwelt on these double structures in order to suggest the romance's efforts to "articulate the unconscious," to probe and unsettle the pentangle symbol, its idealistic ideology, which elides the desiring subject. It is important to mark this part of the narrative as a *character zone*, a discursive network, rather than the adventure of an autonomous individual, because, as was noted above, from a Lacanian perspective, it is not Sir Gawain's repression that is at stake, but rather his emergent role as an ethical directive, an outcome of the testing of pleasure against the register of the *real*. As a powerful parodic device, exploring the sameness and difference of identity, the so-called Exchange of Winnings episode, in the terms of the bargain proposed by the Host to Gawain, puts on trial the very *value* of representation, lays bare the ingredients of the character construct, in the face of the imaginative encounter with the thingness of the object, the kernel of the *real*. Within the episode, which many readers consider the crucial adventure of the romance, the protagonist commits himself again to a verbal contract, which hinges on chivalric *trawþe*, both in terms of the specific virtue of loyalty and truthfulness itself.[28] This time, the mundane circumstance of the exchange, the seemingly light-hearted, even trivial, proposal that host and guest swap winnings at the end of day, provides a context within which to question the ontology of (fictional) character, to search for alternative ways to articulate the new knowledge about a mode of being saturated with the impossible of the *real*. In the Hautdesert zone, then, the Exchange of Winnings episode modifies the "myth of creation" of the kaleidoscopic Green Knight, working toward a role within it for an alterior

27 Also, on the double portrayal, see D.A. Pearsall. "Rhetorical 'Descriptio' in *Sir Gawain and the Green Knight*." *Modern Language Review* 50(1955): 129–34.

28 Two recent introductory books to the *Gawain* poet, Ad Putter's *An Introduction to the Gawain-Poet* (1996) and J.J. Anderson's *Language and Imagination in the Gawain-Poems* (2005), make clear that in contemporary criticism the centrality of the Exchange of Winnings episode is a given.

conception of everyman. Thus, what is most significantly effected here is the transformation of the pentangle knight, the didactic model of the One, into hybrid construction. However, although this transvalued entity is as plastic and mobile as the disorienting green man, it suggests both the fragility and singularity of the human subject. At the end of his "trial," by displaying disloyalty to all Laws, except to his own exceptional vitality, Sir Gawain effectively showcases the mode of being of character in literature, what it is, in fact, that makes that being *tick*.[29]

The methods by which the didactic model is dislocated are not in the form of dismissive criticism but are, in my opinion, best appreciated as an anatomy, a dissection of features of identity, hidden beneath the cloak, or symptom, of the pentangle knight. By interlacing the temptation scenes, the attempted seduction of Gawain by the Lady of Hautdesert on three consecutive days, with accounts of the hunting of wild animals, a doe, a boar and a fox, the narrative again makes use of a doubled structure to suggest differentials, to, in fact, point to its anatomic methods, whereby, as is the case with the animal carcasses, unified identity is "unlaced" ("þenne a wyze þat watz wys upon wodcraftez/to unlace þis bor lufly bigynnez" "then an expert woodsman began knowingly to carve up the boar" 1605–6), unravelled bit by bit, revealing, as does the woodman's craft, multivalence within the single body. In the bedroom scenes, Gawain disorients not only the Lady, who expects the expert in courtly love, in "trweluf craftes" (1527), but a range of common and expert readers as well, who, as Sharon M. Rowley contends, tend to resist ambiguities in the knight's portrayal.[30] According to Rowley, who examines editorial emendations, which limit multivalence in the romance, critics tend to assume Sir Gawain's moral unity, either approving of or condemning his actions according to "the priority of an essential characteristic they see as defining Gawain's identity: his innocence, his Christian *trawþe*, and his misogyny" (166).[31] From a different perspective, but similarly noting the tendency of readers of the romance to elide heterogeneity, ignoring Gawain's many identities, a militant warrior among them, Richard J. Moll avows, "by focusing on a single aspect of Gawain's reputation, his courtesy,

29 I will come back to Zizek's notion of the "ticklish subject," as the one identifying with the kernel of the *real*, with one's own libidinal truth.

30 Sharon M. Rowley. "Textual Studies, Feminism, and Performance in *Sir Gawain and the Green Knight*." *The Chaucer Review* 2 (2003), 159–177.

31 The critics Rowley focuses on as judges of Gawain are David Mills in "An Analysis of the Temptation Scenes in *Sir Gawain and the Green Knight*." *Journal of English and German Philology* 67 (1968), 612–30; Joseph E. Gallagher in "Trawþe and Luf-Talking in *Sir Gawain and the Green Knight*." *Neuphilologische Mitteilungen* 78 (1977), 362–76; Harvey de Roo in "Undressing Lady Bertilak: Guilt and Denial in *Sir Gawain and the Green Knight*." *Chaucer Review* 27 (1993), 305–24.

these [recent] studies deny the multivalent nature of the hero which the poem clearly recognizes" (802).[32]

Indeed, readers' resistance to the hybridity of fictional character, noted here by Rowley and Moll (as well as by Geraldine Heng's feminist analysis, cited above), and the tendency to assume a superior, judgmental position vis-à-vis the artifact, is symptomatic of the very narcissistic identifications that the narrative itself struggles to dismantle. The temptation scenes, in particular, dissect Gawain's identity, assembling the often contradictory facets of his general reputation as the "fine fader of nurture" (919), courteous but chaste, as the expert in "luf-talkyng" (e.g. 926), the aristocratic ladies' man, and as the romance figure, the Lady awaits, the potentially more promiscuous figure whom ladies "keuer her comfort and colen her carez" ("seek for comfort and for the soothing of their longing" 1254). Defending himself against the lady's agressive seduction, Gawain adamantly rejects the romantic image of himself, evoking instead the chivalric code of humble, compassionate and obedient person, placing himself in the position of "seruaunt" (1278), as her Christian knight, rather than courtly lover ("and, soberly your seruaunt, my souerayn I holde yow/And yowre knygt I becom, and Kryst yow forgelde" "I hold myself the servant, submissive to your sovereignty, and I become your knight, may Christ reward you" 1278–79). At the same time, in his rhetorical maneuvers, the good knight becomes entangled himself in the courtly game of love, paradoxically showing himself proficient in many of the attributes he denies ("luf-talkyng" among them) as well as a great performer, even when he is disturbed by the Lady's ruses, playing flawlessly the well-mannered courtier.

If the pentangle knight entered the arena of parodic play as the model of the One, then the intersubjective networks of Hautdesert, crystallized in the temptation scenes, anatomize that oneness, revealing it to be a hybrid, a contingent and incomplete entity. In *Narrative Ethics* (1995), Adam Zachary Newton explains that narrative theory has only recently become concerned with *intersubjectivity*, not primarily because of neglect within literary criticism, but because its status has been negligent within philosophy as well (111).[33] Within contemporary thought, the writings of the ethical philosopher, Emmanuel Levinas, in particular, radically

32 Richard Moll. "Frustrated readers and Conventional Decapitation in *Sir Gawain and the Green Knight*." *The Modern Language Review* 97 (2002), 793–802. Among Moll's recent critical examples are Roy Liuzza's "Names, Reputations and History in *Sir Gawain and the Green Knight*." *Essays in Medieval Studies* 6 (1989), 41–56; and Joerg O. Fichte. "*Historia* and *Fabula*: Arthurian Traditions and Audience Expectations in *Sir Gawain and the Green Knight*." *Festschrift Walter Haug und Brughart Wachinger*, ed. Johannes Janota, Vol 2 (Tübingen: Max Niemeyer, 1992): 589–602.

33 Adam Zachary Newton. *Narrative Ethics* (Cambridge: Harvard University Press, 1995).

re-evaluate the ontological efficacy of intersubjective situations and their formative influences upon the constitution of individual subjects; contrary to rational philosophy, which considers the self-other interaction almost exclusively from the perspective of a universal moral law, that is, as logical and normative, Levinas emphasizes the indeterminacies of such interactions, how ethics comprises contingency, provocation, immediacy and surprise. In Levinas' view a full consciousness of self does not precede and determine the moral situation; rather, as Newton formulates it, "consciousness and even subjectivity follow from, are legitimated by, the ethical summons which proceeds from intersubjective encounter" (12). Hence, subjective identity does not emerge from rationalized containment, but "always remains in some way incomplete [...] because ethical responsibility continually outstrips one's capacity to assume it" (12). Identity, then, is produced in an ethical experience, in a situation of negotiations between self and other; if it cannot be contained and essentialized, it is because it exists in a state of waiting for the Other's summons (12–13).

In the bedroom scenes in *Sir Gawain and the Green Knight*, communicating with a strange Lady, whose motivations, despite the amorous advances, are far from transparent, challenged, provoked and tempted, Gawain's self-containment gives way to a performative mutliplicity. The almost pure immediacy of the temptation episode, the *carpe diem* desperation, reminicent of Andrew Marvell's call to his "coy mistress" to "tear our pleasures with rough strife,/Thorough the iron gates of life," the protagonist dreaming mournfully of "how þat Destiné shuld þat day dele hym his wyrde" ("how destiny would bring his doom the next day" 1752), besieged, when he awakens, by the erotic lures of the Lady of the manor, "who wishes him to come to grief" ("for to have wonnen hym to woge" 1550), – this sudden exposure of the entire libidinal apparatus replaces narcissistic identity with vulnerabiltity and a sense of incompleteness. Thus, no matter how arduously Gawain strives to patrol the borders of his self-knowledge, at the end of his "trial," by accepting the Lady's gift of her girdle, and promising to hide it, he acts against norms, inconsistently and even sinfully, painfully surprising himself, as becomes clear in his guilt-ridden outburst in the poem's last fitt.

Incompleteness, of course, indicates subjective lack, a psychic space inaccessible to conscious knowledge. In the Exchange of Winnings episode, the poetic task is, as I indicated above, to articulate unconscious territory, to probe the symptom of the pentangle knight through a hermeneutic that reveals the truth of desire, the *ticklish* subject. In *Lacan's Medievalism*, Erin Felicia Labbie, briefly surveys Lacan's prevalent concern with formations of the unconscious, and his mounting scepticism about the potential of scientific discourse, of physics or mathematics, for instance, to capture the ineffability of the unknown (192–3). Although, in *Television* (1974), Lacan argues that in hysteria unconscious operation stays almost entirely on the surface of discourse, this presents "a limit case, [as] it also serves to call attention to that which is less overt, less obvious, and more difficult to discern, but nonetheless still present, textually and in the real" (192). Also, in order to underline this intractability of the unconscious as real, Lacan refers to scientific formulations as limit cases, singling out as an error Freud's hope "that one day there would be a thermodynamic able to provide – within the future of science – the unconscious with its posthumous explanation" (*Television* 23; Labbie 193).

Elucidating this scepticism, Labbie helpfully notes that the failure of language and mathematics as sciences of the unconscious hinges on the fact that it is the *energy of the drives* in their nonhuman vitality, in "their transformation and processing that [...] is precisely inarticulable" (193). Nontheless, the dynamism itself of these incalculable processes remain "*evident* in the various forms of language, mathematical, logical, or poetic, hysterical, scientific, or psychotic, that display the textuality of the psyche" (193; emphasis is mine).

As in the perusal generally within the Hautdesert zone of parodic mirrors to foreground subjectivity as divided, the temptation scenes are framed by vignettes from the hunt in order to evoke the animal vitality within Gawain, which drives him, against his normative knowledge, to choose his singular existence over submission to the varieties of substantive Law, which, until that point, have dominated him and restricted his freedom. At the beginning of the romance, although Gawain's offering of himself as the King's substitute in the Beheading Game marks without a doubt a truly heroic act, the human price paid is nontheless exorbitant, its outrageous dimension even openly criticized by the Camelot assembly itself. In fact, the reactions of the courtly gathering frame the start of Gawain's quest, indicated as joyless ("joylez" 542) and anxious ("in longynge þay were" 539) during the All Saints' Day festivities and at the leavetaking itself, expressed as "underground criticism of Arthur" (Andrew and Waldron 1978: gloss 681), as unprecedented protest againt a leader, who "such counsel to take/As knygtez in cauelaciounz on Crystmasse gomnez" ("who follows the course of knights in arguments about Christmas games" 681–2).[34] Partly a chivalric quest, undertaken to uphold the courtly value system, Gawain's ordeal also is designed by Christian morality, a group rescue as well as masochistic self-sacrifice. Examining the relation between arbitrary, insentient Law and the regulated *jouissance* of chivalry, L. O. Aranye Fradenburg calls rescue – the nobleman's obligation to serve as "defender of the faith, the Eucharist, his *patria*, his lord, widows, and orphans" (29) – a *fantasy*, and observes that it is "a powerful means of making sacrifice feel

34 Here, David Baker's observation is pertinent: in spite of the Green Knight's outright challenge to "þe gouernour of þis gang" (225), a knight of lower rank assumes the task; "by assuming the role of protagonist, Gawain ousts Arthur himself" (357).

sublimely good" (29). To risk one's life for the Other entails a complex libidinal dynamic, a reciprocal anxiety whereby the group and the subject enhance their interdependence, both fearing and disavowing constitutional lack. As a pentangle knight, Gawain is trapped within this fetishistic group dynamic.

In the Hautdesert episodes, the protagonist's entrapment within the substantive ideology of the court becomes painfully apparent. In *Sir Gawain and the Green Knight and French Arthurian Romance* (1995), Ad Putter examines hospitality as a crucial ingredient of medieval courtliness, of *courtoisie*, and notes, in particular, how the civilized context of protocol hides the often suspcious, even dangerous, intentions of hosts and guests, especially if confrontations take place between strangers. In chivalric romance, arriving from the hazardous paths of wilderlands and forests, *errant* knights are welcomed into luxurious abodes, at first breathing a sense of security, which

> may be false. For one thing, situations in which strangers take hospitality from strangers have always been permeated with ambiguity and potential conflict. [. .] The etiquette of hospitality in courtly romance [...] attempts to regulate the movements of guest and host, and the very fact that this regulation is deemed necessary should alert us to their underlying danger. (52)

Certainly, while abiding in Bertilak's castle Gawain's behaviour is regulated according to detailed minutae of protocol, constraining him frequently to act against his natural inclinations, to feign mirth when he feels anxious, to play trivial parlour games when his mind is bent on terror, and for the sake of "nurture" ("courtesy" 1661), even though riddled with "perplexity" ("forwondered watz þe wyze" 1660) and "angry with himself" ("wroth with hymseluen" 1660), to cheerfully flirt "how-se-euer þe dede turned/Towrast" ("however much this behavior was against the grain" 1662–3). Appropriated thus by the realm within which he is a stranger, submitting himself absolutely to the hosts' regulations of *courtoisie*, Gawain's status is that of a colonized subject, his specificity as a desiring individual neutralized within the cohesive strategies of the dominating group. Thus, before the acceptance of the gift of the Lady's girdle, the protagonist is trapped within the integrity of the "endeles knot," of the regulated identity of the group, of chivalry, of Christianity, of *courtoisie* and of the microscopic laws of protocol, polite speech, table manners and flirtatious glances.

Against this subjective colonalization, the romance juxtaposes three vignettes from the hunt, undertaken by the host and his compeers on three days prior to Gawain's departure. As in the Green Knight's challenge in the first fitt, the hunting episodes in the form of sporting activity defamiliarize an arbitrary Law at their back, construing hierarchy, participation, cohesion and pleasure. What generates activity is the capricious demand of the host, a seasonal ritual, of course, but at the same time, a parlour-game plot, to relentlessly hunt down three wild animals, a doe, a boar and a fox, which underneath the veneer of good fun hides brutality, mercilessness, risk and the potential sacrifice of lives. Especially, during the ferocious chase after the boar, a remarkably long episode, extending over some one-hundred lines, both the bloodhounds and the hunters are in serious danger, the crazed animal attacking and tearing apart "þe best of his braches" ("the best hounds" 1563), rushing at the archers, who desperately and without avail shoot at him:

> þen, braynwod for bate, on burnez he rasez,/Hurtez hem ful heterly þer he forth hygez;/And mony arged flerat and on lyte drogen. (1461–63)
>
> [Then maddened by the persistent attacks, the boar hurls himself at the archers, dividing their ranks: many were fearful and held back in hesitation]

In the three densely described hunting scenes, the lord of the manor has a central role, epitomized in his "rescue" operation in the boar chase, where he, despite all odds, refuses to give up and "like a bold warrior on the battlefield" ("As burne bold upon bent" 1464), finally slaughters the wild beast, plunges his sword into him, "so that his heart burst" (þat þe hert schynedered" 1594). On the three days of the hunt, the hunters, hounds and the quarry are at the mercy of the lord's caprice, the regulated activity hiding its fault lines of danger, risk and irrational self-aggrandization.[35] In *Sacrifice Your Love*, Fradenburg draws attention to the opacity of the Law in the medieval court, how a royal's will comes to be apprehended as an extention of the courtiers' bodies: "the manner of living," Fradenburg states, "of the court of Henry II of England is completely dependent on the king's movements" (26). Even when individual members are ill-disposed, "have let themselves be bled, or have taken some purgative […] [they] rush forth like madmen […] to get tidings of the king's journey" (26).[36]

The fragility of group members is exploited and regulated for the sake of masking the arbitrary operations of primary Law. In the Hautdesert episodes, by juxtaposing the energetic quarry, the hunted beast, which in spite of its utmost vulnerability, its absolute "colonalization," asserts its exceptional vitality against the brutality of the group, against the protagonist's helplessness, *Sir Gawain and the Green Knight* proposes that the symptom has been inundated by the knowledge of the unconscious, replacing narcissistic gratification with post-transferential identity. At the end of the third temptation scene, it is quite in keeping with

---

35 In *Sir Gawain and the Green Knight and French Arthurian Romance* (1995), Ad Putter notes the urbanized poets' "abhorrence of the forest, and the uncouthness which characterizes it" (50). In my opinion, the abhorrence is implied in the ironized depiction of the "civilized" hunt.

36 Fradenburg is quoting a contemporary letter: Peter Blois' "Letter to the Royal Chaplain of Henry II," in Peter Speed, ed. *Those Who Fought: Anthology of Medieval Sources* (New York: Ithaca, 1996), 52.

the flooding of the narrative with unconscious energy that in agreeing to hide the girdle, Gawain seems unaware of the radical import of his act. However, as a "shadow knot," a replacement for the pentangle, as an emblem of identity, the green girdle evokes the new heterogeneous knowledge the romance wants to generate.[37] The end of the next section will return to the question of the aptness of the girdle as a mark of the "new Narcissus," a sublimated paradox. First, however, it will be necessary to examine further Gawain's singular act, how his *tick*, the enjoyment of his *sinthome* benefits both the one and the many, ethically directs readers into an accommodation to absolute lack.

"Enjoy Your Symptom"

In the manner of the shape-shifting figure of the Green Knight, the discovery of singularity in the romance has a centrifugal effect, upsetting hierarchies and dispelling hegemonic formations. The causal movement proposed here from the unique kernel of the subjective unconscious to hybrid community may appear to defy argumentative logic and may, in fact, be understood as a regression to narcissistic self-sufficiency rather than the liberation of multivalence. Especially, the use made of Lacan's *Sinthome* seminar (1975–6), the last phase of his teaching in topology, by the prominent Joyce scholar Jean-Michel Rabaté to make a case for the Irish writer's "politics of egoism" seems to confirm a conception of literary *jouissance* as solipsistic enclosure, as a modality of Plotinian interiority.[38] One of the few commentators to take seriously the late Lacan's rehabilitation of the previously consistently dismantled ego, Rabaté illustrates Joyce's symptom as a reconstituted Borromean knot, that is, as a psychic weave of the symbolic, imaginary and the real, balanced precariously by the saving grace of "ego scriptor," the writer's egoism.[39] Quite emphatically, Rabaté notes that this infiltration of the outlawed ego

37 The girdle as the pentangle's limber "shadow knot" is one of Geraldine Heng's major points in "Feminine Knots and the Other in *Sir Gawain and the Green Knight*." *PMLA* 3 (1991), 500–514.

38 The *sinthome* is elaborated upon in *Le Séminaire. Livre XXIII. Le sinthome* (1975–6), in *Ornicar?*, 6–11(1976–7). In turn, this seminar is generated from Lacan's lecture on James Joyce, delivered at the instigation of Jacques Aubert, opening the June 1975 International James Joyce Symposium in Paris. The lecture "Joyce le symptôme" is published in Jacques Aubert, ed. *Joyce avec Lacan* (Paris: Navarin, 1987).
For the return of the ego in Lacanian theory, see Jean-Michel Rabaté's *Jacques Lacan: Psychoanalysis and the Subject of Literature* (Palgrave, 2001a) and *James Joyce and the Politics of Egoism* (Cambridge: Cambridge University Press, 2001b).

39 Rabaté notes that the first Lacanian analyst to apprehend with theoretical seriousness the "return to the ego" in the *Sinthome* seminar is Nestor Braunstein. The essays in

into symptomatic structures is "surprising and paradoxical [because] we have to remember that Lacan's entire system is built as a war machine against 'ego psychology'" (2001a: 170). It becomes clear, though, in Rabaté's expositions of both the *Sinthome* seminar (2001a) and of Joycean politics (2001b) that the egoism in question concerns *poetic jouissance*, defensive strategies born of *savoir*, of post-narcissistic knowledge, which works through the misrecognitions of the imaginary to incorporate both a traumatic kernel and intersubjective incompleteness. A telling example from *Jacques Lacan: Psychoanalysis and the Subject of Literature*, elaborated upon from Lacan's frequently quoted dictum that "there is not such thing as a sexual relationship" ("Il n'y a pas de rapport sexual," 1969–70: 134), is Joyce's depiction of marriage in his only play *Exiles*: masochistically, Richard Rowan, the writer's alterego, does not try to prevent his wife's possible affair with an old friend, but proposes, at the end of the play, that they revitalize their love, founded no longer upon the matrimonial institution as security but upon the "living wound" of a conjugal relation; Rabaté telescopes the contours of the post-narcissistic ego:

> Richard and Berta can revise and redefine their love not as a relationship between two complementary male and female partners, but as incommensurably divided subjects who can accept an irreducible difference. That this acceptance creates pain – is even based on pain – is nothing compared with the ethical sense of freedom and empowerment they can experience at the end. (167)[40]

Here, the antagonistic relation, held in suspension within the ethical negotiations of liberated agents, accords with Slavoj Zizek's view of ideology in "The Spectre of Ideology" (1994), where the "progressive tradition" of dialectical practise is criticized for falsely reconciling opposites of, for instance, gender, class and mental states ("reasons-emotions, active-passive, intellect-intution, consciousness-unconscious, *yin-yang*, etc"), ignoring the contentious grounding of all socio-cultural totaltities (75–6).[41] In particular, Zizek targets certain

---

question are "La clínica en el nombre propio," in Helí Morales Ascencio, ed. *El Laberinto de las Estructuras* (Mexico: Siglo 21, 1997), 70–96 and "El ego lacaniano," in Helí Morales and Daniel Gerber *En Las Suplencial del Nombre del Padre* (Mexico: Siglo 21, 1998), 53–74.

"Ego scriptor" is from Ezra Pound's *The Cantos* (London: Faber, 1986), 472.

40 The dictum "il n'y a pas de rapport sexuel" condenses Lacan's view of sexual difference, and does not, of course, signify that the male and female couple are incapable of sexual bonding; what is at stake is rather that "there is no direct, unmediated relation between the male and female sexual position, because the Other of language stands between them as a third party" (Evans, 181). Seminars 17 and 20 (*L'envers de la psychanalyse* and *Encore*) are particularly concerned with sexual difference.

41 Slavoj Zizek. "The Spectre of Ideolgy," in *The Zizek Reader*, eds. Elizabeth Wright and Edmond Wright (Blackwell Publishers, 1999), 53–86. In its original form, this essay introduces *Mapping Ideology*, ed. Slavoj Zizek (London: Verso, 1994), 1–33.

Marxist and feminist critics for performing ideological maneuvers through staking neutral territories for social conflict, synthesizing artificial polarities, and thereby evading "the real of antagonism" (75–6). On the contrary, viewed through a Lacanian/Hegelian lens, social reality is always already self-divided, generated by a non-representational entity, "an impediment which gives rise to ever-new symbolizations by means of which one endeavours to integrate and domesticate it"; *antagonism*, in fact, constitutes the socio-cultural totality, "condemn[ing] these endeavours [at integration] to ultimate failure" (75).

Zizek's analysis helpfully telescopes the narrative process in *Sir Gawain and the Green Knight* from the exclusive narcissistic community at the beginning of the romance to the post-transferential hybrid at the end. As regards literary character as the carrier of this process, here, the *errant* knight, Sir Gawain, the mode of resistance to the hegemonic totality, which elides its agonistic constitution, its *real* rupture, assumes the form of subjective singularity, of the kernel of vital desire. In the romance, during the last interview with the Lady, in accepting the green girdle and thereby defying false consciousness, Sir Gawain becomes a type of a "no-sayer," enunciating the Lacanian *ne*, disrupting group Law through unconscious agency.[42] What is enacted here is a transformation of pathological inclusion in an ideological totality to the pre-ideological *sinthome*, the core of character in literature, the figure or letter, which simultaneously binds readers to the mirror-image of the fiction and undercuts that bond in the enjoyment of irreducible difference.

The mark of singular rupture in the romance is the green girdle itself, after the Lady's gift-giving, substituting the pentangle as the proper trope of character. In recent years, commentators on *Sir Gawain and the Green Knight* have become increasingly aware of its semiotic dimension, of what R.A. Shoaf refers to as "a crisis of interpretation," effected by an excess of meaning, "the 'sygne of surfeit' and the surfeit of signs" (1988: 152–4). Within that overdetermined universe, the emblems of pentangle and girdle play a crucial role, replicating in their juxtapositions the epistemological shifts the narrative undergoes. For both Geraldine Heng (1991) and Catherine Batt (1992), the privileging of the girdle in the second half of the narrative taps into another mode of writing, a version of *écriture féminine* where the ties between signifier and signified, arbitrarily fastened by the pentangle design, are subverted in multivalent opaqueness. An overtly feminist analysis, Heng's "Feminine Knots and the Other *Sir Gawain and the Green Knight*" focuses effectively on the Green Chapel setting toward the end of the romance, noting how "the slipperiness of the girdle as sign" (508) prevents the "potential violence" (508) of male appropriation of meaning; despite

42 See my discussion of the Lacanian subject in relation to negation in Chapter 3.

the Green Knight's claim to the girdle as "my wede" ("garment," 2358) as well as Gawain's moral denunciation of the female donor, and, in fact, of all women's wiles ("Bot hit is no ferly þag a fole madde/And þurg wyles of wymmen be wonen to sorge," 2413–2414), semantic mobility reknots static discourse, sprinkling even the speeches of the male characters with feminine terms – "Twice (1874; 2438) the girdle is called a 'luf-lace,' once (2033) a 'drurye,' glossed by the editors as a 'love-token,' the same word later applied by the poet to the illicit dalliance of Merlin and Morgan" (Heng 507).[43]

There is thus a general critical tendency to oppose the univocal pentangle ideology to the subversive openness of the Lady's green girdle, a tendency attested to not least by R. A. Shoaf's investigation of "the poem as green girdle" in his eponymous book (1984) and by David Baker's assertion that at the end of the knight's quest, as replacement of the pentangle, "the girdle and its description by the poet [...] make a strong case for a secondary interpretation of it as the poem itself" (2003: 359).[44] In particular, Baker's concentration upon the materialistic descriptions of the green girdle, how it is "adorned with green silk, gold-fashioned,/embroidered around the edges, knitted by hand" ("Gered hit watz with grene sylke and with gold schaped,/Nogt bot arounde braydenn, beten with fyngreg" 1833–5), convincingly suggests an analogy of the interwoven text, both in terms of enchaining a story and of the very act of writing, of shaping the ornate letters of a medieval manuscript (359–60). Partly basing his observations upon Michelle Camille's book about thirteenth- and fourteenth-century manuscript marginalia, *Image on the Edge* (1995), Baker makes the strong point that unlike manuscript art in general, placed in the margins so as to draw readers' attention to chirography itself, the decorated letters and the illustrations in *The Pearl Manuscript* (MS Cotton Nero A.x.Art.3) are incorporated in the textual body, upsetting from within, as part of its radical poetic enterprise, "the old hierarchy of spoken above written language, and the granting of the written language as significant in itself" (364). Indeed, the magic-realistic girdle, handcrafted, concrete, earthy, carnal, and at the same time, enigmatic, indeterminate, an enchanted object, associated with the legendary Merlin and King Arthur's half-sister, Morgan le Fay, powerfully evokes the inner workings of the romance, its "speculative turbulence," in Leo Bersani's phrase, a self-divided, oxymoronic

43 Batt views the girdle also as multivalent and open as opposed to the "decorum" of the poem's other spatial designs. Catherine Batt. "Gawain's Antifeminist Rant, the Pentangle and Narrative Space." *The Yearbook of English Studies* 22 (1992), 117–139.

44 R.A. Shoaf. *The Poem as Green Girdle: "Commercium" in Sir Gawain and the Green Knight* (Gainsville: University Presses of Florida, 1984).

narrative space.[45] In psychoanalytic terms, the ascendancy of the girdle in the latter part of *Sir Gawain and the Green Knight*, its usurpation of the place of the pentangle in the protagonist's constitution, attests to the transformation of narcissistic symptom into the *sinthome* of art, from an exlusionary didactic model to aesthetic *jouissance*. The green girdle as the letter of enjoyment knots the second myth of creation in the romance, character as vital oxymoron, as a singular hybrid. In order to further elucidate Sir Gawain's post-narcissistic state, it will be helpful to consider the psychic organization of art from the perspective of Lacan's Borromean knot, especially as this is developed in the twenty-third seminar, *Le Sinthome* (1975–6).[46]

At the risk of over-generalizing, it is possible to trace a tendency within Lacan's investigations of the symptom from a linguistic emphasis to topological explorations. In the 1950s, especially in the *Écrits* essays on language, the symptom is understood as the node of analysis, as the crucial area of signification within the analysand's speech, to be deciphered almost as if it were a coded message, a spoken hieroglyphics. In "The function and field of speech and language in psychoanalysis" (1953), building upon Freud's practice, the analyst is encouraged to "follow the ascending ramification of the symbolic lineage in the text of the patient's free associations" in order to arrive at the symptomatic blockage: "then it is already quite clear that the symptom resolves itself entirely in an analysis of language, because the symptom is itself structured like a language" (59). Increasingly, however, the view of the symptom as a readable code gives way to a depiction of it as an *inscription*, a grammatological fragment, resistant to analysis, but at the same time, singularly tied to the subject's enjoyment, the sustenance, in fact, of libidinal well-being. Especially, following the lecture opening the 1975 International James Joyce Symposium in Paris, this latter understanding of the symptom as a trace of the *real* within the subjective constitution grows into a concern with the psychic organiziaton of writing, or *écriture*, as art. Thus, Joycean creativity, in particular, as manifested in *Finegans Wake*, underpins the revisionary seminar *Le sinthome* (1975–76), that title providing an archaic spelling of the medical symptom, used by Lacan to dispel the pathological aura as well as to generate wordplay: by no means a psychoanalytic "case," Joyce "becomes an exemplary *saint*

45 Leo Bersani. *The Freudian Body: Pschoanalysis and Art* (New York: Columbia University Press, 1986). The phrase is quoted in Heng (1991), 506.

46 *Le Séminaire. Livre XXIII. Le sinthome* (1975–6), in *Ornicar?* 6–11(1976). My discussion will rely to a great extent on issue 13 of *Psychoanalytic Notebooks: A Review of the London Society of the New Lacanian School* (London, 2005), which is devoted to the connection between Lacan and Joyce. See also the excellent entry on the *sinthome* in Dylan Evans' *An Introductory Dictionary of Lacanian Psychoanalysis* (London: Routledge, 1996), 188–190.

homme who, by refusing any imaginary solution, was able to invent a new way of using language to organise enjoyment" (Thurson, 190).

As this chapter has foregrounded, in *Sir Gawain and the Green Knight*, the five-pointed pentangle star, painted on Gawain's shield, in the first part of the romance, constitutes the signifier of truth, normative identity, where the arbitrary connection to a signified, to a semantic ground, is naturalized, effecting both the self-awareness of individual and group. In fact, the interpretive fixity of this "syngne of Salamon" (625) handed down by tradition, Christian, learned and popular, saturates it with didactic purpose, conflating individual desire with public goal. It is in this sense of masking ideological plenitude that the pentangle articulates a symptom of narcissistic politics of exclusion, eliding singularity, by exploiting fantasies of Plotinian self-identity. In the last fitt, during the second arming scene (2025–2045), by juxtaposing "þe gordel of þe grene silk" (2935) to the pentangle sign, and especially by stressing the "thingness" of the belt, its concrete carnality, the way the knight "twined the love-token twice about himself, wrapped it thoroughly about his waist" ("þenn dressed he his drurye double hym aboute,/Swyþe sweþled umbe his swange" 2033–2034), the poem highlights how a libidinal figuration gains ascendancy over abstract imposition. As opposed to the didactically saturated signifier of tradition, the girdle represents character as its *sinthome*, a fragment of the *real* of desire, non-accessible to ideological intrusion, but, as the final scenes of the romance will show, like Joycean knottings, a potential *object a* of art, a cause of the audience's desire to accommodate itself to the otherness within.

Before the romance makes this hybrid appeal to community, it showcases in the episode of the Green Chapel in the last fitt the reknotting of the psychic text, the realignment of the three registers of the symbolic, the imaginary and the real, effected by the infusion of the *sinthome*, of Sir Gawain's liberated singularity. As my epilogue, "'The Indestructible Principle of Life'": Lacan in Woolf's Lighthouse," will show in greater detail, revisionary art often stages practises of artifice such as word-play, tropings and intertextual networks in order to articulate a politics of writing, to deliberately link linguistic renewal, semantics and social change. A remarkably illustrative episode from Jeanette Winterson's *Written on the Body* (1992) performs a drama of the aesthetic knot which propels her novelistic enterprise of revitalizing contemporary romance, of injecting the radical, disruptive nature of love into stale phallogocentric discourse.[47] Interestingly, with regard to the *sinthome* as the dark core of character's *jouissance*, the narrator in Winterson's novel joins together her re-con-

---

47 Jeanette Winterson. *Written on the Body* (London: Vintage, 1992). One of the conondrums of the novel is the gender of the narrator, never revealed.

ception of the lovers' knot and her/his near ecstatic ruminations of the letter L in a medieval illuminated manuscript, encountered in a library at the same time as the passage is written. Suggesting love, the ornate letter nontheless resists understanding, appearing like both an organic maze and a mathematical symbol. On the outside, at its top, stands a pilgrim in "hat and habit," incapable of finding his/her way along routes "woven into shapes of birds and angles" into the heart of L, "which had been formed to make a rectangle out of the double of itself," and which beckons with an inapproachable truth, "the Lamb of God" (88). Despite (or because of) the letter's indeterminate knowledge, creative rapture emanates as the narrator redesigns the knot of love. Testing a variety, – "the simplest pedigree knot, the trefoil, [...] the religious, King Solomon's knot, [...] [the knottings of] carpet makers and cloth weavers" (87) as well as the dangerous, often fatal, noose-like knot of sado-masochistic wrestling in fourteenth and fifteenth-century Italy, fastening "two fighters together with a strong rope, [letting] them beat each other to death" (88) – the narrator writes her/his own version of

> a cord passing around our bodies [with] no sharp twists or sinister turns. [...] I want the hoop around our hearts to be a guide not a terror. I don't want to pull you tighter than you can bear. I don't want the lines to slacken either, the thread paying out over the side, enough rope to hang ourselves. (88)

Clasping the three registers of the symbolic, imaginary and the real with the *sinthome*, the pure *jouissance* of the letter, incomprehensible, yet a generative aesthetic force, Winterson's narrator reknots psychic space, suturing logocentric discourse with her/his private enjoyment. At the same time the intersubjective situation of love here recalls the new model of marriage in Joyce's *Exiles* – a portrayal of Narcissus transformed in ethical negotiations.[48]

In a manner similar to Winterson's ideological maneuvers, in *Sir Gawain and the Green Knight*, the episode of the Green Chapel, the challenger's home territory, showcases the transformation of character as a colonized subject into a singular hybrid, a phenomenon perhaps best described by Homi Bhabba's formulation: "the colonial hybrid is the articulation of the ambivalent space where the rite of power is enacted on the site of desire" (1994: 112).[49] As "rough dwelling" ("rog wonez" 2197), craggy, cavernous, ominous and wild, the environs of the Green Chapel defy rational understanding, the barrow-shaped structure ("berge

48 The intertwinings of the three exigencies, the Real, the Imaginary and the Symbolic (RSI), are concretized in the Borromean Knot, a figure origniating in the heraldic device of the Borromeo family. The formation of the knot includes the clamp of the *sinthome*, the opaque fragment of unconscious desire, preventing dispersal in joyous subjectivation.

49 Homi Bhabba. *The Location of Culture* (New York: Routledge, 1994).

2178) in its midst confusing Gawain, who walks around it, "debating to himself what it might be" ("Debatande with hymself quat hit be mygt" 2179), testing without avail the familiar landscape terms: "And al watz holg inwith, nobot an olde caue/Or a creuisse of an olde cragge – he couþe hi nogt deme/With spelle" ("And it was all hollow within, seeming nothing but and old cavern,/ Or a fissure in an old crag – he could not name it" 2181–2184). In "Gawain's Antifeminist Rant, the Pentangle, and Narrative Space" (1992), Catherine Batt summarily captures the vague, yet dense, patternings of this penultimate narrative space, the bringing to the fore here of the very crisis of interpretation, which underlies the other loci – the Arthurian Court, Hautdesert, the bedroom sets, the wasteland of the *errant* knight, the forests of the hunt (esp. 135–8). At the Green Chapel, interpretive models emerge, intermingle and clash in a kind of overdetermined dissonance: unable to pin down a naturalistic description of the locale, Gawain resorts to both religious language and the observations of a warrior, surmising that this is where "the Devil might say [...] his matins about midnight" ("Here mygt aboute mydnygt/þe Dele his matynnes telle!" 2186–87) as well as a "ground of combat" ("renk" 2206); instead of mounting to the romance's *dénoument*, the verdict expressed here is many-sided, both harsh and benevolent, accusatory of Sir Gawain's breach of loyalty ("lewté you wonted" 2367) as well as absolving him of all blame (Gawain is "As perle bi þe quite pese [...] of prys more [...] bi oþer knygtez" 2364–65); the protagonist's self-recriminations are met with the green man's hearty laughter; even the latter's mastery is undermined through laying the blame on Morgan Le Fey's witchcraft, in turn, uncrowned by the democratic openness of the girdle, belonging to all and none.

The exploratory, semantic density of the Green Chapel episode resembles the revisionary activity of knotting in Winterson's *Written on the Body*, especially in the way a ground is being prepared for inundating official discourse with the mark of the singular subject. The rich ambivalence of the scene dramatizes the encounter of the *real* of desire with paradigms of power, tracing the breakdown of hierarchies through the incorporation of cultural difference. The variegated, shifting patterns Batt points to here can, in my estimation, be profitably understood as the post-colonial "third space of enunication," an intangible zone constructed after liberation, new, unstable, opaque, antagonistic, aspiring to hybrid negotiations. Discussing the conception of cultural difference in "The Commitment to Theory," Homi K. Bhabha cites Frantz Fanon's powerful statement of a third zone in *The Wretched of the Earth* (1967):

> But [native intellectuals] forget that the forms of thought and what [they] feed [...] on, together with modern techniques of information, language and dress have dialectically reorganized the people's intelligences [...] [We] must join the people in that fluctuating movement which they are *just* giving shape to [...] which will be the signal for everything to be called into

> question [...] it is to the zone of *occult instability* where the people dwell that we must come. (168; Bhabha's emphases, 1995: 206–207)[50]

The focus here upon the dialectical "fluctuating movement" of communication between the liberated natives and formations of modernity as well as upon newness and the enigma of dwelling sheds a light on hybrid creation within the Green Chapel episode in *Sir Gawain and the Green Knight.* Empowered through his singular enjoyment, through his irreducible *difference*, Gawain searches, through a variety of enunciatory models, to place the new knowledge, the emerging "fluctuating movement" from the unconscious, within the zone of culture. Thus, even in his reactions to the Green Knight's disclosures about "the other trial" ("þat oþer munt" 2350), the bedroom temptations, Gawain assays, one can even say *ritualizes*, a variety of paradigms of power, which fashion his identity. At first, hearing about Bertilak's and the Lady's conspiracy, the good knight "shrank into himself with shame" ("he schrank for schome" 2372), latching unto the didactic morality of the pentangle, blaming himself for the venial sins of "cowarddyse and couetyse boþe!" (2374); also, as the Green Knight/Bertilak notes ("þou art confessed so clene" 2391), Gawain's moral fervour is articulated in the style of the confessional, in the psychological vocabulary of penitant sinner: "Now am I fawty and falce, and ferde haf ben euer/Of trecherye and untrawþe – boþe bityde sorge/And care!" (Now I am faulty and false, who afraid have ever been of treachery and breaches of loyalty – sorrow and distress will follow" 2382–84). After Bertilak's good-natured reply and "absolution," a surprising shift in attitude takes place, Gawain now, as Batt puts it, "ranting" against women's wiles, grouping himself, in the manner of medieval anti-feminism, among the victims of biblical history, Adam, Solomon, Samson and David, concluding the tirade by excusing himself of all error ("Me þink me burde be excused" 2427). However discourteous that speech may be, it provides an occasion for ritualizing conventional male didacticism upon the site of fragile desire.[51]

Even to a greater extent than Gawain's tentative enunciations, within this penultimate narrative passage, the sign itself of difference, the green girdle traces the mobile trajectory, the "occult instability" of the precondition for hybrid creativity, for the romance's third myth of creation, the *objet d'art* itself as a model of

---

50 Homi K. Bhabba. "Cultural Diversity and Cultural Differences," in Bill Ashcroft, Gareth Griffiths and Helen Tiffin, eds. *The Post–Colonial Reader* (London: Routledge, 1995). 206–207; this excerpt is from Bhabba's "The Commitment to Theory." *New Formations* 5 (1983), 5–23. The expression "Third Space of Enunciation" is Bhabba's.

51 See Batt's article for synopsis of critical opinions about the anti–feminist passage. As Andrew and Waldron observe, many editors and commentators find this reviling of women not in keeping with "the knight of courtesy" (296). .

cultural difference. In "The Commitment to Theory," referring to the Guyanian writer Wilson Harris, Bhabha maps the historical dimension of "the third space of enunciation" as a *void* or, more precisely, as a "misgiving attending every assimilation of contraries" (1996: 209; the phrasing is Harris'), thereby underlining the discursive uncertainties attendant upon the birth of new orders. In *Sir Gawain and the Green Knight*, the girdle figures such a process of uncertainty, the protagonist literally fiddling with it, as if it were some embarassing encumbrance in a farcical play. In shocked reaction to Bertilak's revelations, Gawain at first rejects the "luf-lace," untying its knot ("he kagt to þe knot and þe kest lawsez" 2375), this act preceded by uncompromising words of self-recrimination: "Corsed worth cowarddyse and couetyse boþe!/In yow is vylany and vyse, þat vertue disstryez" ("Cursed be cowardice and couvetousness!/In you is vileness and vice that destroys virtue" 2374–75). However, having exhausted the discourse of moral psychology, the good knight accepts the green belt as a gift from Bertilak, and in conciliatory gestures, wraps it around his own body: now, the girdle turns into a token of personal excess ("in syngne of my surfet I schal se hit ofte" 2433), a reminder of "the flaws and frailties of perverse flesh" ("þe faut and þe fayntyse of þe flesche crabbed" 2435). Further transformations take place on the journey back to King Arthur's court, the shining belt ("þe blykkande belt" 2485) carried like a baldrick in full view "at his side/under his left arm" ("bi his syde,/Loken under his lyfte arme" 2485–86), tied there with a knot. At the very end of the romance, arriving home at last, the publicity of the green figure is attested to, Gawain now compelled to refine his account of it, in fact, to articulate newfound knowledge within communal space. It is noteworthy that within each of these theatrical gestures, as if negotiating a proper name for the *sinthome*, finding it a place in culture, the protagonist enunciates, what can be likened to, post-colonial *misgiving*, first in the form of uncomprehending rage, then in self-doubting humility and finally, in the company of courtiers, in guilty torment and shame ("He groned for gref and grame […] / When he hit schulde schewe, for schame" 2502–04).

There can be no doubt, though, at the end of the romance, that the airing of this misgiving stakes out a province for a new model of cultural difference. In his testimonials before the Arthurian court, Gawain occupies the position of Fanon's liberated native, a zone in the romance of self-divided character, which contaminates the *objet d'art* itself, transforming its initial didactic certainties into incomplete hybridity. Assimilating Sir Gawain's "tick," his vital, yet dark and unknowable core, into their previously exclusive community, the Arthurian court performs a transvaluation of values, in consensual mirth legislating an order of the green girdle, each courtier wrapping the baldrick around him, the "syngne of surfet" turned into the *modus operandi* of ethical communication. Similarly, at a second remove from Arthurian reception, readers are affected by the figure of the green girdle, through the course of the romance directed by its pure *jouissance*, its dark vitality, from mirror-stage identifications to confrontations with their own otherness. Thus, in *Sir Gawain and the Green Knight*, the object of art itself articulates the third myth of creation as Narcissus transformed, operating for readers as their *objet a*, the cause of their desire, prompting them to explore hybridity, to "elude the politics of polarity and emerge as the others of our selves" (Bhabha 1995: 209).

Chapter 10: Epilogue: "The Indestructible Principle of Life": Bergson and Lacan in Woolf's Lighthouse[1]

"intimacy ... which is knowledge"

The vitality of the letter of literature, of the Lacanian *littera*, accrues in the node of character, where the irreducible resistance to symbolization, associated with the materiality of language, is negotiated in sublimated, accommodating tropes – elegaic figurations, parodic reflectors, anamorphosis, hybrid space. The primary Law of signification, the intractability of structures which regulate modes of being, the painful experience of the "incessant sliding of the signified under the signifier" ("The agency of the letter ..." 154), generates strategies of denial, which in the character construct can, through a Lacanian lens, be understood as vitalistic ruptures into insentient linearity. In a short, suggestive essay, "Lacan and the Ideal of Science" (1991), Jean–Claude Milner notes the aptness of Kantian "sophistication" as a solution to the dilemma of modern science, that is, to the predicament of human entrapment within the "infinite literalization" which is the empirical ideal of modernity (38). Kant's conception entails a delicate balance within the mind between a painful truth and fictions of transcendence, and would, according to Milner, explain the tenacity of a belief in the *human* sciences: by positing a limit to materiality, "in fact, all that has been done is to find an illusory solace in the face of a painful truth" (38). As *belles lettres*, literature, in particular, illustrates Kant's sophistication, appropriating, substantifying and energizing the very artifice which constitutes it.[2]

In this epilogue, I propose that modernist vitalism, especially as reflected in Virginia Woolf's life-enhancing aesthetic practice in *To the Lighthouse* (1927), strengthens Lacanian psychoanalysis as an underpinning of the concept of character in literature. Although the question of the influence of vitalist philosophers upon literary modernism is a complex, and even a controversial, one, its implications far from being fully probed in contemporary criticism, there can be little

1 "The indestructible principle of life" is used in connection with Bernard in *The Waves* (1931). The creative thought at the origin of the character imbues the fiction with life. See Bonnie Kime Scott (33–35).

2 The theorem of literature, according to Milner, is "*Letters may be used to spell out what exceeds the letter*" (40). Jean-Claude Milner. "Lacan and the Ideal of Science," in Alexandre Leupin, ed. *Lacan and the Human Sciences* (Lincoln: University of Nebraska Press, 1991), 27–42.

doubt about the impact in the early twentieth century upon British writers and artistis of the French-Jewish thinker, Henry Bergson, about whom Richard Lehan claims: "if the moderns did not have Bergson, they would have had to invent him" (1992: 311).[3] It is, of course, not my intention in this short last chapter to trace in detail the inroads of Bergsonian philosophy into Woolf's fiction but merely to suggest how these writers shared a variety of ontological optimism, respectively theorized and worked towards in *Creative Evolution* (1911) and *To the Lighthouse* (1927).[4] Especially, Bergson's meditation upon the interpenetration of intellect and intuition as a necessary constiutent of a theory of knowledge as well as his vitalist exposition of the "idea of nothing" collate with the elegaic strategies of *To the Lighthouse*, its oscillation between denial and affirmation, finality and vital flow. Confronted with the inertia of matter, both in Bergson's environmentalist, biological understanding and in Woolf's struggle with linearity in the symbolic registrar, these writers articulated a resilient faith in differential modes of knowledge, in mental models which stimulate ethical sensibilities and disinterested leadership. Re-interpreted by Gilles Deleuze as a "philosopher of 'difference'" (Douglas 1992:379), Henri Bergson helps to underline the vitalist implications of the Lacanian perspective on literary character I have developed throughout this book.[5] In particular, in the figure of Mrs Ramsay, the maternal authority in *To the Lighthouse*, the force-field of character is showcased, loss, memory, eros and thanatos interlacing in the discourse of accommodating tropes, which bind readers to the fiction, (potentially) rupturing narcissistic identification through the ethical encounter with a singular multiplex.

3 Richard Lehan. "Bergson and the discourse of the moderns," in *The Crisis in Modernism: Bergson and the Vitalist Controversy*, eds. Frederick Burwick and Paul Douglas (Cambridge: Cambridge University Press, 1992), 306–39. Besides Burwick's and Douglas' historical overview of vitalism in Europe and America, Tom Quirk's recent study *Bergson and American Culture: The Worlds of Willa Cather and Wallace Stevens* (Chapel Hill: The University of North Carolina Press, 1990) provides a platform from which to consider the pre-war cultural investment in Bergsonism. Perhaps, the most revealing guide to Bergson's thought is Gilles Deleuze, who, in the manner of Lacan's appropriation of Freud, re-opens the older philosopher's *oeuvre*, aligning it with contemporary concerns, such as information technology and the cinema. See Deleuze's *Bergsonism*. Trans. Hugh Tomlinson and Barbara Habberjam (New York: Zone Books, 1988). An excellent introduction to Deleuze's Bergsonian heritage is John Marks' *Gilles Deleuze: Vitalism and Multiplicity* (London: Pluto Press, 1998).

4 Henri Bergson. *Creative Evolution*. Trans. Arthur Mitchell (New York: Henry Holt and Company, 1924); Virginia Woolf. *To the Lighthouse* (Penguin Books, 1992). All further references are to these editions and will be incorporated in the text in parenthesis.

5 Paul Douglas. "Deleuze's Bergson: Bergson redux," in Burwick and Douglas, 368–387.

On occasion referred to as a poetics of life, as "a grand biological epic" (Quirk 1990: 57), Bergson's *Creative Evolution* indeed dramatizes the *élan vital*, an imminent force within the real, held hostage by the intellectualism of both science and philosophy, released through a new mode of perception, *intuition*, which alone apprehends flux, motion, the reciprocal enfolding of "the inorganic and the organized" (186). At the very start of his disquisition, Bergson raises the question "what is the precise meaning of the word 'exist'?," reinforcing an earlier conclusion from *Matter and Memory* (*Matière et mémoire* 1896) that authentic existence corresponds to an experience of perpetual, radical change (1924: 1).[6] Even if intellection grasps interiority only as a succession of separate states as if moods, for instance, form mental blocks – sadness, joy, dejection, exhilaration, – the operations of memory, in particular, ceaselessly "convey[ing] something of the past into the present" (2), yield a fluid conception of time as *durée réelle*, as duration itself, inexhaustible transition. In criticizing the turn-of-the-century scientific notion of mechanical temporality, of the chronological measure of subjectivity, Bergson anticipates Lacan's unveiling of the illusoriness of the centered ego. As opposed to the associationist psychology of his day, which, relies to a great extent on Herbert Spencer's mechanistic *Weltanschauung*, on suppositions of Being as static adjustment, Bergson outlined the *moi fondamentale*, the psyche in a state of perpetual Becoming, decentered, transitional and unforeseeable.[7]

If in startling ways Bergson's thoughts about *durée réelle*, especially about memory as the real itself, constituting psychic life, flowing ceaselessly within conscious as well as unconscious life, pressing upon every instance of time, collates with Freud's apprehension of subjective historicity, of a "complex 'time' of space," then the most pregnant articulation of this vital compound, and most relevant for aesthetic figurations, is Gilles Deleuze´s "inorganic life," "a life [which] contains only virtuals. It is made up of virtualities, events, singularities" (1995; 2001: 31).[8] In one of his final essays, "Immanence: A Life" (1995), Deleuze expounds in a lyrical manner a central preoccupation regarding a superior empiricism, that is,

---

6 Henri Bergson. *Matter and Memory*. Trans. Nancy Margaret Paul and W. Scott Palmer (New York: Macmillan, 1911).

7 See Quirk on Bergson's critique of Herbert Spencer and associationist psychology (47–49). As regards a psychoanalytic bent, Bergson intimated Freud's "Copernican revolution": "Bergson foresaw in the psychoanalytic discoveries as wonderful and important 'as have been in the preceding centuries the discoveries of the physical and natural sciences'" (Quirk n2, 260–261); the citation is from Bergson's *Dreams* (1913). Trans. Edwin E. Slosson (New York: B. W. Huebsch, 1914)

8 Gilles Deleuze. "Immanence: A Life," in *Pure Immanence: Essays on A Life*. Trans. Anne Boyman (New York: Zone Books, 2001), 25–33. This edition of Deleuze's final essays includes essays on Hume and Nietzsche.
For Freud's "time of space," see my discussion in chapter two.

a plane of experience, which is both rooted in ordinary perception and traversing this in an experimental search for pre-individualistic logic of sensation. As John Rajchman explains in the introduction to the edition, departing from classical empiricism, which proceeds from solid givens to abstractions, from atomistic particulars to generalities, Deleuze's version of being-in-the-world disrupts the premise of fixed perception, of the Lockean "I," instead problematizing *life*, conceiving it as "a different 'synthesis of the sensible' than the kind that makes possible the conscious self or person" (9).[9] Sharing with French post-structuralism a scepticism toward essentialized subjectivity, Deleuze's enquiries trace divergent philosophical traditions, David Hume's sociological speculations, Bergsonism and William James' pragmatism. In particular, in Hume's exposure of the self as artifice or habit and in Bergson's *élan vital*, the pre-subjective flow of life, "a new or 'superior empiricism' becomes possible, one concerned with what is singular yet 'in-human' in the composition of ourselves" (Rajchman 13). Thus, in Deleuze's essay, the distinction made between the indefinite and the definite, *a life* as depersonalized virtuality and *the life* as participation in a categorical social reality, telescopes the perceptual transformation advocated: the task of experimental thought is to construct a relation between the empirical, lived experience, to the plane of the virtual *élan vital*, to the zone of singular, yet de-personalized, excess.

The intimations of such new relations are, in Deleuze's view, conveyed by the realm of art, by the "logic of sensation" in Francis Bacon's painting, by "the moving image" of the experimental cinema and by "minor" literature, the works of writers such as Kafka, Woolf and Henry James, who "lived with all [their] energies, [...] never ceasing to become" (*A Thousand Plateaus* 1987: 277).[10] Indeed, Rajchman points out that increasingly Deleuze came to understand aesthetic knowledge as liberated sensations, as cognitive and perceptual activity which undermines the premises of "I think" or "I judge": "artworks hit upon something singular yet impersonal in our bodies and brains, irreducible to any pre-existent 'we'" (10). In "Immanence: A Life," a particularly revealing example is culled from Charles Dickens' *Our Mutual Friend* (1865) to elaborate upon this vital synthesis, this energetic singularity: on his deathbed, a villainous character, "a disreputable man, a rouge, held in contempt by everyone" (28), suddenly "attains a sort of beatitude" (29) as a reciprocal sympathy flows between the dying man and his caretakers, a

9 John Rajchman. "Introduction," 7–23.

10 The works in question are *Francis Bacon: The Logic of Sensation*. Trans. Daniel W. Smith (London: Continuum, 1981; 2001); *Cinema-1: The Movement-Image*. Trans. Hugh Tomlinson and Barbara Habberjam (London: Athlone, 1983; 1986); *Cinema-2: The Time-Image*. Trans. Hugh Tomlinson and Robert Galeta (London: Athlone, 1985; 1989); *A Thousand Plateaus: Capitalism and Schizophrenia*. Trans. Brian Massumi (Minneapolis: University of Minnesota Press, 1980; 1987).

disinterested reverence for *a life*, a moment of visceral being: "a life of pure immanence, neutral, beyond good and evil, for it was only the subject that incarnated it in the midst of things that made it good or bad" (29). Revived, the rouge re-enters his lurid existence of petty villainy, an instance of the power of art to channel through character, through a materialistic image, the sense of a differential plane of the empirical pressing upon habitual reality. In the second section of this chapter, I will return to the construction of such an image in *To the Lighthouse*, as Lily, the painter, reflects in a Deleuzian manner upon artistic composition. For the remainder of this section, I want to exmine the empirical Other as conveyed through maternal authority, how a variety of political positions are tested in the novel's first part, "The Window," climaxing in the banquet scene where a community led by disinterested intuition is proposed.

A central, as well as a shifting, object within the critical commentary on the novel, Mrs Ramsay's character tends to polarize views, often leading to evaluations of Victorian patriarchal ideology or, more specifically, of Woolf's own relations as an artist to the mother figure. In a typically polemical essay on the Ramsays' marriage (1981), Jane Lilienfeld succinctly characterizes earlier critics' reactions as "diametrically opposed," as either idealizations of the "angel in the house" or denigrations of ruinous feminine wiles, of Mrs Ramsay as a "feather-brained self-satisfied manipulator" (149).[11] The attitudes of Lilienfeld herself can be said to be representative of the feminist politics of the important 1980's volume, *New Feminist Essays on Virginia Woolf* (1981), where sociololgical evidence is mustered to underscore the patriarchal strategies of oppression in the fiction, how, in the case of *To the Lighthouse*, gender roles in marriage reflect in disturbing detail the domestic ideology of Victorian conduct books and rules of etiquette. According to Lilienfeld, the pressure upon married couples, and especially upon women, to conceal their emotional life, their anger, bitterness, longings, leads to manipulative relationships, petty power-plays with other people's needs and affections: "had [Mrs Ramsay] had some access [...] to self-fulfilment outside the limited domestic sphere, she would not have insisted on her husband's dependence on her, nor dominated Minta, Paul and Lily" (162).

11 Jane Lillenfeld. "Where the Spear Plants Grew: the Ramsays' Marriage in *To the Lighthouse*, in *New Feminist Essays on Virginia Woolf*, ed. Jane Marcus (Lincoln: University of Nebraska Press, 1981), 148–169. Among the enthusiasts Lilienfeld lists David Daiches (*Virginia Woolf* (New York: New Directions, 1963)) and Roger Poole (*The Unknown Virginia Woolf* (London: Cambridge University Press, 1978)); among the detractors are Glenn Pedersenn ("Vision in *To the Lighthouse*." *PMLA* LXXIII (1958), 585–600) and Mitchell Leaska (*Virginia Woolf's Lighthouse: A Study in Critical Method* (New York: Columbia University Press, 1970)).

Although post-1980's criticism often tends to be gender-inflected, more ideologically nuanced readings have been produced of Woolf's fiction, especially in the wake of Toril Moi's *Sexual/Textual Politics* (1985), a major critical intervention, which telescoped writing itself as a political arena, as opposed to the mimetic assumptions about literary language of Anglo-American feminist criticism, in particular (esp. 49–68).[12] Extending Moi's argument into a whole-scale study of Woolf's novels as well as her non-fictional prose, Pamela L. Caughie's *Virginia Woolf & Postmodernism: Literature in Quest & Question of Itself* (1991) productively undermines the high-modernist view of Woolf's art, aligning it more firmly with postmodern fictional explorations, performativity, playful discourse, metafictional strategies and multivocal narrative (19).[13] Particularly valuable is Caughie's emphasis upon Woolf's experimental, relational approach to her narrative worlds, to meaning, perception, knowledge and *écriture féminine*. Thus, a pre-determined reality or categorical conceptions do not shape the novels: "rather, [Woolf] articulates theories as they evolve from her fictional experiments" (20). In contrast to the more direct expositions of short essays such as "Professions for Women" (1942) and "Women and Fiction" (1929), the fictional narratives relativize even the feminist practice they explore and advocate: on the one hand, stands Woolf's "commitment to and promotion of a feminist writing practice, and on the other hand, her reluctance to prescribe such a practice and *her resistance to the desire to prevail*" (19; my emphasis).

Throughout *To the Lighthouse*, it is this experimental, non-mimetic, non-categorical urge which propels the figure of Mrs Ramsay, in the process upsetting deontological presumptions about (human) character, critiquing deterministic morality, which legislates behavior and consigns individuals to limited social roles. Rather than representing the morally proper "angel in the house," the debilitating repressed schemer or the ambivalent mother figure, fertile yet constraining, that is, rather than emerging from what is conventionally given, Mrs Ramsay is experimentally imagined from a position of *not knowing*, from the *terra incognita* of the empirical Other, which contains the pre-subjective matter itself of creation. Indeed, it is something of a critical commonplace that Woolf attacked what Arnold Bennett, one of her targets, referred to as "real" character (quoted in Caughie: 63), in two related prose pieces, "Mr Bennett and Mrs Brown" (1923) and "Character in Fiction" (1924), outlining alternative perceptions, anchored in aesthetic *vision*, rather than recognizable conventions, the habitual psychologi-

12 Toril Moi. *Sexual/Textual Politics: Feminist Literary Theory* (London: Routledge, 1985).

13 Pamela L. Caughie. *Virginia Woolf & Postmodernism: Literature in Quest & Question of Itself* (Urbana: University of Illlinois Press, 1991).

cal and social person (1988: esp. 430–431).[14] In her dismantling of the exhausted nineteenth-century novelistic heritage as tirelessly worked over by the Edwardian writers, H. G. Wells, John Galsworthy and Bennett himself, Woolf most certainly advocates a transcendent empiricism: accepting that "the foundation of good fiction is character-creating, and nothing else," the modern artist quests after a new phenomenon, "a habitable *dwelling-place*" (1988: 388; my empahsis) between the unexplored territory of *a life* and the mundane affairs of such as Mrs Brown, an elderly lady, sitting in the corner of a railway carriage, on the Richmond-Waterloo line (1988: esp. 430). How rapturous vision pursues and experiments with that vital compound – with, for instance, the character's "atmosphere", the intense suffering of Mrs Brown, which "came pouring out like a drought, like a smell of burning" (425) – constitutes the primary ethical endeavour of *To the Lighthouse*, as both the narrative consciousness and its tool of perception, Lily Briscoe, stage the creation of Mrs Ramsay, the uncanny dwelling-place betwen life and art.

Forming a speculative context for modernist character, "Mr Bennett and Mrs Brown" and "Character in Fiction" facilitate connections between Woolf's *vision* as Bergsonian/Deleuzean *intuition*, a philosophical grasp of *élan vital*, singularity itself as a mode of being-in-the world. Throughout the first part of *To the Lighthouse*, "The Window," an undercurrent of thought within the recognizable world of pre-war, quasi-Victorian middle-class family carries with it an exploratory dismantling of rationalistic epistemology, testing new positions for an emergent pre-subjective reality. Thus, early in the novel, complex oppositions are set up between Mr Ramsay's sequential ordering of experience in terms of subjects and objects, in the manner of the English empiricists, Locke, Hume and Berkely, and, one may add, of Woolf's father, Leslie Stephen, and Bergsonian duration, the vital, non-dualistic "time of space," of the wife and mother, Mrs Ramsay.[15] Although the *pater familias* is often presented in mock-heroic terms, as flickering a "lizard's eye" (40) upon the imponderables of existence, his deontological standpoint, the non-speculative logic which propels thought from A to Z, as if it were ranged "like the alphabet […] in twenty-six letters" (39), anchors habitual reality in the novel, constraining perception to the divide between an imperial ego versus the world of objects. It is no coin-

14 The former essay first appeared in "The Literary Review" of the *New York Evening Post*, 17 November 1923; this was revised and expanded to appear as "Character in Fiction" in the *Criterion*, July 1924. *The Essays of Virginia Woolf.* Vol III, ed. Andrew McNeillie (London: The Hogarth Press, 1988).

15 It is important to note that Deleuze problematizes Hume's place within the rationalist tradition, for instance, foregrounding the role fiction and the imagination play in the structuration of the subject. See Constantin V. Boundas' helpful introduction to Deleuze's *Empiricism and Subjectiviy: An Essay on Hume's Theory of Human Nature*. Trans. Constantin V. Boundas (New York: Columbia University Press, 1991).

cidence that one of the few passages in *To the Lighthouse* devoted to Mr Ramsay's thought processes dwells on questions of leadership where a hierarchical model reigns: the inadequate philosopher thinks of himself as a virile conquistador, who leads a company of men into unexplored regions of the earth, a hero "whose temper, neither sanguine nor despondent, surveys with equanimity what is to be and faces it" (40). Scientific intellectualism characterizes the moral vision presented: only those classes of men are fit to lead who master truth, as the end product of rationalistic empiricism; whether that mastery is obtained through plodders of "superhuman strength" or by "the way of genius" (40) is less important than the mental, colonizing heroism. Even if the father's gaze comically falters before the letter R, closing "like the leather eyelid of a lizard" (39), this same gaze demarcates the valuations and moral judgments within the habitual reality of *To the Lighthouse*.

Because constrained to participate in what Emanuelle Levinas has referred to as *the virility* of Being, Mrs Ramsay's differential leadership qualitites, maternal care, nursing talents, sensibility and compassion, are marginalized as inferior values and even distorted as the vices and wiles of an oppressed *dominatrix*.[16] There can be no doubt, though, that through the character of the mother, Woolf's novel experimentally suggests a superior empiricism, associated with femininity as *terra incognita*, as the dark substance to be explored and articulated through mental processes no less rigorous than the father's Polar expeditions. What is of interest here with regard to the psychoanalytic theory of character proposed in my book is the site of Mrs Ramsay as conveyor of disinterested intuition, as ethical directive which guides readers into apprehension of and accommodation to absolute difference. In fact, Woolf's feminist exploration in *To the Lighthouse* telescopes the task of subjectivity as the task of intersubjectivity. The singular life of Mrs Ramsay, elaborated most extensively upon in her solitary communion with the Lighthouse in section 11 of the "Window" section (69–72), must be incorporated as *ethos*, as transvaluative principle, within a communal setting. Within these experimental perimeters, the banquet scene, over which Mrs Ramsay presides, can be profitably understood as an *encounter* in Deleuze's sense of impersonal communication, a post-identificatory celebration of singularity, of *a life*.[17]

16 In "Ethics and the Feminine," Catherine Chalier cites Levinas in *Difficile Liberté* (1976):

To overcome an alienation which, fundamentally, arises from the very virility of the univesal and conquering *logos*, and which stalks even the shadows that could have sheltered it – such would be the ontological function of the feminine, the vocation of her 'who does not conquer.' (53)

Chalier's essay is anthologized in *Re-Reading Levinas*, eds. Robert Bernasconi and Simon Critchely (Bloomington: Indiana University Press, 1991), 119–129.

17 As divorced from individuality, the Deleuzian event or encounter is often presented as indirect discourse; John Marks explains: "The event gives us access to a fourth'

It is possible to claim, following Isobel Armstrong, that the aesthetic effort involved in capturing the singularity of a Mrs Brown or a Mrs Ramsay is that of rethinking "the power of affect in a *cognitive* space" (1995: 403; Armstrong's italics).[18] Although, as we have seen, a certain satirical distance is maintained from Mr Ramsay's deontological *Weltanschauung*, intellection *per se* is not devalued in *To the Lighthouse*, but rather interlaced in complex ways with the potential other affective realm of dark femininity. Here, Gibson's understanding of Jean Rhys' situated fictional discourse, her technique of staging sensibility as both commitment and transient gesture, facilitates a view of Woolf's performative moments of being. Presenting a short passage, focusing on the heroine from *After Leaving Mr Mackenzie* (1930), Gibson draws attention to distortions and slippages on a variety of levels, for instance, as narration shifts from third to second person, as free indirect discourse gives way to an external point of view, as neutral description is overtaken by psychological depth. "Paradoxically," Gibson states, "the disruptions of the flow of sensibility ensure its continuing mobility and free passage" (171). Similarly, in the case of Mrs Ramsay, intuition is performed, climaxing in the two major ontological moments in the first part of the novel, the solitary reverie in section eleven, and the banquet scene in section seventeen, these events, in turn fuelling, Lily's moving image of thought, the new subjective knowledge, in the last part, "The Lighthouse."

In contrast to Mr Ramsay's divisive reality, in section eleven, a kind of a drama of Bergsonian/Deleuzian consciousness takes place, the subject as a site of *not knowing*, "a wedge-shaped core of darkness" (69), opening up to, merging with and becoming enlightened by the luminosity of the objective world. Bergson's relevance for radical empiricism lies not least in his quest for a transformed image of thought, emerging from an elemental world, where the traditional subject-object hierarchy is traversed by "nomadic sensation," by perceptions of the ceaseless mobility of phenomena. The mental model of Mr Ramsay's philosophical heritage, the conception of "consciousness as a searchlight summoning things up from their essential darkness," is interrogated through Bergsonian *élan vital*, where the light of objects guides thought into co-habitation, not conquest (Boundas 1991: 5). To an almost uncanny degree, Mrs Ramsay's ontological moment reflects this birth of consciousness as receptivity to the luminous flow of things, showcasing

---

person; a genuinely impersonal dimension where everything is both collective and private" (41).

18 In *Postmodernity, Ethics and the Novel: From Leavis to Levinas* (London: Routledge, 1999), Andrew Gibson bases his reflections on the place of *sensibility* in ethics upon recent articles by Armstrong: "Textual Harassment: the Ideoloogy of Close Reading, or How Close is Close?" *Textual Practice* 3 (1995), 401–20; "Writing from the Broken Middle: The Post-Aesthetic." *Women: A Cultural Review* 1 (1998), 62–96.

how the "wedge of darkness" folds into and is articulated by "inanimate things; trees, streams, flowers":

> [one] felt they expressed one; felt they became one; felt they knew one, in a sense were one; felt an irrational tenderness thus (she looked at that long steady light) as for oneself. There rose, and she looked and looked with her needles suspended, there curled up off the floor of the mind, rose from the lake of one's being, a mist, a bride to meet her lover. (70–71)

The erotic image evoked in the last line of the mind as lovers' communion radically revises Mr Ramsay's instrumental empiricism. Indeed, throughout the mother's solitary reverie, the figure of the lighthouse as emblematic of vital flow, suggests a libidinal dimension, its "third stroke" interpreted as the one proper to dark femininity, lighting up the mind, bringing it forth in its singularity: meeting "the third stroke [...] it seemed to her like her own eyes meeting her own eyes, searching as she alone could search into her mind and her heart" (70). In rapturous crescendo, the relation of love to the Other becomes more explicit, as Mrs Ramsay's nomadic sensation embraces both lack and bliss, the remorselessness of the lighthouse stroke as well as its "waves of pure delight," the ceaseless rhythm of being-in-the-world (72).

If a new ontological moment is staged here, opening a potential channel between an empirical Other and mundane reality, then the banquet scene in section seventeen elaborates more fully an incorporation of character as *ethos* in a communal setting. What I want, in particular, to stress is that no less than within Mrs Ramsay's reverie a kind of erotic crescendo characterizes the occasion, as the virile desires of ordinary relations are transformed into Deleuzian encounter, a celebration of intuitive communication, led by disinterested *caritas*. At the start of the dinner, gathered around the Ramsays' dining-room table, a cacophany of inner voices seems to reign, each member of the party chained to the "I–I-I," bent on self-preservation and aggressive identifications.[19] Taking her seat at the head of the table, the hostess thinks dejectedly both about the assembly and the meaning of life itself, conceiving only the futility of the domestic reality within which she moves: "But what have I done with my life? thought Mrs Ramsay, [...] she [had] only this – an infinitely long table and plates and knives" (90). Aware of her duties of hospitality, of how "the whole effort of merging and flowing and creating rested on her" (91), she nevertheless feels as if paralyzed, limited to an absolutely mundane vision: "as if a shade had fallen, and, robbed of colour, she saw things truly. The room (she looked around it) was very shabby. There was no beauty anywhere" (91). As if picking up on this solipsistic tune, the diners bewail their own situ-

19 During the dinner scene, the "I–I-I" is attributed to Charles Tansley, whose conversation is marked by a will to assert himself (esp. 115). However, the habitual ego dominates the entire company at the start of the evening.

ation, filled with self-pity, envy, *resentiment* and petty self-gratifications. Thus, Mr Bankes, impatient with the slow progress of the meal, philosophizes no less nihilistically than his hostess, moving in thought from the "trifling" and "boring" occasion to questions about the meaning of life: "What does one live for? Why, one asked oneself, does one take all these pains for the human race to go on? Is it so desirable? Are we attractive as a species? Not so very, he thought" (97). Similarly, Charles Tansley's working-class *resentiment* tends to dominate the early evening mood, his sense of insecurity gnawing at his mind, prompting him to lash out against the "silly, superficial, flimsy" women and "the sort of rot these people wanted him to talk" (93). Even Lily Briscoe's artistic temperament is oppressed by the self-serving ambience, constrained by the condescensions of habitual desires.

Progressively, though, as the evening deepens, candles are lit and the delicious Baeuf en Daube is served, the banquet scene is overtaken by another temporality, by the Bergsonian "time of space," within which static perception gives way to nomadic sensation and condescending mentalities to transferential vital flow. As candle-light replaces twilight, the previously drab dining-room turns into a magic-realist setting, a luminous "island," where "some change at once went through them all, [...] and they were all conscious of making a party together in a hollow, on an island" (106); consisting earlier of narcissistic individuals, the company becomes aware of the celebration of an *event*, of a moment of being open to an impersonal dimension, to a plane without alienating self-identities. Collectively, they sense an ontological shift: "Some weight was taken off them; anything might happen" (106). Connecting this episode to the drama of Mrs Ramsay's singular consciousness, it is possible to follow a libidinal reversal from limiting virile desire, the strife of "each being [...] to presevere in his own being" (Levinas 1976: 104), to utopian longing, the embedding of future good within present experience.[20] In *The Philosophy of the Limit* (1992), Drucilla Cornell emphasizes the progressively emergent identity of the feminine within the masculine symbolic, specifically underlining the need to maintain a proleptic dimension, to continually affirm "the unerasable moment of utopianism" (8) as leverage against the risk of "imprisonment within ontology, foundationalism and their foreclosure on possibility" (Gibson 1999: 174).[21] In the banquet scene in *To the Lighthouse*, as the weight of individuality is lifted from the partygoers' shoulders, utopian temporality floods the occasion. Especially, at the conclusion of the celebration, it is made clear that despite its historical evanescence, the moment in its ideality will last, "partook, she felt, [...] of eternitiy" (114). The aesthetic effort here to incor-

20 Emanuelle Levinas. *Noms propres* (Montpelier: Fata Morgana, 1976); Levinas is citing Spinoza's *Ethics* here.

21 Drucilla Cornell. *The Philosophy of the Limit* (London: Routledge, 1992).

porate the feminine as source of the good has repercussion in futurity, and, as we will see, motivates Lily Briscoe's construction of a new image of thought in the novel's last part.

The shift from an atmosphere of mundane oppression to utopian vision becomes most apparent in the scene's narrational slippage from third person perspective of limited consciousness to the *fourth person*. In *The Logic of Sense* (1969; 1990), envisioning events as "jets of singularities" (53), belonging to "another dimension than that of denotation, manifestation, or signification" (52), Gilles Deleuze replaces Platonic essentialism with differential ideality.[22] Thus, a distinction is not made between a transcendent truth and objective reality, as would inhere in the dual realms of, for instance, "ideal Protestantism and real Lutheranism" (53), but rather an *"aleatory point*" (56) is inhabited, a hybrid, contingent encounter between ranges of elements: "bottlenecks, knots, foyers, and centers; points of fusion, condensation, and boiling; points of tears and joy, sickness and health, hope and anxiety, 'sensitive points'" (52). As the event is realized in discourse, its neutrality, its indirection, is paramount: the pre-individual "they" replaces the "we" of "everyday banality. It is the 'they' of the pure event wherein *it* dies in the same way that *it* rains. The splendour of the 'they' is the splendour of the event itself or of the fourth person" (152).

This kind of transposition of splendid neutrality occurs in the banquet scene in *To the Lighthouse*, imaged first in Mrs Ramsay's sensation of "hover[ing] like a hawk suspended" (114) over the gathering and at the close of the section in the numinous chanting of Charles Elton's poem "Luriana Lurilee." It is important to keep in mind Deleuze's emphasis on the *person* in the congruence of singularities, on *a life* as the interweave of elements. As she rises above the plane of the mundane, Mrs Ramsay re-enters the empirical other of her solitary reverie, but now within intersubjectivity, as the directive of the good within a community. In her imagined bird-like shape, the hostess experiences the pure bliss of nurture: she "float[s] in an element of joy which filled every nerve of her body fully and sweetly, [...] for it arose, she thought, looking at them all eating there, from husband and children and friends" (114). The erotic birth of consciousness allegorized in the communion with the lighthouse, is here depicted as the loving interfacing of the dual dimensions of the real: lit up by the "third stroke" of the world's luminosity, emerging from her feminine darkness as *ethos*, an ethical directive, Mrs Ramsay metamorphoses into a mobile, hybrid fourth person, climbing and sinking "like a hawk" on the waves of air, floating "like a flag in an element of joy," then imperceptibly merging with the "fume rising upwards" from the Baeuf en Daube,

22 Gilles Deleuze. *The Logic of Sense*. Trans. Mark Lester (London: The Athlone Press, 1990).

emanating finally into "a light stealing under water so that it ripples and the reeds in it and the minnows [...] and the sudden silent trout are all lit up hanging, trembling" (114–116). This complex metaphoric drama stages character as *élan vital* itself, as the flow of life is channelled through it, encompassing the elements, the waves of air and water, the creatures on land and beneath the surface of the ocean, and the domestic realm itself, with its banalities, laughter, earthenware pots and plates of food. The ethical consciousness binding together singularities is celebrated in the fourth person of the (Deleuzian) event.

That *a life*, rather than individualities, is at the center of the banquet scene, crystallizes in the ceremonial reciting of poetry at the end of the meal. The sweeping rhythms of Mrs Ramsay's mental activity, the cascades of birds rising and falling, of light penetrating under water, of the delicate movement of trout, are in these concluding moments transposed into the language of poetry, "the rhythm and the ring of exaltation and melancholy" in the reciting voice (120). It seems entirely in keeping with the activity of this novel, so intent on *shaping* what is "liable always to shapelessness" (Lee 1991: xl), to endow the dining assembly with the features of a religous service, perfomed "in some Roman Catholic cathedral" (120).[23] Indeed, dome-like shapes punctuate the narrative, especially in Lily's thoughts about Mrs Ramsay's figure as the center of her art, articulated beautifully in "The Lighthouse" section as "one of those globed compacted things over which thought lingers, and love plays" (209); thus, as the music of Elton's seductive words sweeps over and carries with them the celebrants, this aleatory occasion is turned into "the event of language," into a coming into being of "the univocity of language, in the form of the undetermined infinitive, without person, without present, without any diversity of voice. It is poetry itself" (*The Logic of Sense* 185). The implication of the poetic letter in vital flow is underscored as each member of the company finds in it his and her *unheimliche* home, experiencing "relief and pleasure [...] as if this were, at last, the natural thing to say, this were their own voice speaking" (120). Directed to this point of disinterested sympathy, the singuarities of the event merge in the empirical other of poetry, which articulates *a life*, generating reverence, humility, vulnerability and generous care.

The Virtual "There Is"

Propelled by the desire to shape loss and the grieving for loved ones into literary figuration, Woolf's novel substantiates character's ontological identity, aesthetically underpinning its locus as psychoanalytic directive. Acutely aware of *To*

23 Hermione Lee. "Introduction." *To the Lighthouse* (Penguin Boooks, 1992), ix-xliii.

the Lighthouse as a work of mourning, prompted to call it "Elegy" rather than a novel and experiencing its writing as a kind of "talking cure," tapping into and "express[ing] some very long felt and deeply felt emotion" (Lee 1996: 80), Woolf penetrates character in art as both the wellspring of personal consolation and the aesthetic modality of *object a*, a fantasized *something*, a sustenance of vital being across the irreducible lack which grounds it.[24] At the heart of the last part of the novel, "The Lighthouse," are aesthetic reflections upon the work involved in imaging this paradoxical composite, in imbuing it with libidinal purity, the magnetic pull of disinterested *jouissance*. In her introduction to the 1992 Penguin edition, Hermione Lee considers how the task of the new writing undertaken here is to channel the "secret language" of the mother, the unified, rhythmic and sensuous speech of childhood, into paternal law, "to rediscover the true language of the garden" within adult reality (xxxviii). My discussion here, centered on Lily's painting of Mrs Ramsay, will also take into account this subtext of the maternal *chora*, but is specifically focused upon its conditioning of a transformed image of thought, a transvaluative directive in the language of fiction.

The novel's perceptual tool, Lily Briscoe opens "The Lighthouse" section with a "think-act" (Smythe 1992: 72), an interiorized mobile quest and questioning, fuelled by the loss of a loved one and the libido of grief.[25] The very first sentence of the section asks the question, "What does it mean then, what can it all mean?," a philosophical enigma which steers Lily's activity as she strives to aesthetically model "[everything] she wanted to say [...] about life, about death; about Mrs. Ramsay" (193). The urgency of this task, an inflection of Bergsonian intellectual intuition, appears, in the confrontation of the painter with the blank canvas, as a kind of primal scene of art, within which character emerges as ethically empowered by maternal sensibility. Like Freud's grandson, depicted in *Beyond the Pleasure Principle*, who compensates for his mother's absences by master-

24 Woolf's psychoanalytic comment on her novel is recorded in "A Sketch of the Past" (1939–1940):

I ceased to be obsessed by my mother. I no longer hear her voice; I do not see her. I suppose that I did for myself what psychoanalysts do for their patients. I expressed some very long felt and deeply felt emotion. And in expressing it I explained it and laid it to rest. (cited in Hermione Lee. *Virginia Woolf* (London: Chatto&Windus, 1996), 80

In the last part of *To the Lighthouse*, struggling against emptiness, the painter, Lily Briscoe, affirms the something that eventually will image both eros and thanatos (e.g. 171; 209).

25 "Think-act" is Karen Smythe's coinage, paralleled with J. L. Austin's "speech-act" or "doing things with words" (72). Quite rightly, in Lily's case, actively *thinking*, rather than verbally communicating, absence, performs a virtual reality, especially in memory scenes. Karen Smythe. "Virginia Woolf's Elegaic Enterprise." *NOVEL: A Forum on Fiction* 1 (1992): 64–79.

ing signifiers, the painter shapes the unspeakable desire for infantile symbiosis in accommodating images, which inscribe primary loss in vitalized constructions. What Lily is shown to achieve, despite her humble denigration of her painting as a "scrawl," fit only to "be hung in the attics" (195), is sublime *prosopopoeia*, a representation of the *very impossibility* of the Real, or, in the words of Slavoj Zizek, discussing the Kantian Sublime, "*a form in which negation as such assumes positive existence*" (2002: 144; Zizek's emphasis).[26] In *To the Lighthouse*, character is grasped by philosophical intuition as vital phenomenon: it is a maternal letter, inscribing loss, desire and poetic mastery.

Because art here is driven by *think-acts*, by Bergsonian inquisition, Lily's methods are comparable to those of Hegel and Wittgenstein, whom Zizek summons as theatrical thinkers, bent on staging existential problems rather than arguing exclusively in abstract terms. In *For they know not what they do: Enjoyment as a Political Factor*, Zizek contends "in [...] (Hegelian) words" that "the only solution of a philosophical problem is its displacement," supporting this with the scenic nature of the Wittgensteinian example: instead of tackling problems directly and asking, for instance, "'What is *the real nature* of remembering, imagining, calculating?'," drawn thereby "into the blind alley of fruitless ruminations about different kinds of 'mental events,'" Wittgenstein proposes that a kind of life theory replaces abstraction: "'What are *the circumstances when we say of someone* 'He suddenly *remembered* where he had left his hat,' 'He *imagined* the house he wanted,' or He *calculated* the number in his head?'" (145; Zizek's emphasis). Significantly, Zizek adds that such concreteness does not operate as "'illustration' of general proposition" but should be taken as "'scenic presentations,'" as, in fact, subversive acts, "rendering manifest [...] unspoken presupposition" and overturning fixed categories of thought (145).

In ways similar to the philsophical theater, in constructing a new image of thought, Lily's method of *tunnelling*, of digging into the (Freudian) "time of space," clears up psychic territory for "scene-making," where the memoralization of a singular life, of Mrs Ramsay's actuality as wife, mother, hostess and friend, evokes and transmits the maternal good as source of desire in art, as sublime *object a*.[27] In *Refiguring Modernism: Postmodern Feminist Readings of Woolf, West, and Barnes* (1995), Bonnie Kime Scott makes the apt remark abut Woolf's

26 Slavoj Zizek. *For they know not what they do: Enjoyment as a Political Factor* (Londno: Verso, 1991; 2002).

27 This activity of spatializing time is perfectly summed up in one of Lily's memories of Mrs. Ramsay, "that scene on the beach" (174):

The moment at least seemed extraordinarily fertile. [Lily] rammed a little hole in the sand and covered it up, by way of burying in it the perfection of the moment. It was like a drop of silver in which one dipped and illumined the darkness of the past. (187)

excavating techniques, that they work along with "a sense of what was connected to what, a process directed toward wholeness through inclusiveness" (16).[28] Digging out the "beautiful cave behind" Mrs Ramsay, Lily is ushered into a dynamic creative mode, where the central pulse is the oscillation between intimacy and distance, between human singularity and impersonal vistas, exemplified in the novel in the artist's own physical movements between the intensity of the canvas and the "distance and blue" of the island seascape (esp. 197).[29] Indeed, immersed in this creative rhythm, Lily undergoes an accommodating process within which the narcissistic wound of primary loss is ethically activated as responsible knowing of others. What is achieved in Lily's communication with the past is a kind of choral center in art, Scott's tunnelling wholeness, a new image of thought flowing through the maternal figure. At the beginning of the process, suffering like a helpless child, Lily's desire is expressed in inarticulate pain, in the "ignominous cry" – "'Mrs Ramsay!' […] 'Mrs Ramsay'" (196), – an appeal which, from a Lacanian view, can be compared to the analysand's hermeneutic quest. A productive interpretative method in the psychoanalytic situation involves what Lacan calls *punctuation*, where the listening analyst steers a speaker into an understanding of his own undifferentiated discourse or signifying chain by parcelling it out in defamiliarizing ways, for instance, by abrupt interruptions, by revealing silences or by terminating the sessions at climactic moments. By listening subversively, the analyst mobilizes the meaning of destructively fixated speech; he "renews it or upsets it" through alternative modes of punctuation (*Écrits* 99).

Scene-making in "The Lighthouse" section renews Lily's understanding, undercutting the fixity of a presumed sovereign knower through the staging of momentary flashes into truth. Digging out Mrs Ramsay from "the darkness of the past" (187), Lily as artist, child, analysand and/or observer is directed into a kind of fragmentary, yet integrated, hermeneutics, assimilating a kaleidoscopic truth through the aesthetic punctuating tactics of the maternal "not all," of non-universalizable Woman, who compassionately grasps moments of being, aware of

---

In the introduction to the 1992 Penguin edition, Hermione Lee discusses Woolf's penchanct for "scene making": It is her "'natural way of marking the past'" (xxii; the citation is culled from Woolf's autobiographical writings, collected posthumously in *Moments of Being*). Virginia Woolf. *Moments of Being: Unpublished Autobiographical Writings of Virginia Woolf*, ed. Jeanne Schulkind (London: Chatto&Windus, 1976).

28 Bonnie Kime Scott. *Refiguring Modernism: Postmodern Feminist Readings of Woolf, West and Barnes* (Bloomington: Indiana University Press, 1995).

29 The phrase "beautiful caves behind […] characters" is taken from a diary entry on *Mrs Dalloway* (1925), quoted in Scott (16).

the impossiblity of saying "the whole truth."[30] In this last section of the novel, the precarious hold on many-sided truths replicates in philosophical scene-making the aleatory ethical encounter investigated in "The Window." Even if the maternal figure is physically absent from several of the memories Lily stages, her animating directive dominates the composition. Thus, Lily's memory flashes of William Bankes and of the Rayleys, Paul and Minta, are less based on positivistic truth than on recognition and reverence for these characters' irreducible otherness; their representations are epiphanic, suffused with singularity, not sites of identification, analysis and judgment. Lily's think-act about Paul and Minna dramatizes their disintegrating marriage, positioning them in delicate harmony, first in lovers' quarrel, the simmering violence suggested by their attitudes, the wife "eating her sandwich, annoyingly," the husband "in his pyjamas carrying a poker in case of burglars," speaking "indignant, jealous words" (188). Later, resigned to the end of love, the Rayleys are depicted in an act of cooperation when their car breaks down: by their gestures, it can be intimated that "it was all right now. They were in 'in love' no longer; " the careful juxtaposition within the image convinces us that the couple are friendly, without sexual tension, Paul sitting "on the road mending the car" and Minta handing "him the tools – business-like, straightforward, friendly" (189).

The aesthetic consciousness which dictates the points of this image, which is at the center of this character zone, is marked by disinterested affection, by what I want to term, an *other-regarding* constitution. Similarly, within Lily's memory scenes, the very viscerality of William Bankes and Charles Tansley is rendered, the scientist's attentive intelligence and the political passion of the reformed misogynist, this "atmosphere" of the characters, in the manner of Mrs Brown, "pouring out like a drought, like a smell of burning" ("Character in Fiction" 425). The transvalued observer, capable of such reverential acts of imagining others, is crucially located in the maternal figure, memorialized by Lily as the "scene on the beach" (esp. 174–5; 186–7), an inflection of the numinous dinner party in the "Window" section. Here, the painter dips into the harmonious moment, entering this realm of the mind, this suspended "drop of silver" (187), as if through the gate

30 Lacan's controversial claim, "il n'y a pas La femme" ("there is no such thing as Woman), should, of course, not be taken as a denigration of women as non-entities, but rather a celebratory view of their non-categoricality. It's the definite article in the statement – *La* – which is stressed, and Lacan's practice is to strike this out every time it precedes *femme*. Note this statement from "Conférence à Géneve sur le symptôme" (1975), quoted by Evans: women "do not lend themselves to generalization, even to phallocentric generalization" (221). Jacques Lacan. "Conférence à Géneve sur le symptôme." *Les Block-Notes de la pscychanalyse* (Brussel, 1975). The expression "not all" (*pas-toute*) is Lacan's from *Encore* (1972–3: 13).

of the elegaic *otium*, accommodation to loss in the *hour of peace*. In "Virginia Woolf's Elegaic Enterprise" (1992), Karen Smythe traces the change from the conventional pastoral faith in the comforts of the natural world to the modernist awareness of consolation as precarious substitution, as "*prosopopeic* 'visions'" (73). As shown both in *To the Lighthouse* and *Mrs. Dalloway*, visions may "ceaselessly float up, pace beside, put their faces in front of the actual thing"; despite this artifice, however, the imagined faces often overpower "the solitary traveller [... ,] taking away from him the sense of the earth, the wish to return, and giving him for substitute a general peace" (*Mrs Dalloway* 85).[31] Such is the magnetic pull of character as vitalist metaphor: it promises a dwelling in language within the hour of peace, the realm of pure desire for the other's good.

That this *otium* on the beach is ethically saturated is emphasized in Lily's painting, her spatializing of the moment as a place of worship: "Lily, painting steadily, felt as if a door had opened, and one went in and stood gazing silently about in a high cathedral place, very dark, very solemn" (186). At the center, choregraphing the respectful harmonies of the scene, dissolving the petty enmities of Charles and Lily, tranforming the virile desires of everyday reality into a condition of "friendhip and liking" (175), is Mrs Ramsay "watching them" (175), "silent [...] uncommunicative" (186–7), the source itself of the aesthetic analyst's disinterested desire.

As *To the Lighthouse* elaborates on the transformed image of thought, infusing it with maternal sensibility, the choral rhythms of the banquet scene in "The Window" carry into the creative activities of the last part, sounded on almost every level of the narrative, from the think-act to the painter's touch, from physical movement to observance, from closeness to distance, from interiority to cosmic vistas. Above, I noted how Lily Briscoe, confronted with the blank canvas, undergoes an accommodating process within which the narcissistic drive for indentification is both acknowledged and transmuted into a condition of ethical responsibility. For instance, the impersonal compassion of the mother seems inscribed in the artist's movement between singularity and distance, between the intensity of the one and the choral perspective which encompasses the aleatory event. In an insightful essay, "Mr. Carmichael and Lily Briscoe: The Rhythm of Creativity in *To the Lighthouse* "(1983), J. Hillis Miller notes the oscillations in Woolf's novel between "interpolation, the filling of gaps between here and there, this and that, [...] [and] extrapolation, the projection out into the unknown of a life force, a consturctive force, whether moral, collective, or artistic" (167).[32] The central dilemma

31 Virginia Woolf. *Mrs Dalloway* (New York: Harcourt, 1925). The example is given by Smythe.

32 J. Hillis Miller. "Mr Carmichael and Lily Briscoe: The Rhythm of Creativity in *To the Lighthouse*," in *Modernism Reconsidered*, ed Robert Kiely (Cambridge: Harvard

within this novel, as persistently within Woolf's *oeuvre*, according to Miller, is whether this *élan*, this vital force sustains creative effort within habitual reality or "whether such rhythm as there is outside human constructing beats out no more than the measure of approaching death" (168). Although the modernist house of fiction offers only a precarious dwelling in *prosopopeia*, in vitalist metaphors, by inundating its very cosmology with the rhythms of the maternal body, *To the Lighthouse* directs readers to the living event of language, to their *unheimliche* home in the nurturing object of art. That Mrs. Ramsay's illuminating guidance is affirmatively extrapolated into a superior empiricism, into a realm beyond socio-cultural difference, is attested to in the daughter's, Cam's, meditation upon global rhythm, upon the delicate balance she perceives between the island, her family's private resort, glimpsed from afar, and the universe at large, "Greece, Rome, Constantinople," "shapes of a world not realized" (205). Moving in her mind, like Lily, between intimacy and distance, Cam glimpses the irreducible multiplicity of phenomena, the "place in the universe" of the little island, "shaped something like a leaf stood on end with the gold sprinkled waters flowing in and about it" (205). Increasingly, "the slumbrous shapes" in the young girl's mind will become illuminated, sustained by the creative effort, which accommodates all difference in the measure of Being.

University Press, 1983), 167–189.

Bibliography

Aldington, Richard. "Introduction." *St Mawr and The Virgin and the Gipsy* (Penguin Books, 1950).

Alexiou, Margaret. *The Ritual Lament in Greek Tradition* (Cambridge: Cambridge University Press, 1974).

Anderson, J.J. *Language and Imagination in the Gawain Poems* (Manchester: Manchester University Press, 2005).

Andrew, Malcolm and Ronald Waldron, eds. *The Poems of the Pearl Manuscript: Pearl, Cleanness, Patience, Sir Gawain and the Green Knight* (Berkeley: University of California Press, 1978).

Aristotle. *The Rhetoric and The Poetics of Aristotle*. Trans. W. Rhys Roberts and Ingram Bywater (New York: The Modern Library, 1954).

Armstrong, Isobel. "Textual Harassment: The Ideology of Close Reading, or How Close is Close?" *Textual Practice* 3 (1995), 401–420.

– "Writing from the Broken Middle: The Post-Aesthetic." *Women: A Cultural Review* 1 (1998), 62–96.

Aubert, Jacques, ed. *Joyce avec Lacan* (Paris: Navarin, 1987).

Austin, J.L. *How to Do Things with Words* (Oxford: Oxford University Press, 1962).

Baker, David. "The Gödel in *Gawain*: Paradoxes of Self-Reference and the Problematics of Language in *Sir Gawain and the Green Knight*." *The Cambridge Quarterly* 4 (2003), 349–366.

Bakhtin, M.M. *The Dialogic Imagination*. Trans. Caryl Emerson and Michael Holquist (Austin: University of Texas Press, 1981).

– *Problems of Dostoevski's Poetics*. Trans. Caryl Emerson (Minneapolis: University of Minnesota Press, 1984).

Bamback, Charles. "Heidegger, Technology and the Homeland." *The Germanic Review* 78 (2003), 267–282.

Barnes, Julian. *England, England* (London: Jonathan Cape, 1998).

Barthes, Roland. *S/Z: An Essay*. Trans. Richard Miller (New York: Hill and Wang, 1974). Trans. Stephen Heath (New York: Hill and Wang, 1977).

Bates, Stanley. "Character." *The Oxford Handbook of Philosophy and Literature* (Oxford: Oxford University Press, 2009), 393–419.

Bateson, Gregory. *Steps to an Ecology of Mind* (Chicago: University of Chicago Press, 1972).

Batt, Catherine. "Gawain's Antifeminist Rant, the Pentangle and Narrative Space." *The Yearbook of English Studies* 22 (1992), 117–139.

Bauman, Richard. *Verbal Art as Performance* (Prospect Heights: Waveland Press, 1977).

Bede. *A History of the English Church and People.* Trans. Leo Sherley-Price (Penguin Books, 1955).

Belanoff, Patricia A. "*Ides ... geomrode giddum*: The Old English Female Lament." *Medieval Women's Song: Cross-cultural Approaches*, eds. Anne L. Klinck and Ann Marie Rasmussen (Philadelphia: University of Pennsylvania Press, 2002), 29–46.

– "Women's Songs, Women's Language: *Wulf and Eadwacer* and *The Wife's Lament.*" *New Readings on Women in Old English Literature*, eds. Helen Damaci and Alexandra Hennesey Olsen (Bloomington: Indiana University Press, 1990), 193–203.

Benjamin, Walter. "The Storyteller." *Illuminations.* Trans. Harry Zohn (Fontana, 1970), 83–109.

– "The Work of Art in the Age of Mechanical Reproduction." *Illuminations* (1955). Trans. Harry Zohn (Fontana, 1970), 219–253.

Bennett, Helen T. "Exile and the Semiosis of Gender in Old English Elegies." *Class and Gender in Early English Literature*, eds. Britton J. Harwood and Gillian R. Overing (Bloomington: Indiana University Press, 1994), 43–58.

Benson, Larry. "The Literary Character of Anglo-Saxon Fromulaic Poetry." *Publications of the Modern Language Association* 81 (1966), 334–341.

Bergson, Henri. *Creative Evolution.* Trans. Arthur Mitchell (New York: Henry Holt and Company, 1924).

– *Dreams.* Trans. Edwin E. Slosson (New York: B.W. Huebsch, 1914).

– *Matter and Memory.* Trans. Nancy Margaret Paul and W. Scott Palmer (New York: Macmillan, 1911).

Bernard, Catherine and Graham Swift. "An Interview with Graham Swift." *Contemporary Literature* 38 (1997), 217–231.

Bersani, Leo. *The Freudian Body: Psychoanalysis and Art* (New York: Columbia University Press, 1986).

– *A Future for Astyanax: Character and Desire in Literature* (Boston: Little Brown, 1976).

Bhabha, Homi. " The Commitment to Theory." *New Formations* 5 (1983), 5–23.

– "Cultural Diversity and Cultural Differences." *The Post-Colonial Reader*, eds. Bill Ashcroft, Gareth Griffiths and Helen Teffin (London: Routledge, 1995), 155–158.

– *The Location of Culture* (New York: Routledge, 1994).

– Of Mimicry and Man: The Ambivalence of Colonial Discourse." *Modern Literary Theory*, eds. Philip Rice and Patricia Waugh (London: Arnold, 1989), 380–387.
Bjork, Robert E. "Sundor æt rune: The Voluntary Exile of 'The Wanderer.'" *Neophilologus*, 73 (1989), 119–129.
Bliss, Alan and Allen J. Frantzen. "Integrity of *Resignation*." *The Review of English Studies* 27 (1976), 385–402.
Bloomfield, Morton W. "The From of *Deor*." *PMLA* 79 (1964), 534–541.
Bolton, W.F. "Boethius, Alfred and 'Deor' Again." *Modern Philology* 69 (1972). 222–227.
Bosworth, Joseph. *Anglo-Saxon Dictionary*, ed. T. Northcote Toller (Oxford: Clarendon Press, 1992).
Bowie, Malcolm. *Lacan* (Cambridge: Harvard University Press, 1991).
Bracher, Mark. *Lacan, Discourse and Social Change: A Psychoanalytic Cultural Criticism* (Ithaca: Cornell University Press, 1993).
Bradley, A.C. *Shakespearean Tragedy* (1905) (London: McMillan, 1995).
Bradley, S.A.J., ed. *Anglo-Saxon Poetry* (Everyman, 1995).
Bragg, Morgan. *The New Politics of Conflict Resolution: Responding to Difference* (New York: Palgrave, 2008).
Braunstein, Nestor. "La cliínica en el nombre propio." *El Libertinto de las Estructuras*, ed. Heli Morales Ascencio (Mexico: Siglo 21, 1997), 70–96.
– "El ego lacaniano." *En las Suplencial del Nombre del Padre*, eds. Heli Morales and Daniel Gerber (Mexico: Siglo 21, 1998), 53–74.
Burrow, J.A. *A Reading of Sir Gawain and the Green Knight* (London: Routledge, 1965).
Caughie, Pamela L. *Virginia Woolf and Postmodernism: Literature in Quest & Question of Itself* (Urbana: University of Illinois Press, 1991).
Chaitin, Gilbert D. *Rhetoric and Culture in Lacan* (Cambridge: Cambridge University Press, 1996).
Chalier, Catherine. "Ethics and the Feminine." *Re-Reading Levinas*. Ed. Robert Bernasconi and Simon Critchely (Bloomington: Indiana University Press, 1991), 119–129.
Champion, Margrét Gunnarsdóttir. "Cracked Voices: Identification and Ideology in Graham Swift's *Waterland*." *Critique: studies in contemporary fiction* 45 (2003), 34–42.
– "From Plaint to Praise: Language as Cure in 'The Wanderer.'" *Old English Literature: Critical Essays*, ed. R.M. Liuzza (New Haven: Yale University Press, 2002), 328–352.
– "Reception Theory and Medieval Narrative: Reading *Pearl* as a Novel." *Neophilologus* 76 (1992), 629–637.

Chatman, Seymour. *Story and Discourse: Fiction and Film* (Ithaca: Cornell University Press, 1978).
Chaucer, Geoffrey. *Chaucer's Translation of Boethius's De Consolatione Philosophiae*, ed. Richard Morris (Kessinger Publishing, 2001).
Cixous, Hélèn. "The Character of 'Character.'" *New Literary History* 5 (1974), 282-402.
Clemoes, Peter. "*Mens absentia cogitans* in *The Seafarer* and *The Wanderer*." *Medieval Literature and Civilization: Studies in Memory of G.N. Garmonsway* (London: The Athlone Press, 1969), 62–77.
Cohen, Anthony P. "Culture as Identity: An Anthropologist's View." *New Literary History* 24 (1993), 195–209.
Cohen, Jeffrey J. *Of Giants* (Minneapolis: Minnesota University Press, 1999).
Cook, Patrick. "The Bonds of Exile in 'The Wanderer'." *Neophilologus* 80 (1996), 127–137.
Copjec, Joan. *Read My Desire: Lacan against the Historicists* (Cambridge: The MIT Press, 1994).
Cornell, Drucilla. *The Philosophy of the Limit* (London: Routledge, 1992).
Cross, J.E. "On the Genre of 'The Wanderer'." *Essential Articles for the Study of Old English Poetry*, eds. Jess B. Bessinger and Stanley J. Kahrl (Hamden: Archon Books, 1968), 515–526.
Curry, George. "Narrative and the Psychology of Character." *The Journal of Aesthetics and Art Criticism* 67(2009), 61–71.
Daiches, David. *Virginia Woolf* (New York: New Directions, 1981).
Dayan, Daniel. "The Tudor-Code of Classical Cinema." *Movies and Methods*, ed. Bill Nichols (Berkely: University of California Press, 1976), 438–45.
Deleuze, Gilles. *Bergsonism*. Trans. Hugh Tomlinson and Barbara Habberjam (New York: Zone Books, 1988).
– *Cinema – 1: The Movement Image*. Trans. Hugh Tomlinson and Barbara Habberjam (London: Athlone, 1986).
– *Cinema – 2: The Time-Image*. Trans. Hugh Tomlinson and Robert Galeta (London: Athlone, 1985; 1989).
– *Empiricism and Subjectivity: An Essay on Hume's Theory of Human Nature*. Trans. Constantin V. Boundas (New York: Columbia University Press, 1995).
– *Francis Bacon: The Logic of Sensation*. Trans. Daniel W. Smith (London: Continuum, 1981; 2001).
– *The Logic of Sense*. Trans. Mark Lester (London: The Athlone Press, 1990).
– *Pure Immanence: Essays on Life*. Trans. Anne Boyman (New York: Zone Books, 2001).
– *A Thousand Plateaus: Capitalism and Schizophrenia*. Trans. Brian Massumi (Minneapolis: Universit of Minnesota Press, 1980; 1987).

Derrida, Jacques. *Of Spirit: Heidegger and the Question*. Trans. Geoffrey Bennington and Rachel Bowlby (Chicago: University of Chicago Press, 1989).
Doane, A.N. "Heathen Form and Christian Function in *The Wife's Lament*." *Medieval Studies* 28 (1966), 77–91.
– and Carol Braun Pasternack, eds. *Vox intexta: Orality and Textuality in The Middle Ages* (Madison: The University of Wisconsin Press, 1991).
Dochery, Thomas. *Reading (Absent) Character: Towards a Theory of Characterization in Fiction* (Oxford: Clarendon Press, 1983).
Douglas, Paul. "Deleuze's Bergson: Bergson redux." *The Crisis in Modernism: Bergson and the Vitalist Controversy* (Cambridge: Cambridge University Press, 1992), 368–388.
Dronke, Peter. *Medieval Lyric* (New York: Harper and Row, 1969).
Drury, Shadia B. *Alexandre Kojève: The Roots of Postmodern Politics* (New York: St Martin Press, 1994).
Earl, James W. "*Beowulf* and the Origin of Civilization." *Speaking Two Languages: Traditional Disciplines and Contemporary Theory in Medieval Studies*, ed. Alan Frantzen (Albany: State University of New York Press, 1991), 65–89.
Eckstrom, Lisa. "Moral Perception and the Chronotope: The Case of Henry James." *Bakhtin in Contexts: Acrosss the Disciplines*, ed. Amy Mandelker (Evanston: Northwestern University Press, 1995), 99–116.
Eliason, Norman. "*Deor* – A Begging Poem?" *Medieval Literature and Civilization: Studies in Memory of G.N.* Garmonsway, eds. D.A. Pearsall and R.A. Waldron (London: The Athlone Press, 1969), 55–61.
Evans, Dylan. *An Introductory Dictionary of Lacanian Psychoanalysis* (London: Routledge, 1996).
Exeter Book, eds. George Philip Krapp and Elliott van Kirk Dobbie (New York: George Routledge and Sons, 1936).
Felman, Shoshana. "Beyond Oedipus: The Specimen Story of Psychoanalysis." *Psychoanalytic Criticism,* ed. Maud Ellman (London: Longman, 1994), 76–102.
– "Turning the Screw of Interpretation." *Yale French Studies*. 55/56 (1977), 94–207.
Fichte, Joerg O. "*Historia* and *Fabula*: Arthurian Traditions and Audience Expectations in *Sir Gawain and the Green Knight*." *Festschrift Walter Haugh and Brughart Wachinge*, ed. Johannes Jonota, Vol 2 (Tübingen: Max Niemeyer, 1992), 589–602.
Fink, Bruce. *A Clinical Introduction to Lacanian Psychoanalysis: Theory and Technique* (Cambridge: Harvard University Press, 1997).
– *The Lacanian Subject: Between Language and Jouissance* (Princeton: Princeton University Press, 1995).

– "Reading *Hamlet* with Lacan." *Lacan, Politics, Aesthetics*, eds. Richard Feldstein and Willy Apollon (Albany: SUNY Press, 1996), 181–198.

Finnegan, Ruth. *Oral Poetry: Its Nature, Significance and Social Context* (Cambridge: Cambridge University Press, 1977).

– *Literacy and Orality: Studies in the Technology of Communication* (Oxford: Basil Blackwell, 1988).

Foley, John Miles. "Epic and Charm in Old English and Serbo-Croatian Oral Tradition." *Comparative Criticism* 2 (1980), 71–92.

– *Immanent Art: From Structure to Meaning in Traditional Oral Epic* (Bloomington: Indiana University Press, 1991).

– ed. *Oral Traditional Literature: A Fest-schrift for Albert Bates Lord* (Columbia: Slavica Publishers, 1981).

– "Orality, Textuality, and Interpretation." *Vox intexta: Orality and Textuality in the Middle Ages*, eds. A. N. Doane and Carol Braun Pasternack (Madison: The University of Wisconsin Press, 1991), 34–45.

– *The Singer of Tales in Performance* (Bloomington: Indiana University Press, 1995)

Foot, Sarah. "The Making of *Angelcynn*: English Identity before the Norman Conquest." *Old English Literature: Critical Essays*, ed. R.M. Liuzza (New Have: Yale University Press, 2002), 51–78.

Fowler, Elizabeth. *Literary Character: The Human Figure in Early English Writing* (Ithaca: Cornell University Press, 2003).

Fradenburg, L.O. Aranye. *Sacrifice your Love: Psychoanalysis, Historicism, Chaucer* (Minneapolis: University of Minnesota Press, 2005).

– and Carla Freccero. "Introduction: Caxton, Foucault and the Pleasure of History." *Premodern Sexualities*, eds. Louise Fradenburg and Carla Freccero (New York: Routledge, 1996), xiii-xxiv.

– "We are Not Alone: Psychoanalytic Medievalism," in *New Medieval Literatures*. Vol II, eds. Rita Copeland, David Lawton and Wendy Scase (Oxford: Clarendon Press, 1998), 249–276.

Freud, Sigmund. *Beyond the Pleasure Principle*. Trans. James Strachey (New York: Norton, 1961).

– *Civilization and its Discontents*. Trans. James Strachey (W.W: Norton, 1961).

– "The Dynamics of Transference" (1912). *SE* XII (London: Hogarth Press, 1958).

– *The Ego and the Id*. Trans. Joan Riviere (New York: W.W. Norton, 1960).

– "Fragment of an Analysis of a Case of Hysteria" (1905). *SE* VII (London: Hogarth Press, 1953).

– *Group Psychology and the Analysis of the Ego*. Trans. James Strachey (New York: W.W. Norton, 1955).

– *Inhibitions, Symbol and Anxiety* (1926). *SE* XX (London: Hogarth Press, 1959).
– *Leonardo Da Vinci and a Memory of his Childhood SE* Vol XI (London: Hogarth, 1957).
– "Observations on Transference Love" (1915). *SE* Vol. XII. Ed. and trans. James Strachey (London: Hogarth Press, 1958).
– "On Narcissism: An Introduction" (1917). *Collected Papers* Vol 4. Trans. Joan-Riviere (New York: Basil Books, 1959), 30–59.
– *On Sexuality: Three Essays on the Theory of Sexuality*. Trans. James Strachey (Penguin Books, 1987).
– *An Outline of Psycho-Analysis* (1939). *SE* XXII (London: Hogarth Press, 1964).
– "Mourning and Melancholia" (1917). *Collected Papers* Vol. 4. Trans. Joan Riviere (New York: Basil Books, 1959), 152–170.
– "Remembering, Repeating and Working Through" (1914). *SE* XII (London: Hogarth Press, 1958).
– "Splitting of the Ego in the Process of Defense" (1938). *SE* XXIII (London: Hogarth Press, 1966).
– and Joseph Breuer. *Studies in Hysteria* (1895). *SE* II (London: Hogart Press, 1955).
– *Three Case Histories*, ed. Philip Rieff (New York: Collier Books, 1963).
– *Totem and Taboo* (1913). *SE* Vol XIII (London: Hogarth Press, year?)
– "The Uncanny" (1919). *Collected Papers*. Vol 4. Trans. Joan Riviere (New York: Basic Books, 1959), 368–407.
– "The Unconscious" (1915). *SE* XIV. Trans James Strachey (London: Hogarth Press, 1957).
Frow, John. "Spectacle Binding: On Character." *Poetics Today* 7(1986), 227–250.
Gallagher, Joseph E. "Trawþe and Luf-Talking in *Sir Gawain and the Green Knight*." *Neophilologische Mitteilungen* 78 (1977), 362–276.
Galloway, Andrew. "Dream-Theory in 'The Dream of the Rood' and 'The Wanderer'." *The Review of English Studies* 180 (1994), 475–485.
Gay, Peter. *Freud: A Life for our Time* (London: J.M. Dent &Sons, 1988).
Gechner, G.T. *Einige Ideen zur Schöpfung – und Entwichlungsgeschichte des Organismen* (Leipzig, 1873).
Gibson, Andrew. *Postmodernity, Ethics and the Novel: From Leavis to Levinas* (London: Routledge, 1999).
Giovannelli, Alessandro. "In Sympathy with Narrative Characters." *The Journal of Aesthetics and Art Criticism* 67(2009), 83–95.
Godden, M.R. "Anglo-Saxons on the Mind." *Old English Literature*, ed. R.M. Liuzza (New Haven: Yale University Press, 2002), 284–314.

le Goff, Jacques. *The Medieval Imagination*. Trans. Arthur Goldhanner (Chicago: The University of Chicago Press, 1958).

Goffman, Erving. *Frame Analysis: An Essay on the Organization of Experience* (New York: Harper&Row, 1974)

Gossman. Lionel. "History as Decipherment: Romantic Historiography and the Discovery of the Other." *Studies in Historical Change* 18(1986), 23–57.

Granon-Safont, Jeanne. *La topologie ordinaire de Jacques Lacan* (Paris: Point Hors Ligne, 1985).

Greenfield, S.B. "The Formulaic Expression of the Theme of 'Exile' in Anglo-Saxon Poetry." *Essential Articles for the Study of Old English Poetry*, eds. Jess B. Bessinger and Stanley J. Kahrl (Hamden: Archon Books, 1968), 515–526.

– "*Sylf*, Seasons, Structure and Genre in *The Seafarer*." *Anglo-Saxon England 9* (1981), 199–213.

– "'The Wanderer': A Reconsideration of Theme and Structure." *Journal of English and Germanic Philology* 50 (1951).

Grosz, Elizabeth. *Sexual Subversions: Three French Feminists* (Sidney: Allen&Unwin, 1989).

Hamlyn, D.W. *The Penguin History of Western Philosophy* (Penguin Books, 1987).

Harbus, Antonia. "Deceptive Dreams in 'The Wanderer'." *Studies in Philology* 93 (1996), 164–179.

Harris, Joseph. "*Deor* and its Refrain: Preliminaries to an Interpretation." *Traditio* 43 (1987), 23–53.

– "A Note on eorðscræfe/eorðsele and Current Interpretations of *The Wife's Lament*." *English Studies* 58 (1977), 204–208.

Head, Dominic. *The Cambridge Introduction to Modern Fiction, 1950–2010* (Cambridge: Cambridge University Press, 2002).

Heatt, A. Kent. "*Sir Gawain*: Pentangle, Luf-Lace, Numerical Structure." *Papers on Language and Literature* 4 (1968), 339–359.

Heng, Geraldine. "Feminine Knots and the Other in *Sir Gawain and the Green Knight*." *PMLA* 3 (1991), 500–514.

Henry, P.L. *The Early English and Celtic Lyric* (London: Allen and Unwin, 1966).

Hiett, Constance B., ed. and trans. *Beowulf and Other Old English Poems* (Bantam Books, 1967).

Homer, Sean. *Jacques Lacan* (London: Routledge, 2003).

Horner, Shari. "Enclosed Subjects: *The Wife's Lament* and the Culture of Early Monasticism." *Old English Literature: Critical Essays*, ed. R.M. Liuzza (New Haven: Yale University Press, 2002), 381–391.

Hough, Graham. *The Dark Sun* (London: Duckworth, 1956).

Howe, Nicholas. "The Cultural Construction of Reading in Anglo-Saxon England." *Old English Literature: Critical Essays*, ed. R.M. Liuzza (New Haven: Yale University Press, 2002), 284–314.

Hutcheon, Linda. *Narcissistic Narrative: The Metafictional Paradox* (New York: Methuen, 1980).

– *A Poetics of Postmodernism: History, Theory, Fiction* (New York: Routledge, 1988).

– *The Politics of Postmodernism* (London: Routledge, 1989).

Hymes, Del. "*In vain I tried to tell you*": *Essays in Native American Ethnopoetics* (Philadelphia: University of Pennsylvania Press, 1981).

Jakobson, Roman. "Shifters, Verbal Categories, and the Russian Verb" (1957). *Selected Writings* Vol 2 (The Hague: Mouton, 1971), 130–147.

Kalnins, Mara. "Symbolic Seeing: Lawrence and Heraclitus." *D.H. Lawrence: Centenary Essays*, ed. Mara Kalnins (Bristol: Bristol Classical Press, 1986), 173–190.

Kennedy, Charles W., ed. and trans. *An Anthology of Old English Poetry* (New York: Oxford University Press, 1960).

Ker, W.P. *Medieval English Literature* (London: Oxford University Press, 1955).

Kershaw, Nora, ed. and trans. *Anglo-Saxon and Norse Poems* (Cambridge: Cambridge University Press, 1922).

Keynes, S and M. Lapidge, eds and trans. *Alfred the Great: Asser's 'Life of King Alfred' and Other Contemporary Sources* (Harmondsworth, 1986).

Killingmo, Bjørn. "Relational-oriented Character Analysis: A Position in Contemporary Psychoanalysis. *Scandinavian Psychological Review* 30 (2007), 76–83.

Klein, W.F. "Purpose and Poetics of 'The Wanderer' and'The Seafarer'." *Anglo-Saxon Poetry: Essays in Appreciation for John C. McGalliard*, ed. Lewis E. Nicholson and Dolores Warwick Frese (London: University of Notre Dame Press, 1975), 208–223.

Klinck, Anne L. *The Old English Elegies: A Critical Edition and Genre Study* (Montreal: McGill Queen's University Press, 1992).

– "*Resignation*: Exile's Lament or Penitent's Prayer?" *Neophilologus* 71 (1987), 423–430.

Kristeva, Julia. *Black Sun*. Trans. Leon S. Roudiez (New York: Columbia University Press,1989).

– *New Maladies of the Soul* (New York: Colunbia University Press, 1995).

– *Powers of Horror*. Trans. Leon S. Roudiez (New York: Columbia University Press, 1982).

– *Revolution in Poetic Language*. Trans. Margaret Waller (New York: Columbia University Press, 1984).

– *Tales of Love*. Trans. Leon S. Roudiez (New York: Columbia University Press, 1987).
– "Within the Microcosm of the Talking Cure," in *Psychiatry and the Humanities*, eds. T. Gore and M. Waller (New Haven: Yale Univrersity Press, 1983), 33–48.
– "Women's Time." *The Kristeva Reader*, ed. Toril Moi. Trans. Alice Jardin and Harry Blake (New York: Columbia University Press, 1986), 188–211.
– "Word, Dialogue and Novel." *The Kristeva Reader*, ed. Toril Moi. Trans. Alice Jardin, Thomas Gora and Leon Roudiez (New York. Columbia University Press, 1986), 34–61.
Labbie, Erin Felicia. *Lacan's Medievalism* (Minneapolis: University of Minnesota Press, 2006).
Lacan, Jacques. "Conférence à Géneve sur le symptom." *Les Block-Notes de la pscychanalyse* (Brussel, 1975).
– "Desire and the Interpretation of Desire in *Hamlet*." Trans. James Hulbert. *Yale French Studies* 55/56 (1977), 11–52.
– *Écrits*. Trans. Alan Sheridan (New York: W. W. Norton, 1977).
– *Encore*. Le Séminare. Livre XX. 1972–73, ed. Jacques-Alan Miller (Paris: Seuil, 1975).
– *The Ethics of Psychoanalysis: The Seminar of Jacques Lacan: Book VII*. Trans. Dennis Potter (New York: Routledge, 2008).
– *The Four Fundamental Concepts of Psycho-Analysis* (1964). Trans. Alan Sheridan (Penguin Books, 1977).
– *Freud's Papers on Techniques*, 1953–54. The Seminar. Book I. Trans. John Forrester (New York: Norton; 1988).
– *Le Moi dans la théorie de Freud et dans la technique psychoanalytique*. Le Seminaire. Livre II (Paris: Seuil, 1978).
– *The Other Side of Psychoanalysis: The Seminar of Jacques Lacan, Book XVII*. Trans. Russell Grigg (New York: W.W. Norton, 2007).
– *La relation d'object*. Le Séminaire. Livre IV, ed. Jacques-Alain Miller (Paris: Seuil, 1994).
– *Le sinthome*. Le Séminaire. Livre XXIII. 1975/76, in Ornicar? 6–11 (1976–7).
– *Le transfer*. Le Séminaire. Livre VIII, 1960–61, ed. Jacques-Alain Miller (Paris: Seuil, 1991).
Lapidge, Michael. "Textual Criticism and the Literature of Anglo-Saxon England." *Bulletin of the John Rylands University Library of Manchester* 73 (1991), 17–45.
Laplanche, Jean and Jean-Bertrand Pontalis. *The Language of Psychoanalysis*. Trans. Donald Nicholson Smith (London: Hogarth Press and the Institute of Psychoanalysis, 1973).

Latour, Bruno. *We Have Never Been Modern.* Trans. Catherine Porter (Cambridge: University of Harvard Press, 1993).
Lawrence, D.H. *The Letters of D.H. Lawrence*, ed. J.T. Boulton et al (Cambridge: University Press, 1979–85).
– *Phoenix*, ed. E.D. MacDonald (London: Heineman, 1936).
– *St Mawr* (1925). *St Mawr and The Virgin and the Gipsy* (Penguin Books, 1950).
– *Studies in Classical American Literature* (1932). (New York: Viking Press, 1969).
Lawrence, W.W. "*The Wanderer* and *The Seafarer*." *Journal of English and German Philology* 4 (1902), 460–80.
Leaska, Mitchell. *Virginia Woolf's Lighthouse: A Study in Critical Method* (New York: Columbia University Press, 1970).
Lemaire, Anika. *Jacques Lacan.* Trans. David Macey (London: Routledge, 1977).
Lee, Alvin A. *Gold-Hall and Earth-Dragon: Beowulf as Metaphor* (Toronto: University Toronto Press, 1998).
Lee, Hermione. "Introduction." *To the Lighthouse* (Penguin Books, 1992), ix-xliii.
– *Virginia Woolf* (London: Chatto&Windus, 1996).
Lees, Clara A. and Gillian Overing. "Birthing, Bishops and Fathering Poets: Bede, Hild and the Relations of Cultural Production." *Old English Literature: Critical Essays*, ed. R.M. Liuzza (New Haven: Yale University Press, 2002), 125–156.
Lehan, Richard. "Bergson and the discourse of the moderns." *The Crisis in Modernism: Bergson and the Vitalist Controversy*, eds. Frederick Burwick and Paul Douglas (Cambridge: Cambridge University Press, 1992), 306–39.
Lench, Elinor. "*The Wife's Lament*: A Poem of the Living Dead." *Comitatus* 1 (1970), 3–23.
Leslie, A.F, ed. *Three Old English Elegies* (Manchester: Manchester University Press, 1961).
Lessing, Doris. *Love, Again* (London: Flamingo, 1996).
Levinas, Emanuelle. *Noms propres* (Montpellier: Fata Morgana, 1976).
Lillenfeld, Jane. "Where the Spear Plant Grew: The Ramsays' Marriage in *To the Lighthouse*." *New Feminist Essays on Virginia Woolf*, ed. Jane Marcus (Lincoln: University of Nebraska Press, 1981), 148–169.
Linley, Arthur. "Pinning Gawain Down: The Misediting of *Sir Gawain and the Green Knight*." *Journal of English and Germanic Philology* 96 (1997), 26–42.
Liuzza, Roy. "Names, Reputation and History in *Sir Gawain and the Green Knight*." *Essays in Medieval Studies* 6 (1989), 41–56.
Lochrie, Karma. "Wyrd and the Limits of Human Understanding: A Thematic Sequence In the *Exeter Book*." *Journal of English and Germanic Philology* 85 (1986), 323–331.

Lord, Albert B. *The Singer of Tales* (Cambridge: Harvard University Press, 1960).
Luminasky, R.M. "Dramatic Structure of the Old English 'Wanderer'." *Neophilologus* 34 (1950), 104–112.
Lunacharsky, A. *On Literature and Art* (Moscow: Progress Publishers, 1973).
Magoun, Francis P. "The Oral-Formulaic Character of Anglo-Saxon Narrative Poetry." *Speculum* 28 (1953), 446–467.
Malone, Kemp, ed. *Deor* (New York: Appleton-Century-Crofts, 1966).
– "Two English *Frauenlieder*." *Studies in Old English Literature*, ed. Stanley B. Greenfield (Eugene: University of Oregon Press, 1963), 106–117.
Mandel, Jerome. *Alternative Readings in Old English Poetry* (New York: Peter Lang, 1987).
– "Exemplum as Refrain: The Meaning of 'Deor'." *Yearbook of English Studies* 7 (1977), 1–9.
Margolin, Uri. "Individuals in Narrative Worlds: An Ontological Perspective." *Poetics Today* 11 (Winter, 1990), 843–871.
Markland, Murray F. "Boethius, Alfred and Deor." *Modern Philology* 66 (1968).
Marks, John. *Gilles Deleuze: Vitalism and Multiplicity* (London: Pluto Press, 1998).
McKeon, Richard. *Introduction to Aristotle* (New York: Random House, 1947).
Miller, J. Hillis. "Mr Carmichael and Lily Briscoe: The Rhythm of Creativity in *To the Lighthouse*." *Modernism Reconsidered*, ed. Robert Kiely (Cambridge: Harvard University Press, 1983), 167–189.
Miller, Jacques-Alain. "Suture." *Screen* 18.4 (1977/78), 24–34.
Mills, David. "Analysis of the Temptation-Scenes in *Sir Gawain and the Green Knight*." *Journal of English and German Philology* 67 (1968), 612–30.
Milner, Jean-Claude. "Lacan and the Ideal of Science." *Lacan and the Human Sciences*, ed. Alexandre Leupin (Lincoln: University of Nebraska Press, 1991), 27–42.
Milowicki, Edward J. and R. Rawdon Wilson. "Ovid through Shakespeare: The Divided Self." *Poetics Today* 16 (Summer 1995), 217–252.
Mitchell, Juliet. *Psychoanalysis and Feminism* (Penguin Books, 1974).
Moffat, Douglas. "Anglo-Saxon Scribes and Old English Verse." *Speculum* 67 (1992), 805–27.
Moll, Richard. "Frustrated Readers Conventional Decapitation in *Sir Gawain and the Green Knight*." *The Modern Language Review* 97 (2002), 793–802.
Moi, Toril. *Sexual/Textual Politics: Feminist Literary Theory* (London: Routledge, 1985)
– *The Kristeva Reader* (New York: Columbia University Press, 1986). .
Morel, Genevève. "Fundamental Phantasy and the Symptom as a Pathology of the Law." *The Center for Freudian Analysis and Web Journal* Summer (www.cfar.org.uk, 2008).

Muhall, Stephen. "Introduction." *Heidegger and Being and Time* (London: Routledge, 1996), 1–33.

Newton, Adam Zachary. *Narrative Ethics* (Cambridge: Harvard University Press, 1995).

Niles, John D. "The Problem of the Ending of *The Wife's Lament*." *Speculum* 78 (2003), 1107–1150.

O'Keeffe, Katherine O'Brien. "The Performing Body and the Oral Literate Continuum: Old English Poetry." *Teaching Oral Traditions*, ed. John Miles Foley (New York: The Modern Language Association, 1998), 46–58.

– *Visible Song: Transitional Literacy in Old English Verse* (Cambridge: Cambridge University Press, 1990).

Oliver, Kelly. *Witnessing: Beyond Recognition* (Minneapolis: University of Minnesota Press, 2001).

– and Steve Edwin, eds. *Between the Psyche and the Social: Psychoanalytic Social Theory* (Lanham: Rowan&Littlefield Publishers, 2002).

Ong, Walter. *Orality and Literacy: The Technologizing of the Word* (London: Methuen, 1982).

Opland, Jeff. *Anglo-Saxon Poetry: A Study of the Traditions* (New Haven: Yale University Press, 1980).

Orgel, Stephen. "Not on his picture but his book." *Times Literary Supplement* (August 2003).

Orton, Peter. "The Form and Structure of *The Seafarer*." *Old English Literature: Critical Essays*, ed. R.M. Liuzza (New Haven: Yale University Press, 2002), 353–380.

Overing, Gillian R. *Language, Sign and Gender in Beowulf* (Carbondale: Southern Illinois University Press, 1990).

Ovid. *Metamorphoses*. Trans. Mary M. Innes (Penguin Classics, 1955).

Oxford Dictionary Online (www.dictionary.oed.com).

Paris, Bernard Jay. *Imagined Human Beings: A Psychological Approach to Character and Conflict* (New York: New York University Press, 1998).

Parkes, Malcolm. *Pause and Effect: An Introduction to the History of Punctuation in the West* (Berkely: University of California Press, 1993).

Parry , Adam. *The Making of Homeric Verse: The Collected Papers of Milman Parry* (Oxford: Clarendon Press, 1971).

Pasternack, Carol Braun. *The Textuality of Old English Poetry* (Cambridge: Cambridge University Press, 1995).

Paxman, Jeremy. *The English: A Portrait of a People* (London: Michel Joseph, 1998).

Pearsall, Derek. "Rhetorical 'Descriptio' in *Sir Gawain and the Green Knight*." *Modern Language Review* 50 (1995), 129–134.

Pedersen, Glenn. "Vision in *To the Lighthouse. PMLA* LXXIII (1958), 585–600.
Phelan, James. *Reading People, Reading Plots: Character, Progression and the Interpretation of Narrative* (Chicago: Universtiy of Chicago Press, 1989).
– *Narrative as Rhetoric: Technique, Audiences, Ethics, Ideology* (Colombus: Ohio State University Press, 1996).
Poole, Adrian. "Graham Swift and the Mourning After." *An Introduction to Contemporary Fiction. International Writing in English since 1970* (Polity Press, 1999), 150–167.
Poole, Roger. *The Unknown Virginia Woolf* (London: Cambridge University Press, 1978).
Pope, John C. "Dramatic Voices in 'The Wanderer' and 'The Seafarer'."*Franciplegius: Medieval and Linguistic Studies in Honour of Francis Peabody Magoun Jr.*, eds. J.B Bessinger Jr. and Robert P. Creed (New York: New York University Press, 1965), 164–193.
– "Paleography and Poetry: Some Solved and Unsolved Problems of the Exeter Book." *Medieval Scribes: Manuscripts and Libraries: Essays Presented to N.R. Ker*, eds. M.B. Parkes and Andrew Watson (London: Scholar Press, 1978).
– "Second Thoughts on the Interpretation of 'Seafarer'." *Anglo-Saxon England* 9 (1974), 75–86.
– ed. *Seven Old English Poems* (New York: Norton, 1981).
Porter, Joseph A. "Character and Ideology in Shakespeare." *Shakespeare Left and Right*, ed. Ivo Kamps (New York: Routledge, 1991)
Pound, Ezra. *The Cantos* (London: Faber, 1986).
Propp, Vladimir. *Morphology of the Folktale* (1928). Trans. L. Scott (Austin: University of Texas Press, 1986).
Psychoanalytic Notebooks: A Review of the London Society of the New Lacanian School 13 (London: Vintage, 1992).
Putter, Ad. *Sir Gawain and the Green Knight and French Arthurian Romance* (Oxford: Clarendon Press, 1995).
– *An Introduction to the Gawain Poet* (London: Longman, 1996).
Quirk, Tom. *Bergson and American Culture: The Worlds of Willa Cather and Wallace Stevens* (Chapel Hill: The University of North Carolina Press, 1990).
Rabaté, Jean-Michel. *Jacques Lacan: Psychoanalysis and the Subject of Literature* (Palgrave, 2001).
– *James Joyce and the Politics of Egoism* (Cambridge: Cambridge University Press, 2001).
Rajchman, John. "Introduction." *Pure Immanence: Essays on Life*. Trans. Anne Boyman (New York: Zone Books, 2001), 7–23.
Reineke, Martha J. *Sacrificed Lives: Kristeva on Women and Violence* (Bloomington: Indiana University Press, 1997).

Renoir, Alan. "Descriptive Techniques in *Sir Gawain and the Green Knight.*" *Orbis Literarum* 13 (1958), 126–132.

– "A Reading Context for 'The Wife's Lament'." *Anglo-Saxon Poetry: Essays in Appreciation for John C. McGalliard*, ed. Lewis E. Nicholson and Dolores Warwick Frese (London: University of Notre Dame Press, 1975), 224–241.

Ricoeur, Paul. "The Metaphorical Process as Cognition, Imagination, and Feeling." in *On Metaphor*, ed. Sheldon Sacks (Chicago: University of Chicago Press, 1979), 141–157.

Rimmon-Kenan, Shlomith. *Narrative Fiction: Contemporary Poetics* (Colombus: Ohio University Press, 1983).

De Roo, Harvey. "Undressing Lady Bertilak: Guilt and Denial in *Sir Gawain and the Green Knight.*" *Chaucer Review* 27 (1993), 305–326.

Rose, Jacqueline. "Introduction." – II. *Feminine Sexuality and the école freudienne*, eds. Juliet Mitchell and Jacqueline Rose (New York: W.W. Norton, 1982), 27–57.

Rowley, Sharon M. "Textual Studies, Feminism and Performance in *Sir Gawain and The Green Knight.*" *The Chaucer Review* 2 (2003), 159–177.

Sacks, Peter. *The English Elegy* (Baltimore: The Johns Hopkins University Press, 1985).

de Saussure, Ferdinand. *Cours de linguistique générale* (1915; Paris: Payot, 1965).

Scarry, Elaine. *The Body in Pain: The Making and Unmaking of the World* (New York: Oxford University Press, 1985).

Schaefer, Ursula. "Hearing from Books: The Rise of Fictionality in Old English Poetry." *Vox intexta: Orality and Textuality in the Middle Age*, eds. A. N. Doane and Carol Braun Pasternack (Madison: The University of Wisconsin Press, 1991).

Scott, Bonnie Kime. *Refiguring Modernism: Posmodern Feminist Readings of Woolf, West and Barnes* (Bloomington: Indiana Univeristy Press, 1995).

Shoaf, R.A. *The Poem as Green Girdle: "Commercium" in Sir Gawain and the Green Knight* (Gainesville: University of Florida Press, 1984).

– "The 'Sygne of Surfet' and the Surfeit of Signs in *Sir Gawain and the Green Knight.*" *The Passing of Arthur: Essays in Arthurian Tradition*, ed. Wiliam Sharpe (New York: Garland, 1988), 152–169.

Shücking, Levin L. "Das angelsächische Elegiendichtung." *Englische Studien* 73 (1938), 1–31.

Shippey, T.A. *Old English Verse* (London: Hutchinson, 1972).

Sjögren, Lars. *Sigmund Freud: Mannen och verket* (Natur och Kultur, 1997).

Smithers, G.V "The Meaning of *The Seafarer* and *The Wanderer.*" *Medium Aevum* 3 (1957), 137–153.

Smythe, Karen. "Virginia Woolf's Elegaic Enterprise." *NOVEL: A Forum on Fiction* 1 (1992), 64–79.

Sophocles. *Antigone.* (Penguin, 1982).

Spearing, A.C. *The Gawain Poet: A Critical Study* (Cambridge: Cambridge University Press, 1970).

Stanley, E.G. "Old English Poetic Diction and the Interpretation of *The Wanderer, The Seafarer* and *The Penitent's Prayer. Essential Articles for the Study of Old English Poetry*, eds. Jess. B. Bessinger and Stanley J. Kahrl (Hamden: Archer Books, 1968), 488–514.

Strohm, Paul. *Theory and the Premodern Text* (Minneapolis: University of Minnesota Press, 2002).

Swift, Graham. *Ever After* (New York: Picador, 1992).

– *Last Orders* (Picador, 1996).

– *Waterland* (1983; rev. ed. New York: Picador, 1992).

Tedlock, Dennis. *The Spoken Word and the Work of Interpretation* (Philadelphia: The University of Pennsylvania Press, 1983).

Todorov, Tzvetan. *The Poetics of Prose.* Trans. Richard Howard (Ithaca: Cornell University Press, 1977).

Tolkien, J.R. "Introduction." *Sir Gawain and the Green Knight, Pearl and Sir Orfero.* Trans. J.R. Tolkien (London: George Allen&Unwen, 1975), 13–24.

Tripp, Raymond P. "The Narrator as Revenant: A Reconsideration of Three Old English Elegies." *Papers on Language and Literature* 8 (1972), 339–361.

Turner, Victor. *The Ritual Process: Structure and Anti-structure* (Ithaca: Cornell University Press, 1977).

The Vercelli Book, ed. George Philip Krapp (London: George Routledge and Sons, 1932).

Walker-Peckey, Faye. "'Frige Hwæt Ic Hatte': 'The Wife's Lament' as Riddle." *Papers on Language and Literature* 28 (1992): 242–266.

Weber, Samuel. *Demarcating the Disciplines* (Minneapolis: University of Minnesota Press, 1986)

Weinsheimer, Joel. "Theory of Character: *Emma.*" *Poetics Today* 1(Autumn, 1979), 185–211.

Whitelock, Dorothy. "The Interpretation of 'The Seafarer'." *Franciplegius: Medieval and Linguistic Studies in Honour of Francis Peabody Magoun Jr.*, eds, J.B. Bessinger Jr. and Robert P. Creed (New York: New York University Press, 1965), 442–447.

Wilden, Anthony. *Speech and Language in Psychoanalysis* (Baltimore: The Johns Hopkins University Press, 1968).

Winnberg, Jakob. *An Aesthetic of Vulnerability: The Sentimentum and the Novels of Graham Swift* (Gothenburg: The University of Gothenburg Press, 2001).

Winterson, Jeanette. *Written on the Body* (London: Vintage, 1992).
Wollheim, Richard. *Freud* (Fontana Press, 1971).
Woolf, Virginia. "Character in Fiction" (1924). *The Essays of Virgina Woolf.* Vol III, ed. Andrew McNeillie (London: The Hogarth Press, 1988).
– "The Fleeting Portrait." *Granite and Rainbow* (London: Hogarth Press, 1958), 216–224.
– *Moments of Being: Unpublished Autobiographical Writings of Virginia Woolf,* ed. Jeanne Schulkind (London: Chatto&Windus, 1976).
– "Mr Bennett and Mrs Brown" (1923). *The Essays of Virginia Woolf.* Vol III, ed. Andrew McNeillie (London: The Hogarth Press, 1998).
– *Mrs Dalloway* (New York: Harcourt, 1925).
– *To the Lighthouse* (Penguin Books, 1992).
Zizek, Slavoj. *Enjoy Your Symptom: Jacques Lacan in Hollywood and Out* (London: Routledge, 1992).
– *For they know not what they do: Enjoyment as a Political Factor* (London: Verso, 1991; 2002).
– *Looking Awry: An Introduction to Jacques Lacan through Popular Culture* (Cambridge: MIT Press, 1991).
– *Sublime Object of Ideology* (New York: Verso, 1989).
– *The Zizek Reader*, eds. Elizabeth Wright and Edmond Wright (Blackwell Publishers, 1999), 53–86.
Zumthor, Paul. *Toward a Medieval Poetics.* Trans. P. Bennett (Minneapolis: University of Minnesota Press, 1992).

www.ingramcontent.com/pod-product-compliance
Ingram Content Group UK Ltd.
Pitfield, Milton Keynes, MK11 3LW, UK
UKHW041825100926
8556IPUK00002B/25

9 783631 644379